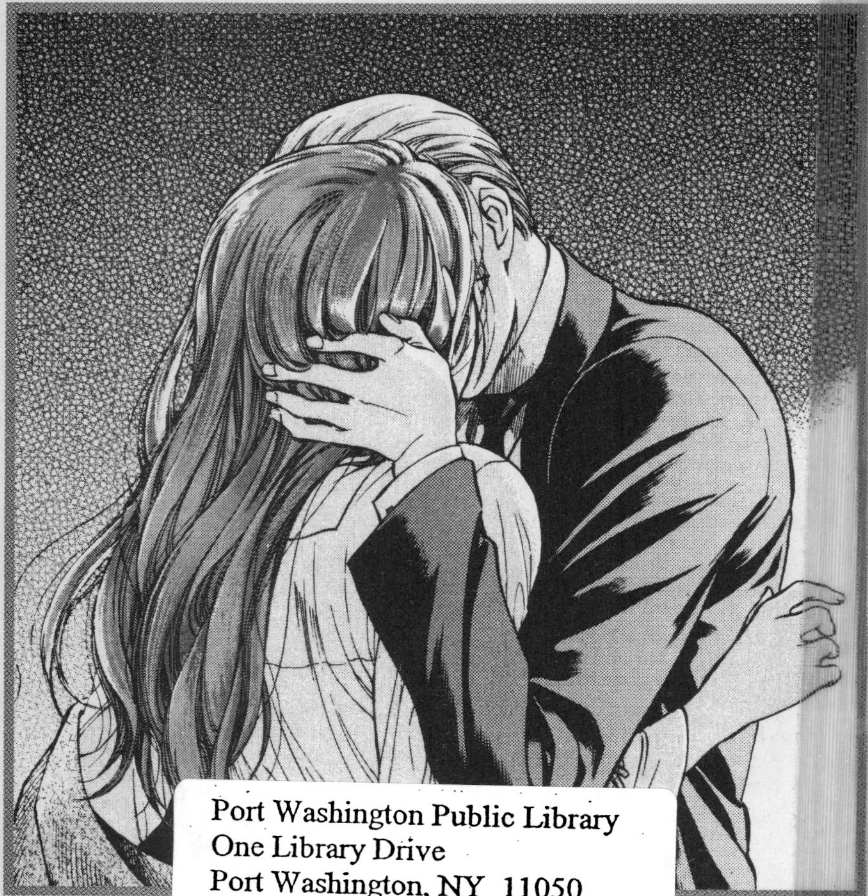

EMMA

Volume 7

By Kaoru Mori

-Contents-

Chapter 44 The Dawn....................................003

Chapter 45 The New World...........................021

Chapter 46 Hand in Hand............................047

Chapter 47 The Meredith Family Maids......073

Chapter 48 The Favor...................................107

Chapter 49 Eleanor at Night........................141

Chapter 50 The Showdown...........................159

Chapter 51 The Feelings of Two People.......193

The Final Chapter The Blessed Flowers......227

Afterword...266

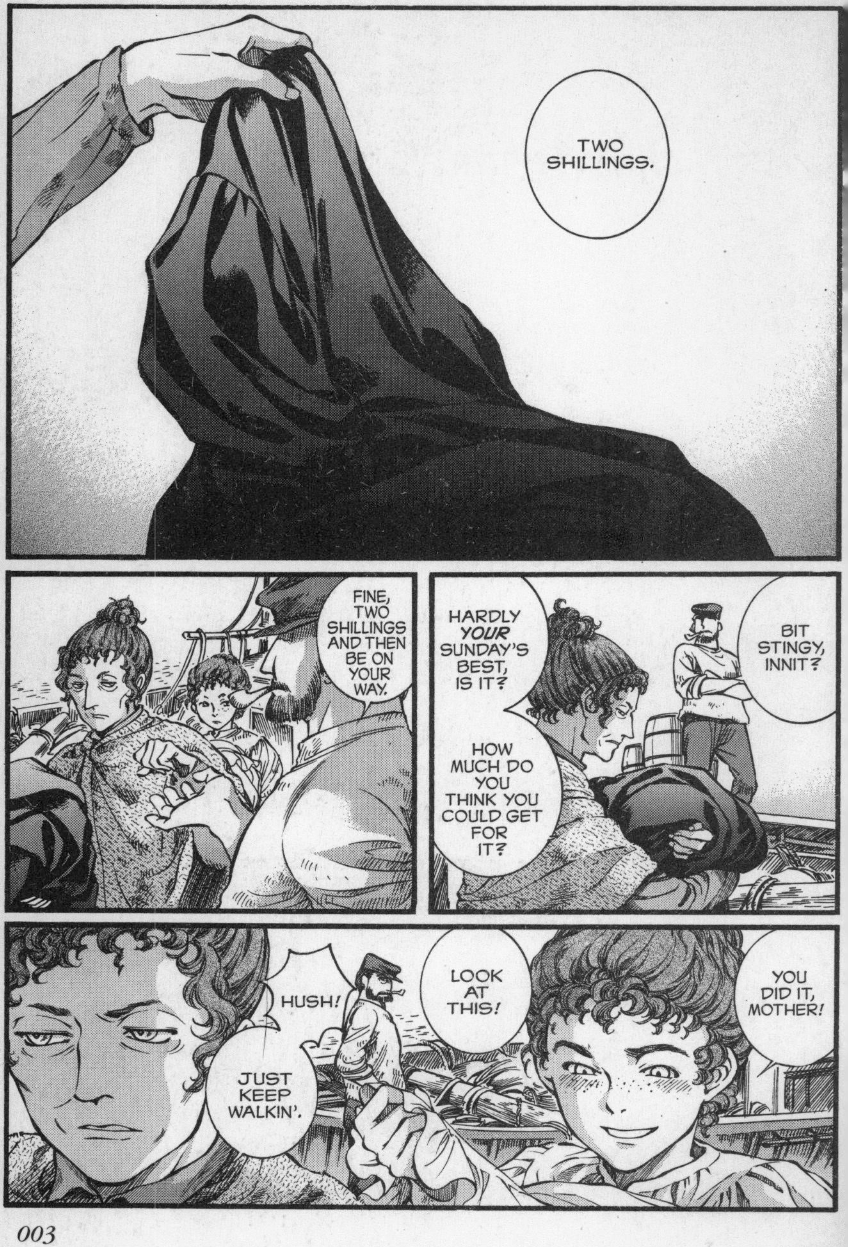
TWO SHILLINGS.
BIT STINGY, INNIT?
HARDLY *YOUR* SUNDAY'S BEST, IS IT?
HOW MUCH DO YOU THINK YOU COULD GET FOR IT?
FINE, TWO SHILLINGS AND THEN BE ON YOUR WAY.
YOU DID IT, MOTHER!
LOOK AT THIS!
HUSH!
JUST KEEP WALKIN'.

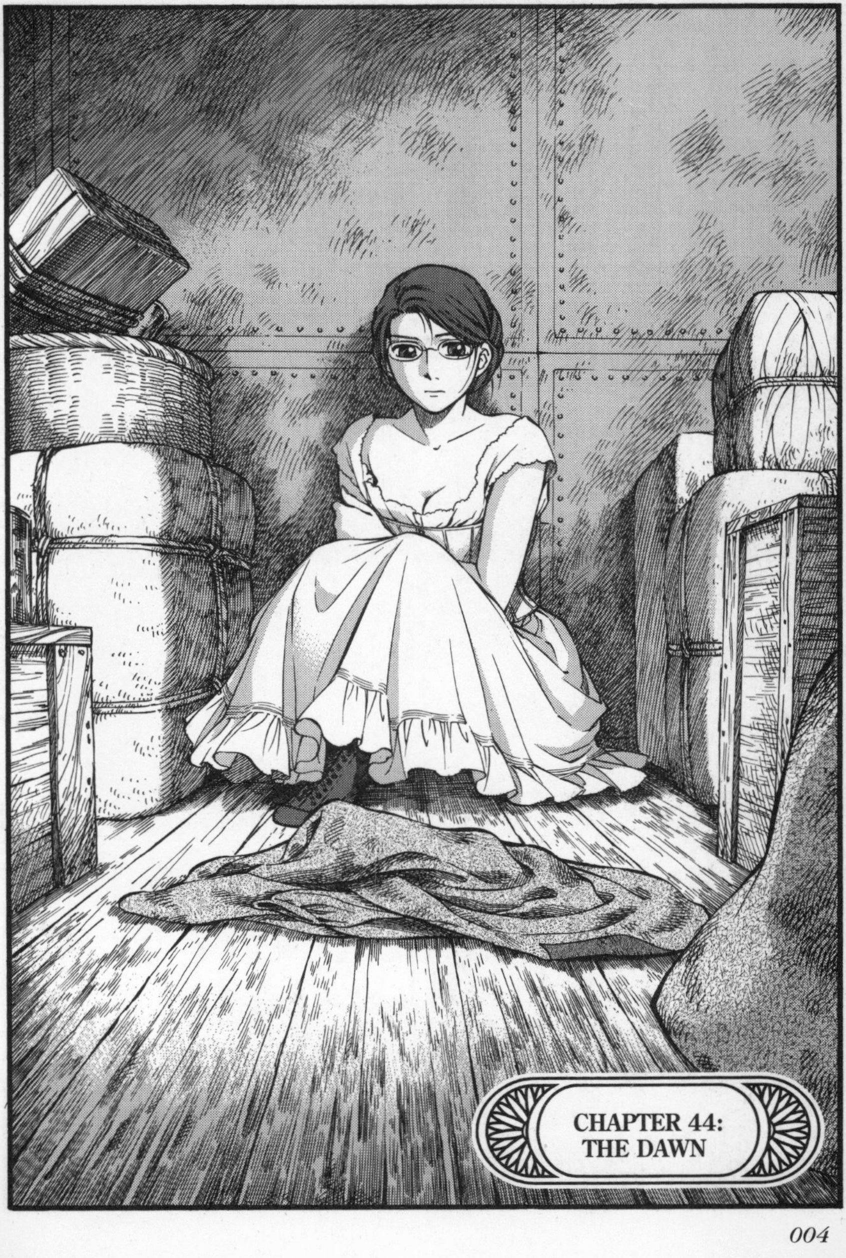
CHAPTER 44:
THE DAWN

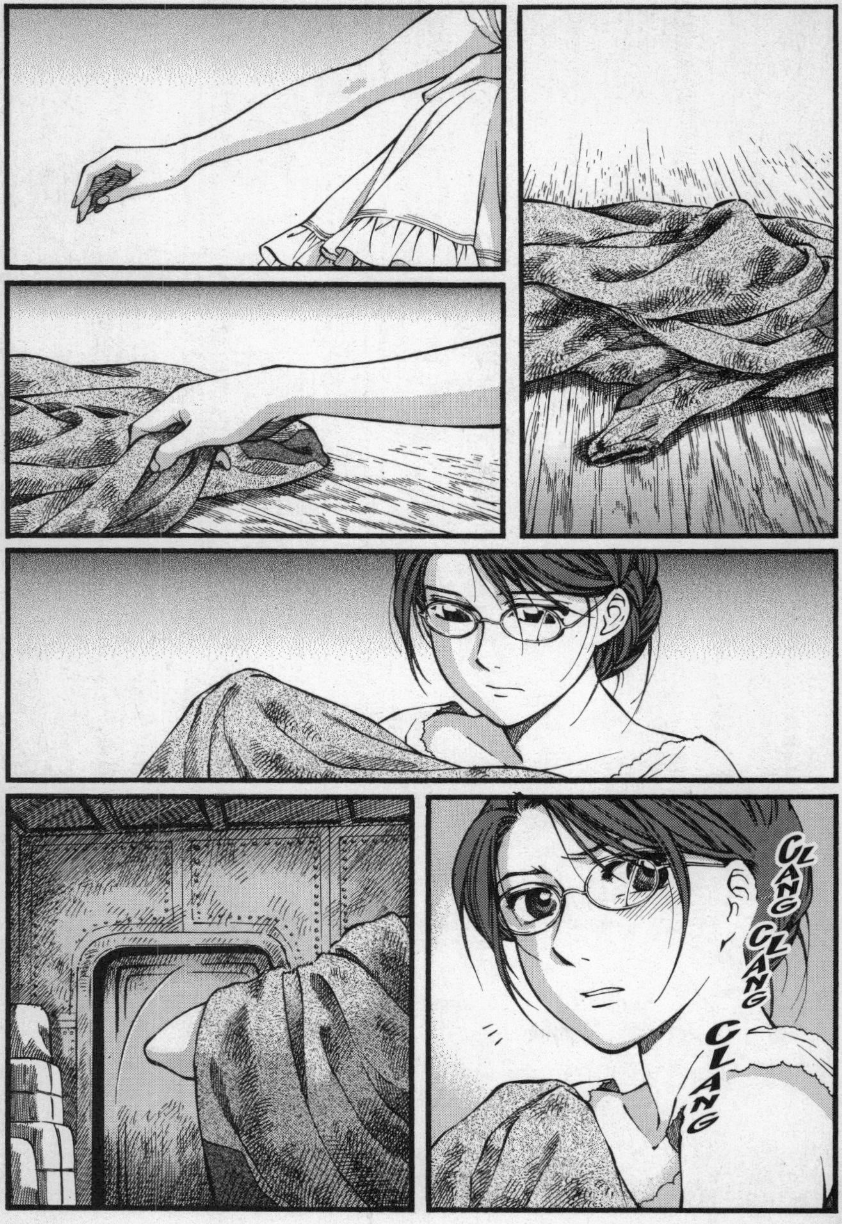
CLANG CLANG CLANG

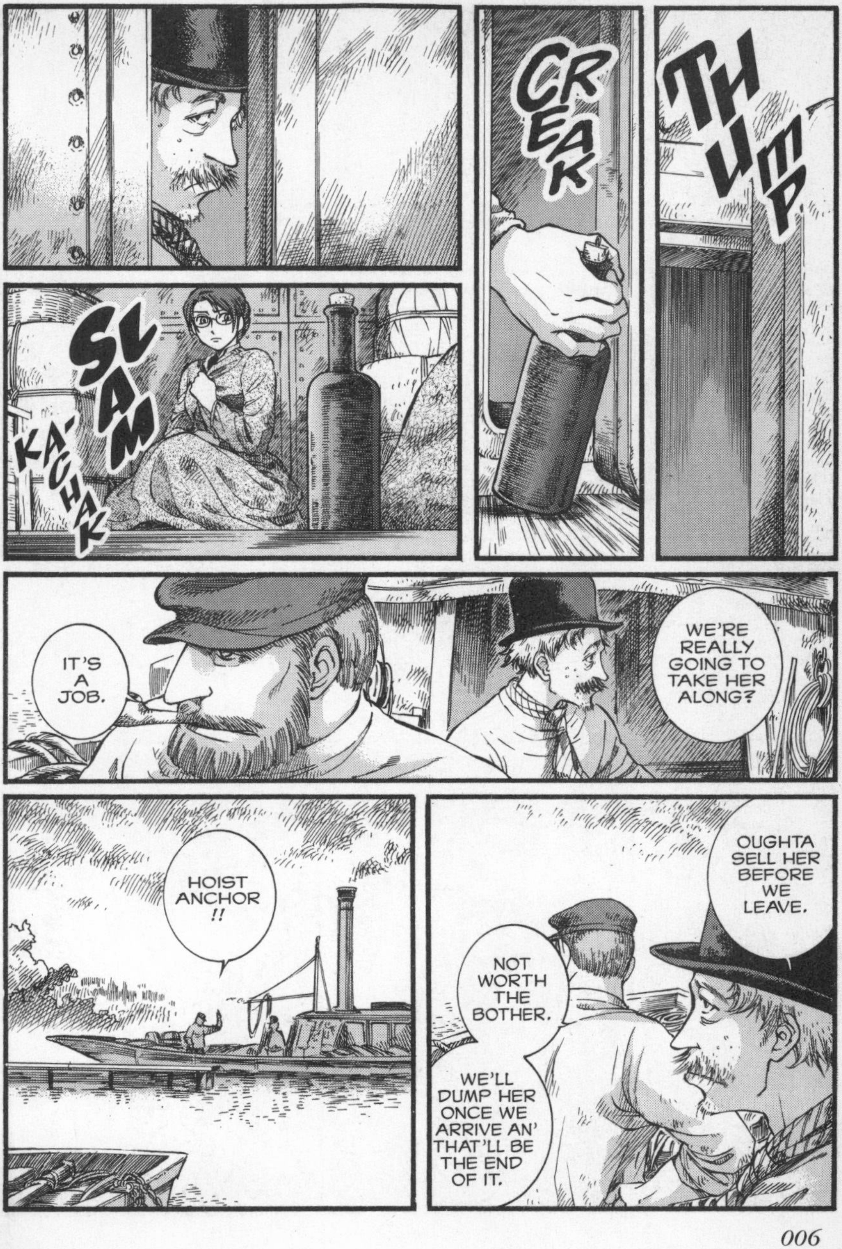
THUMP
CREAK
SLAM
KA-CHAK
WE'RE REALLY GOING TO TAKE HER ALONG?
IT'S A JOB.
OUGHTA SELL HER BEFORE WE LEAVE.
NOT WORTH THE BOTHER.
WE'LL DUMP HER ONCE WE ARRIVE AN' THAT'LL BE THE END OF IT.
HOIST ANCHOR !!

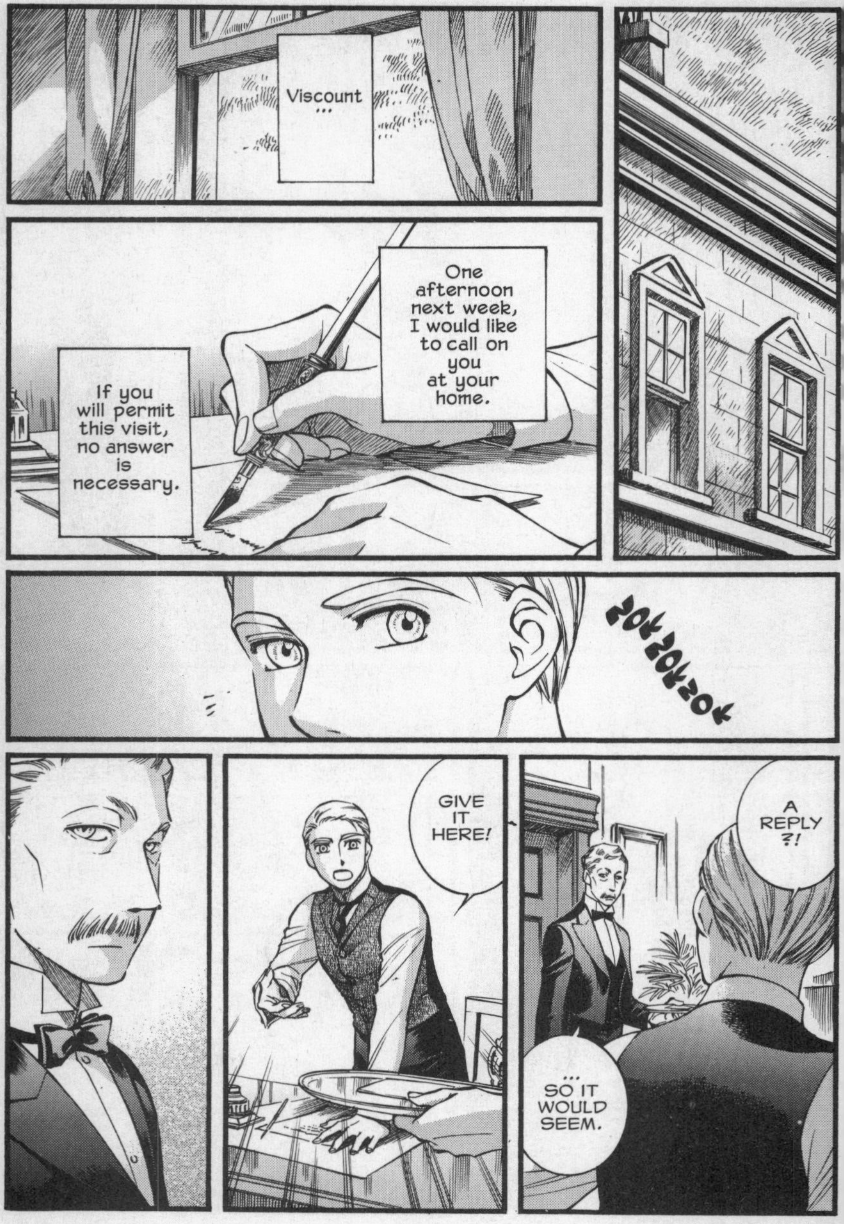
Viscount ...
One afternoon next week, I would like to call on you at your home.
If you will permit this visit, no answer is necessary.
A REPLY ?!
... SO IT WOULD SEEM.
GIVE IT HERE!

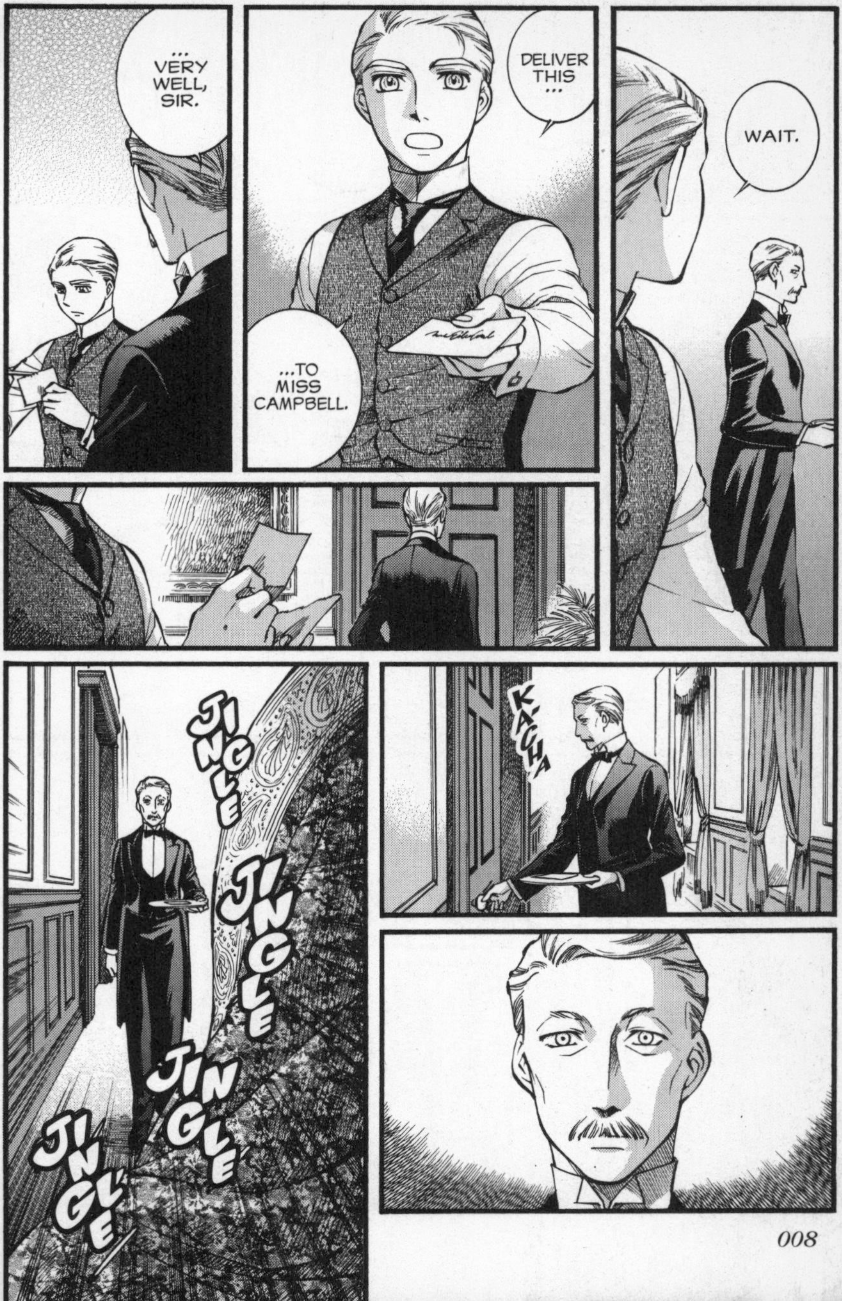
WAIT.
DELIVER THIS ...
...TO MISS CAMPBELL.
... VERY WELL, SIR.
KACHA
JINGLE
JINGLE
JINGLE
JINGLE

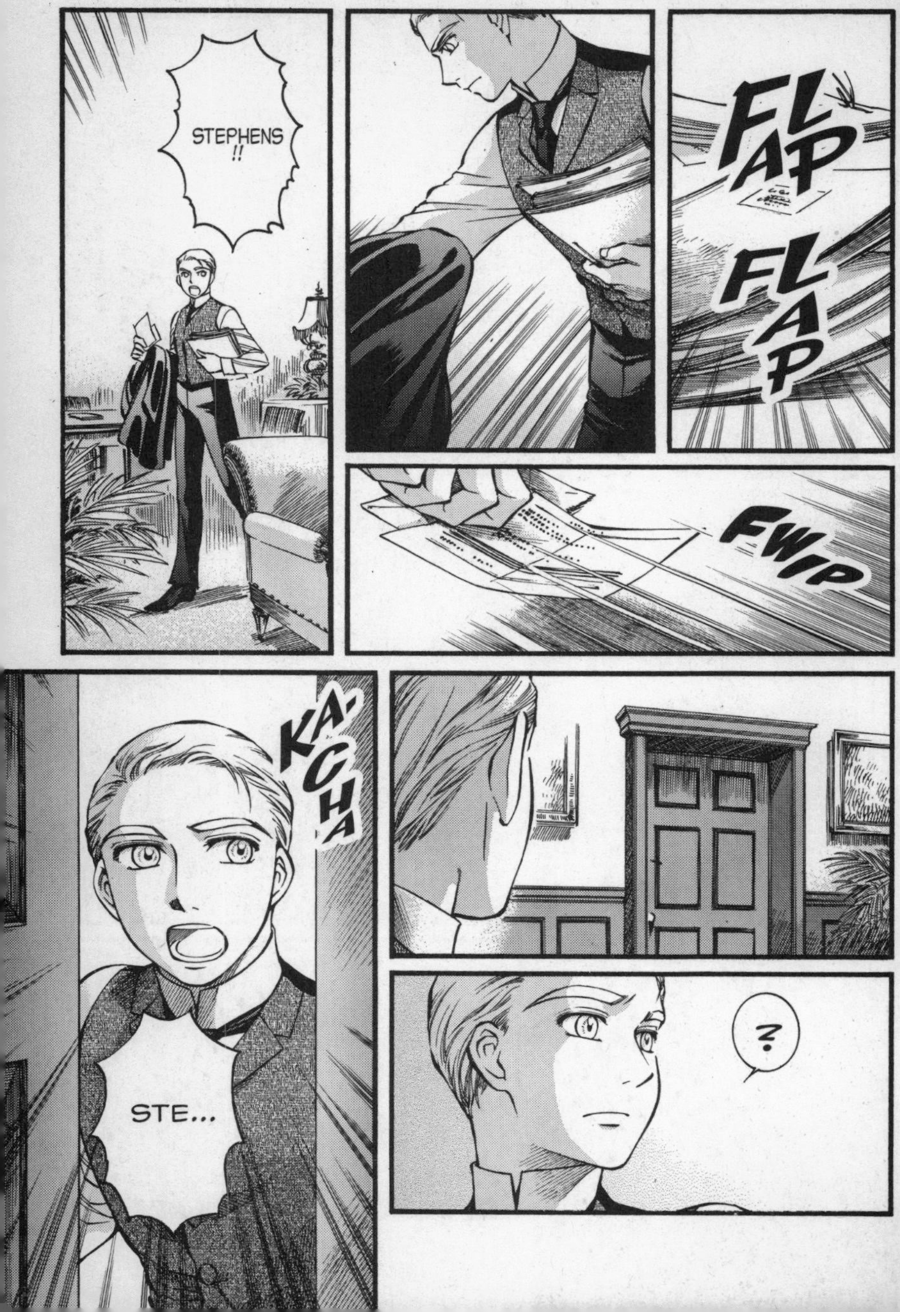
FLAP
FLAP
FWIP
STEPHENS !!
?
KA-CHA
STE...

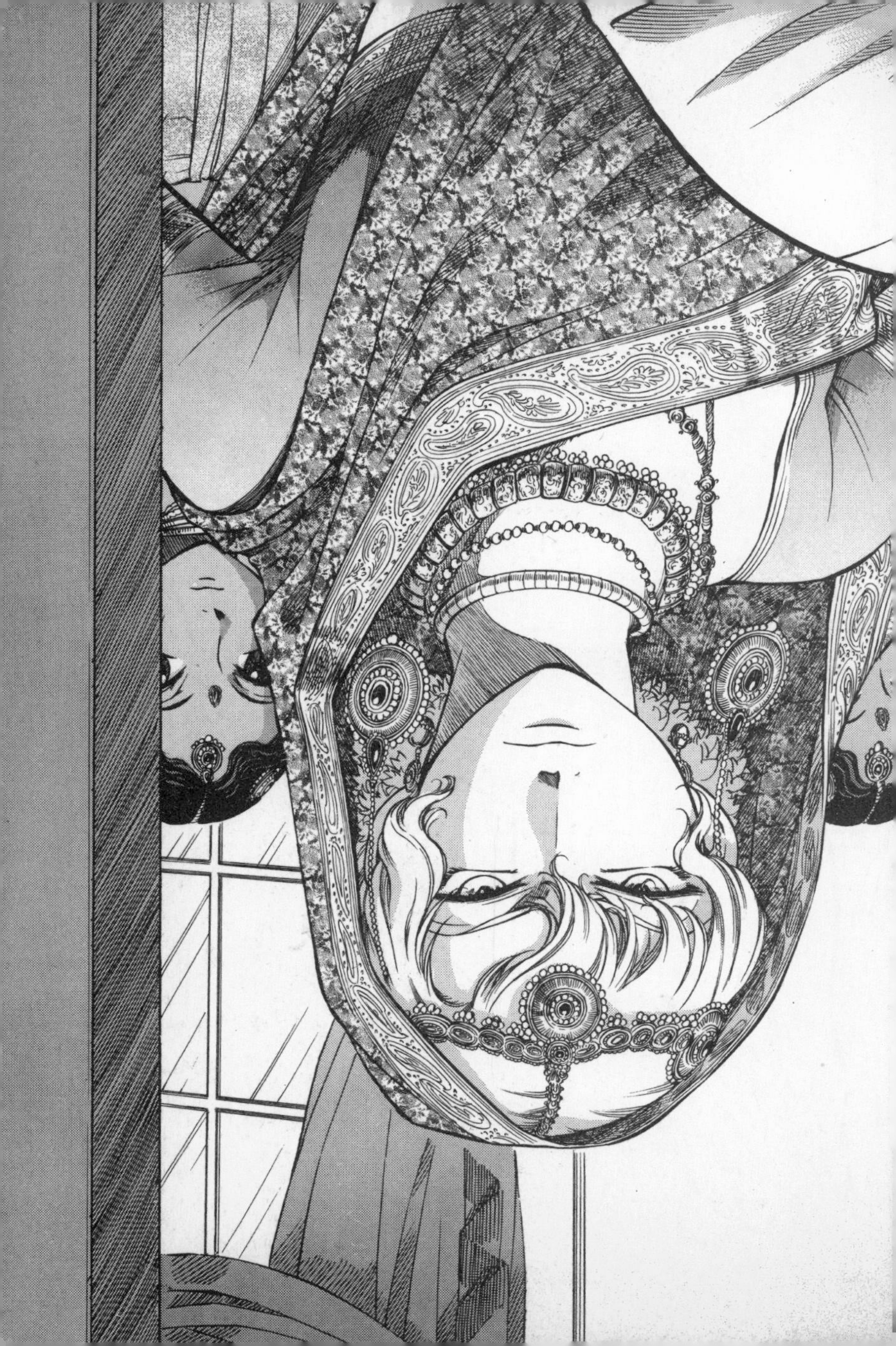

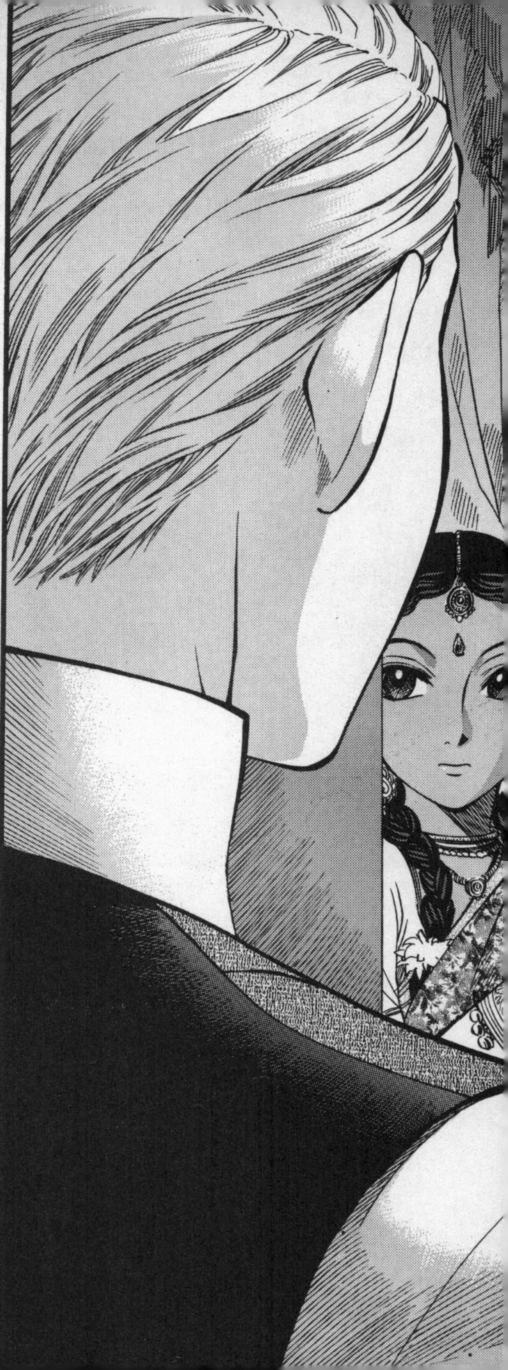
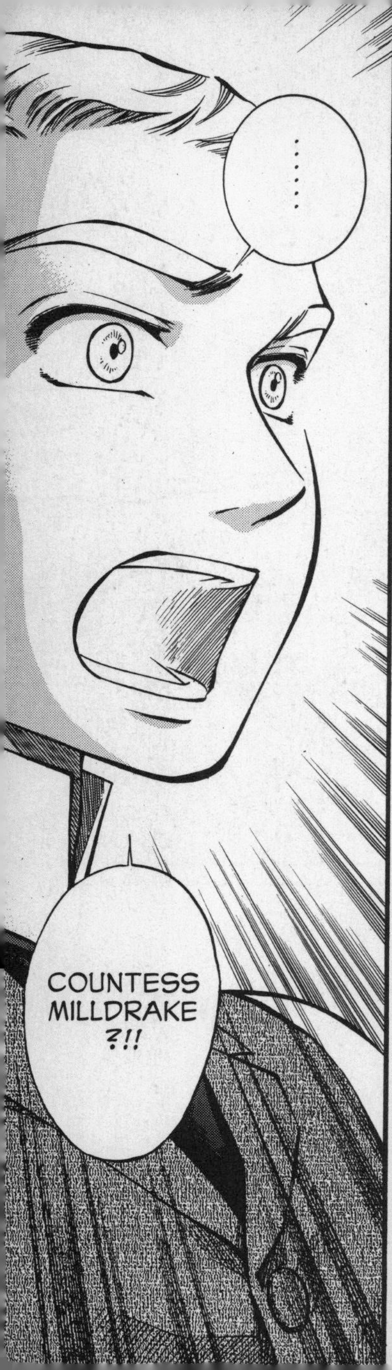
......
COUNTESS MILLDRAKE ?!!

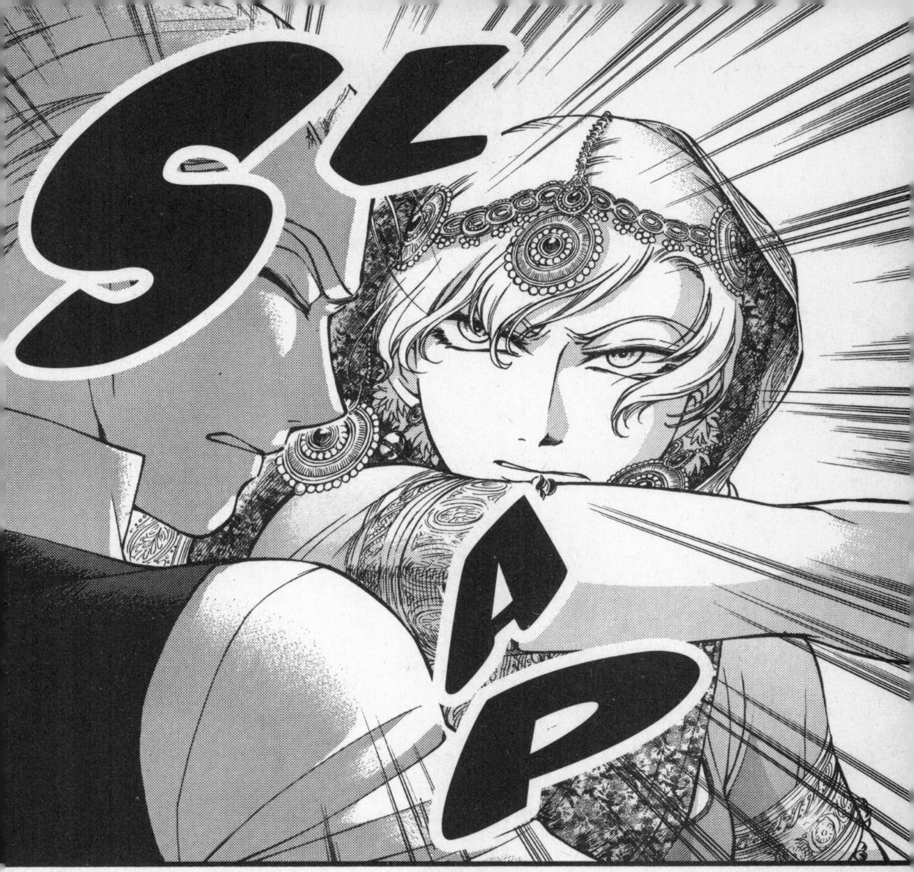
SLAP
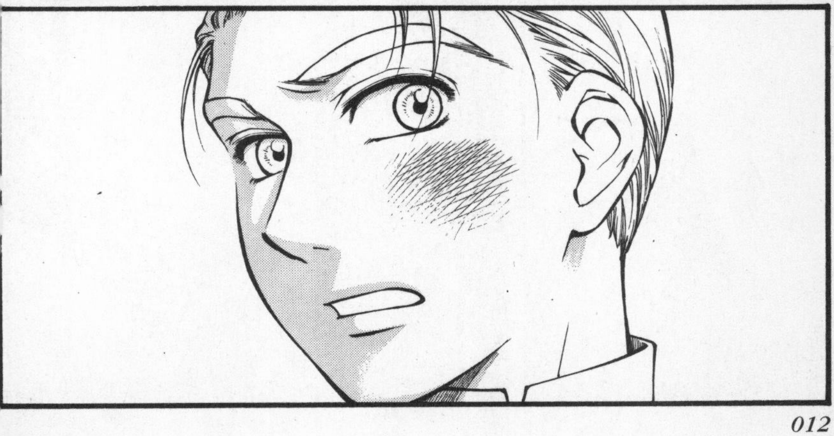

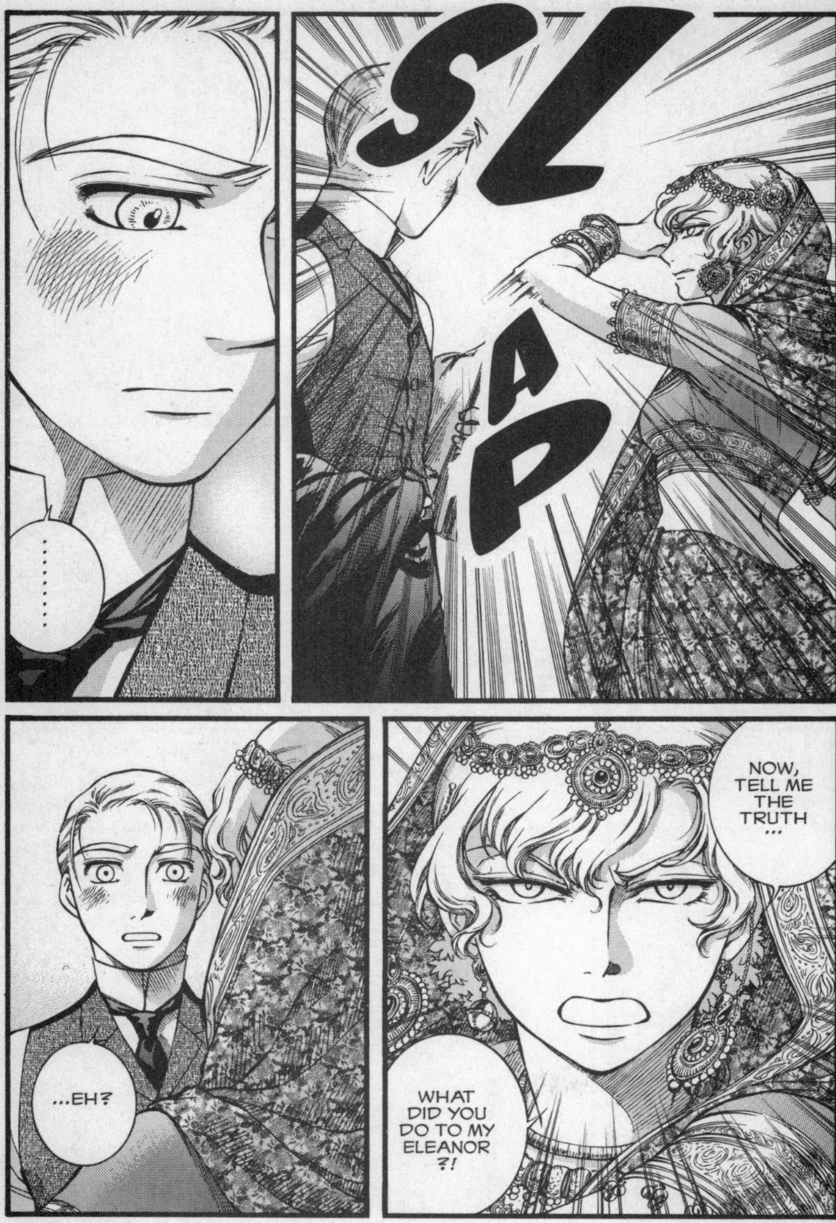
SLAP
......
NOW, TELL ME THE TRUTH ...
WHAT DID YOU DO TO MY ELEANOR ?!
...EH?

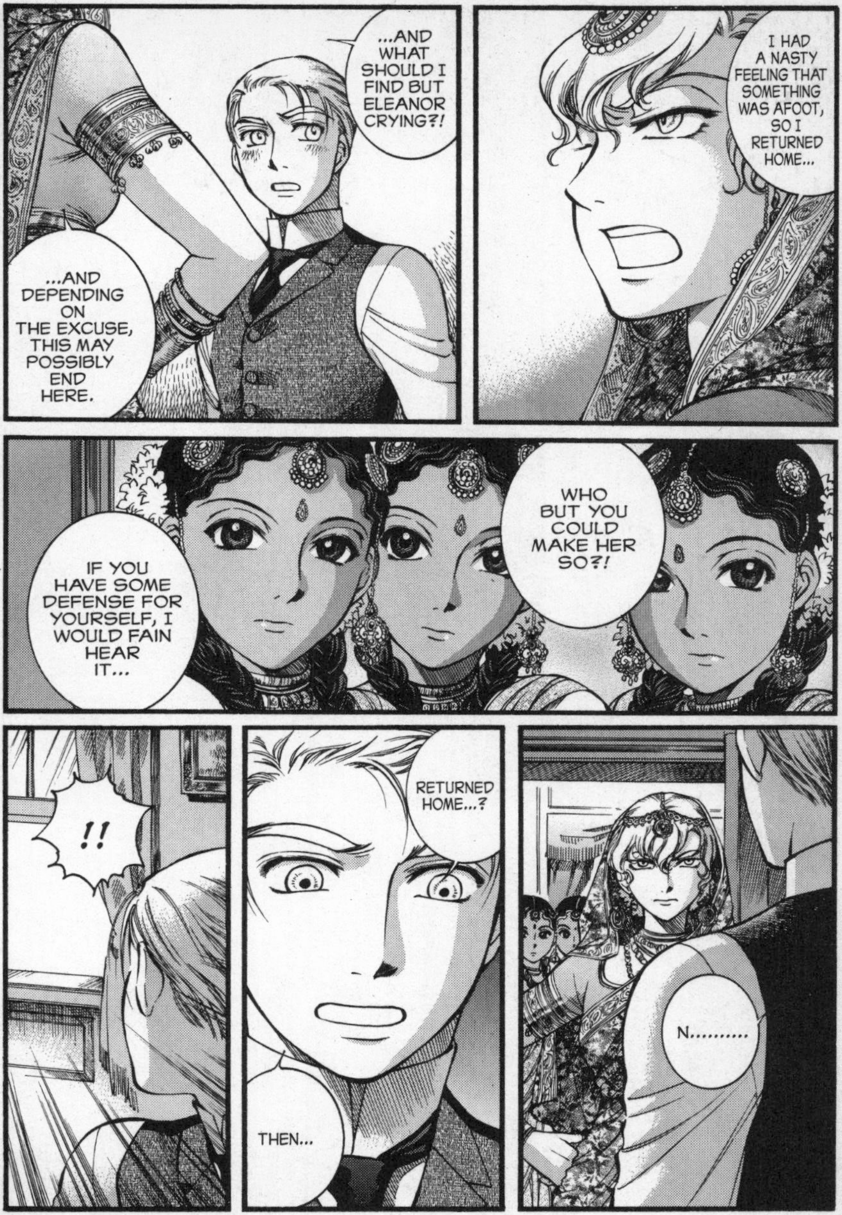
I HAD A NASTY FEELING THAT SOMETHING WAS AFOOT, SO I RETURNED HOME...
...AND WHAT SHOULD I FIND BUT ELEANOR CRYING?!
...AND DEPENDING ON THE EXCUSE, THIS MAY POSSIBLY END HERE.
WHO BUT YOU COULD MAKE HER SO?!
IF YOU HAVE SOME DEFENSE FOR YOURSELF, I WOULD FAIN HEAR IT...
N..........
RETURNED HOME...?
THEN...
!!

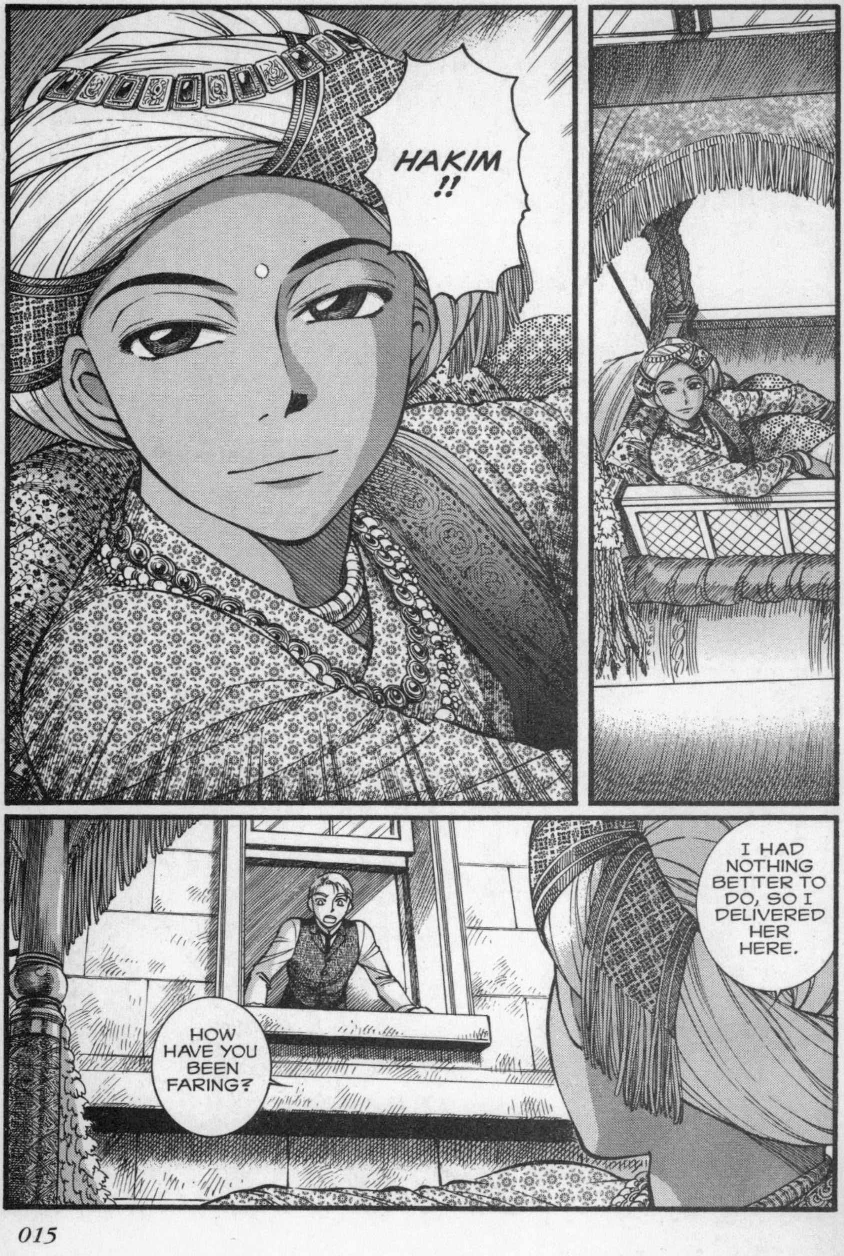
HAKIM !!
I HAD NOTHING BETTER TO DO, SO I DELIVERED HER HERE.
HOW HAVE YOU BEEN FARING?

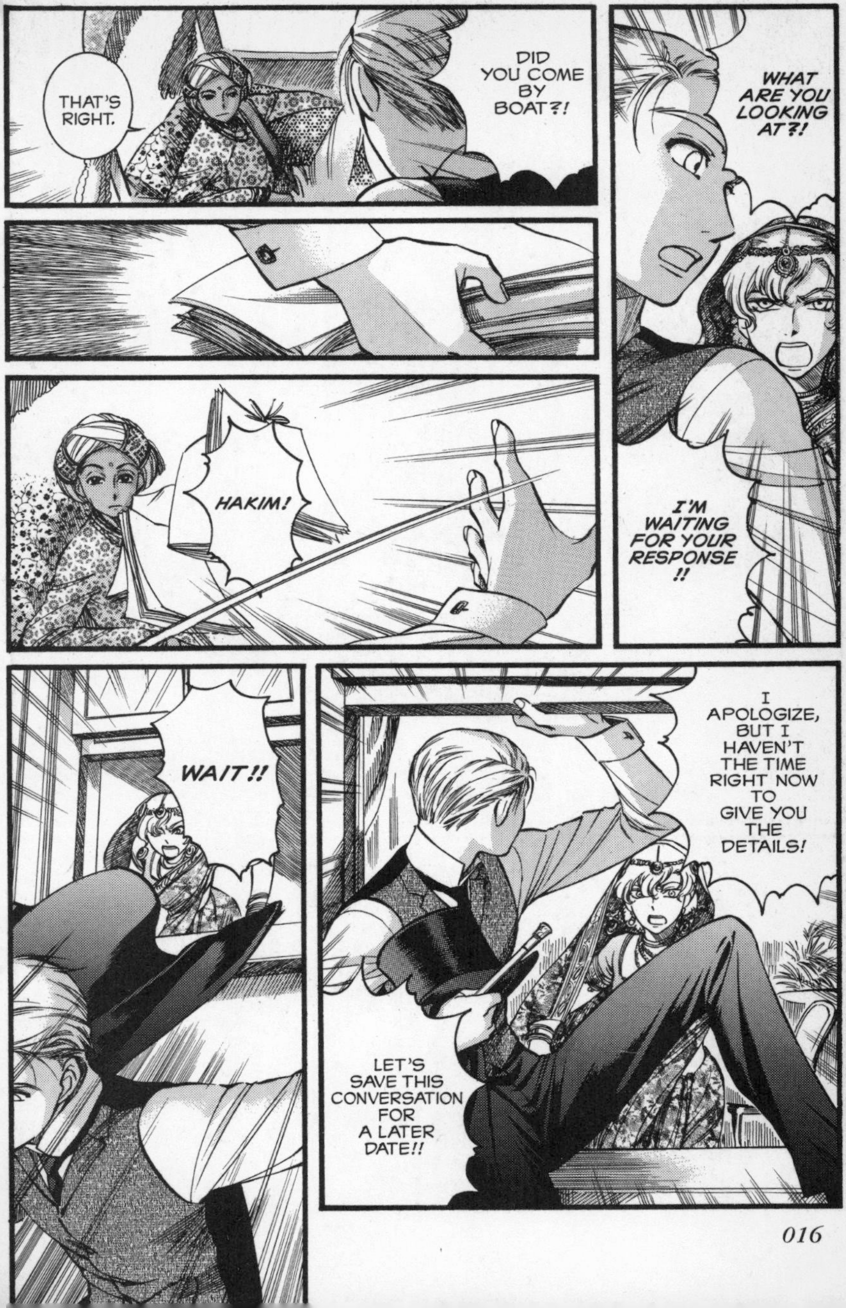
WHAT ARE YOU LOOKING AT?!
I'M WAITING FOR YOUR RESPONSE!!
DID YOU COME BY BOAT?!
THAT'S RIGHT.
HAKIM!
I APOLOGIZE, BUT I HAVEN'T THE TIME RIGHT NOW TO GIVE YOU THE DETAILS!
LET'S SAVE THIS CONVERSATION FOR A LATER DATE!!
WAIT!!

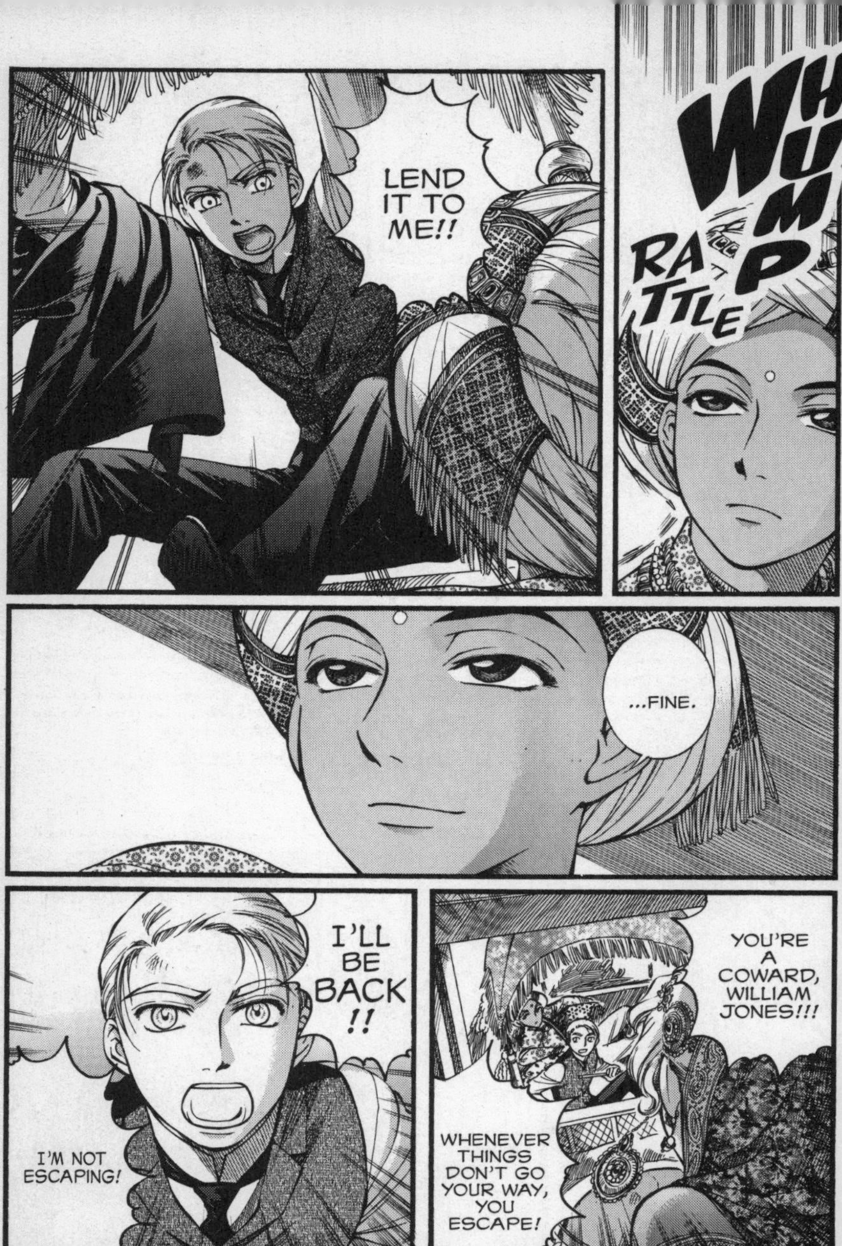
WHUMP
RATTLE
LEND IT TO ME!!
...FINE.
YOU'RE A COWARD, WILLIAM JONES!!!
WHENEVER THINGS DON'T GO YOUR WAY, YOU ESCAPE!
I'LL BE BACK!!
I'M NOT ESCAPING!

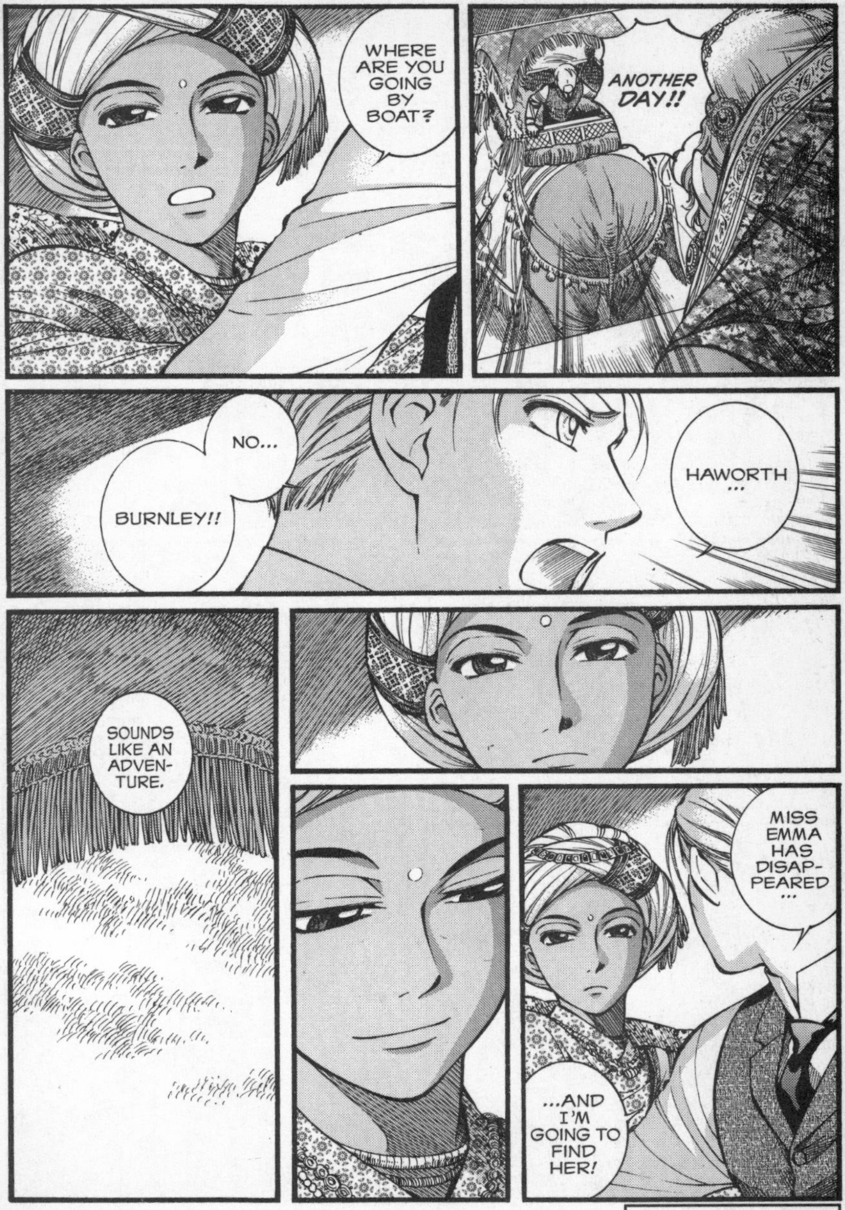
ANOTHER DAY!!
WHERE ARE YOU GOING BY BOAT?
HAWORTH ...
NO...
BURNLEY!!
MISS EMMA HAS DISAP-PEARED ...
...AND I'M GOING TO FIND HER!
SOUNDS LIKE AN ADVEN-TURE.

Chapter Forty Four:
The End

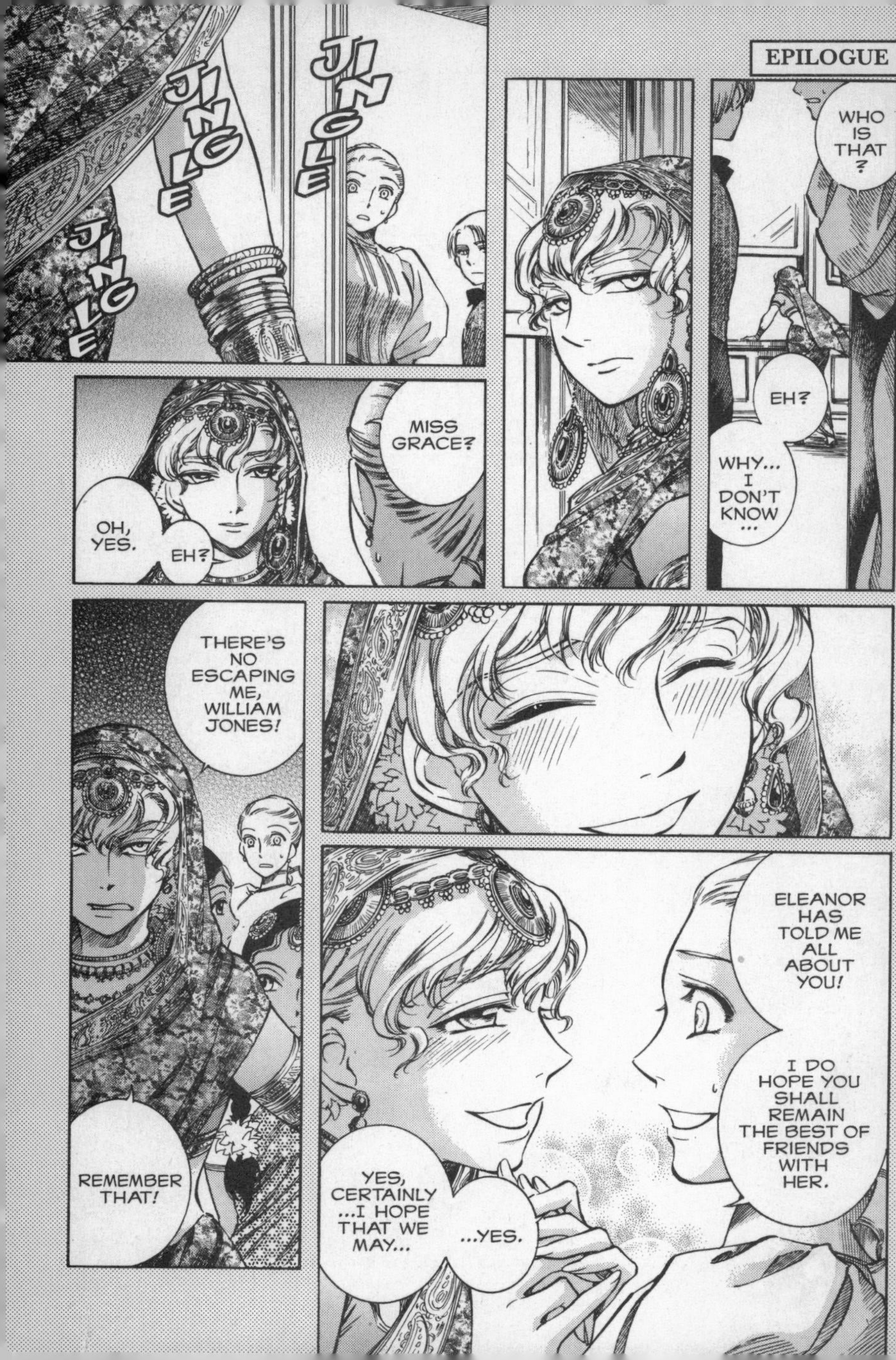
WHO IS THAT?
EH?
WHY... I DON'T KNOW...
JINGLE
JINGLE
JINGLE
MISS GRACE?
OH, YES.
EH?
ELEANOR HAS TOLD ME ALL ABOUT YOU!
I DO HOPE YOU SHALL REMAIN THE BEST OF FRIENDS WITH HER.
YES, CERTAINLY ...I HOPE THAT WE MAY...
...YES.
THERE'S NO ESCAPING ME, WILLIAM JONES!
REMEMBER THAT!

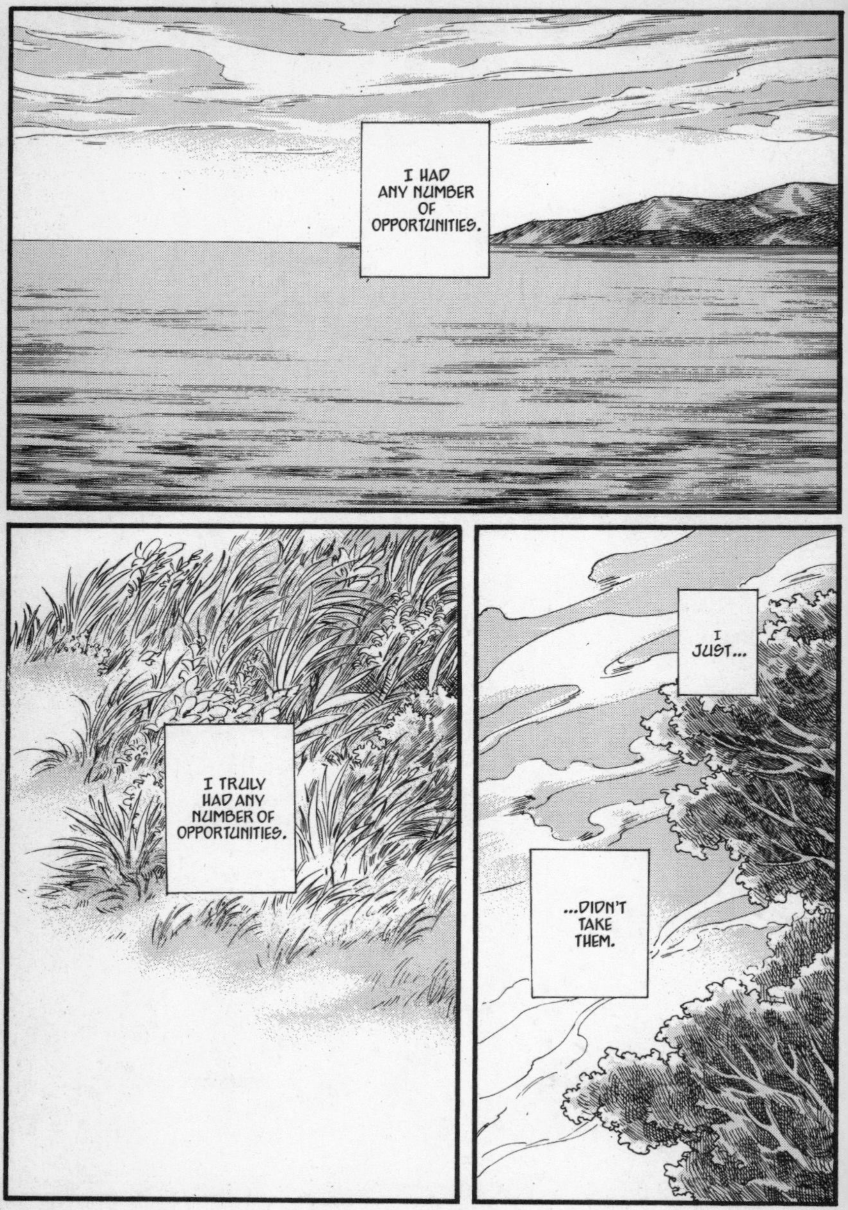
I HAD ANY NUMBER OF OPPORTUNITIES.
I TRULY HAD ANY NUMBER OF OPPORTUNITIES.
I JUST...
...DIDN'T TAKE THEM.

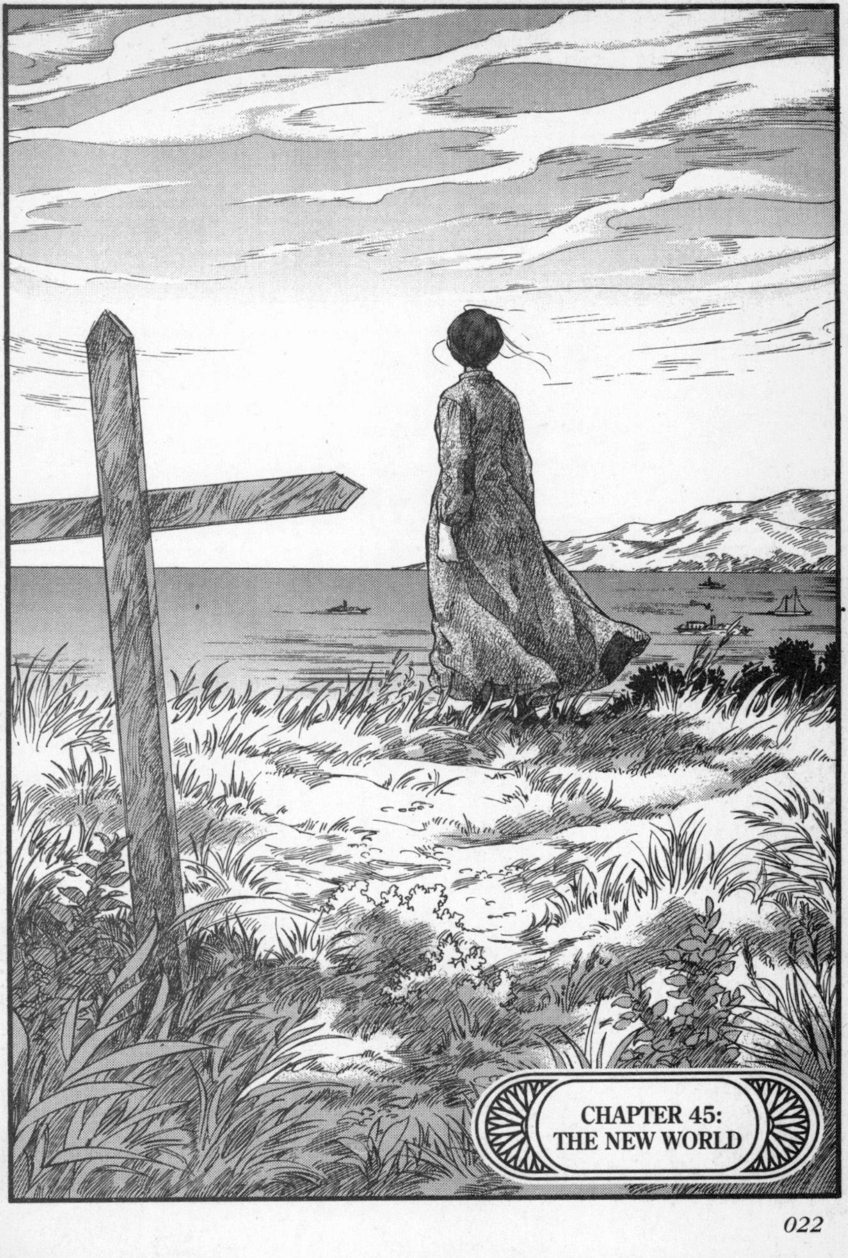
CHAPTER 45:
THE NEW WORLD

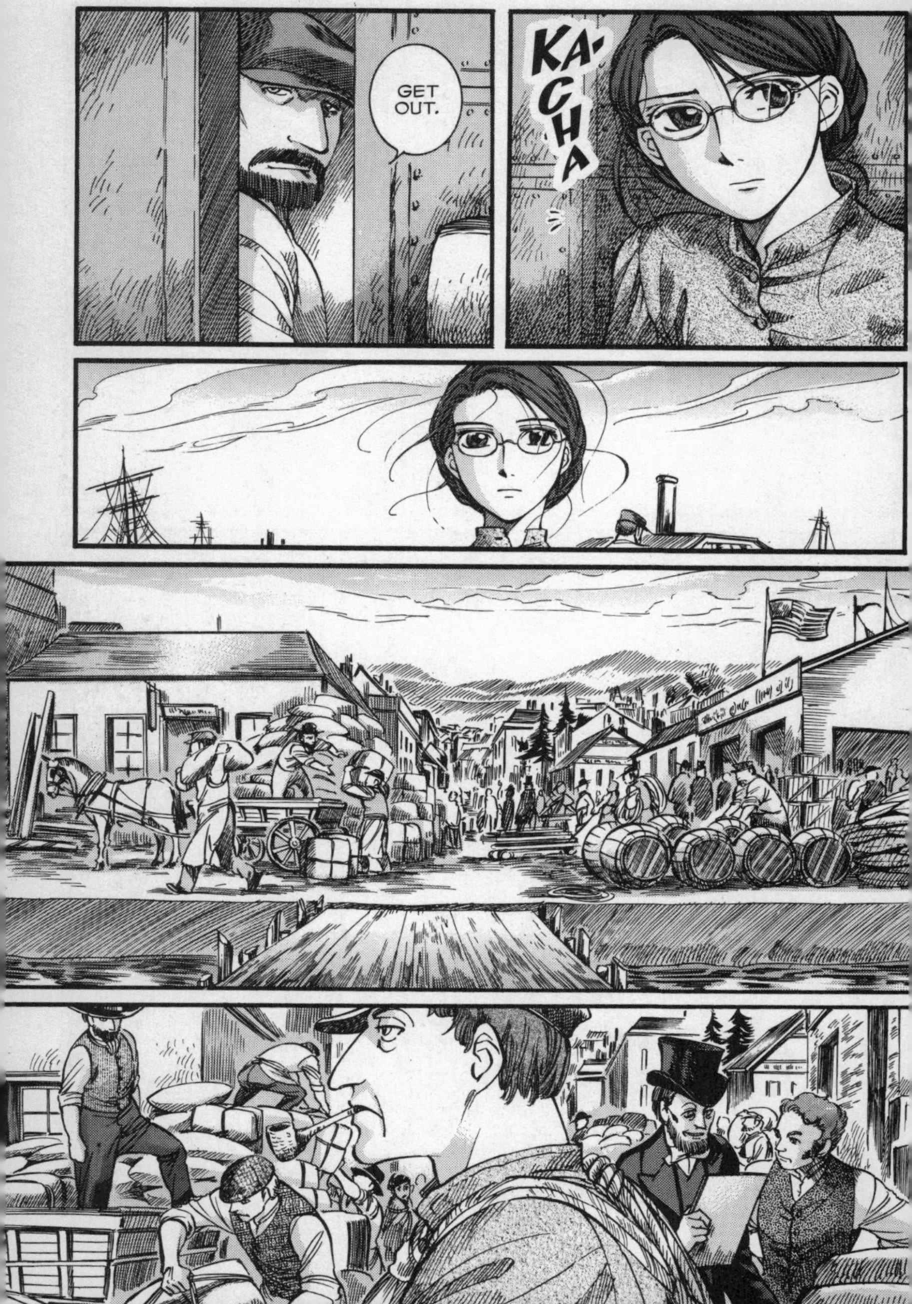
KA-CHA
GET OUT.

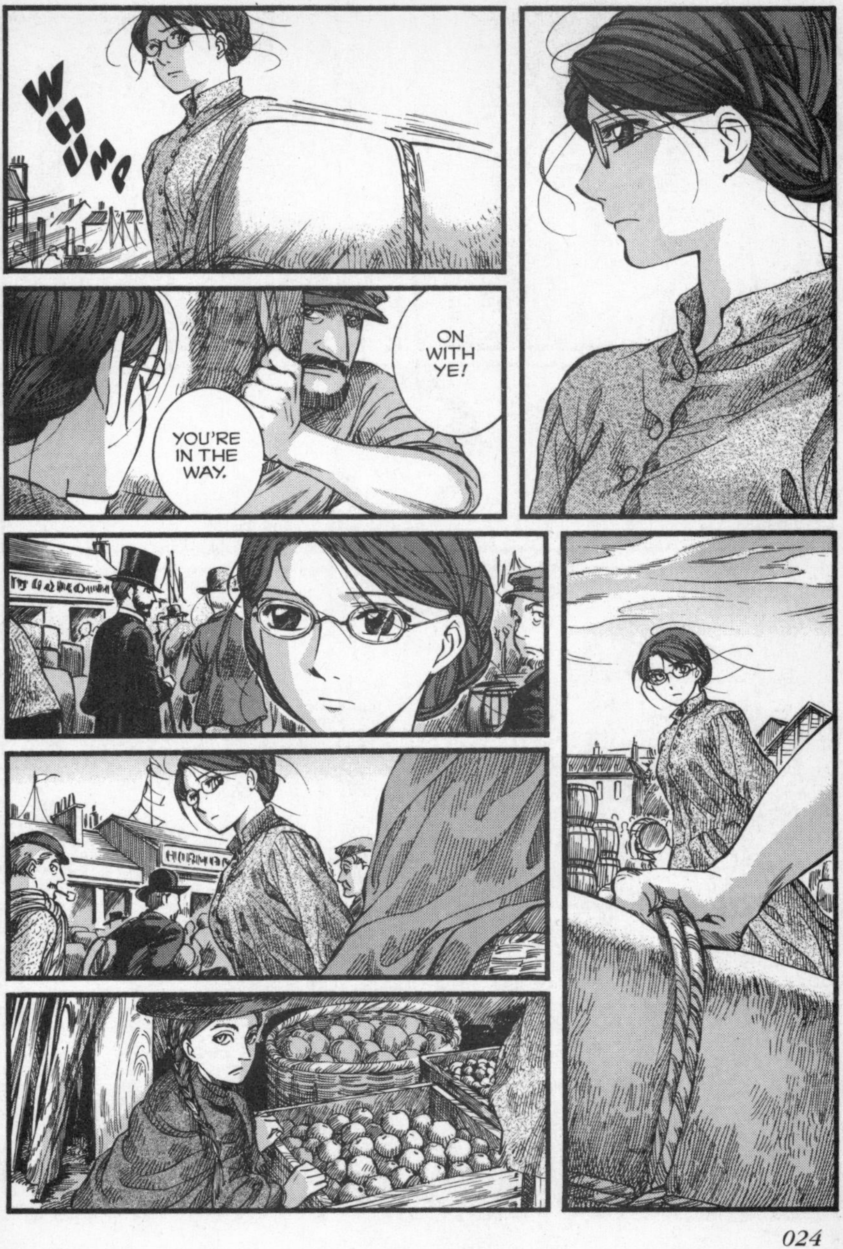
WHUMP
ON WITH YE!
YOU'RE IN THE WAY.

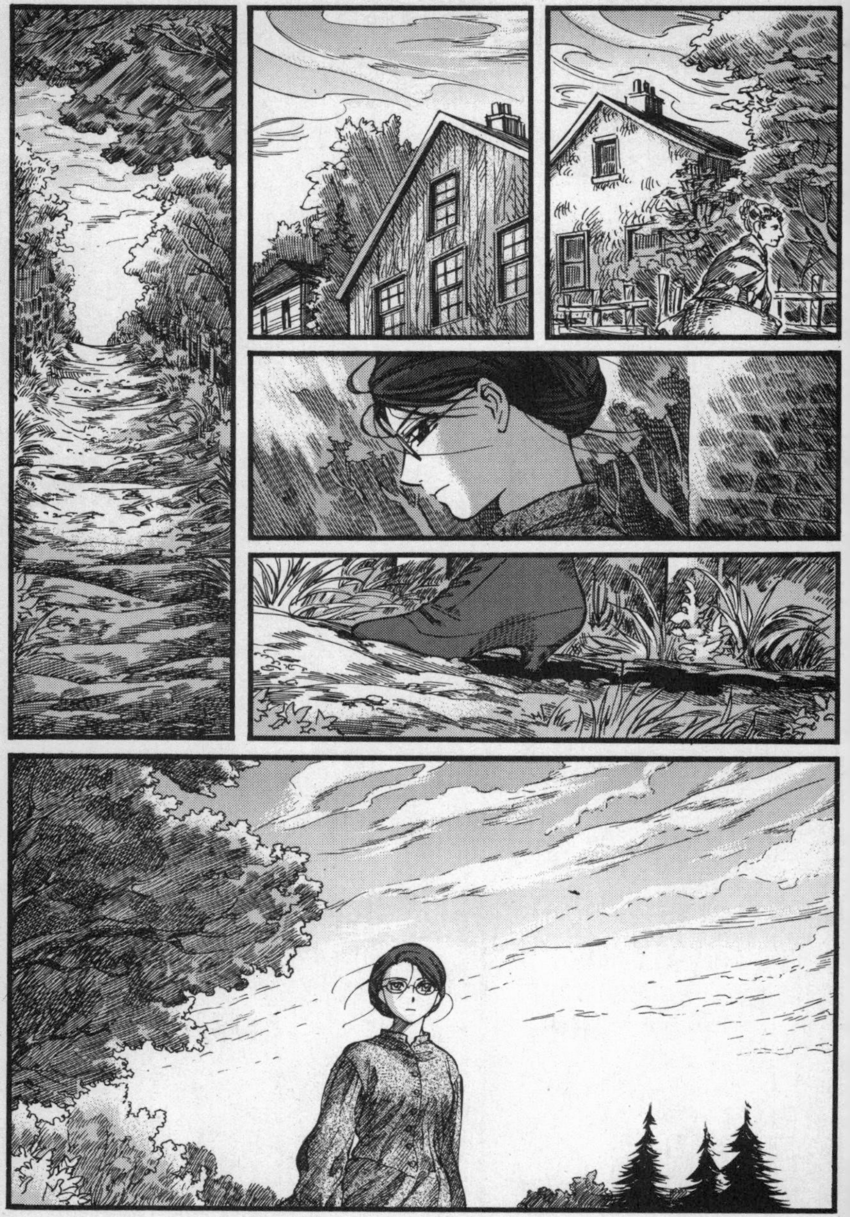

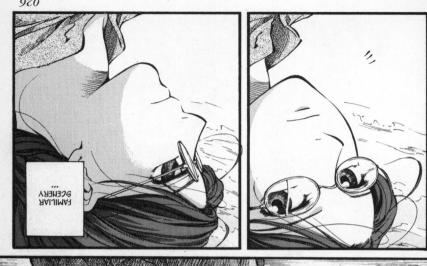

FAMILIAR SCENERY...

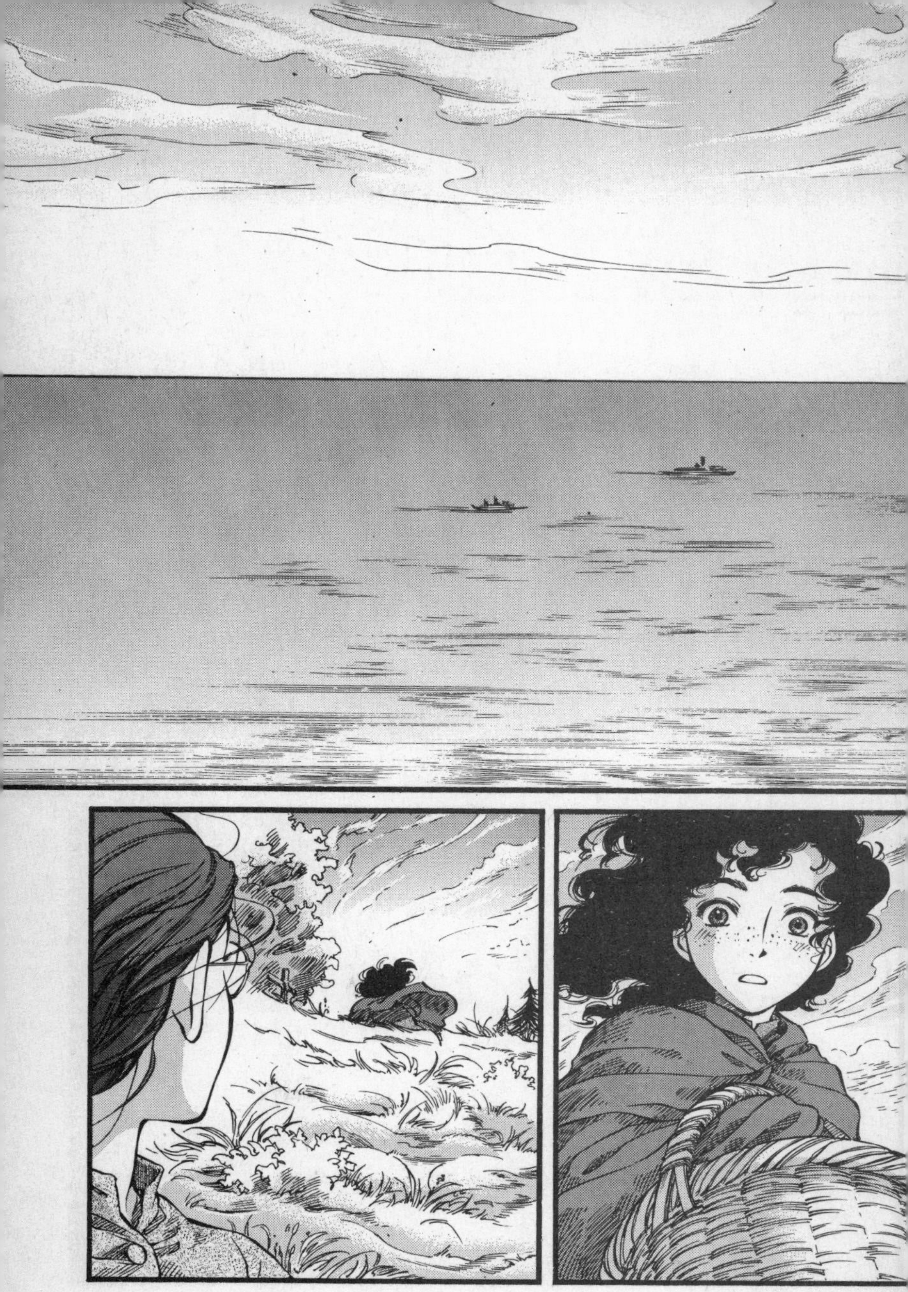

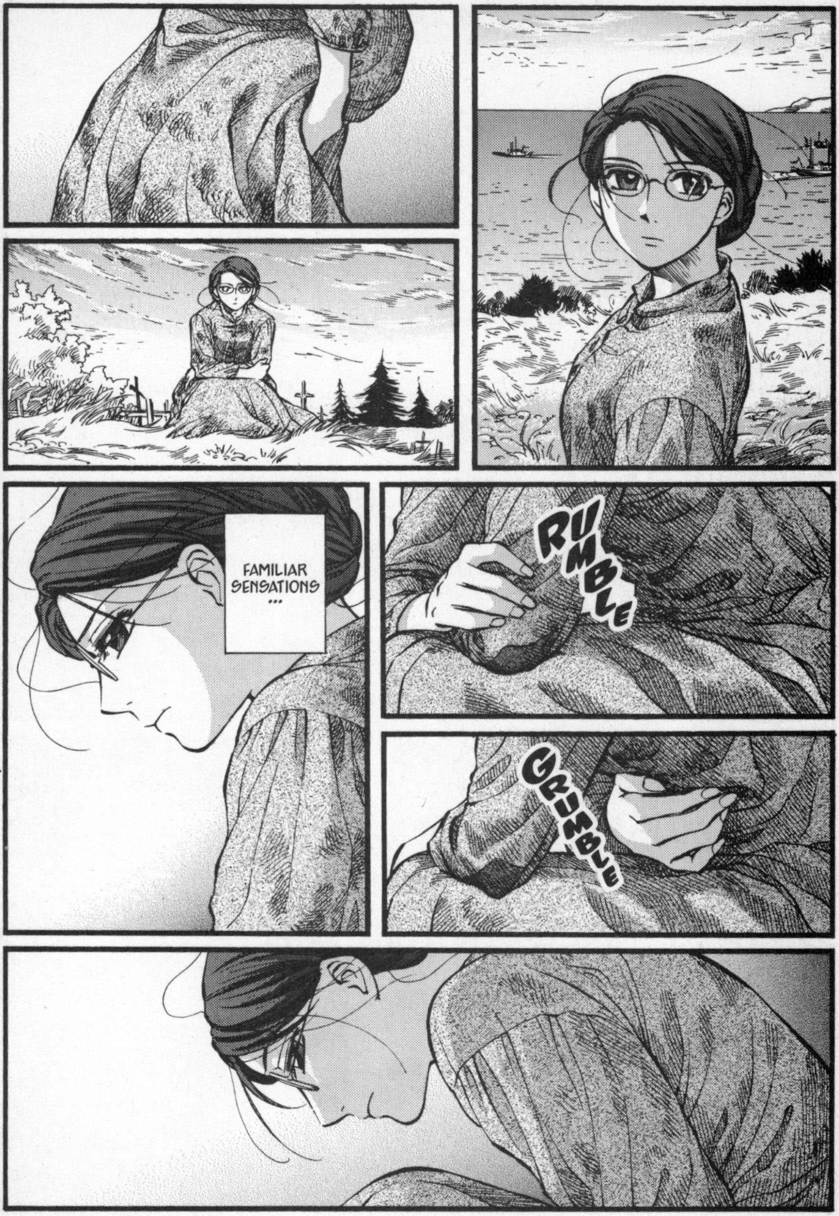
RUMBLE
GRUMBLE
FAMILIAR SENSATIONS ...

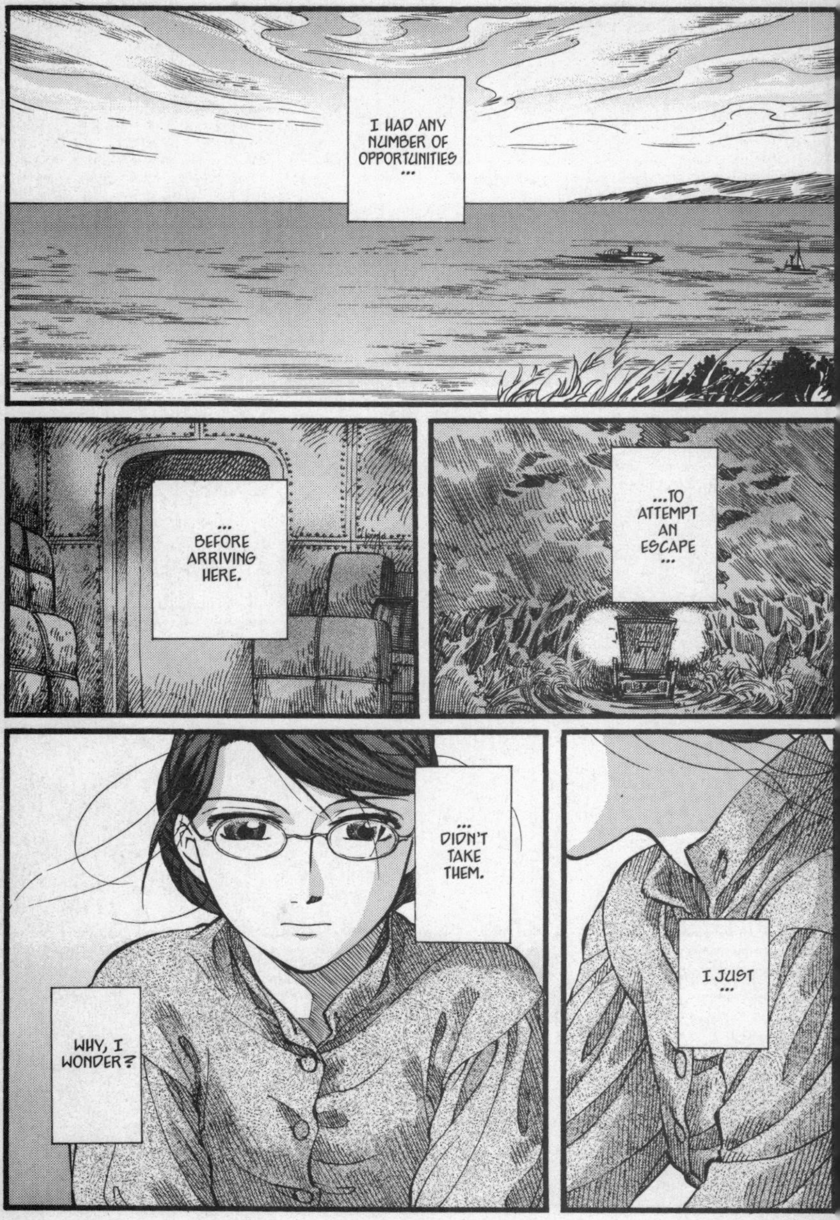
I HAD ANY NUMBER OF OPPORTUNITIES ...
...TO ATTEMPT AN ESCAPE ...
... BEFORE ARRIVING HERE.
I JUST ...
... DIDN'T TAKE THEM.
WHY, I WONDER?

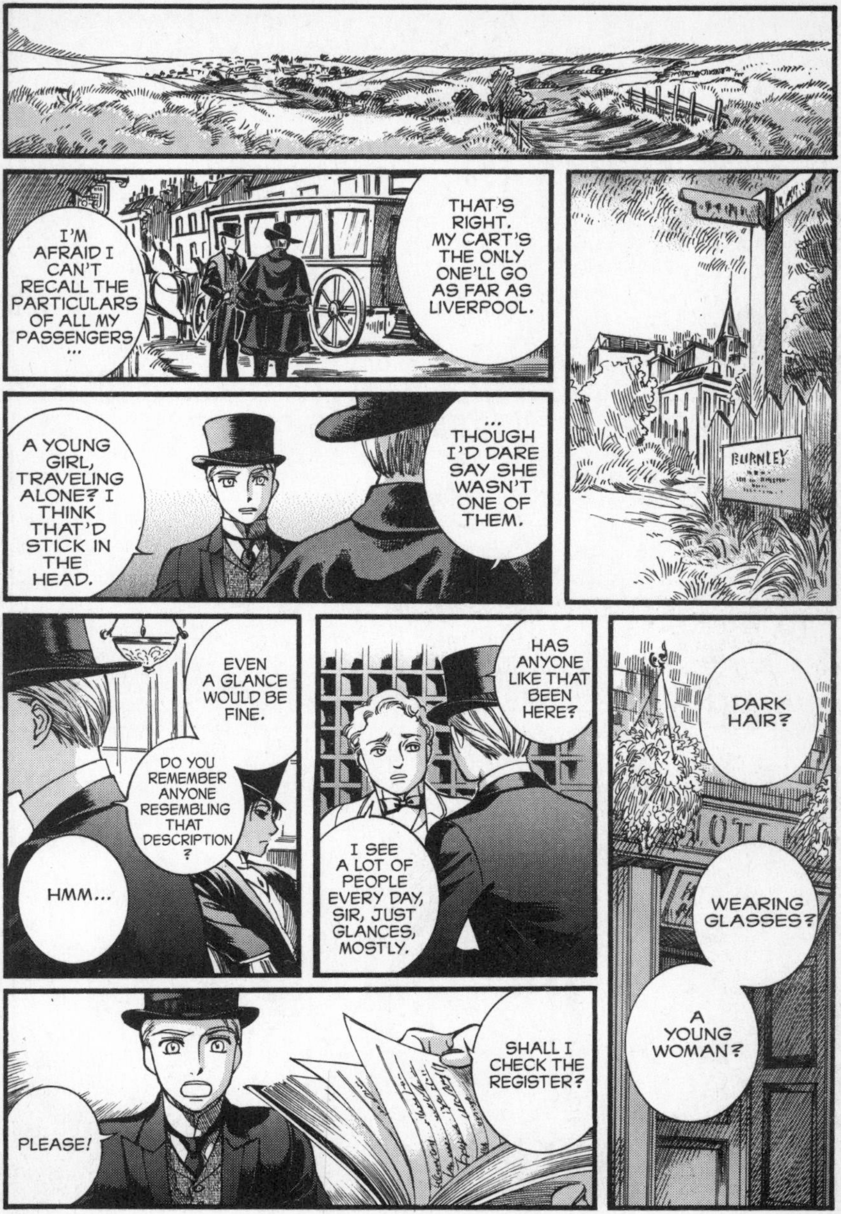
BURNLEY
THAT'S RIGHT. MY CART'S THE ONLY ONE'LL GO AS FAR AS LIVERPOOL.
I'M AFRAID I CAN'T RECALL THE PARTICULARS OF ALL MY PASSENGERS...
... THOUGH I'D DARE SAY SHE WASN'T ONE OF THEM.
A YOUNG GIRL, TRAVELING ALONE? I THINK THAT'D STICK IN THE HEAD.
DARK HAIR?
WEARING GLASSES?
A YOUNG WOMAN?
HAS ANYONE LIKE THAT BEEN HERE?
I SEE A LOT OF PEOPLE EVERY DAY, SIR, JUST GLANCES, MOSTLY.
EVEN A GLANCE WOULD BE FINE.
DO YOU REMEMBER ANYONE RESEMBLING THAT DESCRIPTION?
HMM...
SHALL I CHECK THE REGISTER?
PLEASE!

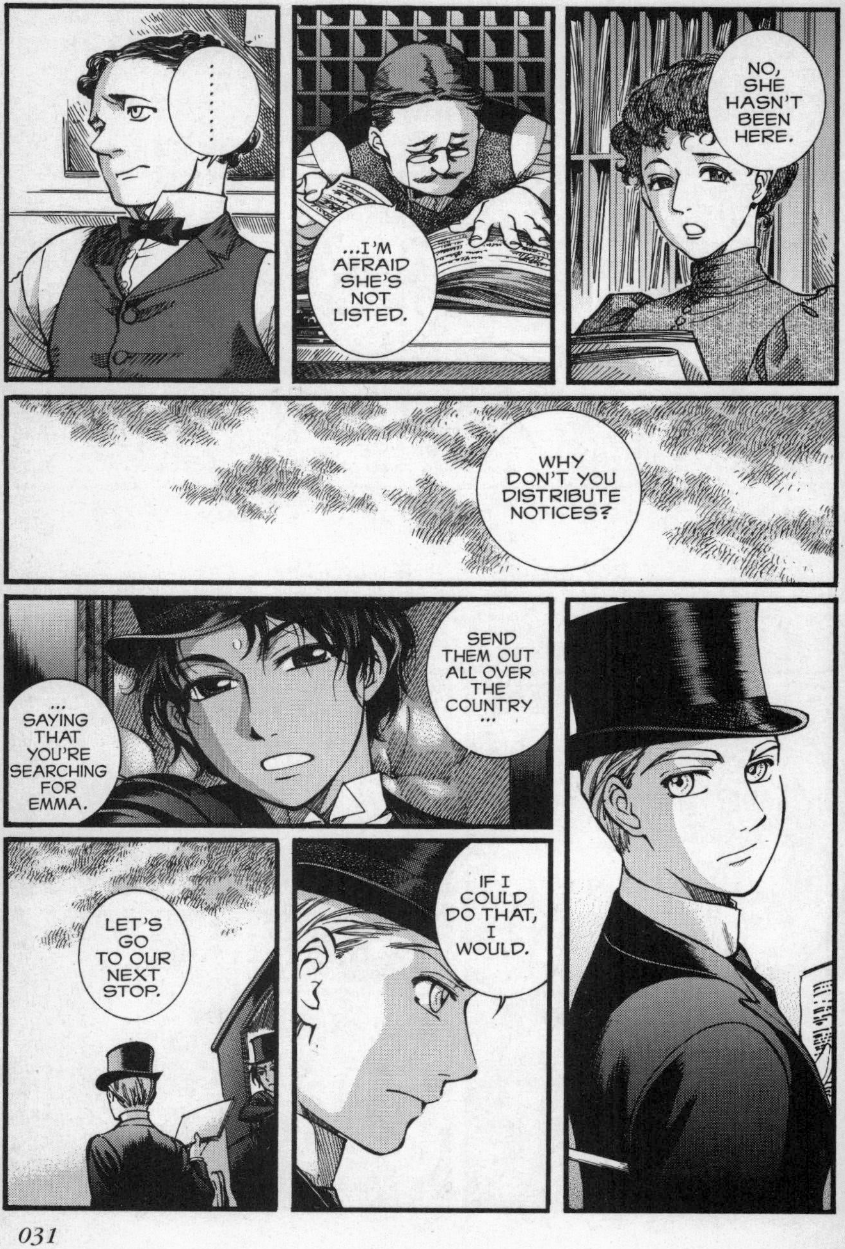
NO, SHE HASN'T BEEN HERE.
...I'M AFRAID SHE'S NOT LISTED.
......
WHY DON'T YOU DISTRIBUTE NOTICES?
SEND THEM OUT ALL OVER THE COUNTRY ...
... SAYING THAT YOU'RE SEARCHING FOR EMMA.
IF I COULD DO THAT, I WOULD.
LET'S GO TO OUR NEXT STOP.

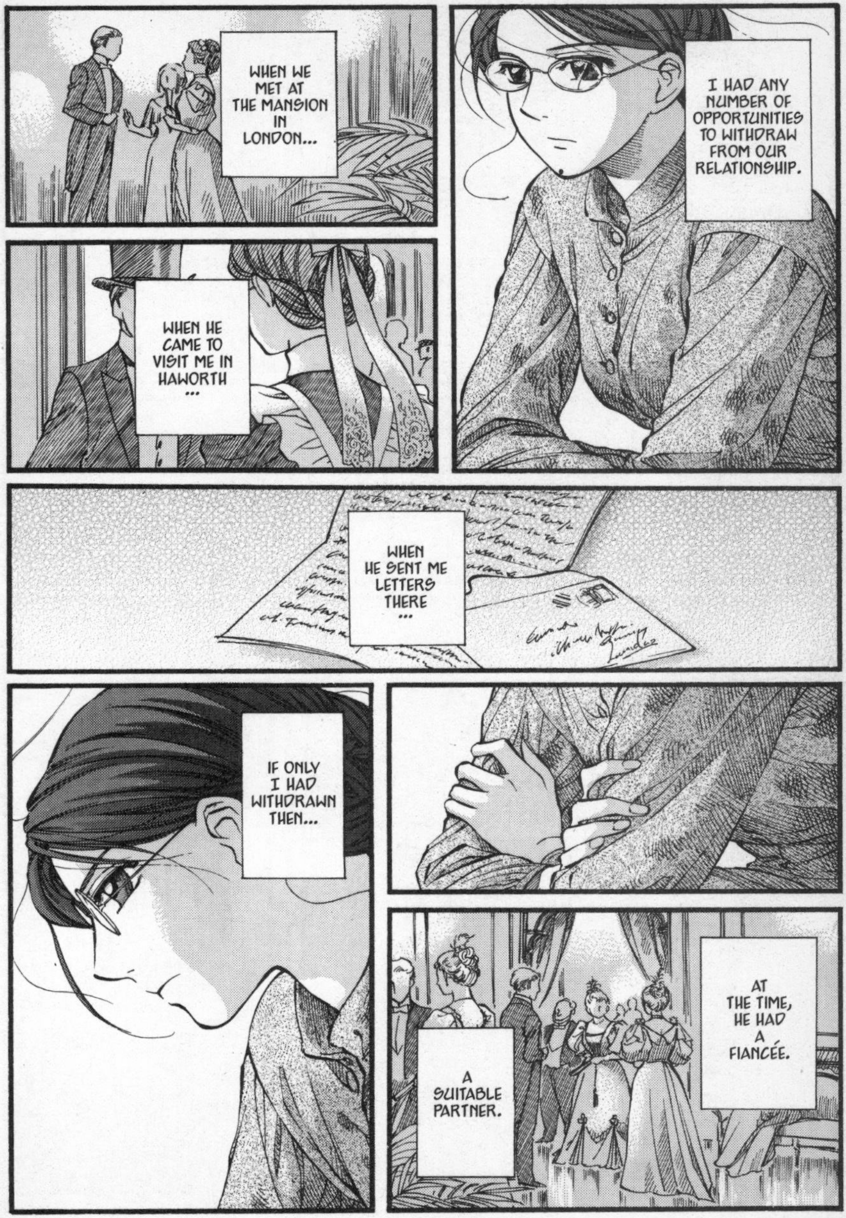
I HAD ANY NUMBER OF OPPORTUNITIES TO WITHDRAW FROM OUR RELATIONSHIP.
WHEN WE MET AT THE MANSION IN LONDON...
WHEN HE CAME TO VISIT ME IN HAWORTH ...
WHEN HE SENT ME LETTERS THERE ...
AT THE TIME, HE HAD A FIANCÉE.
A SUITABLE PARTNER.
IF ONLY I HAD WITHDRAWN THEN...

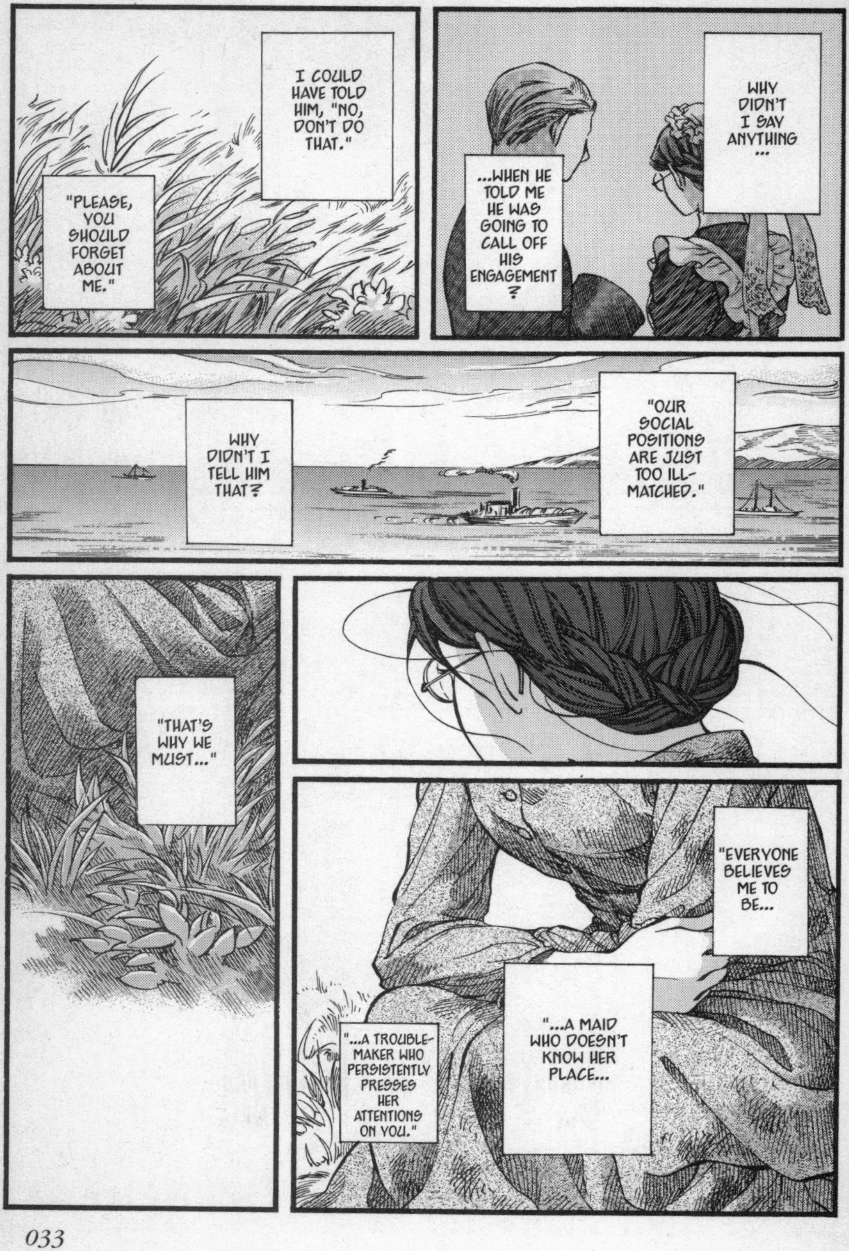
WHY DIDN'T I SAY ANYTHING ...
...WHEN HE TOLD ME HE WAS GOING TO CALL OFF HIS ENGAGEMENT?
I COULD HAVE TOLD HIM, "NO, DON'T DO THAT."
"PLEASE, YOU SHOULD FORGET ABOUT ME."
"OUR SOCIAL POSITIONS ARE JUST TOO ILL-MATCHED."
WHY DIDN'T I TELL HIM THAT?
"EVERYONE BELIEVES ME TO BE...
"...A MAID WHO DOESN'T KNOW HER PLACE...
"...A TROUBLE-MAKER WHO PERSISTENTLY PRESSES HER ATTENTIONS ON YOU."
"THAT'S WHY WE MUST..."

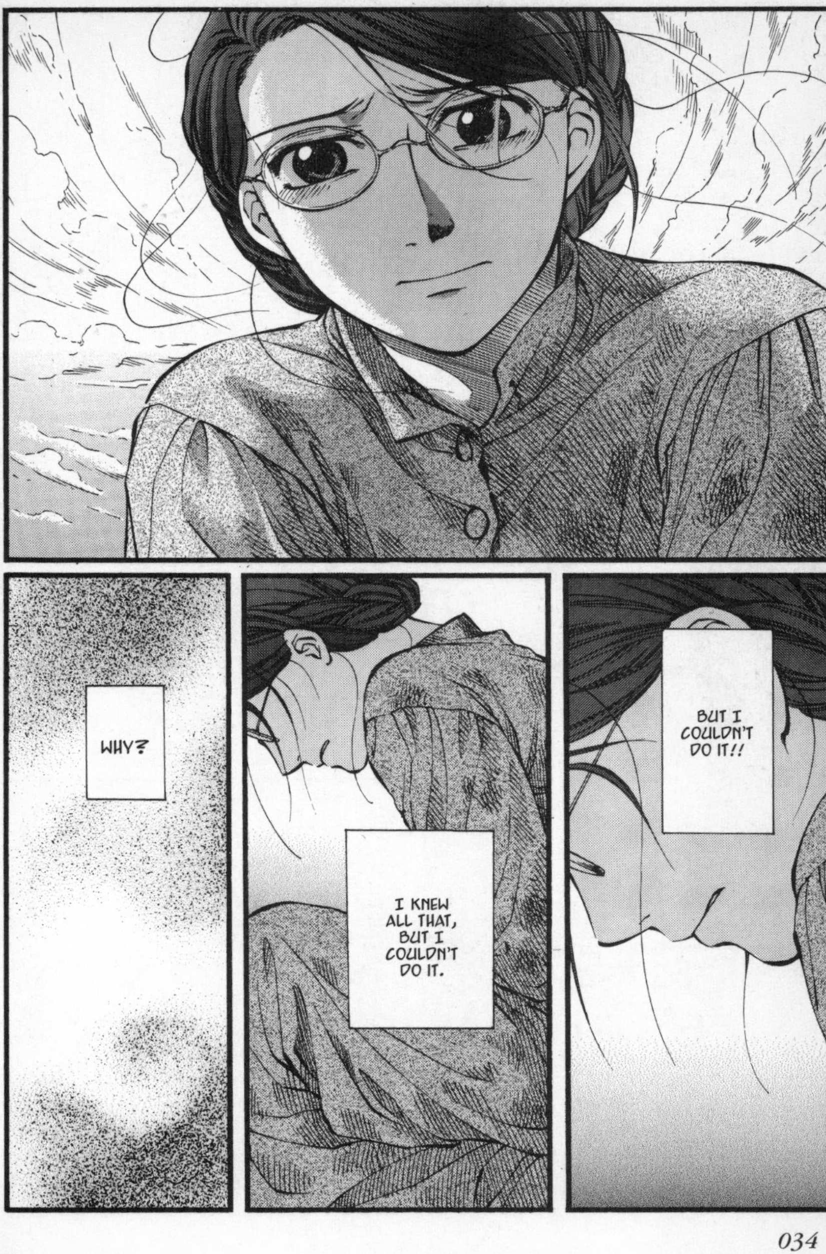
BUT I COULDN'T DO IT!!
I KNEW ALL THAT, BUT I COULDN'T DO IT.
WHY?

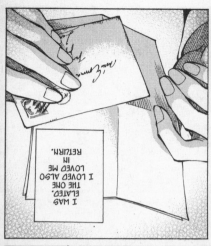

BECAUSE I *LOVE* YOU!!
BECAUSE I WAS *HAPPY*.
I WAS ELATED. THE ONE I LOVED ALSO LOVED ME IN RETURN.
I WAS THRILLED TO BE ABLE TO EXPRESS MY FEELINGS TO THE MAN I LOVED.

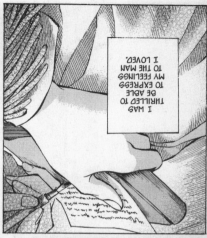

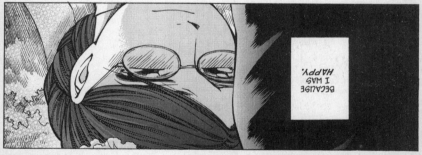

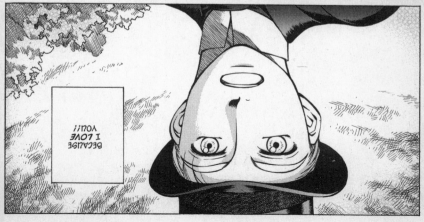

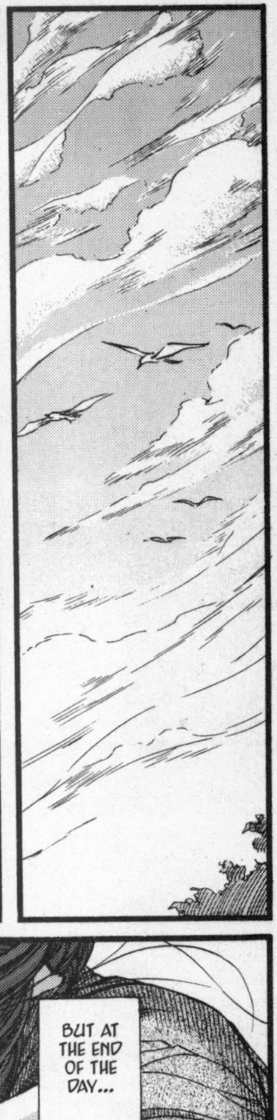

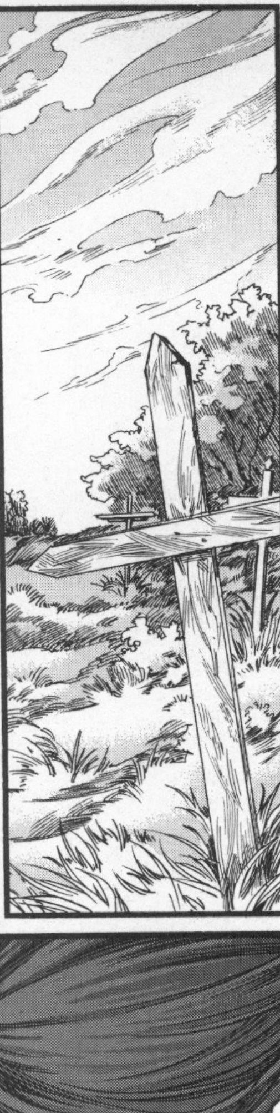

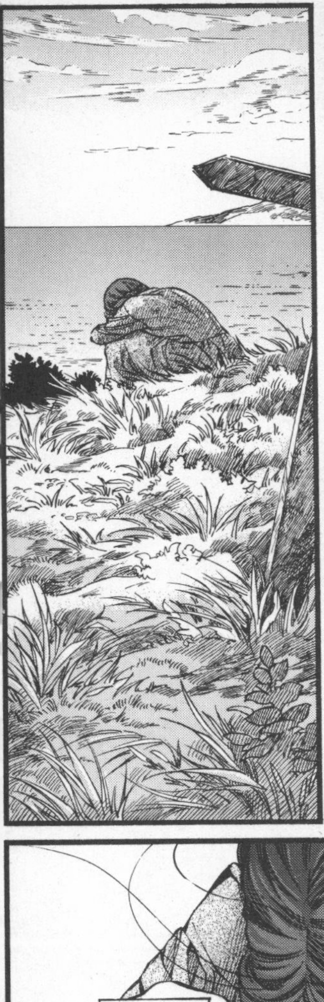

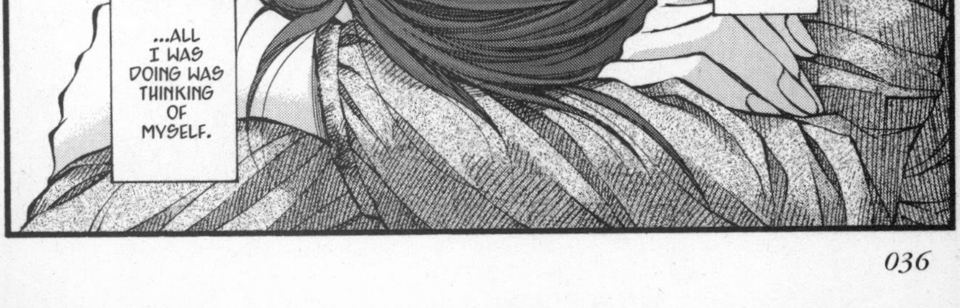
BUT AT THE END OF THE DAY...
...ALL I WAS DOING WAS THINKING OF MYSELF.

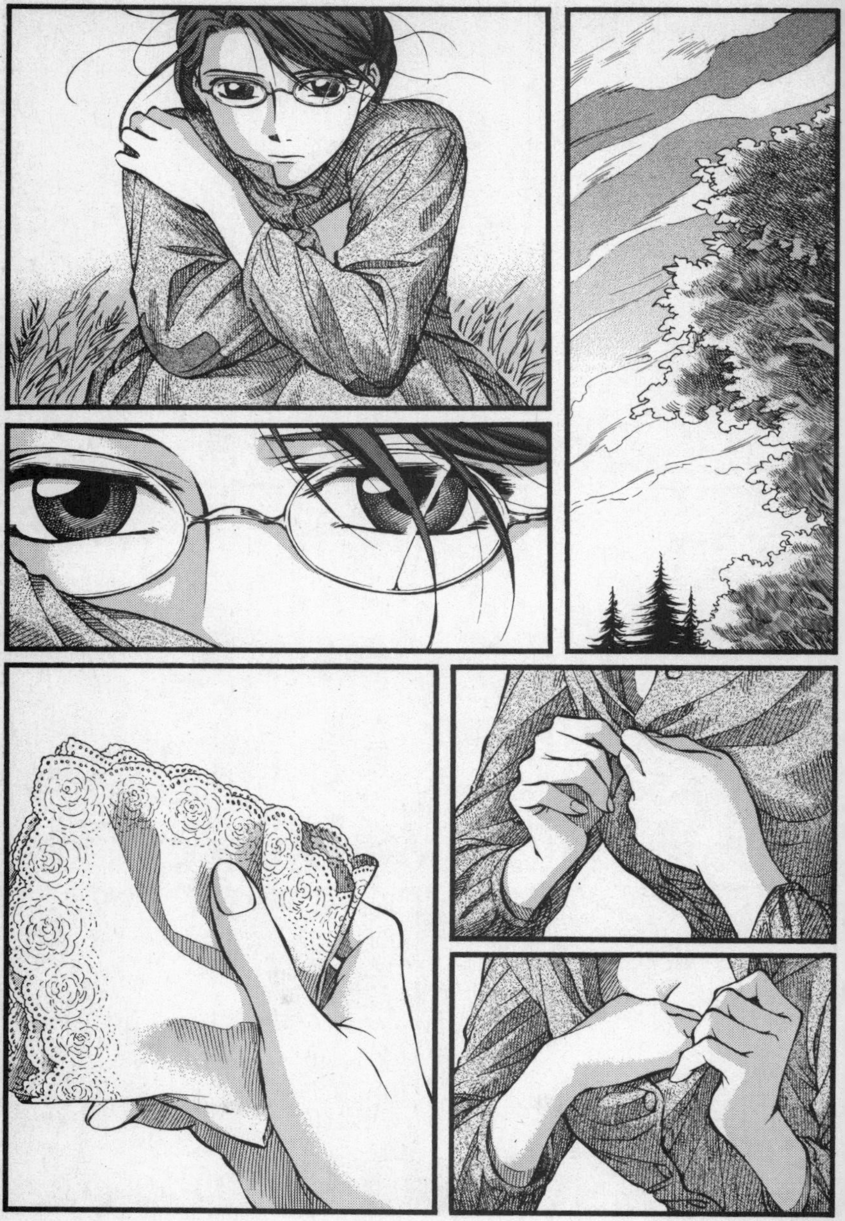

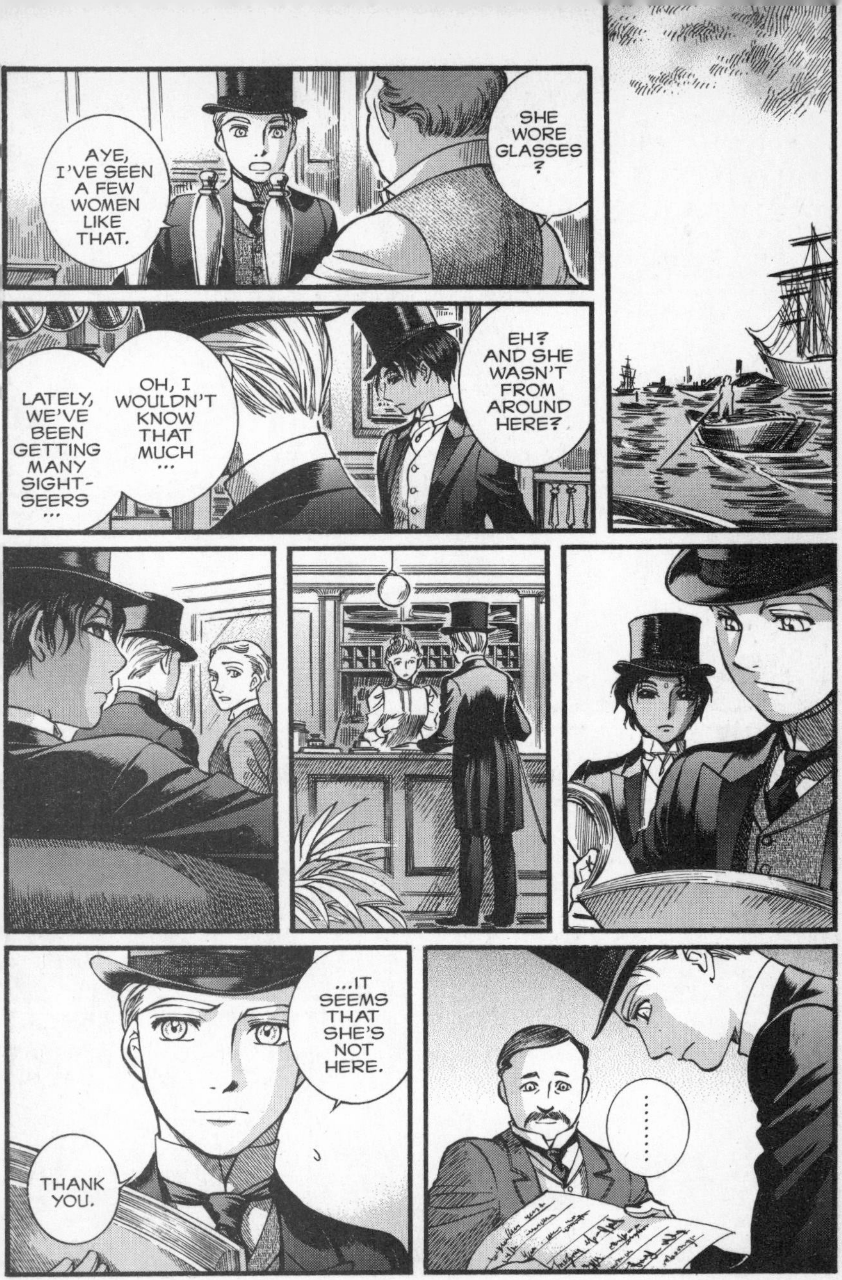
SHE WORE GLASSES?
AYE, I'VE SEEN A FEW WOMEN LIKE THAT.
EH? AND SHE WASN'T FROM AROUND HERE?
OH, I WOULDN'T KNOW THAT MUCH ...
LATELY, WE'VE BEEN GETTING MANY SIGHT-SEERS ...
......
...IT SEEMS THAT SHE'S NOT HERE.
THANK YOU.

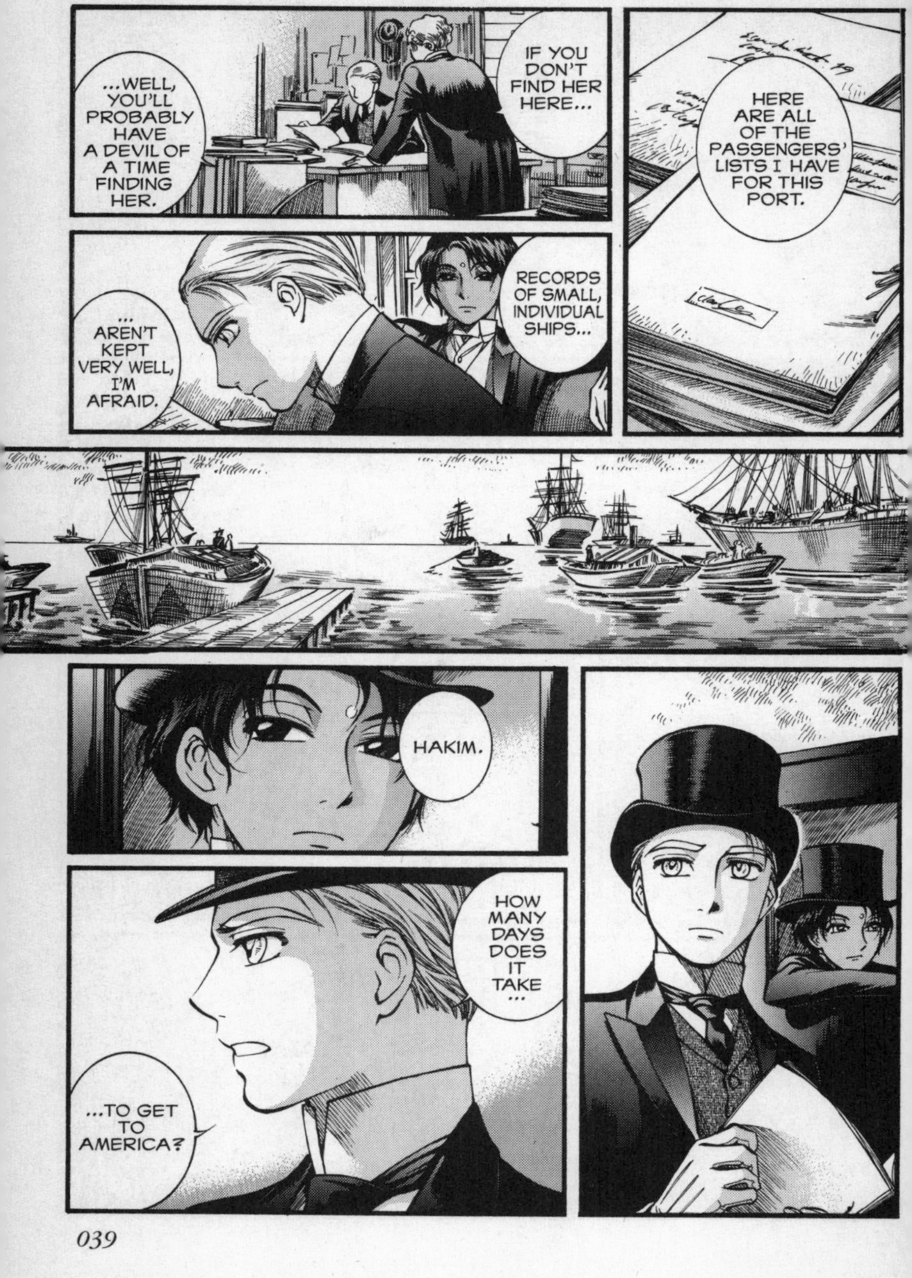
HERE ARE ALL OF THE PASSENGERS' LISTS I HAVE FOR THIS PORT.
IF YOU DON'T FIND HER HERE...
...WELL, YOU'LL PROBABLY HAVE A DEVIL OF A TIME FINDING HER.
RECORDS OF SMALL, INDIVIDUAL SHIPS...
...AREN'T KEPT VERY WELL, I'M AFRAID.
HAKIM.
HOW MANY DAYS DOES IT TAKE...
...TO GET TO AMERICA?

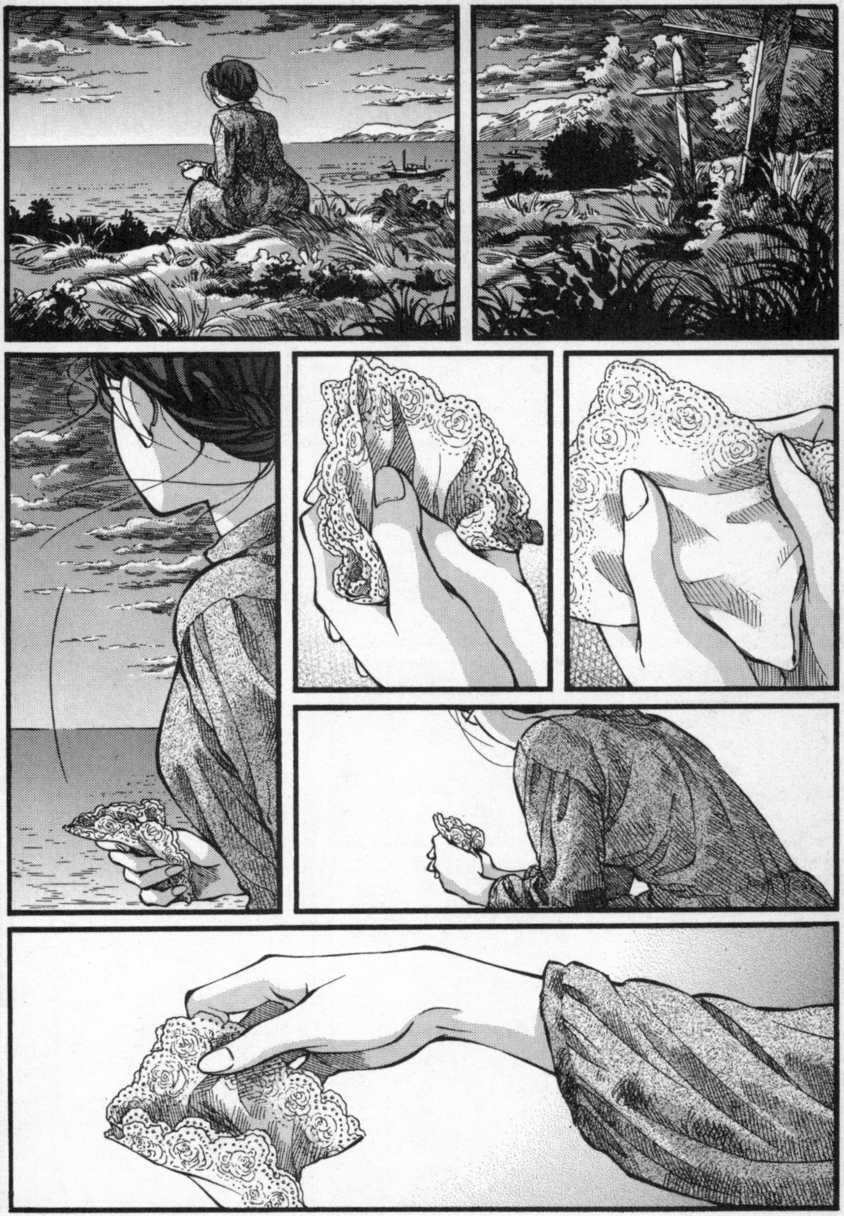

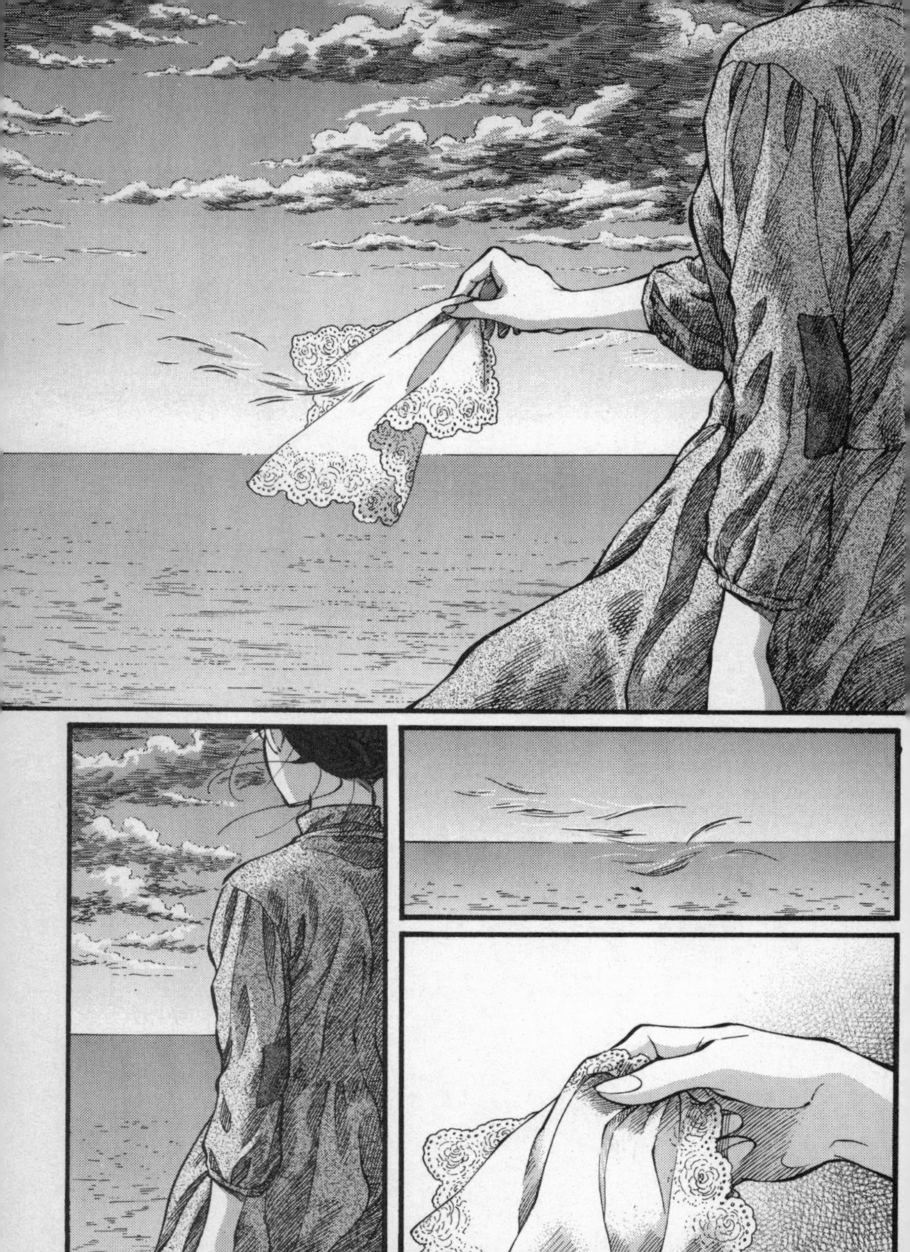

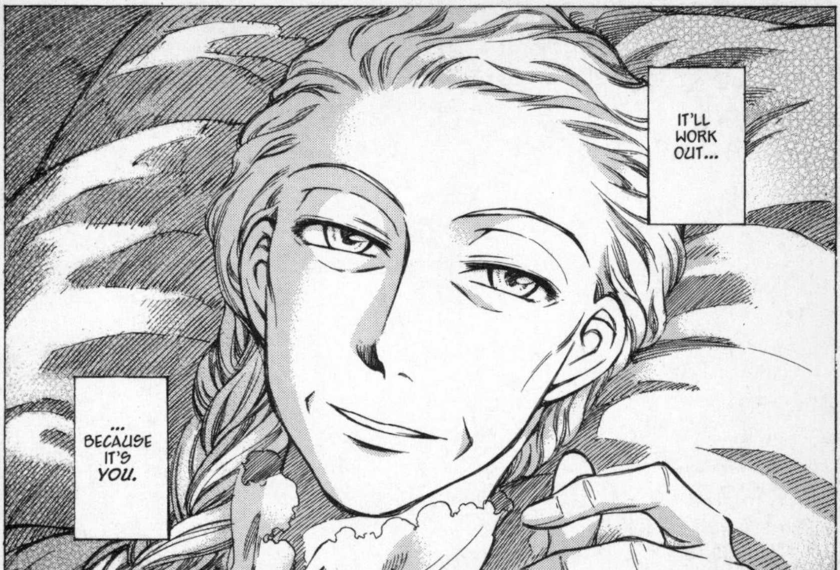
IT'LL WORK OUT...
... BECAUSE IT'S *YOU.*

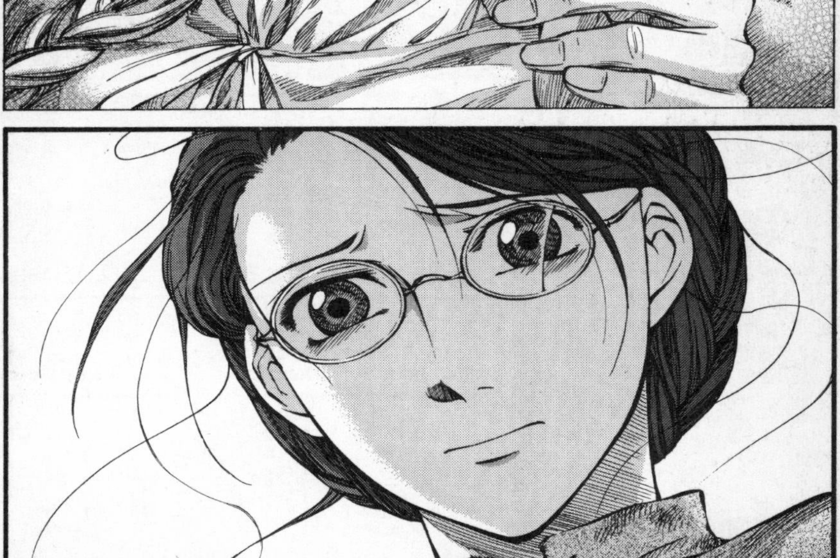

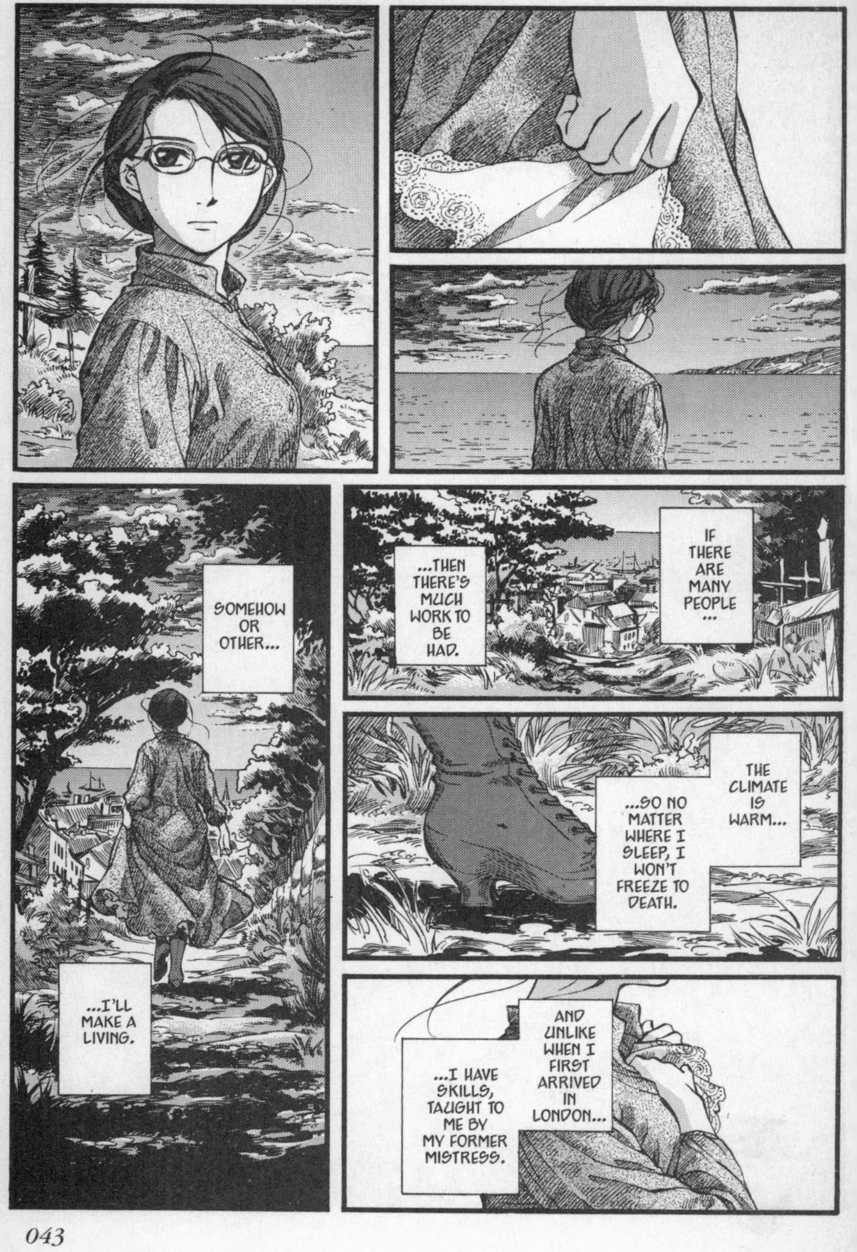
IF THERE ARE MANY PEOPLE ...
...THEN THERE'S MUCH WORK TO BE HAD.
THE CLIMATE IS WARM...
...SO NO MATTER WHERE I SLEEP, I WON'T FREEZE TO DEATH.
AND UNLIKE WHEN I FIRST ARRIVED IN LONDON...
...I HAVE SKILLS, TAUGHT TO ME BY MY FORMER MISTRESS.
SOMEHOW OR OTHER...
...I'LL MAKE A LIVING.

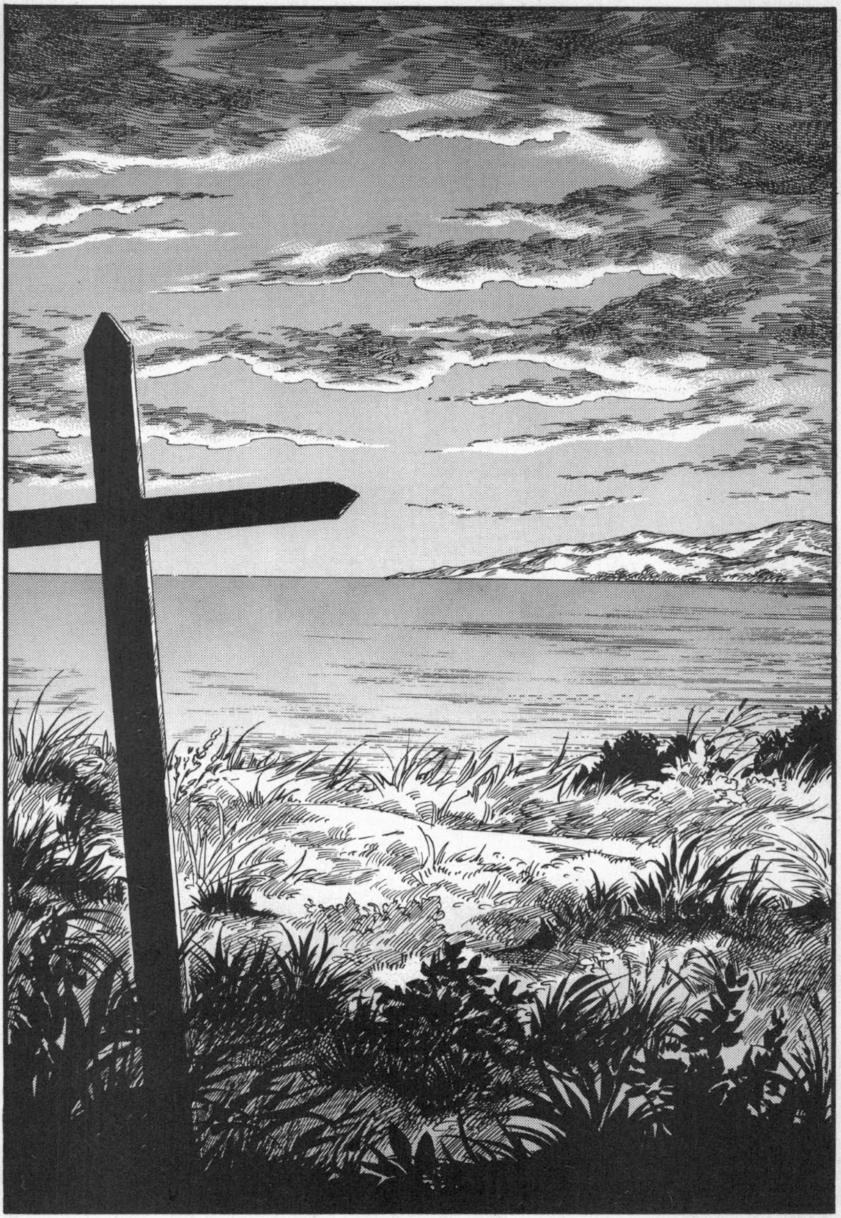

Chapter Forty Five: The End

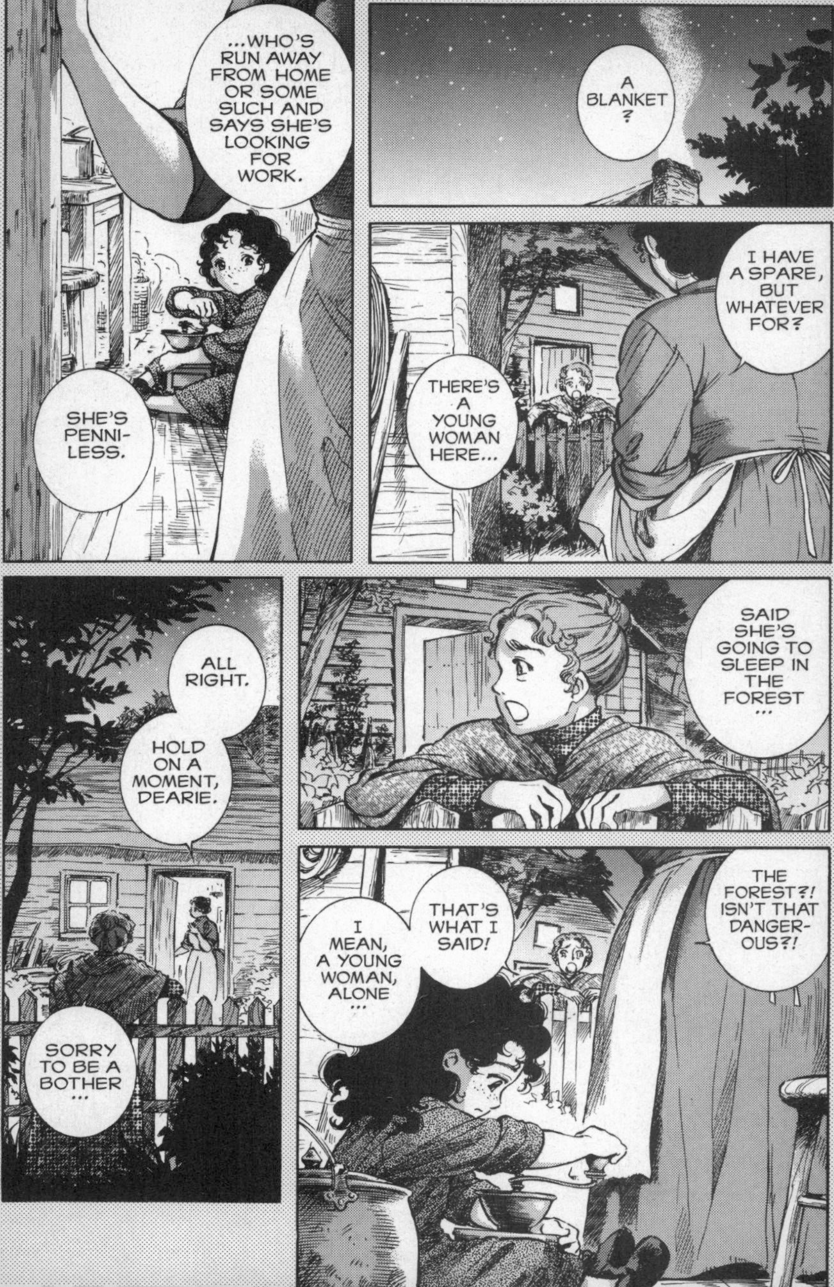
A BLANKET?
I HAVE A SPARE, BUT WHATEVER FOR?
THERE'S A YOUNG WOMAN HERE...
...WHO'S RUN AWAY FROM HOME OR SOME SUCH AND SAYS SHE'S LOOKING FOR WORK.
SHE'S PENNILESS.
SAID SHE'S GOING TO SLEEP IN THE FOREST...
THE FOREST?! ISN'T THAT DANGEROUS?!
THAT'S WHAT I SAID!
I MEAN, A YOUNG WOMAN, ALONE...
ALL RIGHT.
HOLD ON A MOMENT, DEARIE.
SORRY TO BE A BOTHER...

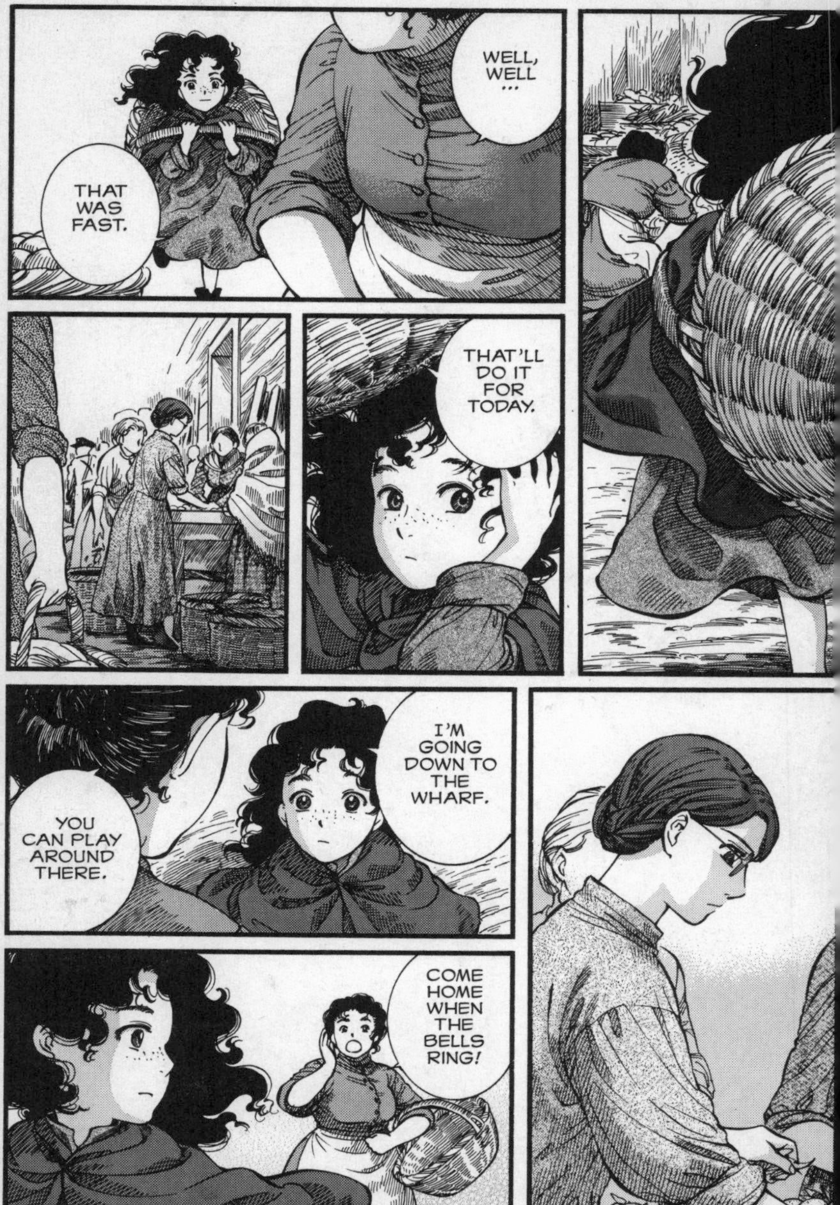
WELL, WELL ...
THAT WAS FAST.
THAT'LL DO IT FOR TODAY.
I'M GOING DOWN TO THE WHARF.
YOU CAN PLAY AROUND THERE.
COME HOME WHEN THE BELLS RING!

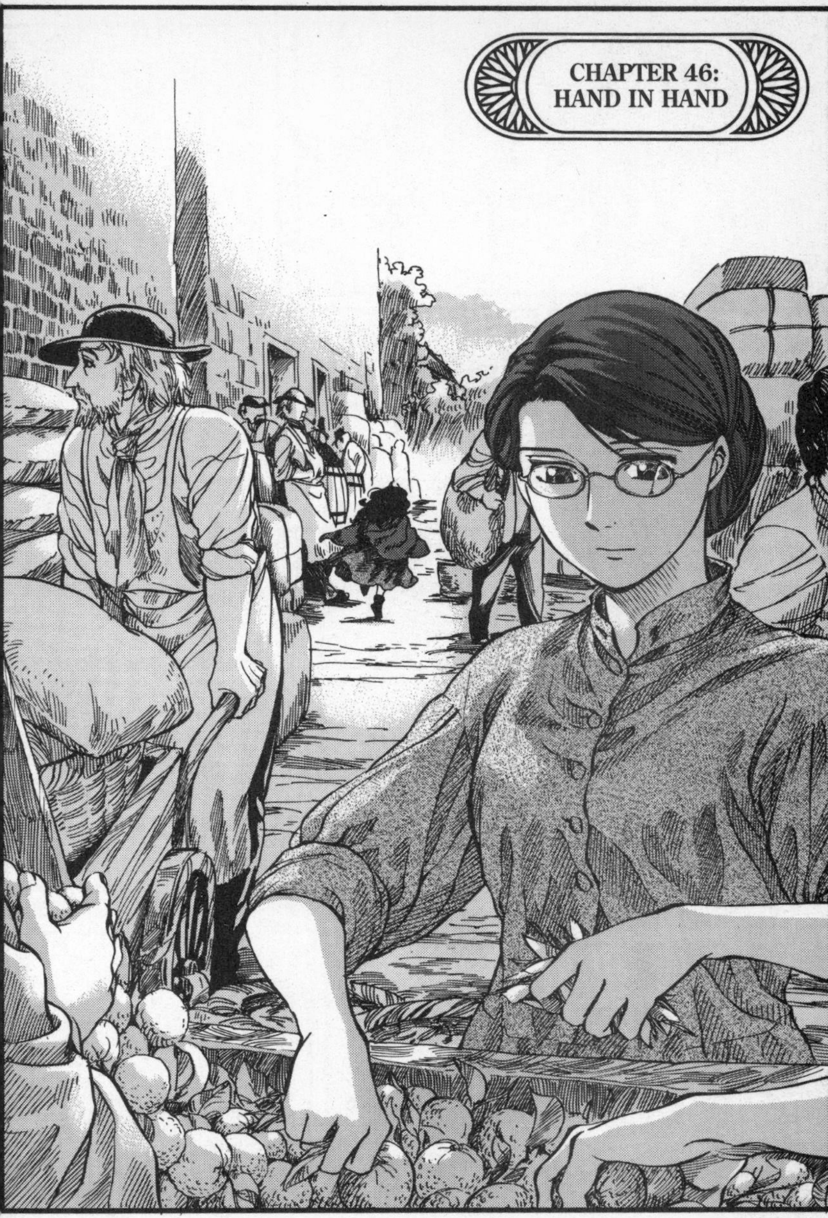
CHAPTER 46:
HAND IN HAND

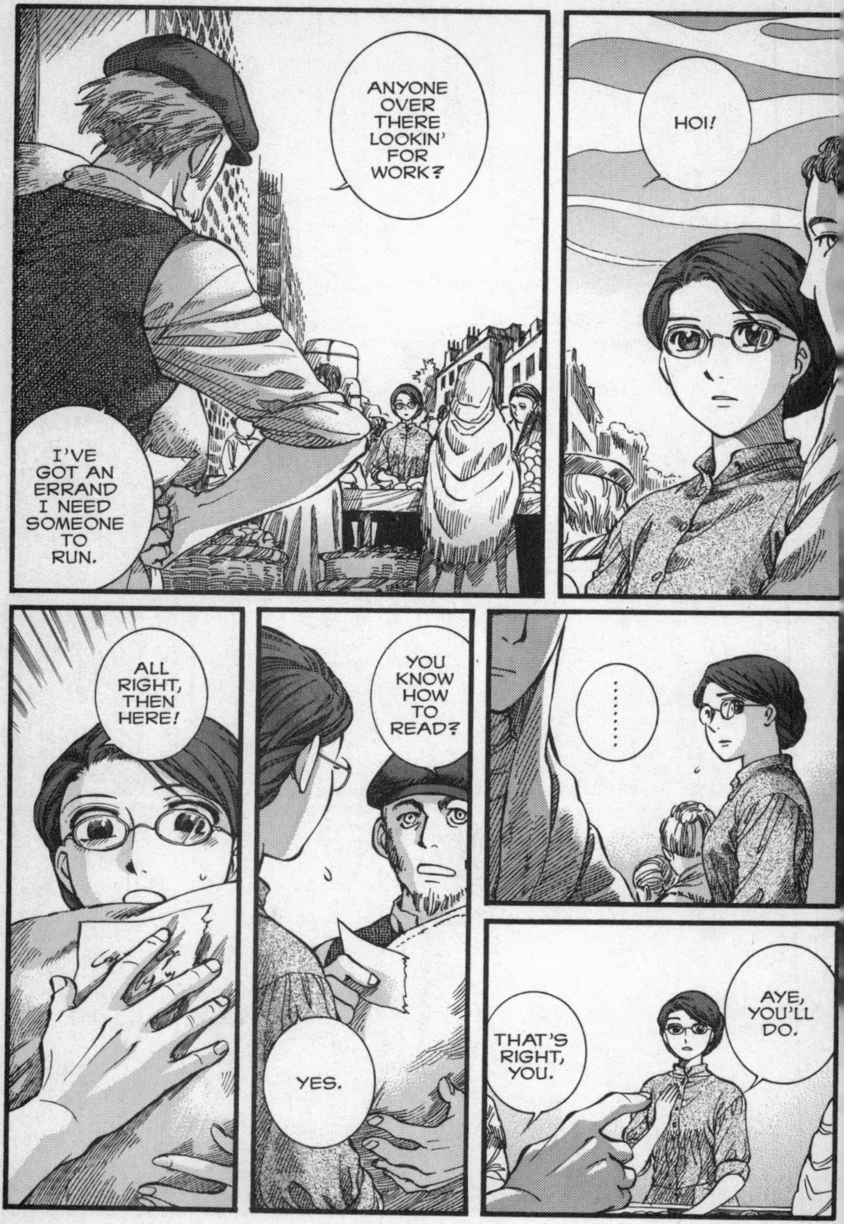
HOI!
ANYONE OVER THERE LOOKIN' FOR WORK?
I'VE GOT AN ERRAND I NEED SOMEONE TO RUN.
......
AYE, YOU'LL DO.
THAT'S RIGHT, YOU.
YOU KNOW HOW TO READ?
YES.
ALL RIGHT, THEN HERE!

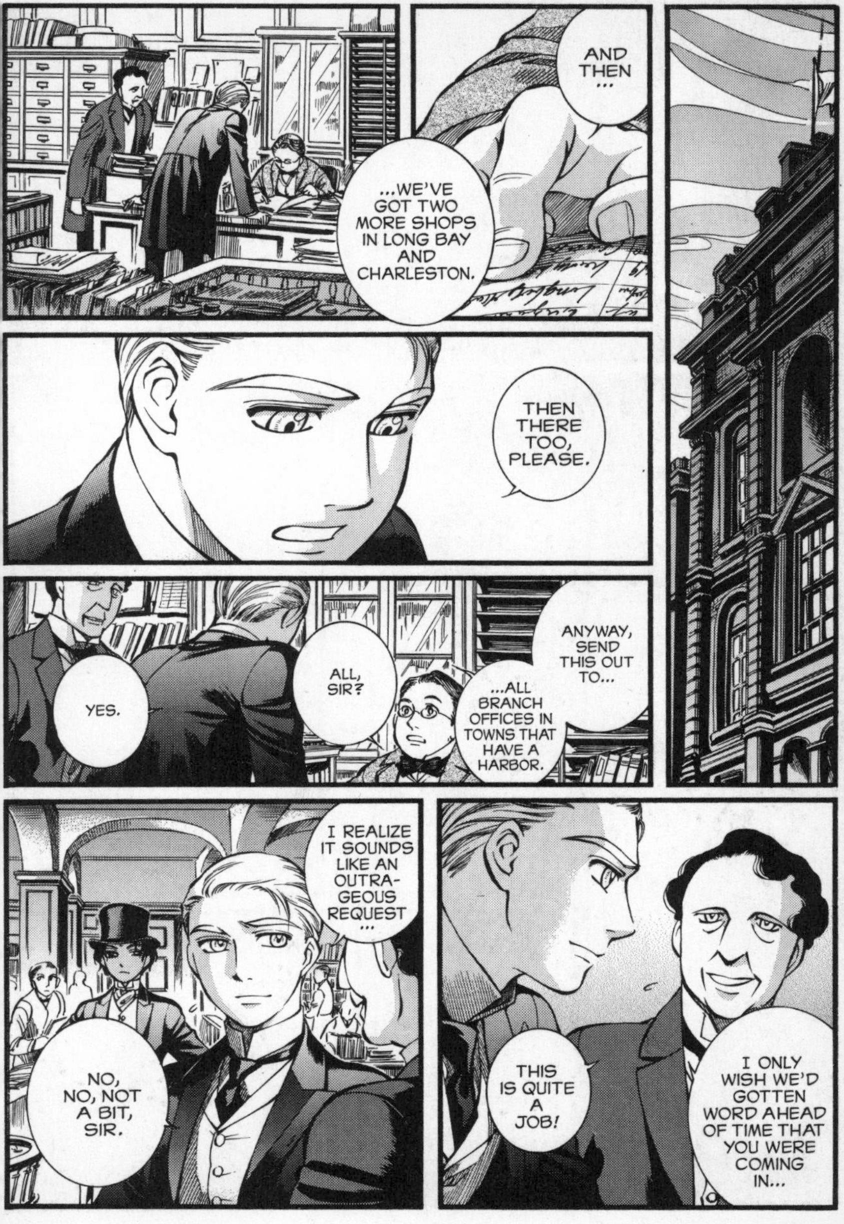
AND THEN ...
...WE'VE GOT TWO MORE SHOPS IN LONG BAY AND CHARLESTON.
THEN THERE TOO, PLEASE.
ANYWAY, SEND THIS OUT TO...
...ALL BRANCH OFFICES IN TOWNS THAT HAVE A HARBOR.
ALL, SIR?
YES.
I ONLY WISH WE'D GOTTEN WORD AHEAD OF TIME THAT YOU WERE COMING IN...
THIS IS QUITE A JOB!
I REALIZE IT SOUNDS LIKE AN OUTRA-GEOUS REQUEST ...
NO, NO, NOT A BIT, SIR.

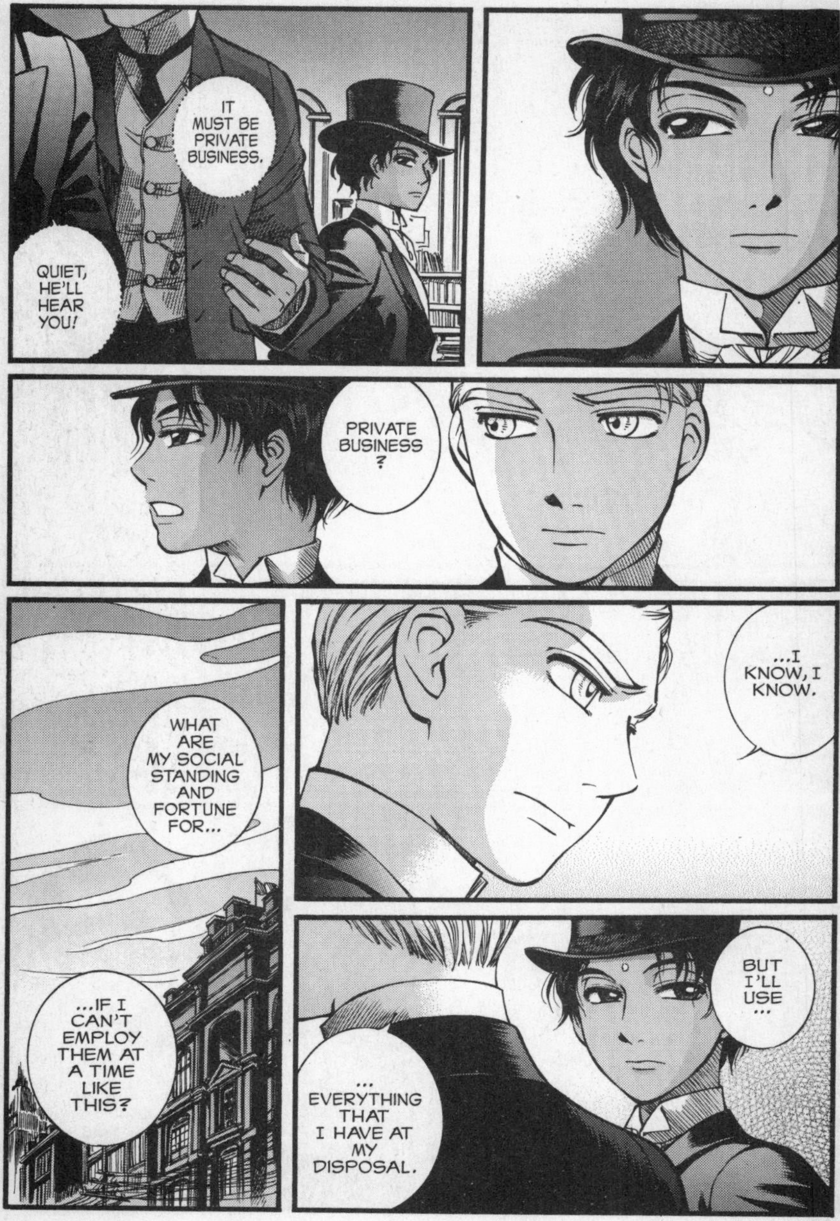
IT MUST BE PRIVATE BUSINESS.
QUIET, HE'LL HEAR YOU!
PRIVATE BUSINESS?
...I KNOW, I KNOW.
BUT I'LL USE...
...EVERYTHING THAT I HAVE AT MY DISPOSAL.
WHAT ARE MY SOCIAL STANDING AND FORTUNE FOR...
...IF I CAN'T EMPLOY THEM AT A TIME LIKE THIS?

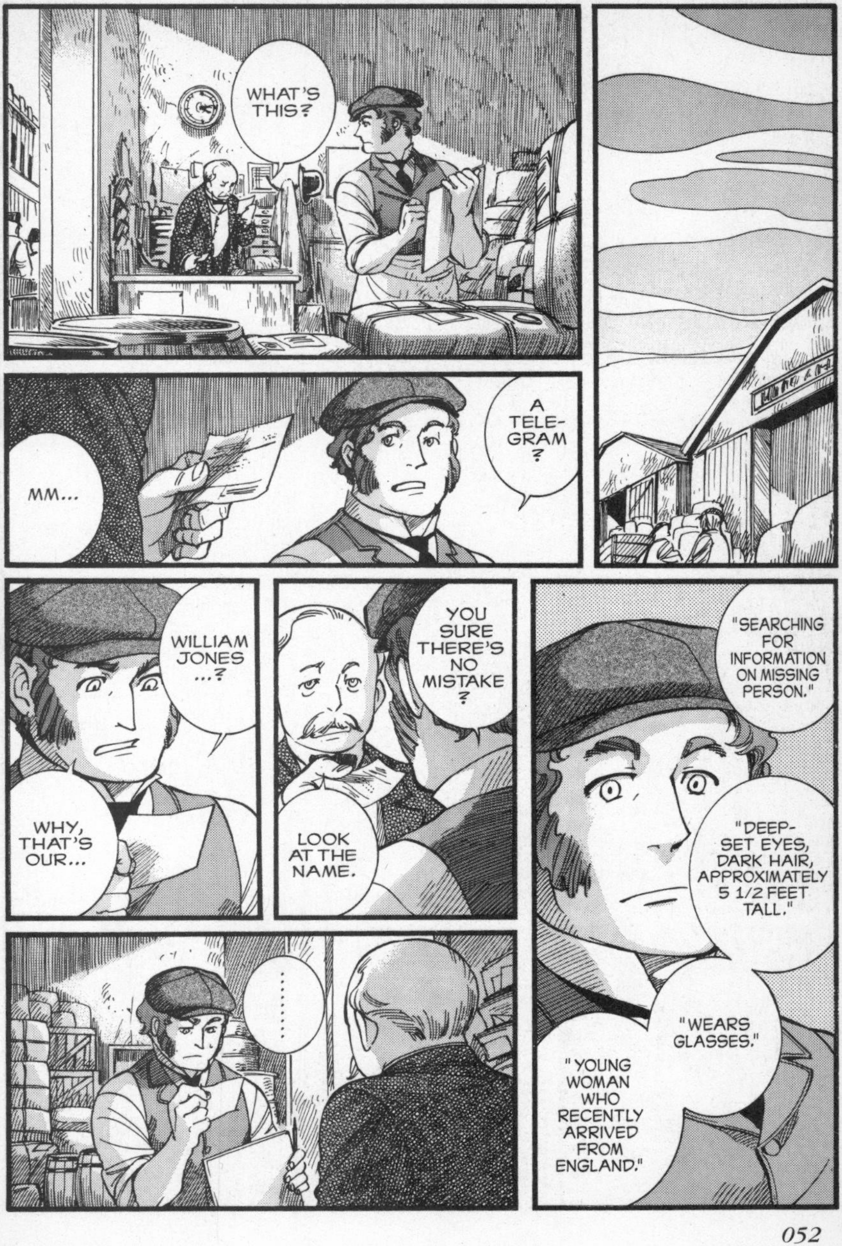
WHAT'S THIS?
A TELE-GRAM?
MM...
"SEARCHING FOR INFORMATION ON MISSING PERSON."
"DEEP-SET EYES, DARK HAIR, APPROXIMATELY 5 1/2 FEET TALL."
"WEARS GLASSES."
"YOUNG WOMAN WHO RECENTLY ARRIVED FROM ENGLAND."
YOU SURE THERE'S NO MISTAKE?
LOOK AT THE NAME.
WILLIAM JONES ...?
WHY, THAT'S OUR...
......

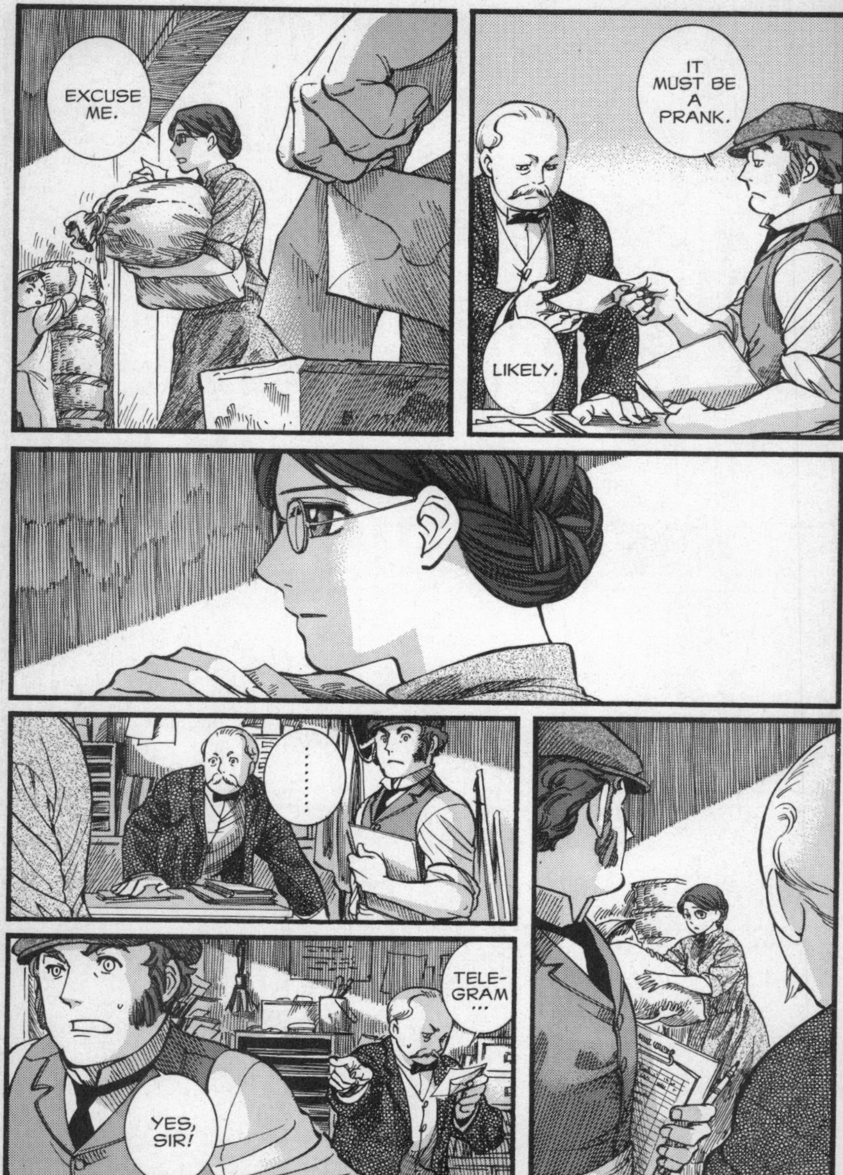
IT MUST BE A PRANK.
LIKELY.
EXCUSE ME.
......
TELE-GRAM...
YES, SIR!

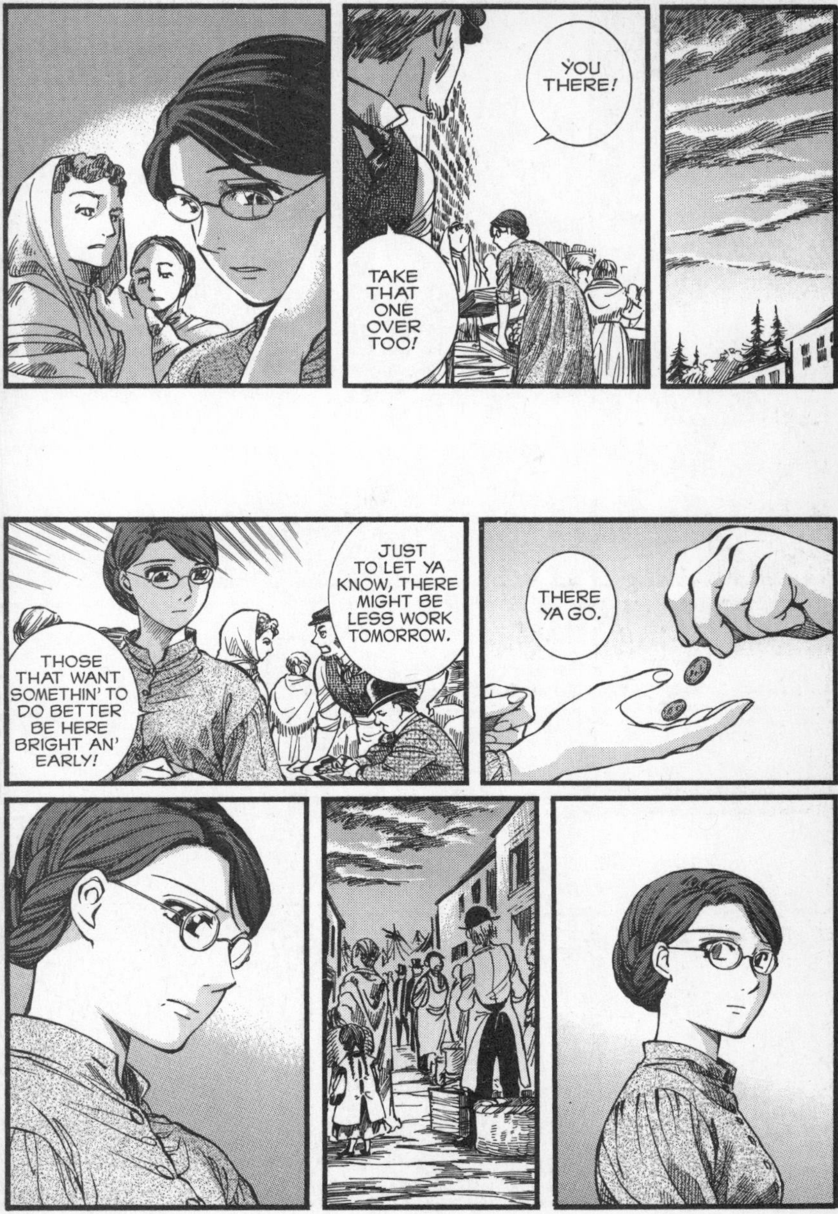
YOU THERE!
TAKE THAT ONE OVER TOO!
THERE YA GO.
JUST TO LET YA KNOW, THERE MIGHT BE LESS WORK TOMORROW.
THOSE THAT WANT SOMETHIN' TO DO BETTER BE HERE BRIGHT AN' EARLY!

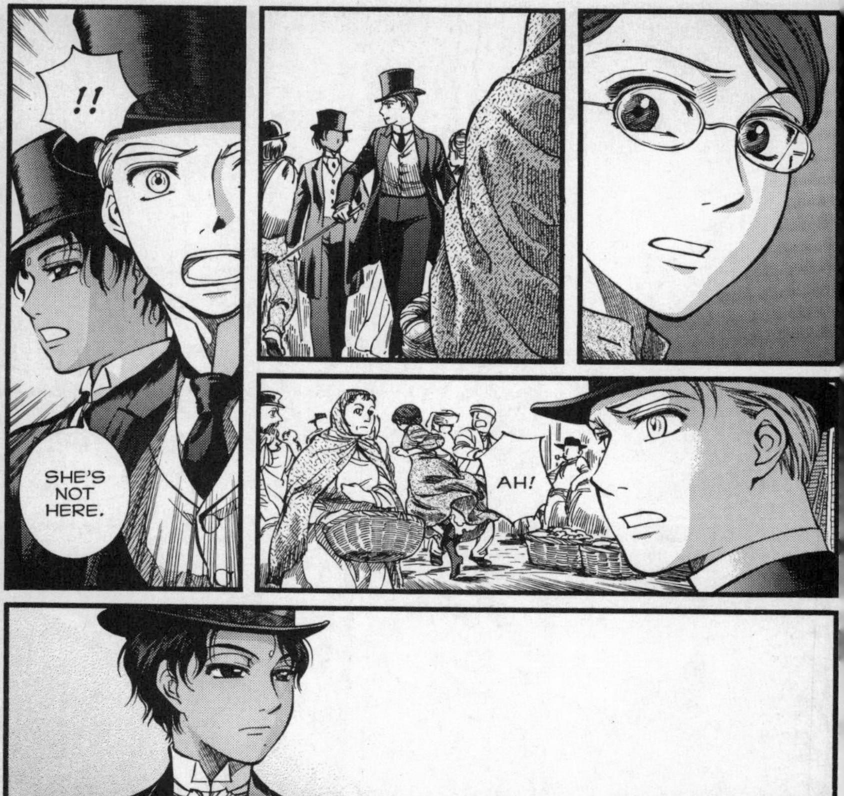
AH!
!!
SHE'S NOT HERE.
......
... SHE WAS HERE.

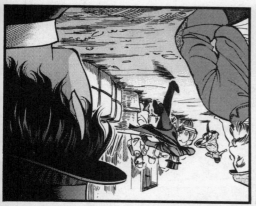

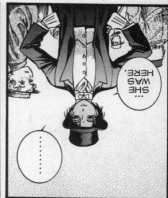

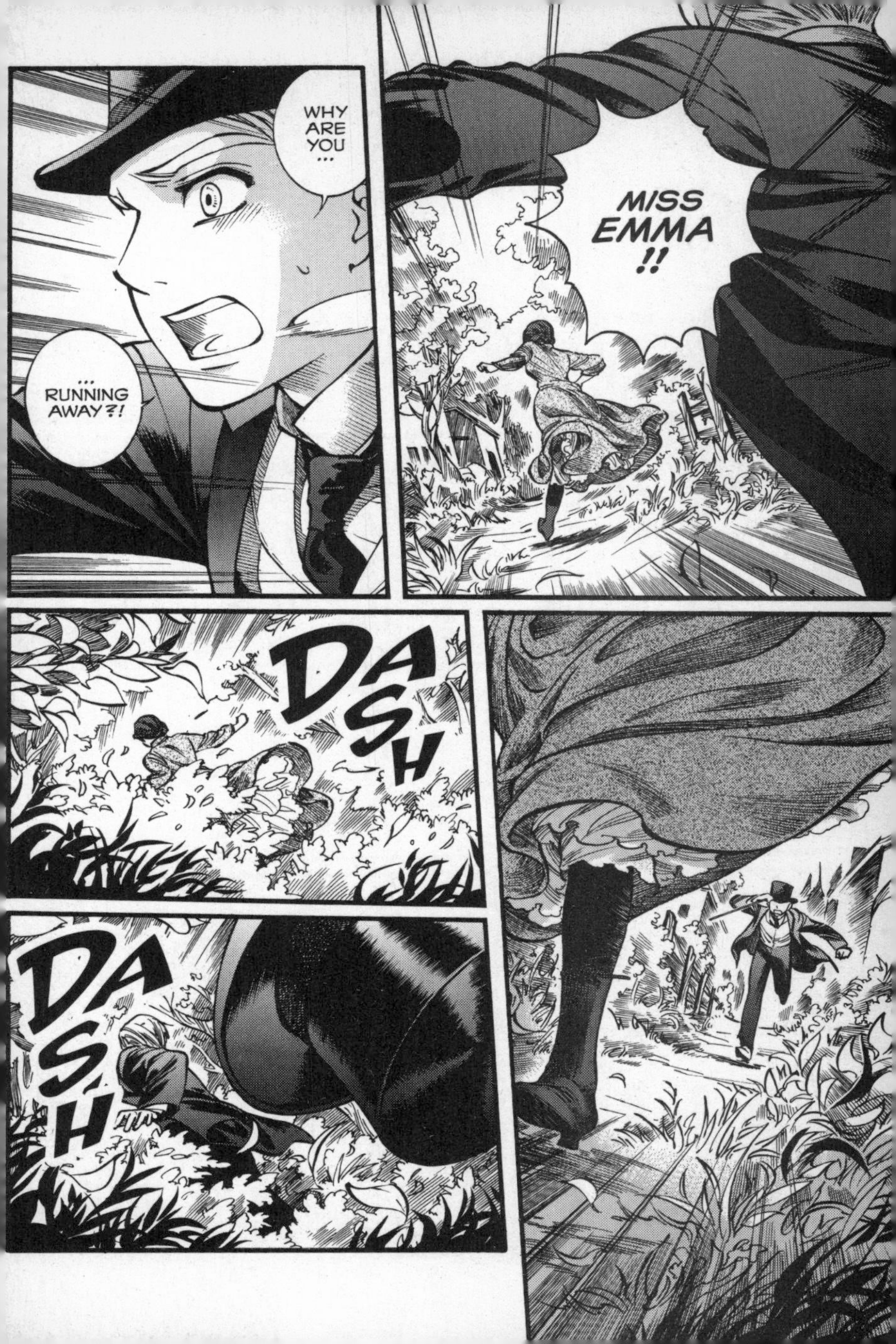
MISS EMMA !!
WHY ARE YOU ...
... RUNNING AWAY?!
DASH
DASH

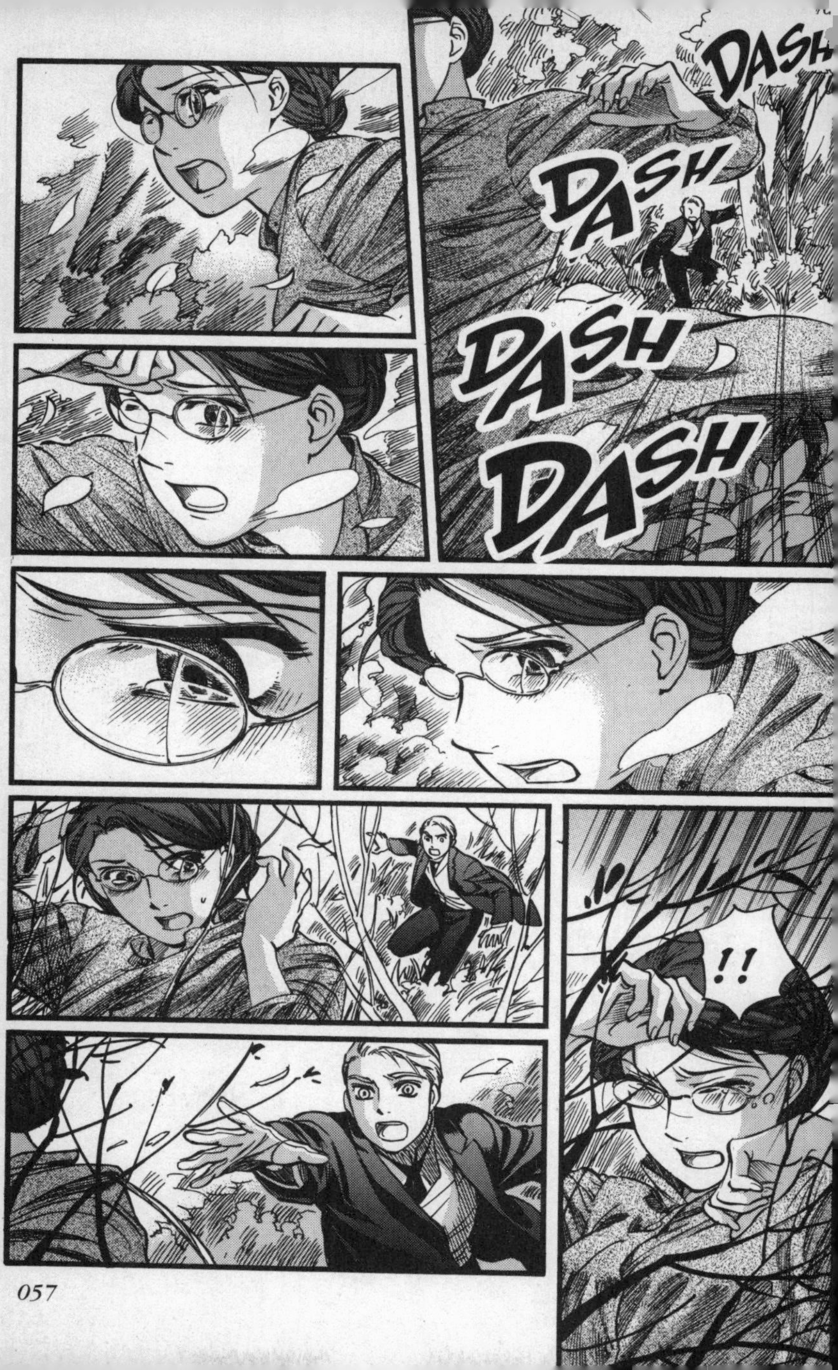
DASH
DASH
DASH
DASH
!!

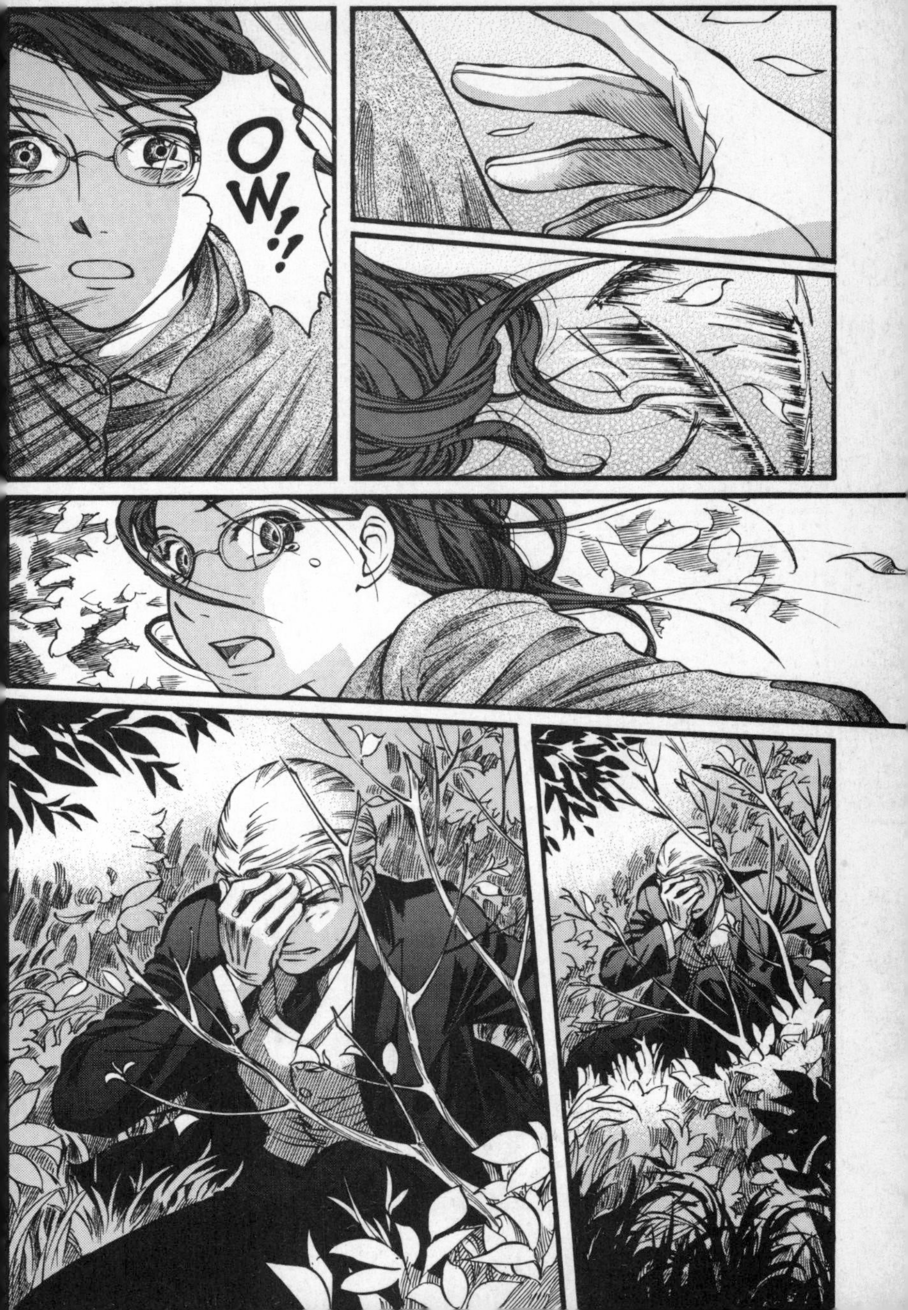
OW!!

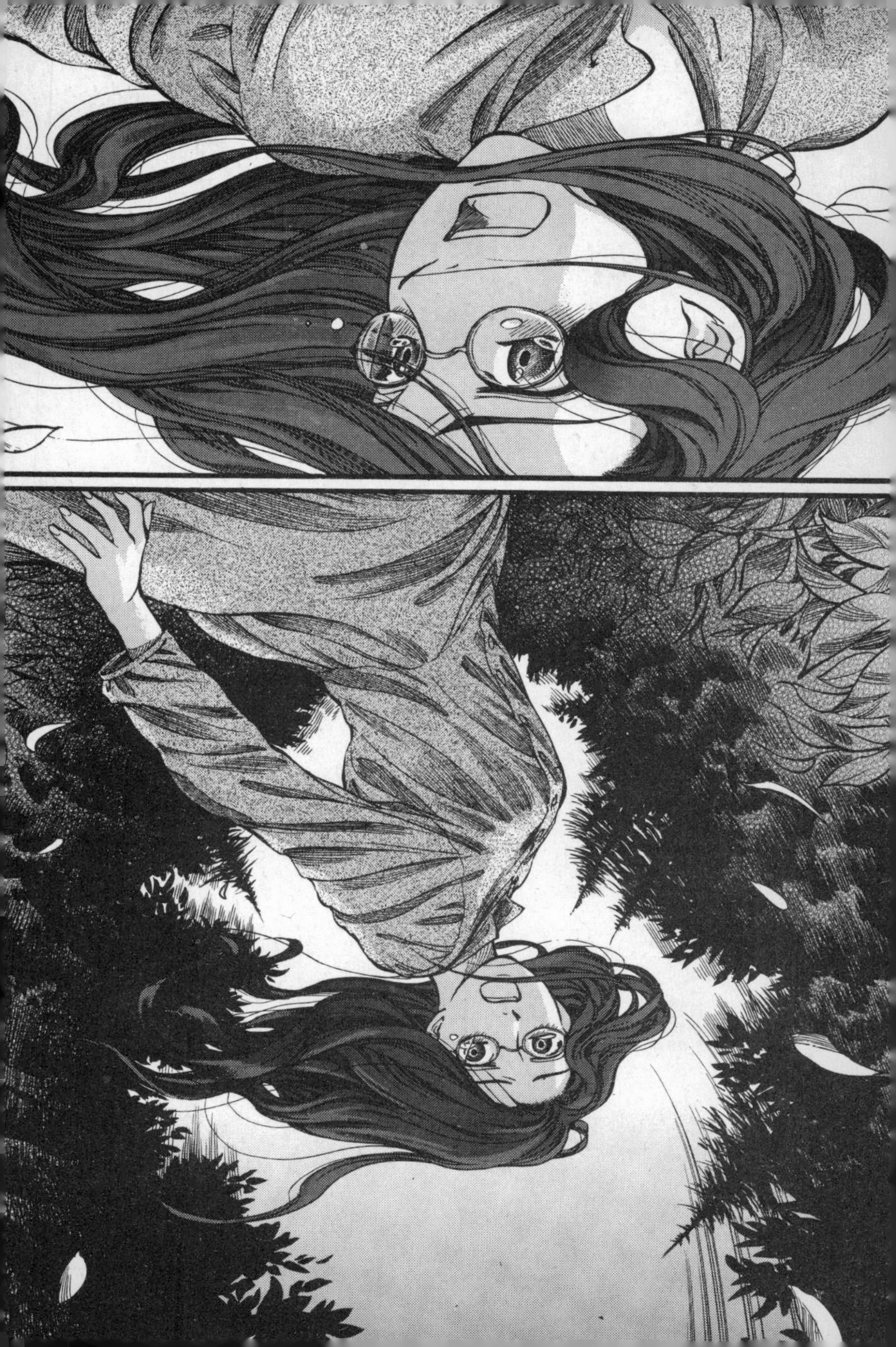

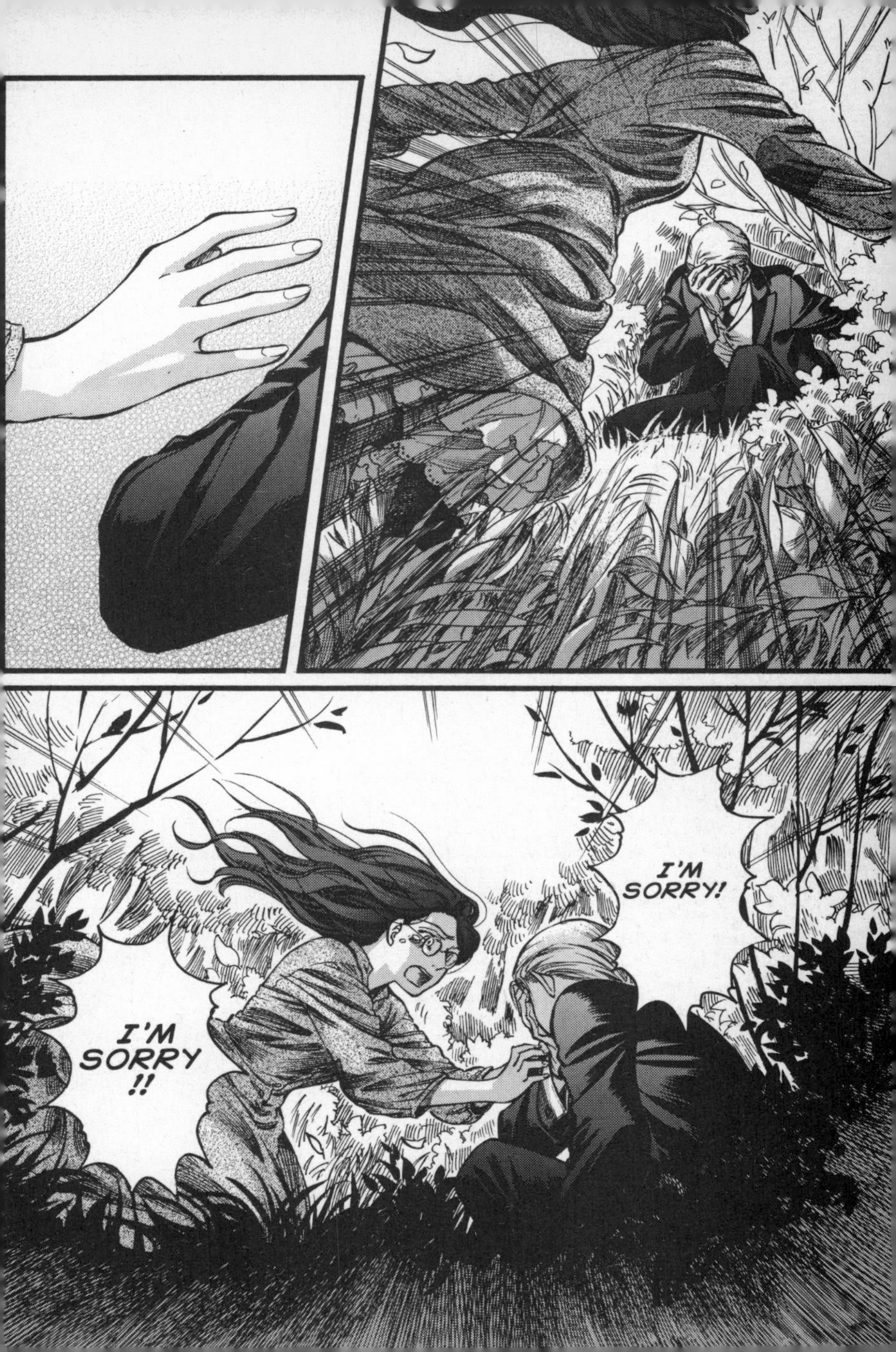
I'M SORRY!
I'M SORRY !!

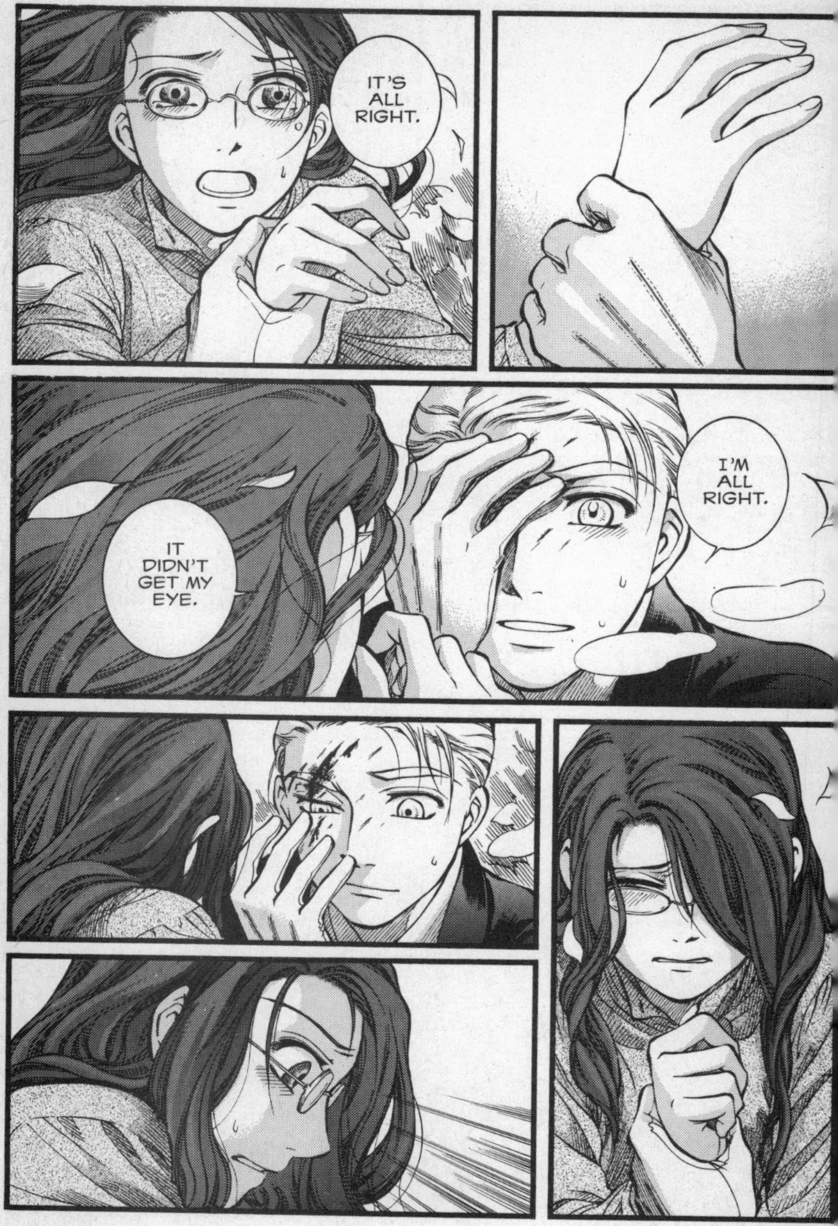
IT'S ALL RIGHT.
I'M ALL RIGHT.
IT DIDN'T GET MY EYE.

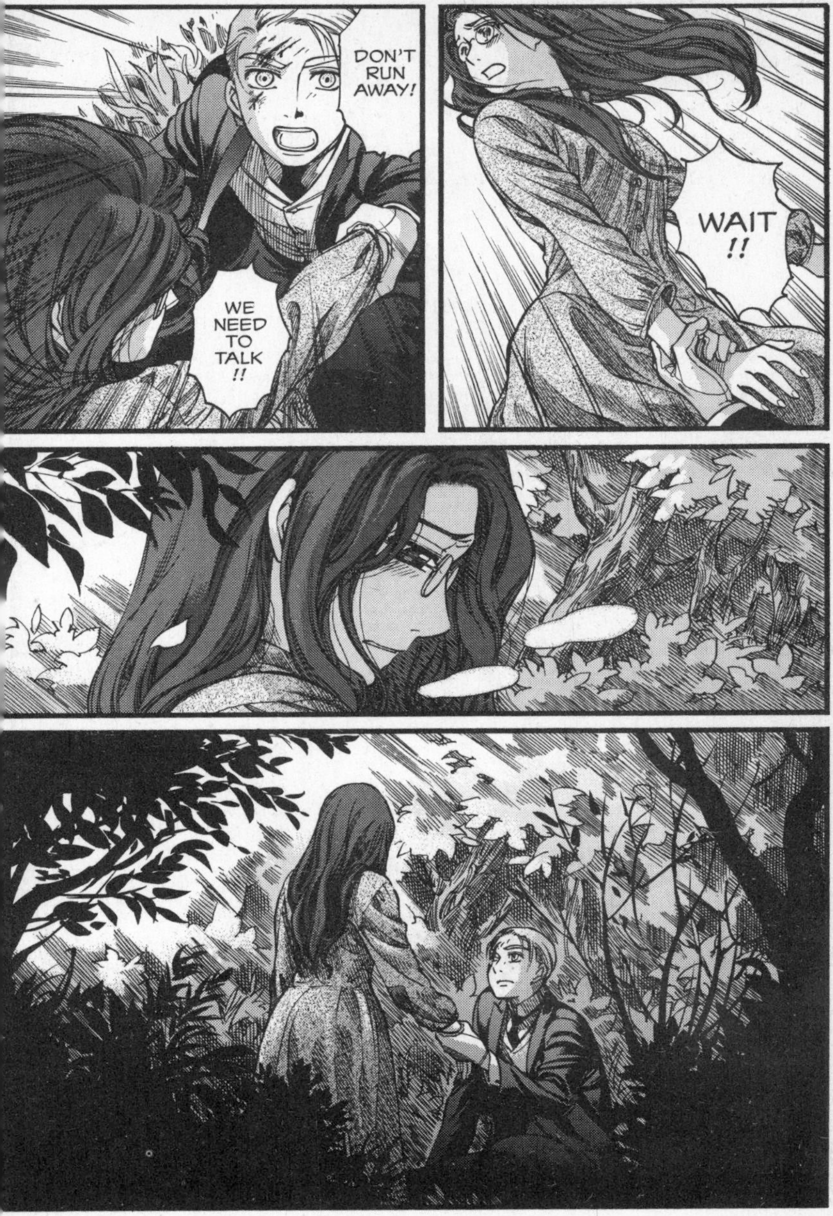
WAIT !!
DON'T RUN AWAY!
WE NEED TO TALK !!

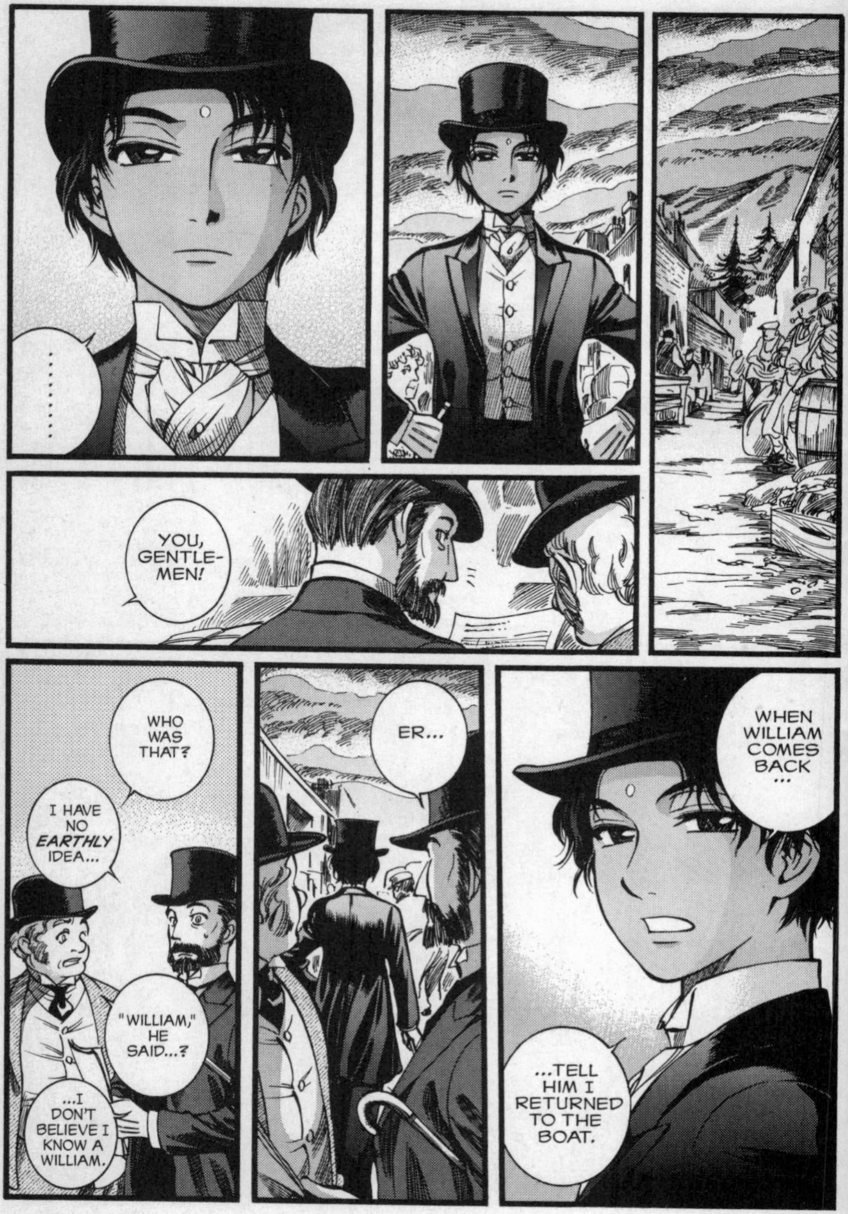
......
YOU, GENTLE- MEN!
WHEN WILLIAM COMES BACK ...
...TELL HIM I RETURNED TO THE BOAT.
ER...
WHO WAS THAT?
I HAVE NO EARTHLY IDEA...
"WILLIAM," HE SAID...?
...I DON'T BELIEVE I KNOW A WILLIAM.

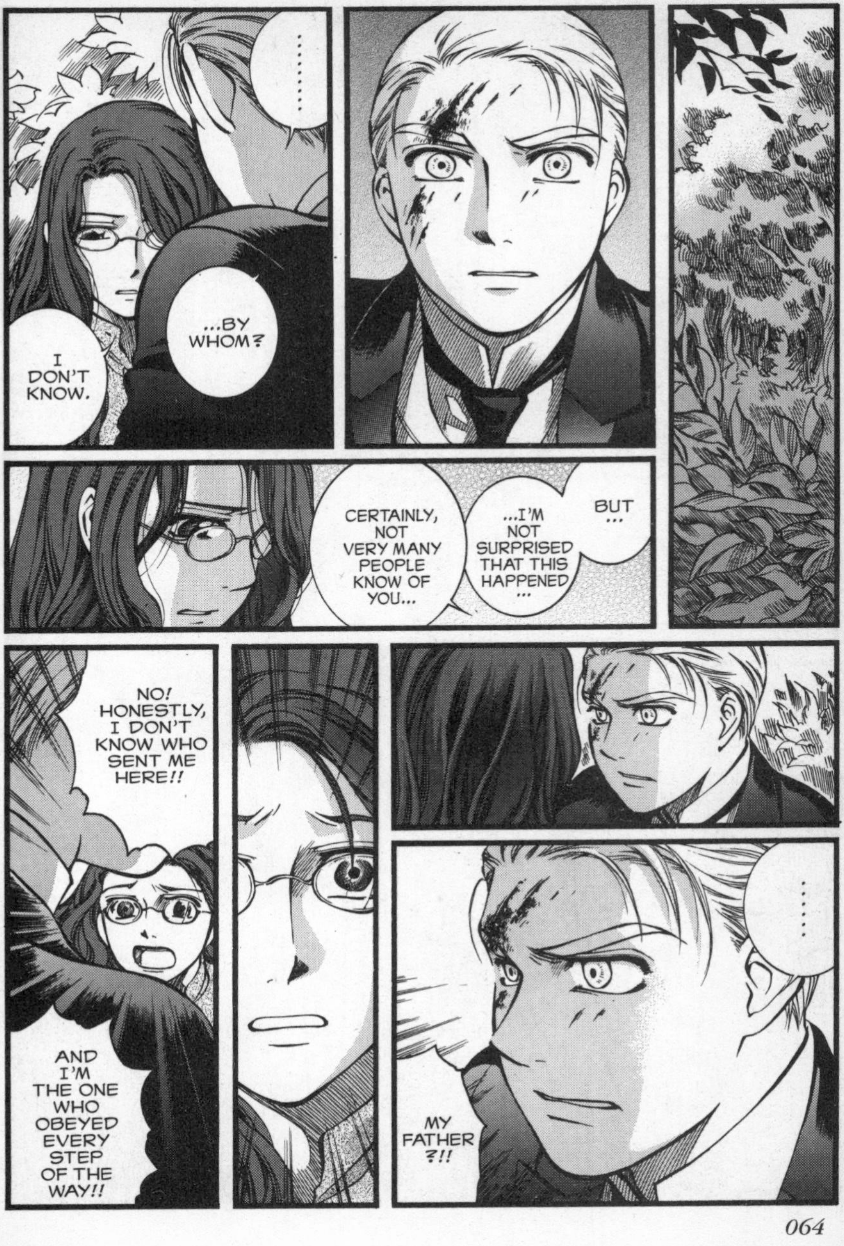
......
...BY WHOM?
I DON'T KNOW.
BUT ...
...I'M NOT SURPRISED THAT THIS HAPPENED ...
CERTAINLY, NOT VERY MANY PEOPLE KNOW OF YOU...
......
MY FATHER ?!!
NO! HONESTLY, I DON'T KNOW WHO SENT ME HERE!!
AND I'M THE ONE WHO OBEYED EVERY STEP OF THE WAY!!

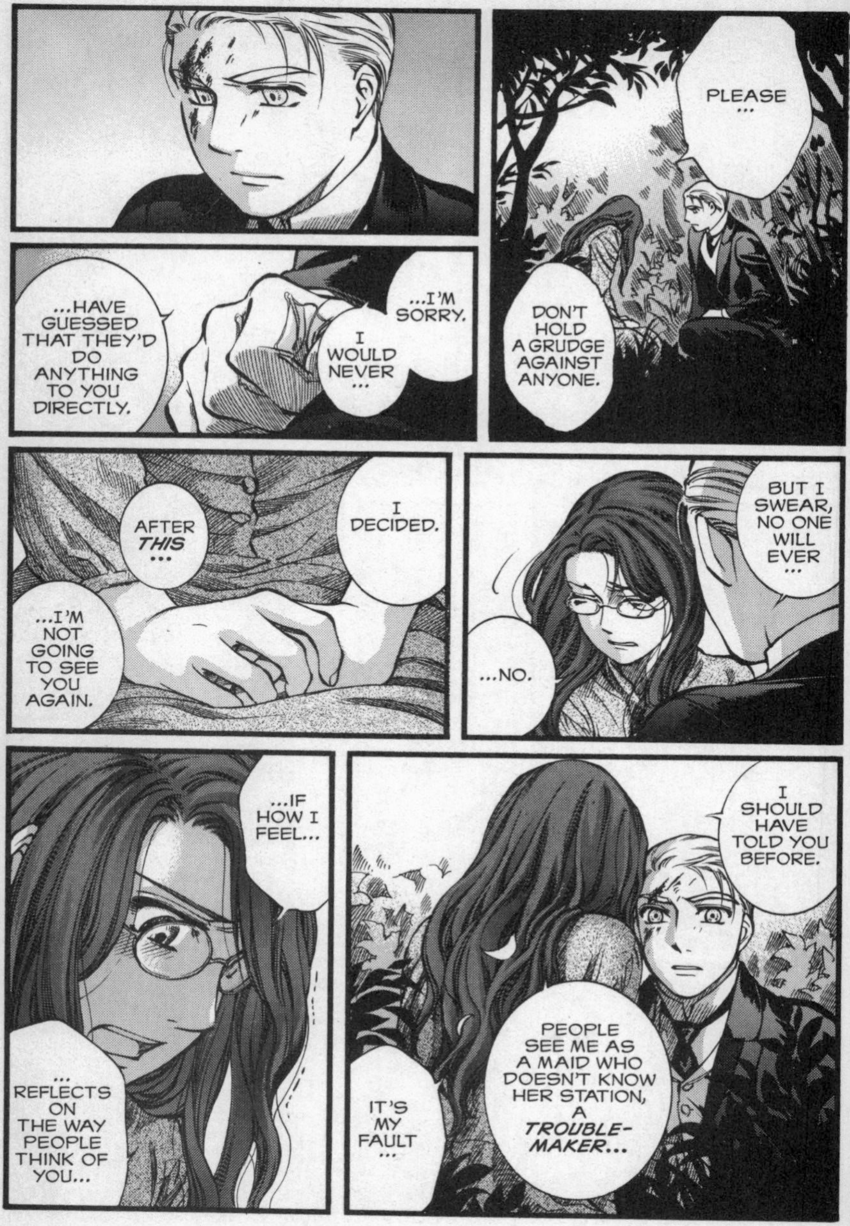
PLEASE ...
DON'T HOLD A GRUDGE AGAINST ANYONE.
...I'M SORRY.
I WOULD NEVER ...
...HAVE GUESSED THAT THEY'D DO ANYTHING TO YOU DIRECTLY.
BUT I SWEAR, NO ONE WILL EVER ...
...NO.
I DECIDED.
AFTER *THIS* ...
...I'M NOT GOING TO SEE YOU AGAIN.
I SHOULD HAVE TOLD YOU BEFORE.
PEOPLE SEE ME AS A MAID WHO DOESN'T KNOW HER STATION, A *TROUBLE-MAKER*...
IT'S MY FAULT ...
...IF HOW I FEEL...
... REFLECTS ON THE WAY PEOPLE THINK OF YOU...

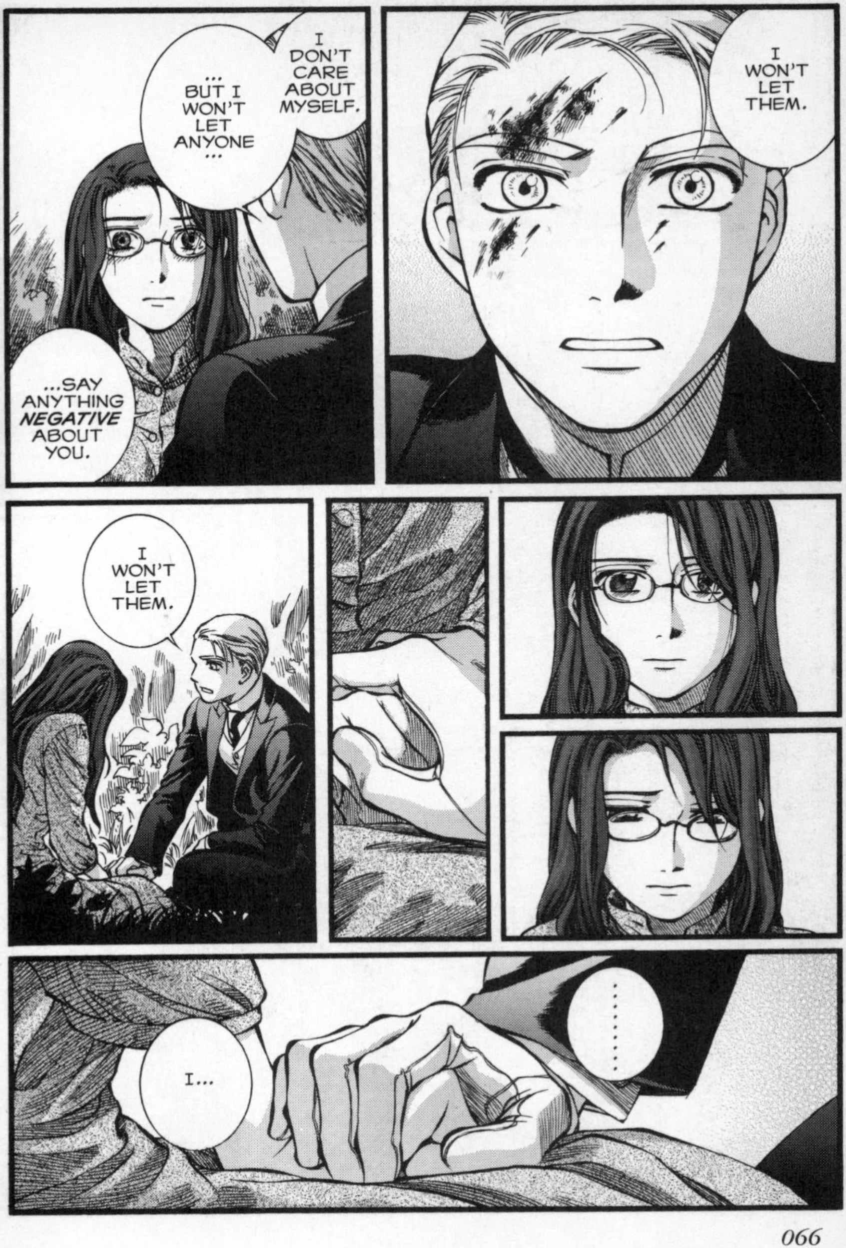
I WON'T LET THEM.
I DON'T CARE ABOUT MYSELF.
... BUT I WON'T LET ANYONE ...
...SAY ANYTHING ***NEGATIVE*** ABOUT YOU.
I WON'T LET THEM.
I...
....

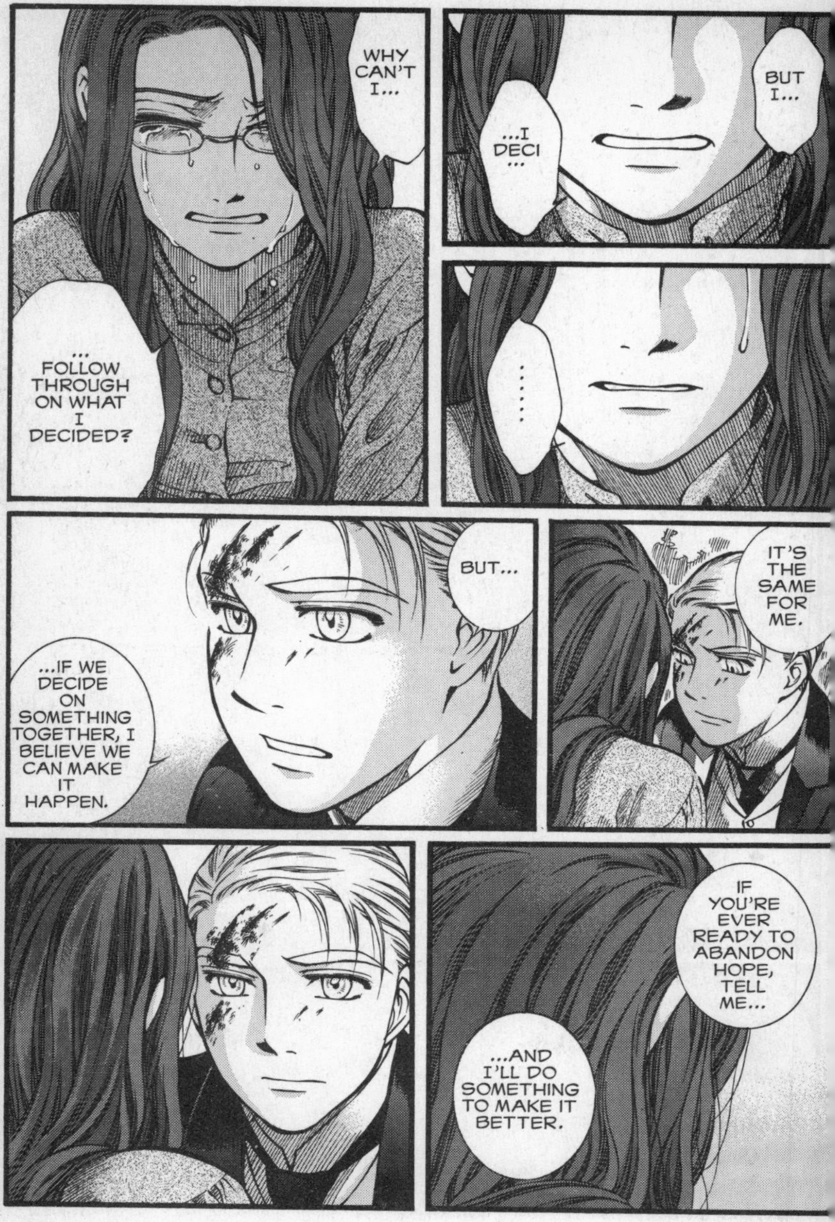
BUT I...
...I DECI...
......
WHY CAN'T I...
...FOLLOW THROUGH ON WHAT I DECIDED?
IT'S THE SAME FOR ME.
BUT...
...IF WE DECIDE ON SOMETHING TOGETHER, I BELIEVE WE CAN MAKE IT HAPPEN.
IF YOU'RE EVER READY TO ABANDON HOPE, TELL ME...
...AND I'LL DO SOMETHING TO MAKE IT BETTER.

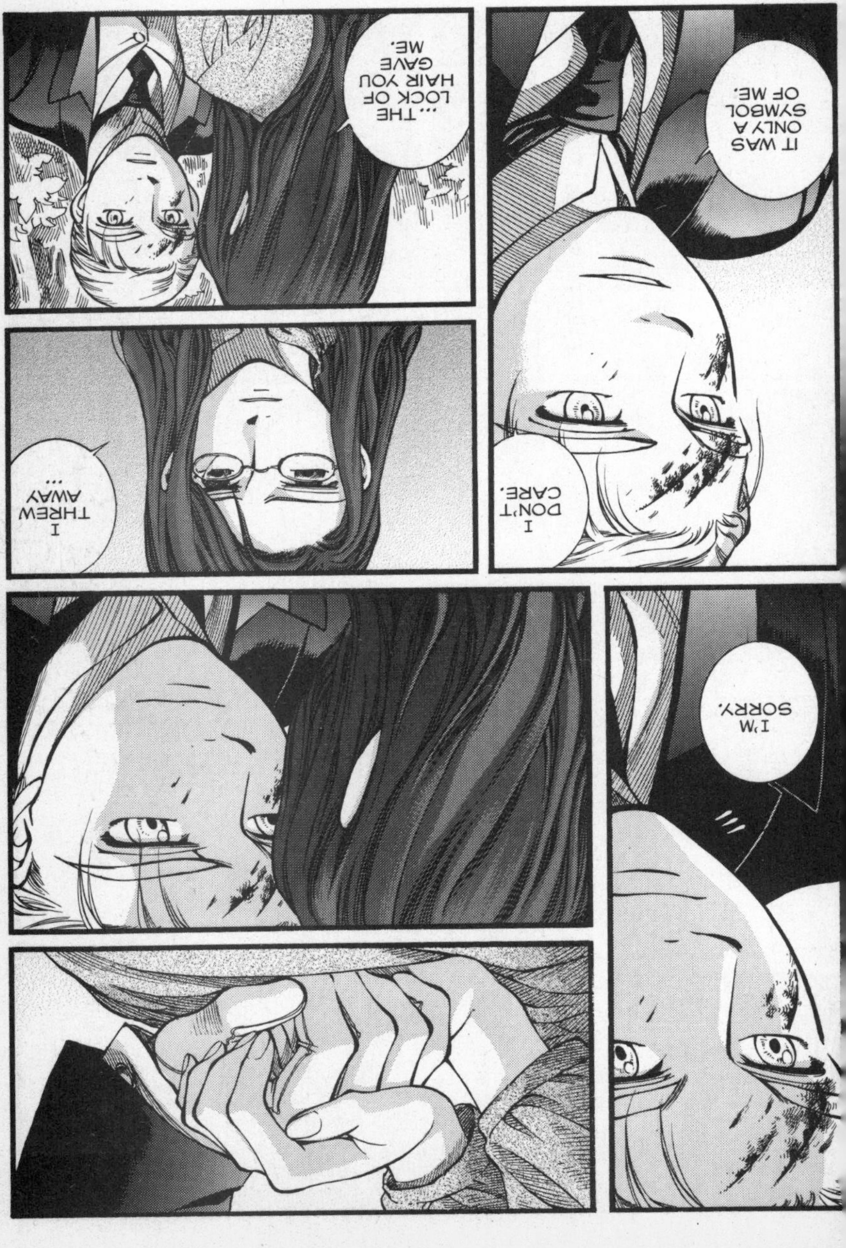
I'M SORRY.
I THREW AWAY ...
...THE LOCK OF HAIR YOU GAVE ME.
I DON'T CARE.
IT WAS ONLY A SYMBOL OF ME.

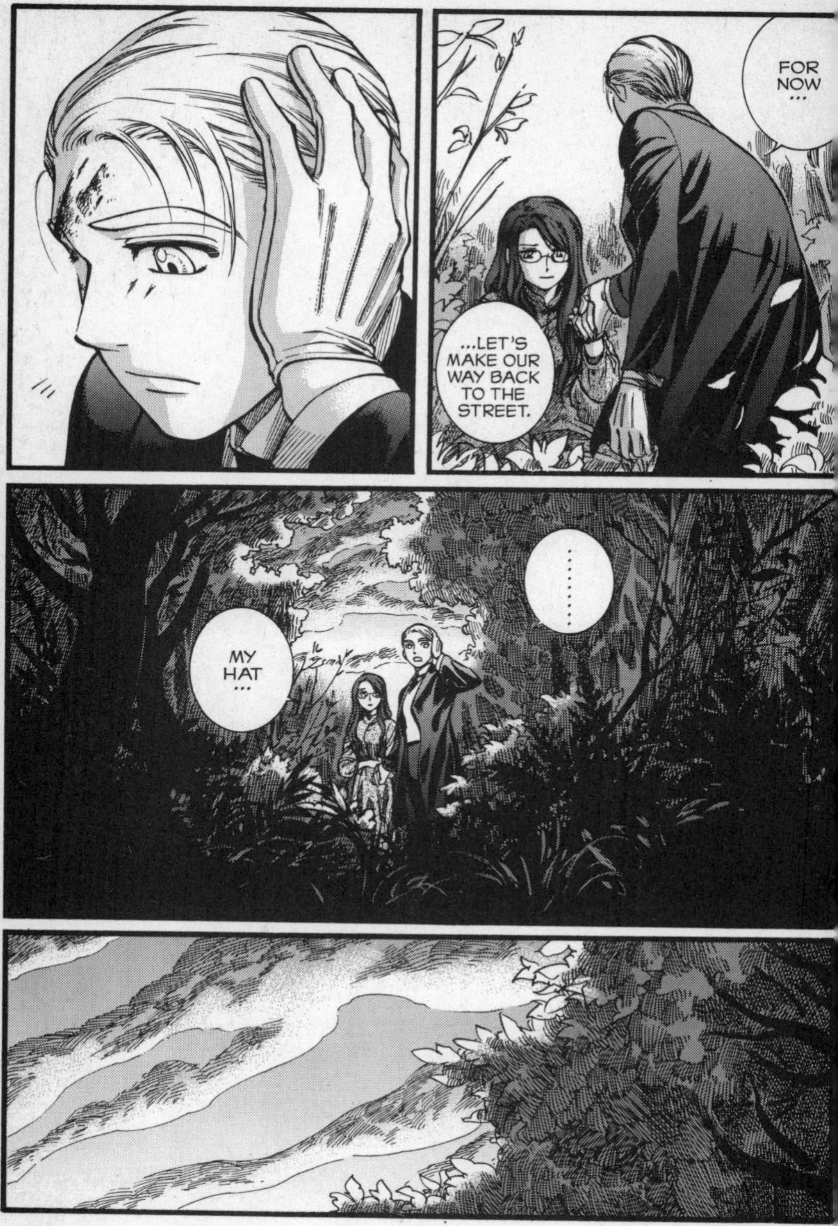
FOR NOW ...
...LET'S MAKE OUR WAY BACK TO THE STREET.
......
MY HAT ...

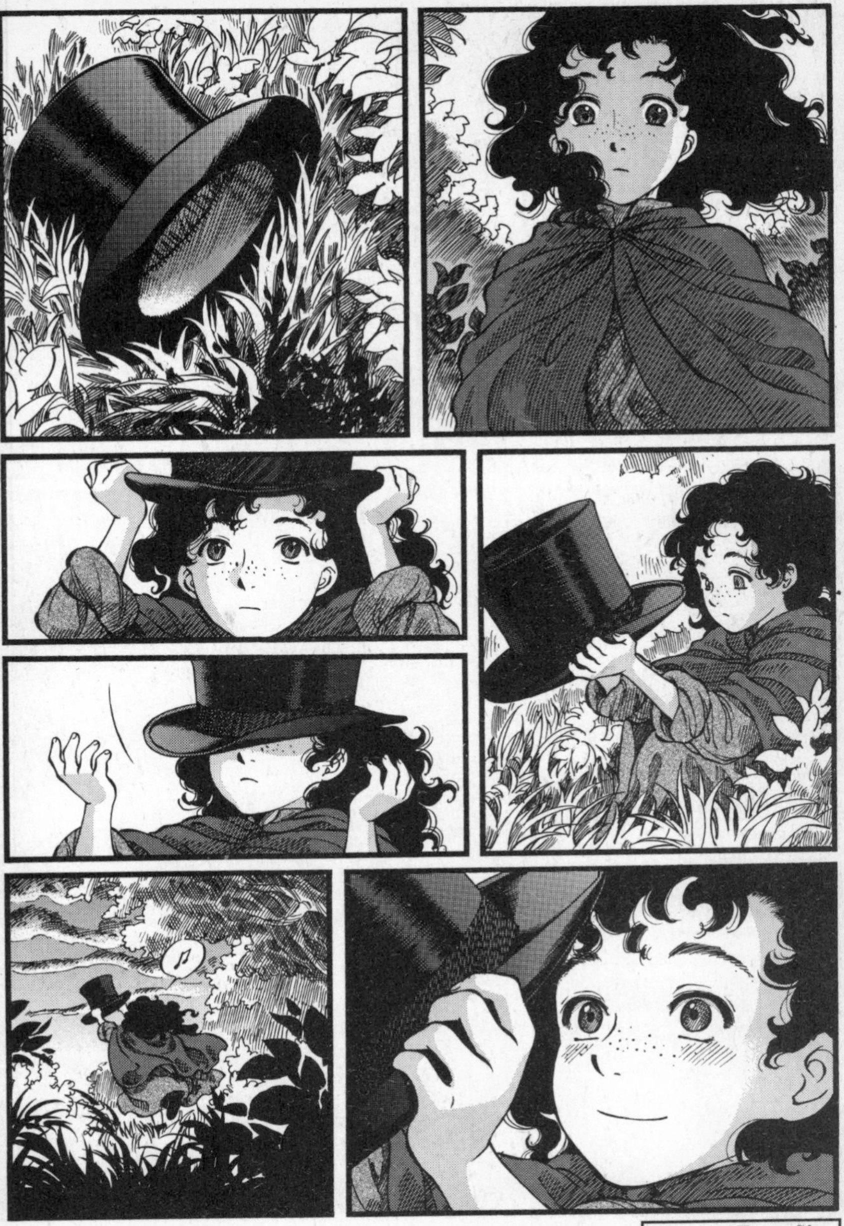

Chapter Forty Six:
The End

EPILOGUE

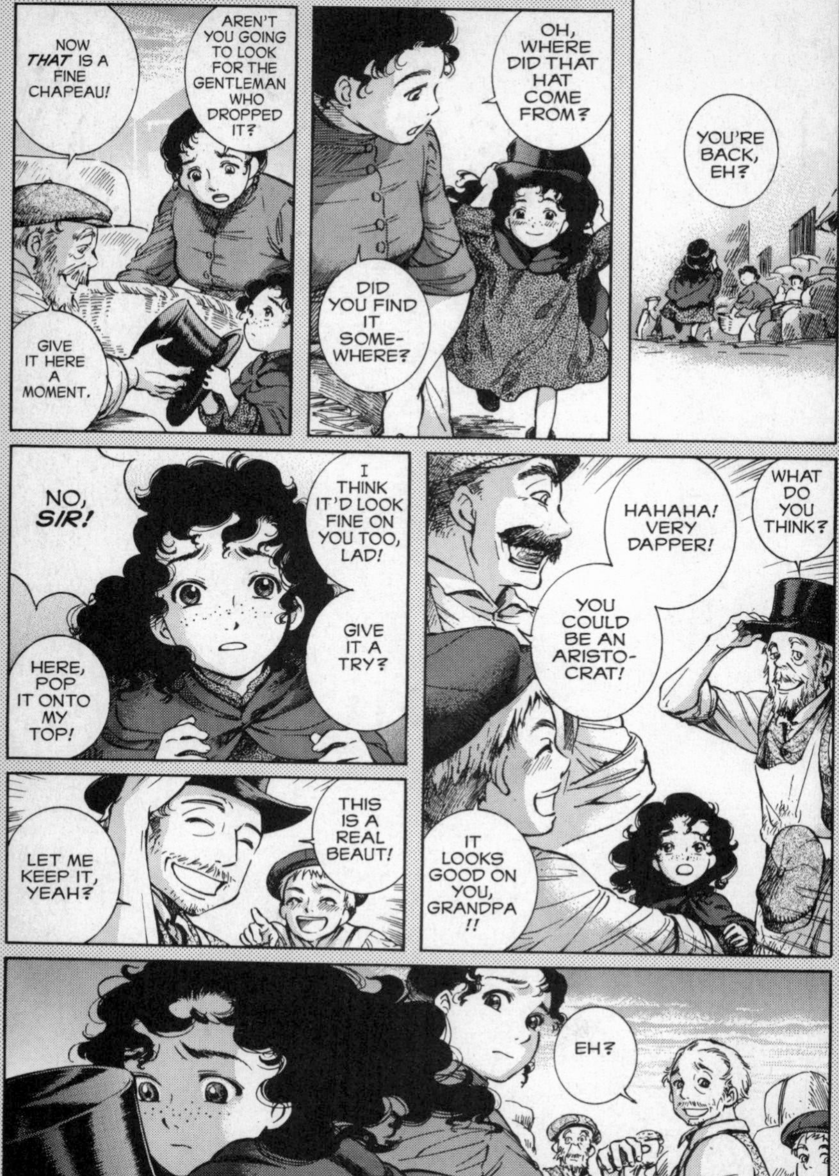
YOU'RE BACK, EH?
OH, WHERE DID THAT HAT COME FROM?
DID YOU FIND IT SOME-WHERE?
NOW *THAT* IS A FINE CHAPEAU!
AREN'T YOU GOING TO LOOK FOR THE GENTLEMAN WHO DROPPED IT?
GIVE IT HERE A MOMENT.
WHAT DO YOU THINK?
HAHAHA! VERY DAPPER!
YOU COULD BE AN ARISTO-CRAT!
IT LOOKS GOOD ON YOU, GRANDPA!!
I THINK IT'D LOOK FINE ON YOU TOO, LAD!
GIVE IT A TRY?
NO, *SIR!*
HERE, POP IT ONTO MY TOP!
THIS IS A REAL BEAUT!
LET ME KEEP IT, YEAH?
EH?

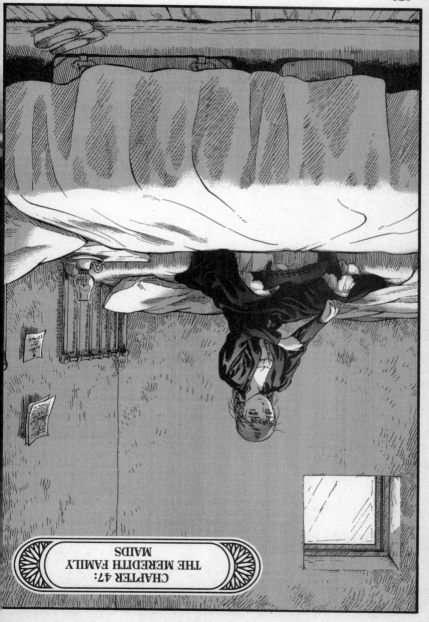

CHAPTER 47:
THE MEREDITH FAMILY
MAIDS

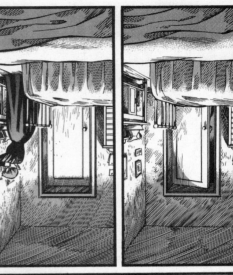

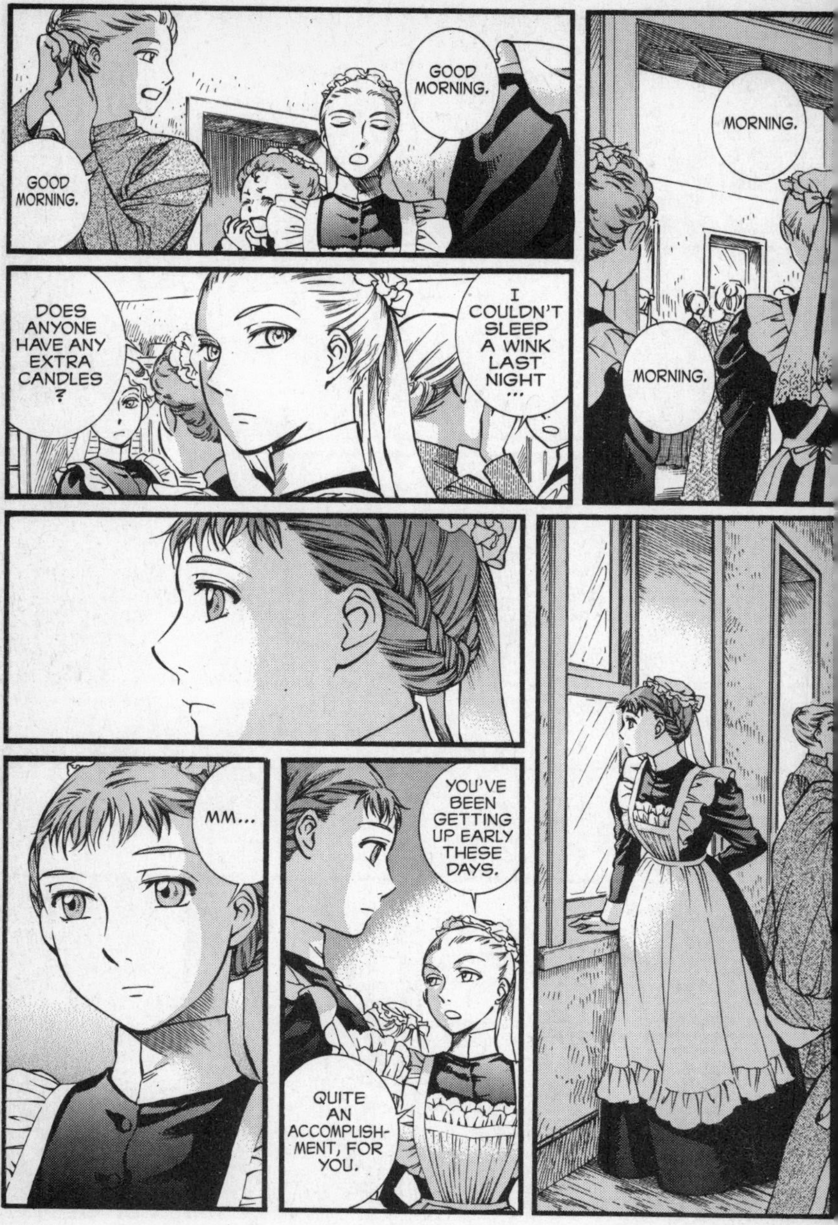
MORNING.
MORNING.
GOOD MORNING.
GOOD MORNING.
I COULDN'T SLEEP A WINK LAST NIGHT...
DOES ANYONE HAVE ANY EXTRA CANDLES?
YOU'VE BEEN GETTING UP EARLY THESE DAYS.
QUITE AN ACCOMPLISHMENT, FOR YOU.
MM...

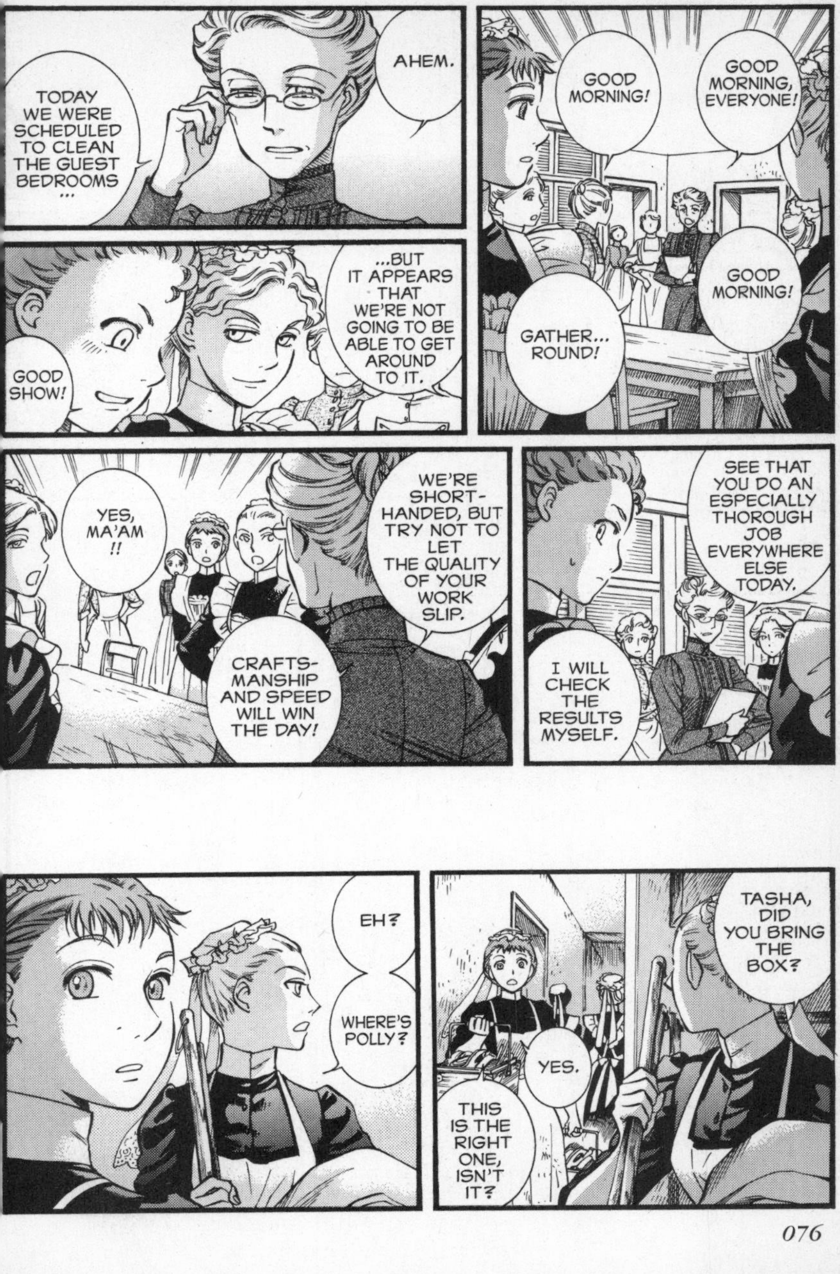
GOOD MORNING, EVERYONE!
GOOD MORNING!
GOOD MORNING!
GATHER... ROUND!
AHEM.
TODAY WE WERE SCHEDULED TO CLEAN THE GUEST BEDROOMS ...
...BUT IT APPEARS THAT WE'RE NOT GOING TO BE ABLE TO GET AROUND TO IT.
GOOD SHOW!
SEE THAT YOU DO AN ESPECIALLY THOROUGH JOB EVERYWHERE ELSE TODAY.
I WILL CHECK THE RESULTS MYSELF.
WE'RE SHORT-HANDED, BUT TRY NOT TO LET THE QUALITY OF YOUR WORK SLIP.
CRAFTS-MANSHIP AND SPEED WILL WIN THE DAY!
YES, MA'AM !!
TASHA, DID YOU BRING THE BOX?
YES.
THIS IS THE RIGHT ONE, ISN'T IT?
EH?
WHERE'S POLLY?

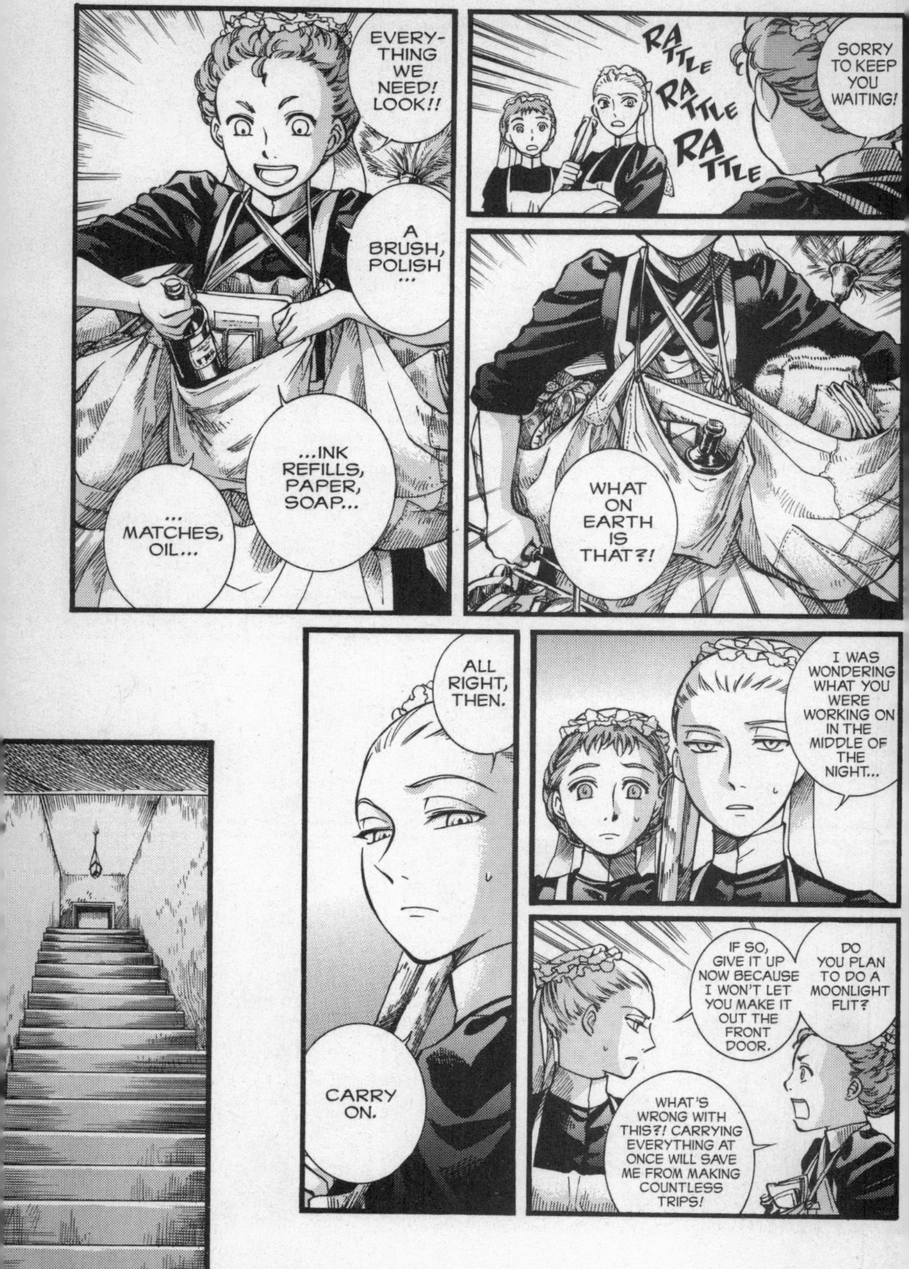
SORRY TO KEEP YOU WAITING!
RATTLE RATTLE RATTLE
EVERY-THING WE NEED! LOOK!!
A BRUSH, POLISH...
...INK REFILLS, PAPER, SOAP...
...MATCHES, OIL...
WHAT ON EARTH IS THAT?!
I WAS WONDERING WHAT YOU WERE WORKING ON IN THE MIDDLE OF THE NIGHT...
DO YOU PLAN TO DO A MOONLIGHT FLIT?
IF SO, GIVE IT UP NOW BECAUSE I WON'T LET YOU MAKE IT OUT THE FRONT DOOR.
WHAT'S WRONG WITH THIS?! CARRYING EVERYTHING AT ONCE WILL SAVE ME FROM MAKING COUNTLESS TRIPS!
ALL RIGHT, THEN.
CARRY ON.

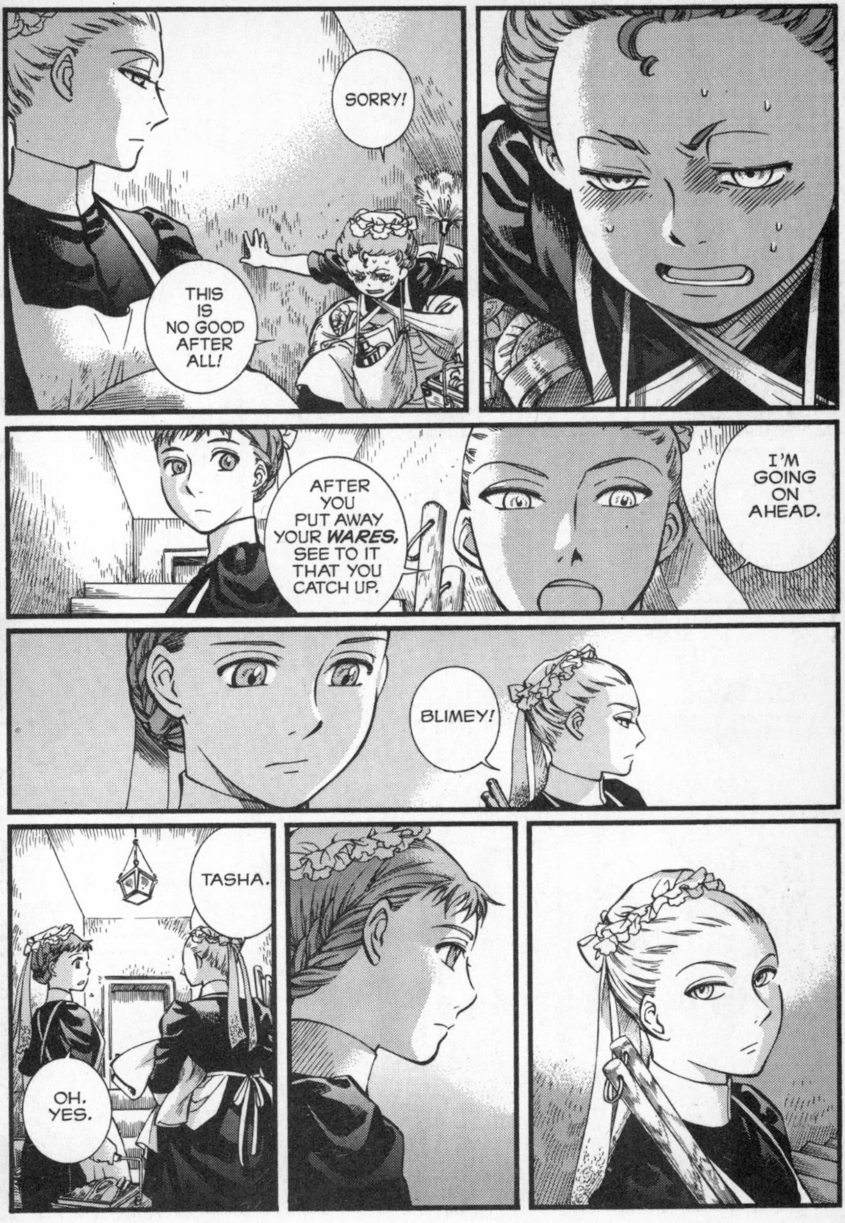
SORRY!
THIS IS NO GOOD AFTER ALL!
I'M GOING ON AHEAD.
AFTER YOU PUT AWAY YOUR WARES, SEE TO IT THAT YOU CATCH UP.
BLIMEY!
TASHA.
OH. YES.

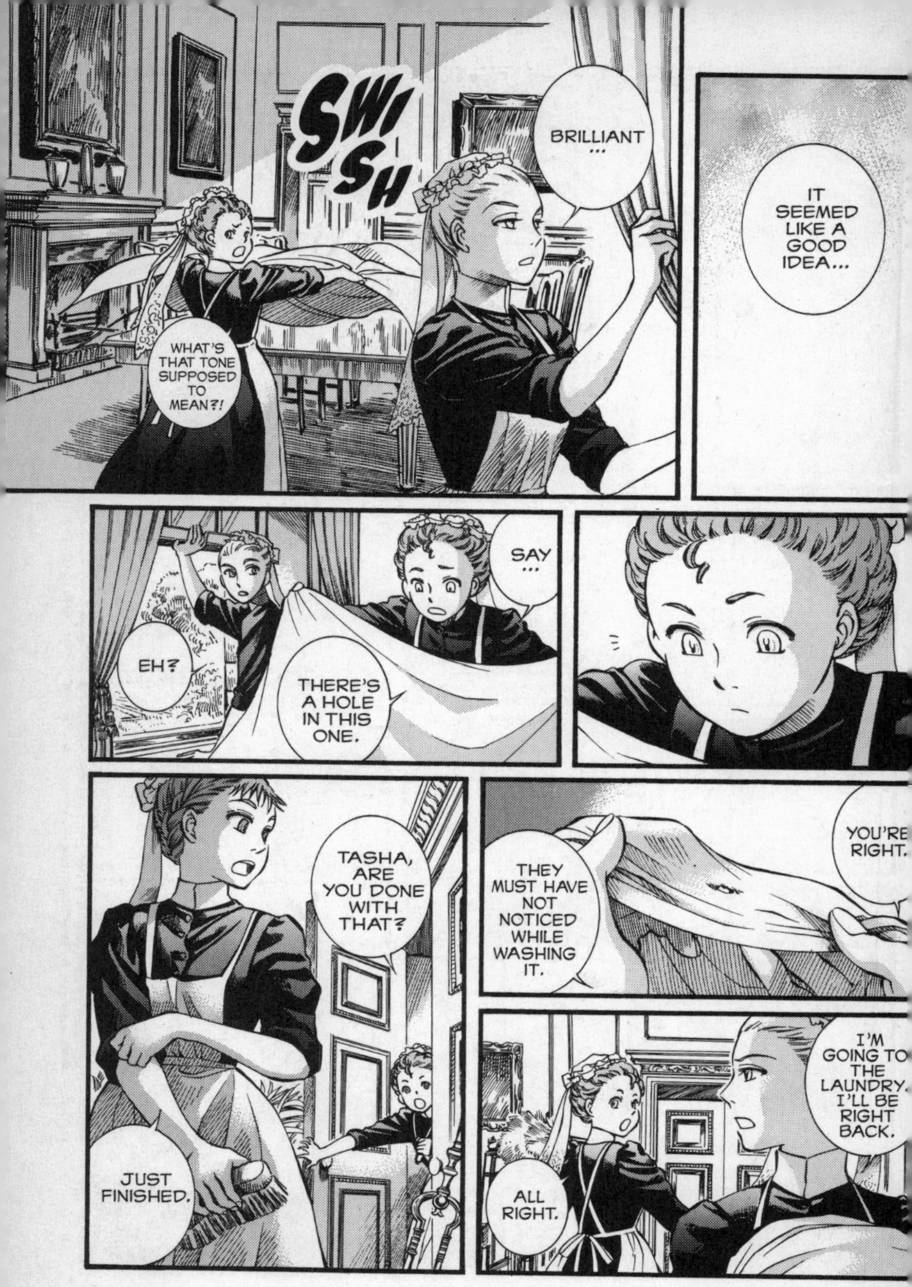
IT SEEMED LIKE A GOOD IDEA...
BRILLIANT ...
SWISH
WHAT'S THAT TONE SUPPOSED TO MEAN?!
SAY ...
THERE'S A HOLE IN THIS ONE.
EH?
YOU'RE RIGHT.
THEY MUST HAVE NOT NOTICED WHILE WASHING IT.
I'M GOING TO THE LAUNDRY. I'LL BE RIGHT BACK.
ALL RIGHT.
TASHA, ARE YOU DONE WITH THAT?
JUST FINISHED.

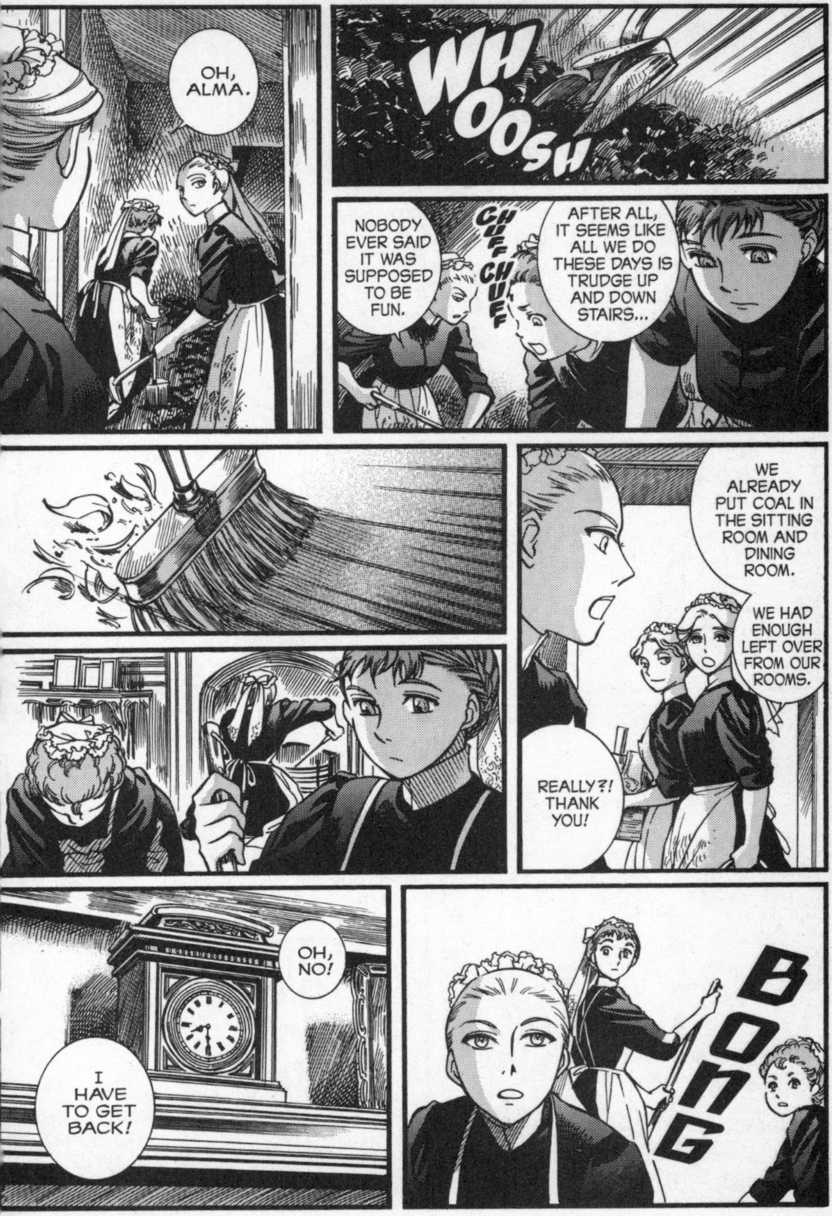
WHOOSH
AFTER ALL, IT SEEMS LIKE ALL WE DO THESE DAYS IS TRUDGE UP AND DOWN STAIRS...
CHUFF CHUFF CHUFF
NOBODY EVER SAID IT WAS SUPPOSED TO BE FUN.
OH, ALMA.
WE ALREADY PUT COAL IN THE SITTING ROOM AND DINING ROOM.
WE HAD ENOUGH LEFT OVER FROM OUR ROOMS.
REALLY?! THANK YOU!
BONG
OH, NO!
I HAVE TO GET BACK!

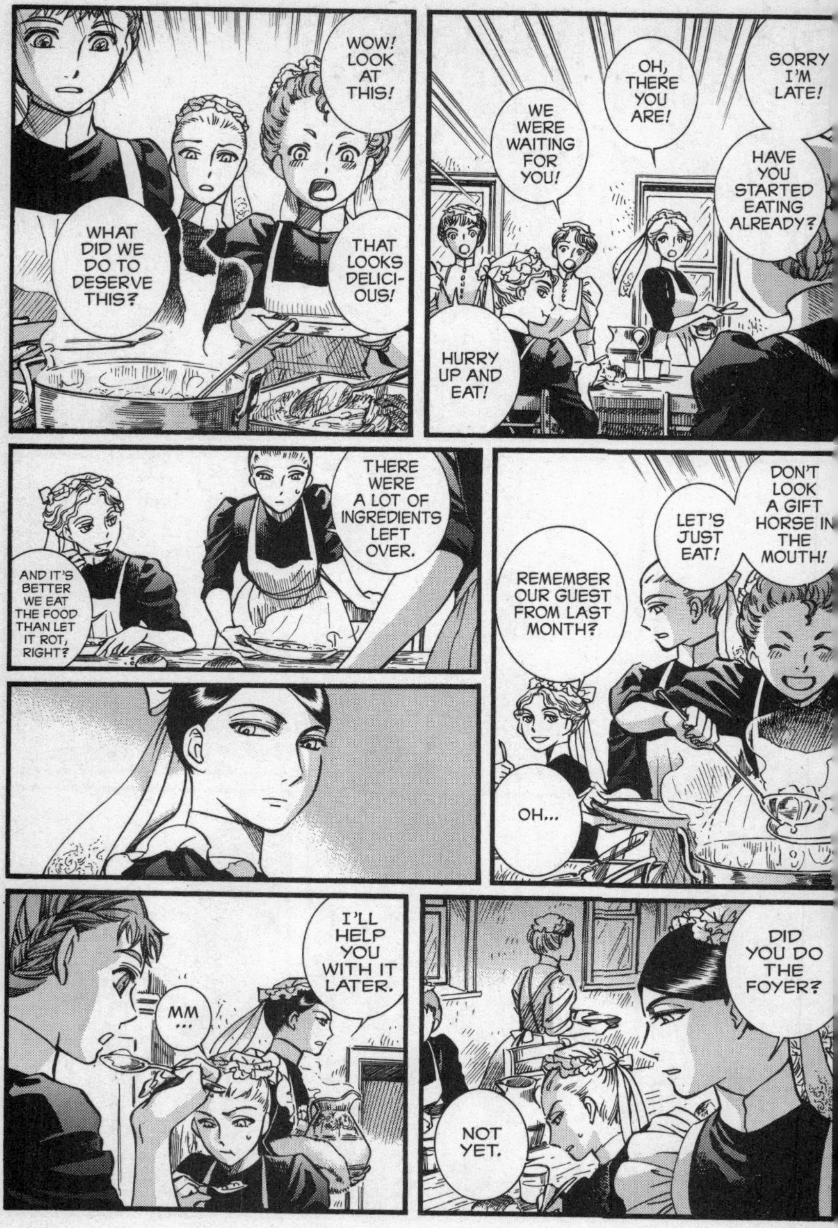
SORRY I'M LATE!
HAVE YOU STARTED EATING ALREADY?
OH, THERE YOU ARE!
WE WERE WAITING FOR YOU!
HURRY UP AND EAT!
WOW! LOOK AT THIS!
THAT LOOKS DELICI-OUS!
WHAT DID WE DO TO DESERVE THIS?
DON'T LOOK A GIFT HORSE IN THE MOUTH!
LET'S JUST EAT!
REMEMBER OUR GUEST FROM LAST MONTH?
OH...
THERE WERE A LOT OF INGREDIENTS LEFT OVER.
AND IT'S BETTER WE EAT THE FOOD THAN LET IT ROT, RIGHT?
DID YOU DO THE FOYER?
NOT YET.
I'LL HELP YOU WITH IT LATER.
MM ...

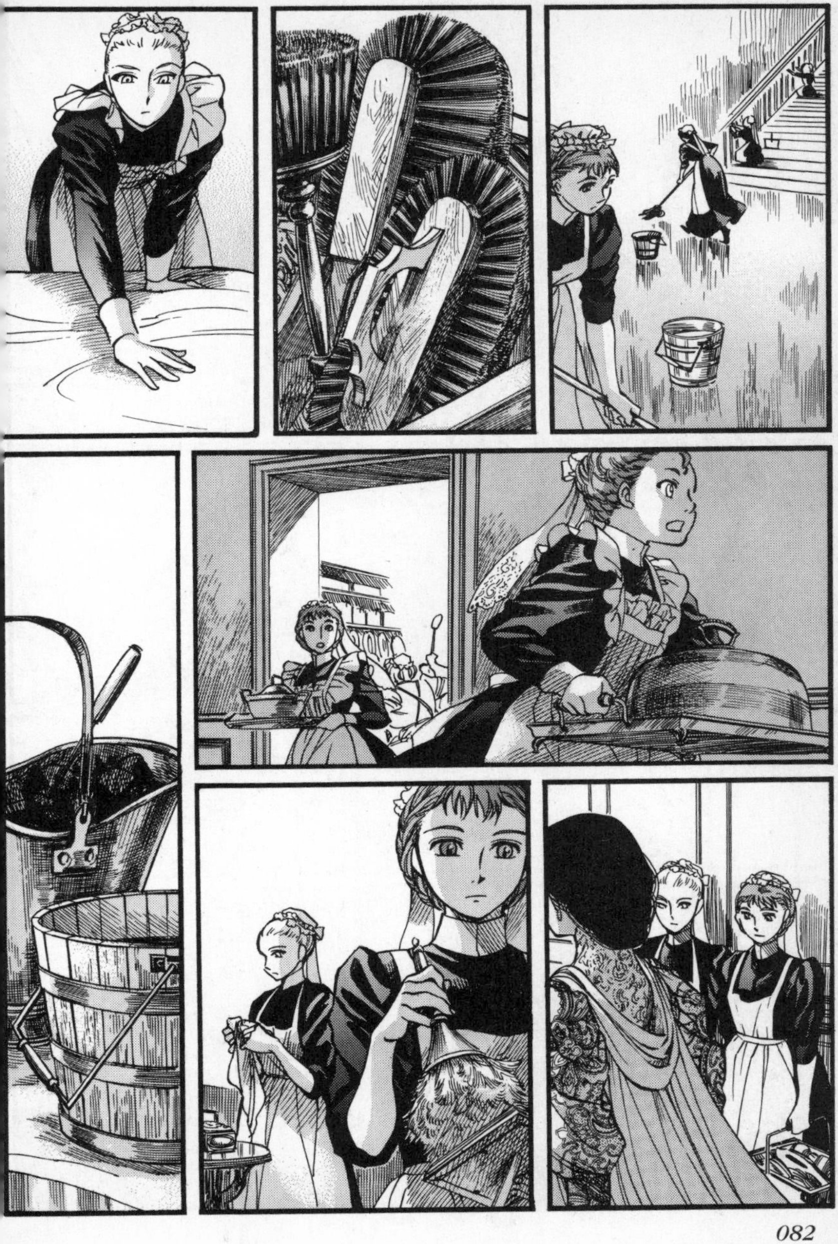

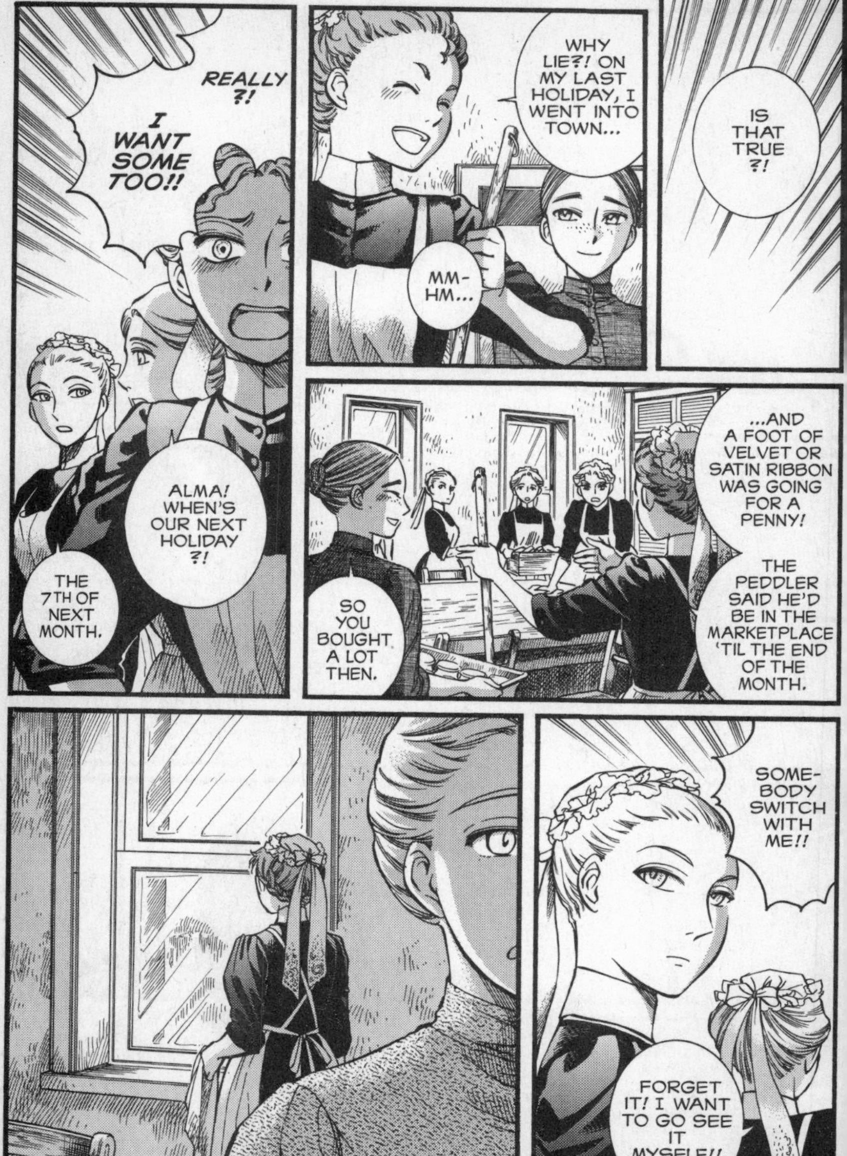
IS THAT TRUE ?!
WHY LIE?! ON MY LAST HOLIDAY, I WENT INTO TOWN...
MM-HM...
REALLY ?!
I WANT SOME TOO!!
ALMA! WHEN'S OUR NEXT HOLIDAY ?!
THE 7TH OF NEXT MONTH.
...AND A FOOT OF VELVET OR SATIN RIBBON WAS GOING FOR A PENNY!
THE PEDDLER SAID HE'D BE IN THE MARKETPLACE 'TIL THE END OF THE MONTH.
SO YOU BOUGHT A LOT THEN.
SOME-BODY SWITCH WITH ME!!
FORGET IT! I WANT TO GO SEE IT MYSELF!!

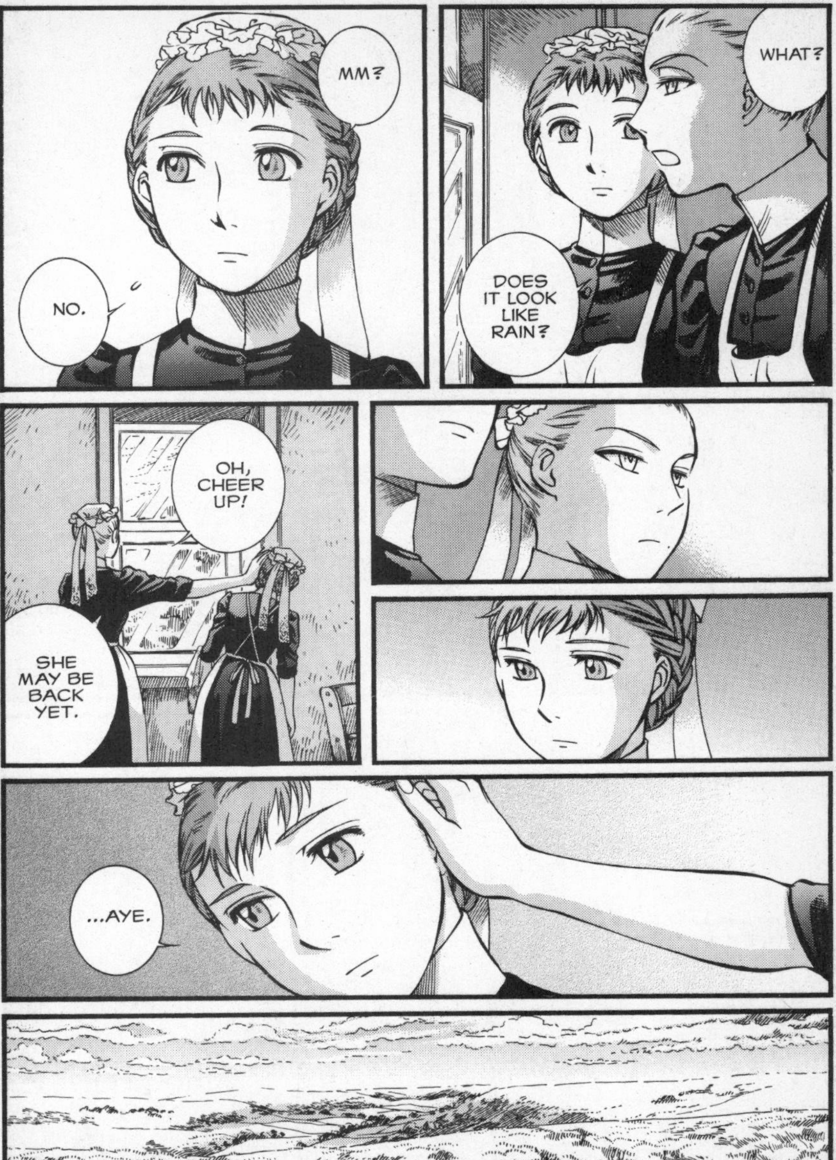
WHAT?
DOES IT LOOK LIKE RAIN?
MM?
NO.
OH, CHEER UP!
SHE MAY BE BACK YET.
...AYE.

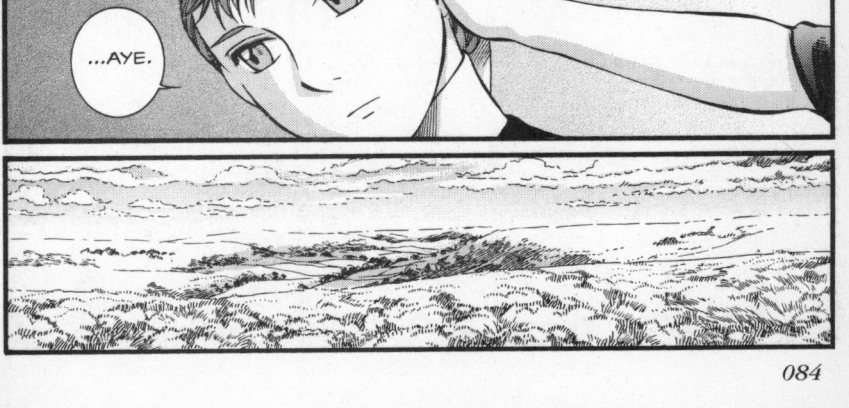

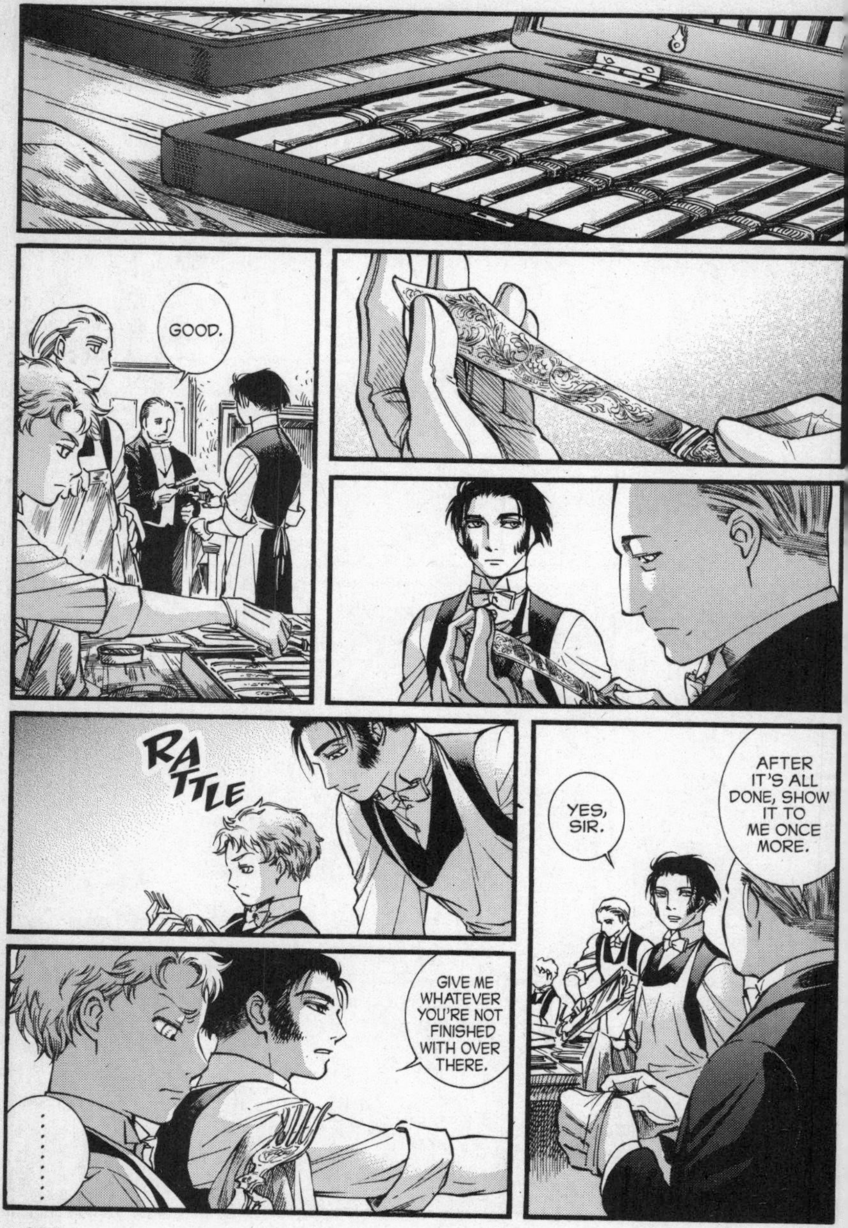
GOOD.
AFTER IT'S ALL DONE, SHOW IT TO ME ONCE MORE.
YES, SIR.
RATTLE
GIVE ME WHATEVER YOU'RE NOT FINISHED WITH OVER THERE.
......

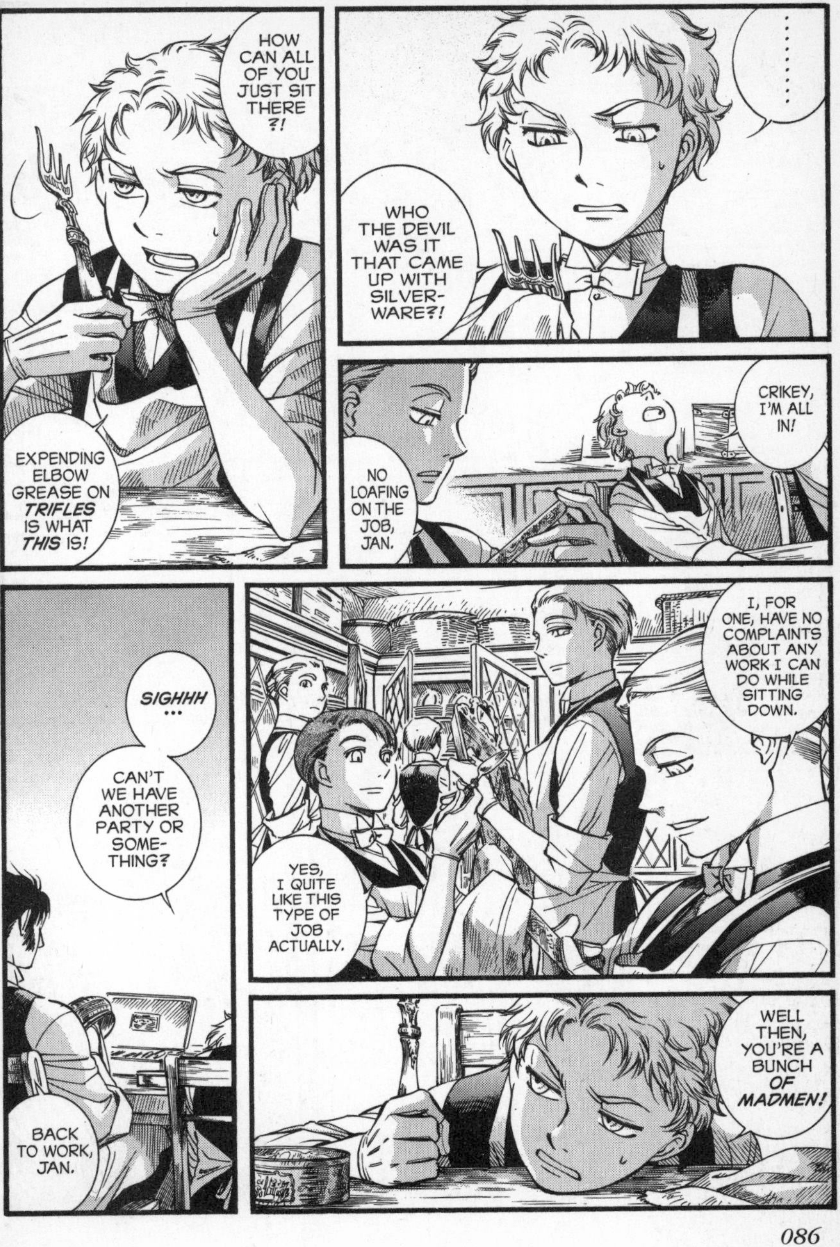
HOW CAN ALL OF YOU JUST SIT THERE ?!
EXPENDING ELBOW GREASE ON ***TRIFLES*** IS WHAT ***THIS*** IS!
....
WHO THE DEVIL WAS IT THAT CAME UP WITH SILVER-WARE?!
CRIKEY, I'M ALL IN!
NO LOAFING ON THE JOB, JAN.
SIGHHH...
CAN'T WE HAVE ANOTHER PARTY OR SOME-THING?
YES, I QUITE LIKE THIS TYPE OF JOB ACTUALLY.
I, FOR ONE, HAVE NO COMPLAINTS ABOUT ANY WORK I CAN DO WHILE SITTING DOWN.
WELL THEN, YOU'RE A BUNCH ***OF MADMEN!***
BACK TO WORK, JAN.

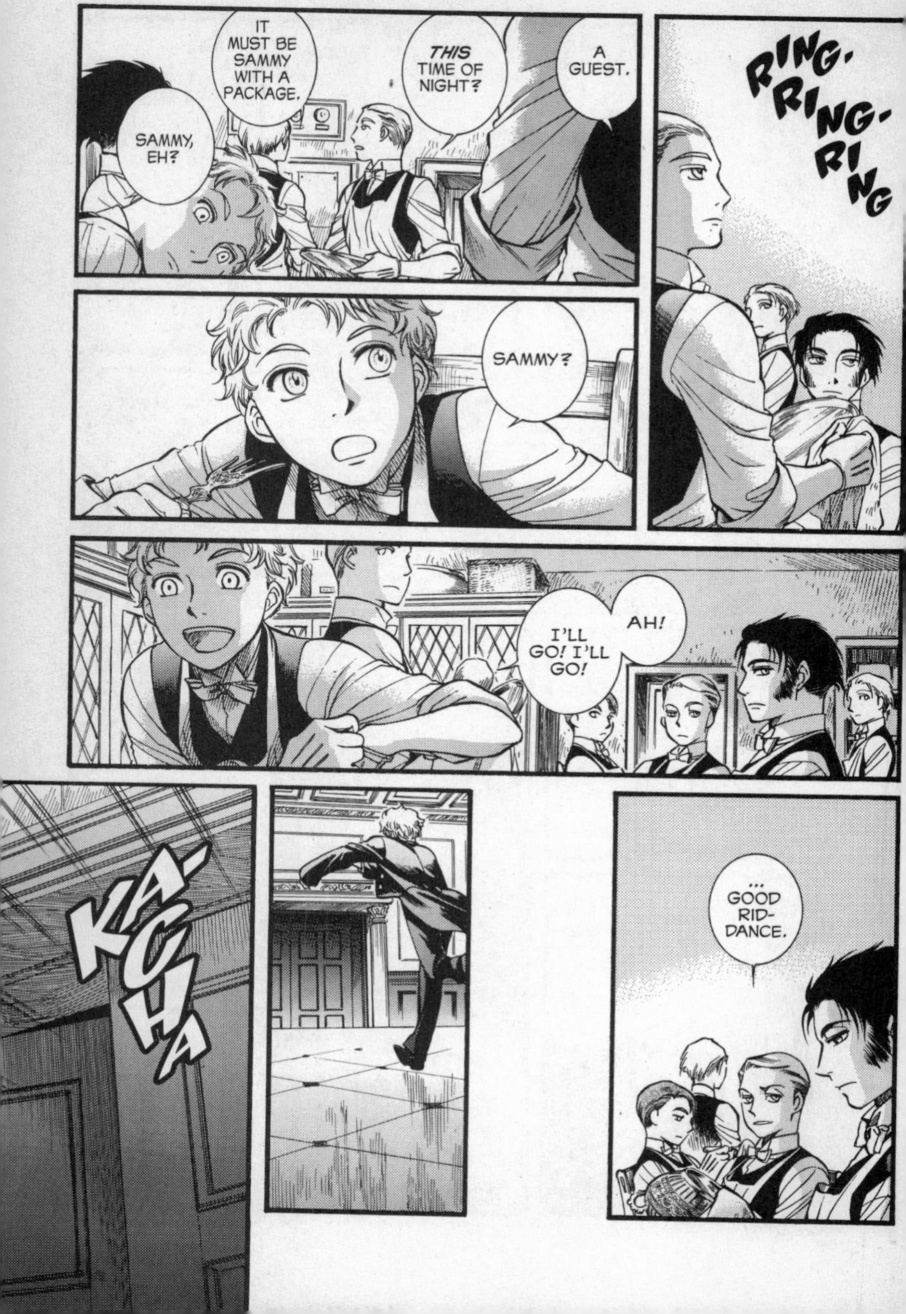
RING-RING-RING
A GUEST.
THIS TIME OF NIGHT?
IT MUST BE SAMMY WITH A PACKAGE.
SAMMY, EH?
SAMMY?
AH!
I'LL GO! I'LL GO!
... GOOD RID-DANCE.
KA-CHA

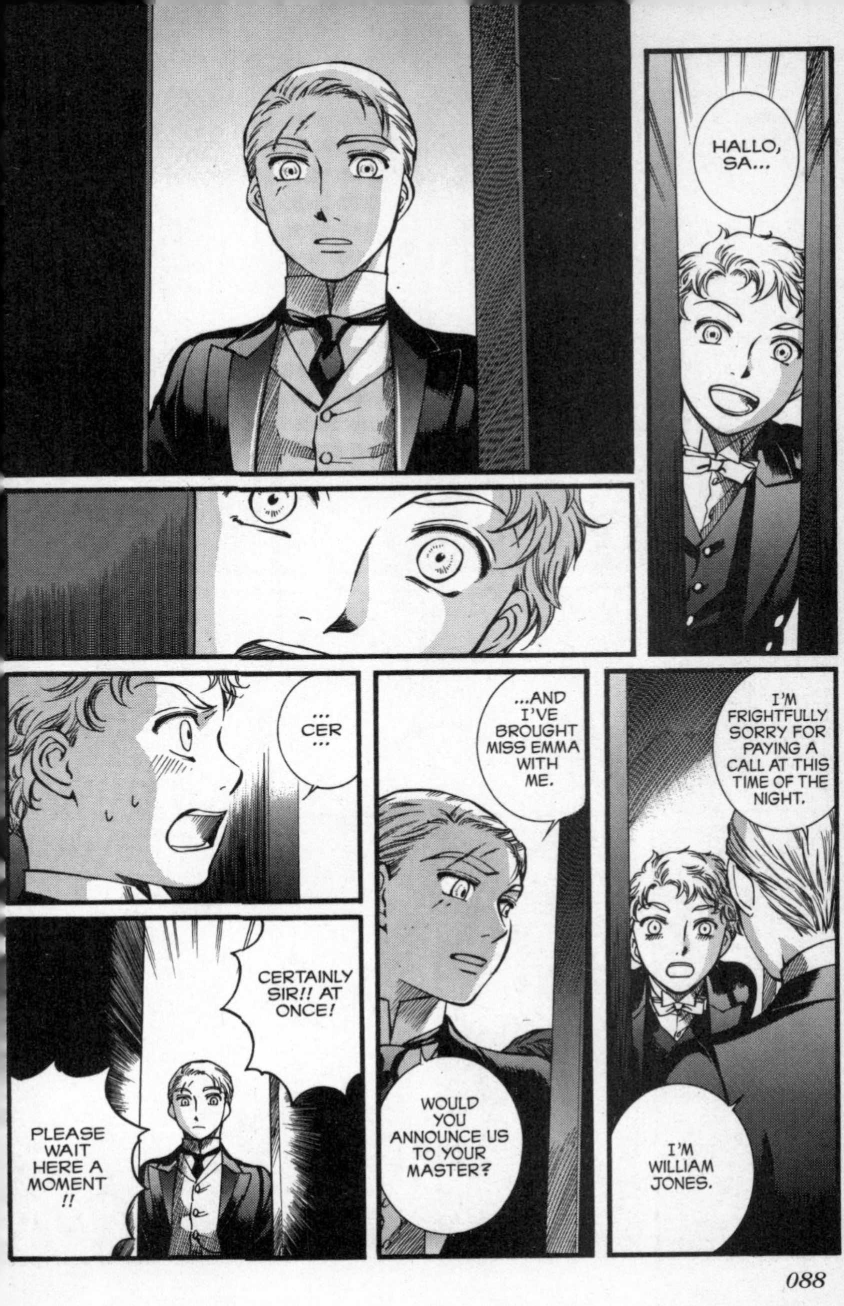
HALLO, SA...
I'M FRIGHTFULLY SORRY FOR PAYING A CALL AT THIS TIME OF THE NIGHT.
I'M WILLIAM JONES.
...AND I'VE BROUGHT MISS EMMA WITH ME.
WOULD YOU ANNOUNCE US TO YOUR MASTER?
... CER ...
CERTAINLY SIR!! AT ONCE!
PLEASE WAIT HERE A MOMENT !!

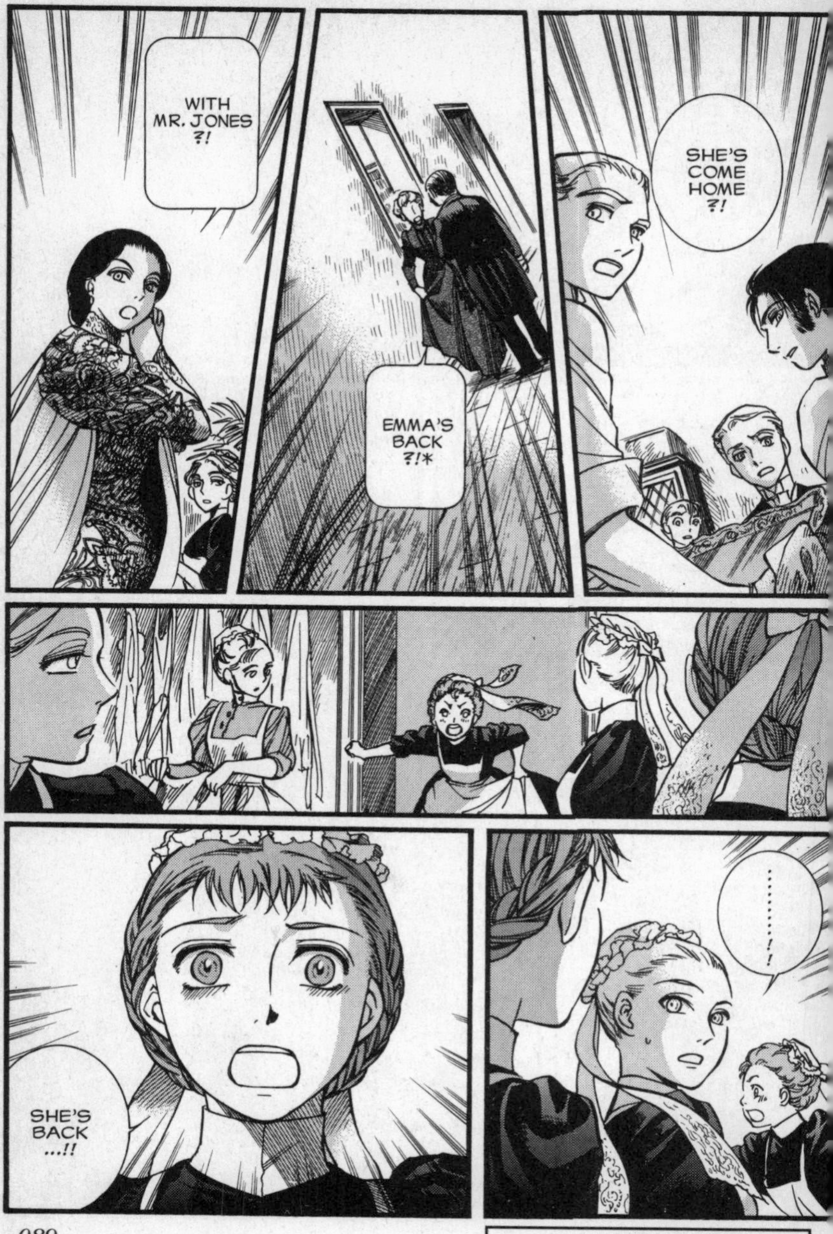
SHE'S COME HOME ?!
EMMA'S BACK ?!*
WITH MR. JONES ?!
......!!
SHE'S BACK ...!!

* ALL SQUARISH BALLOONS DENOTE GERMAN SPEECH

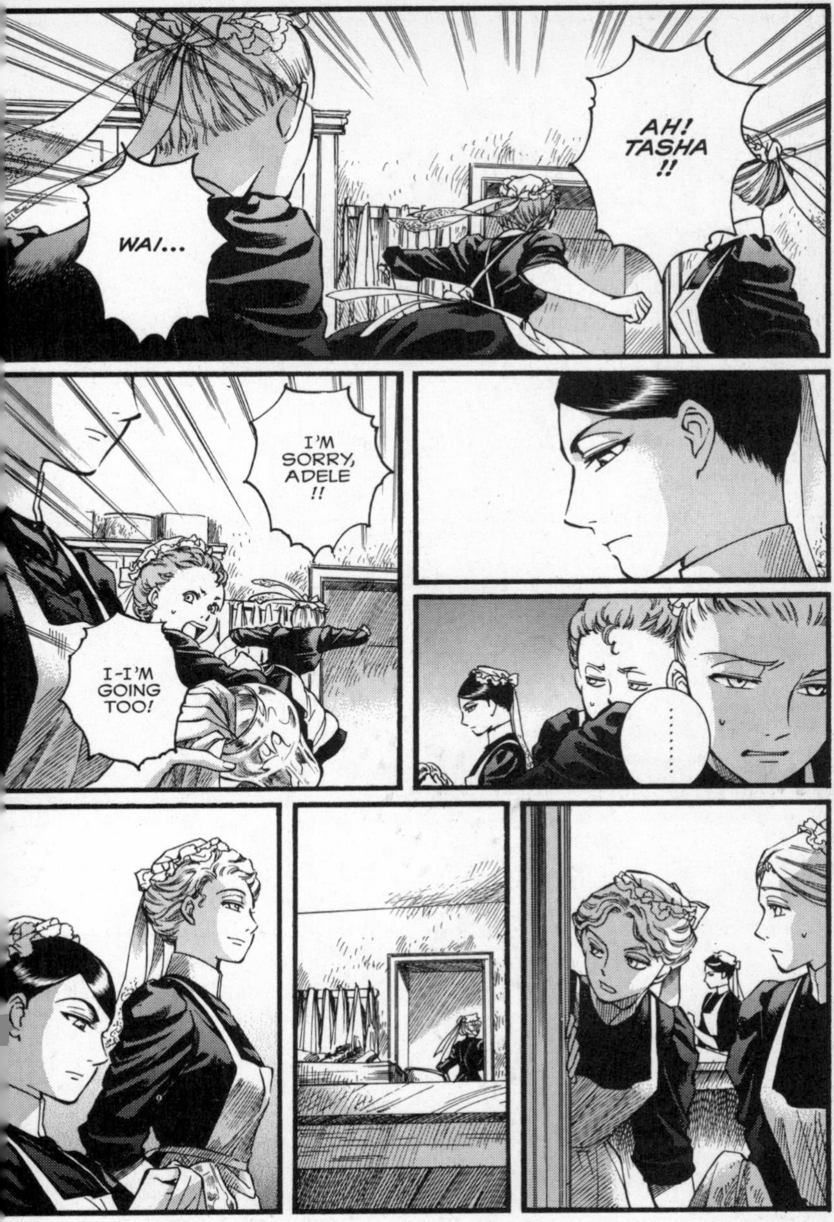
AH! TASHA !!
WAI...
......
I'M SORRY, ADELE !!
I-I'M GOING TOO!

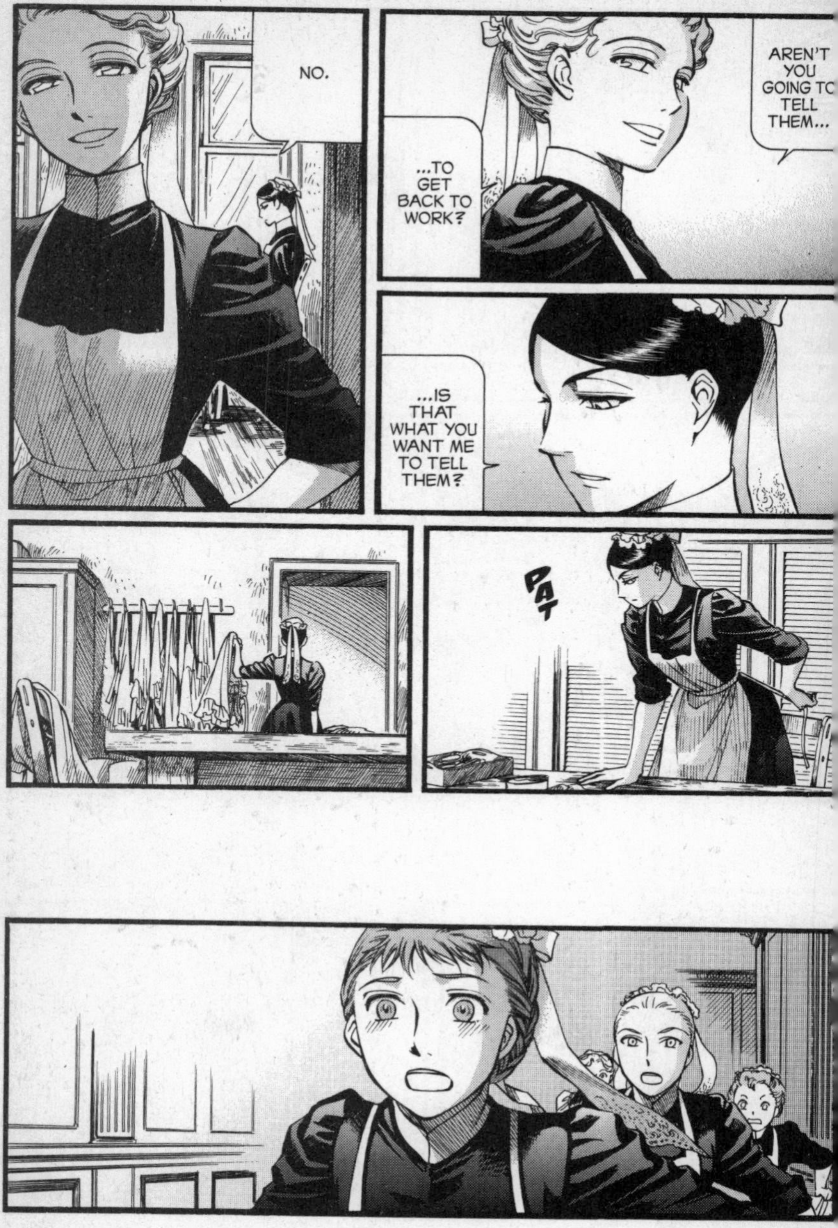
AREN'T YOU GOING TO TELL THEM...
...TO GET BACK TO WORK?
...IS THAT WHAT YOU WANT ME TO TELL THEM?
NO.
PAT

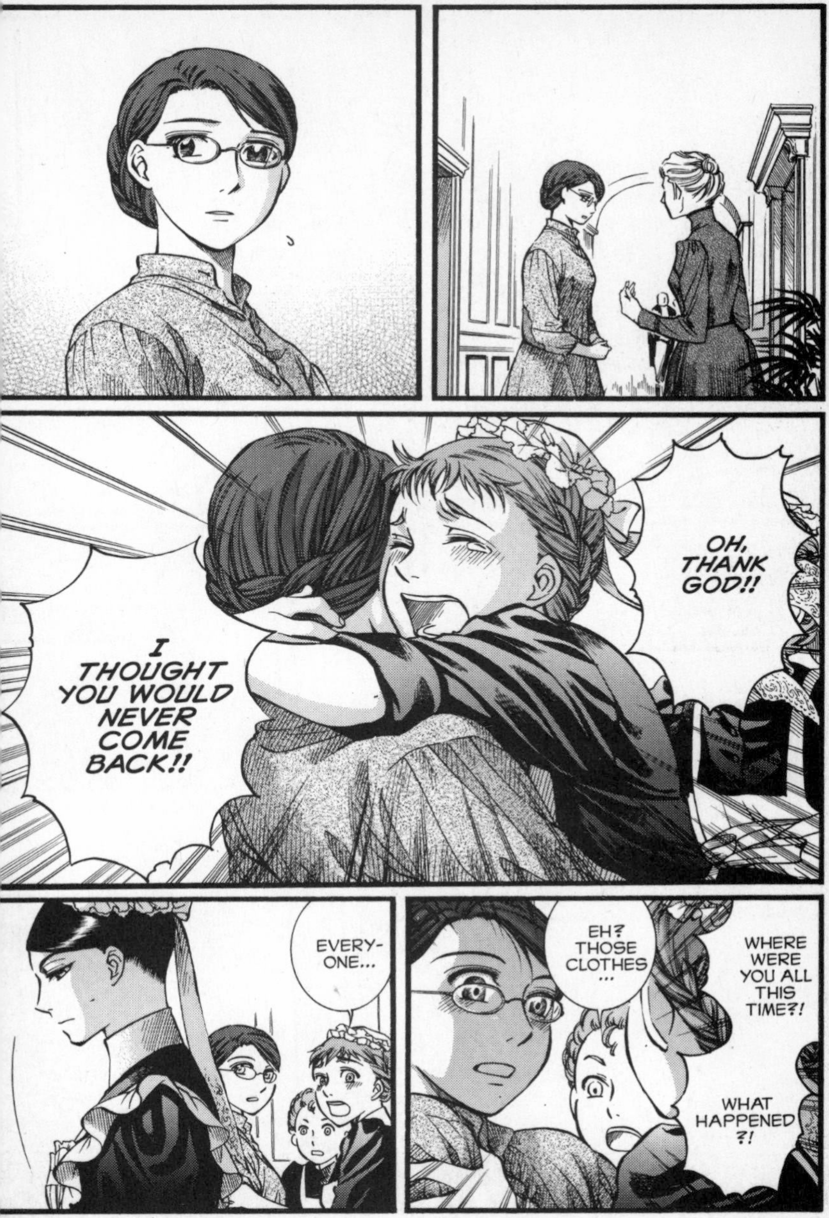
OH, THANK GOD!!
I THOUGHT YOU WOULD NEVER COME BACK!!
WHERE WERE YOU ALL THIS TIME?!
WHAT HAPPENED?!
EH? THOSE CLOTHES ...
EVERY-ONE...

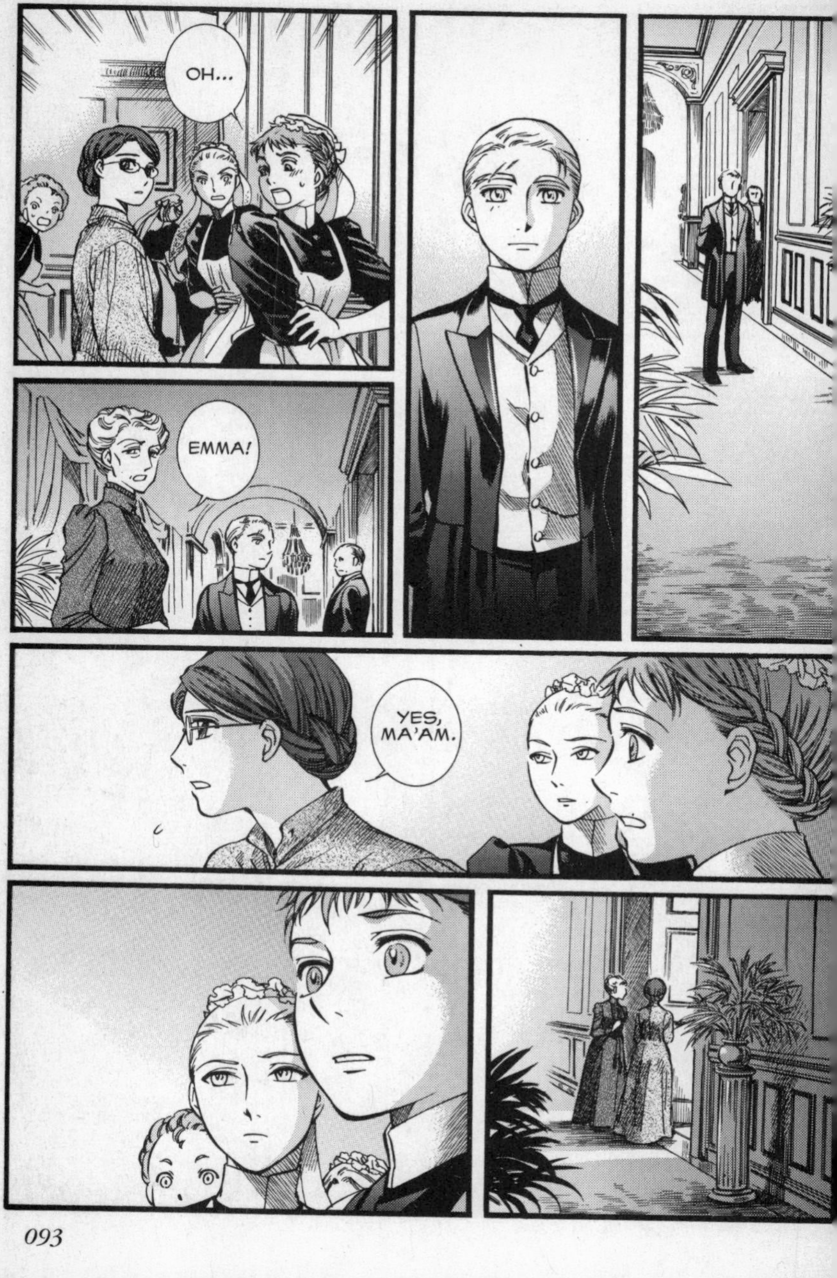
OH...
EMMA!
YES, MA'AM.

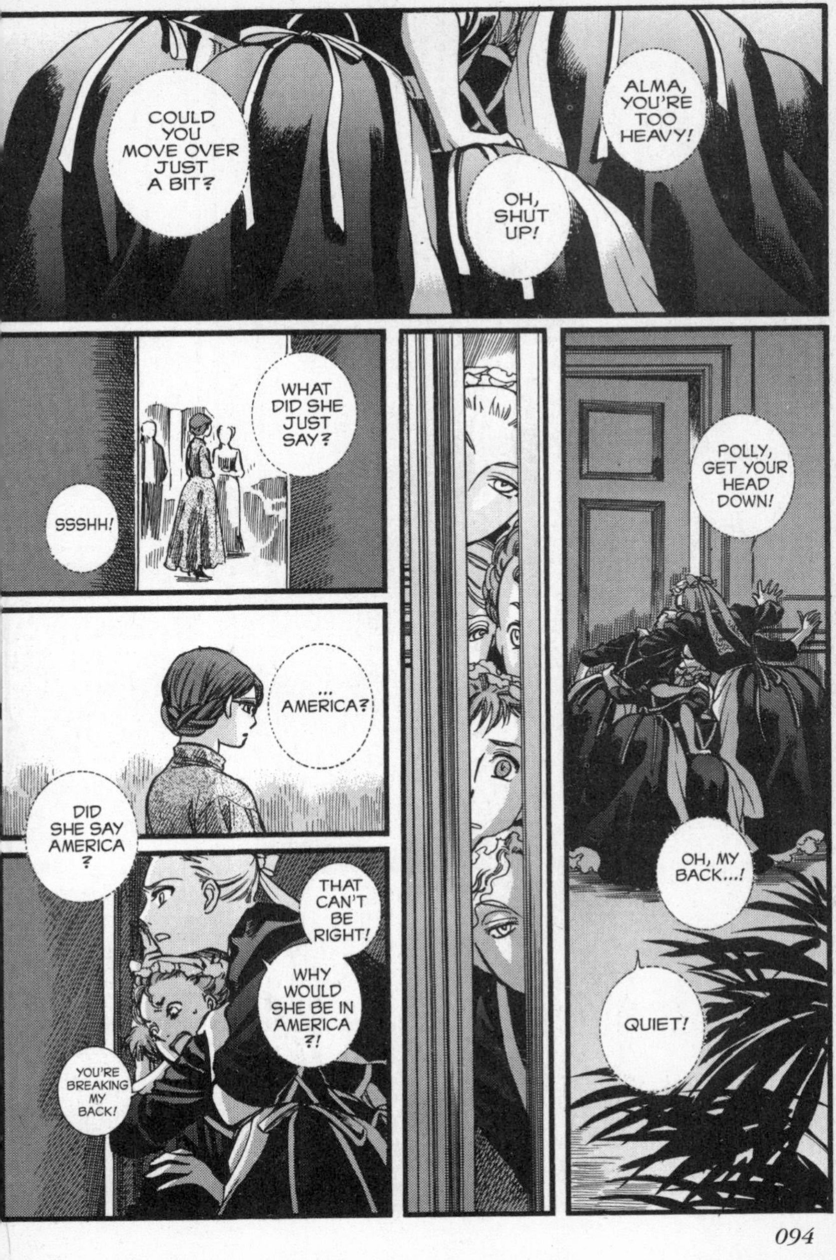
ALMA, YOU'RE TOO HEAVY!
OH, SHUT UP!
COULD YOU MOVE OVER JUST A BIT?
POLLY, GET YOUR HEAD DOWN!
OH, MY BACK...!
QUIET!
WHAT DID SHE JUST SAY?
SSSHH!
... AMERICA?
DID SHE SAY AMERICA?
THAT CAN'T BE RIGHT!
WHY WOULD SHE BE IN AMERICA?!
YOU'RE BREAKING MY BACK!

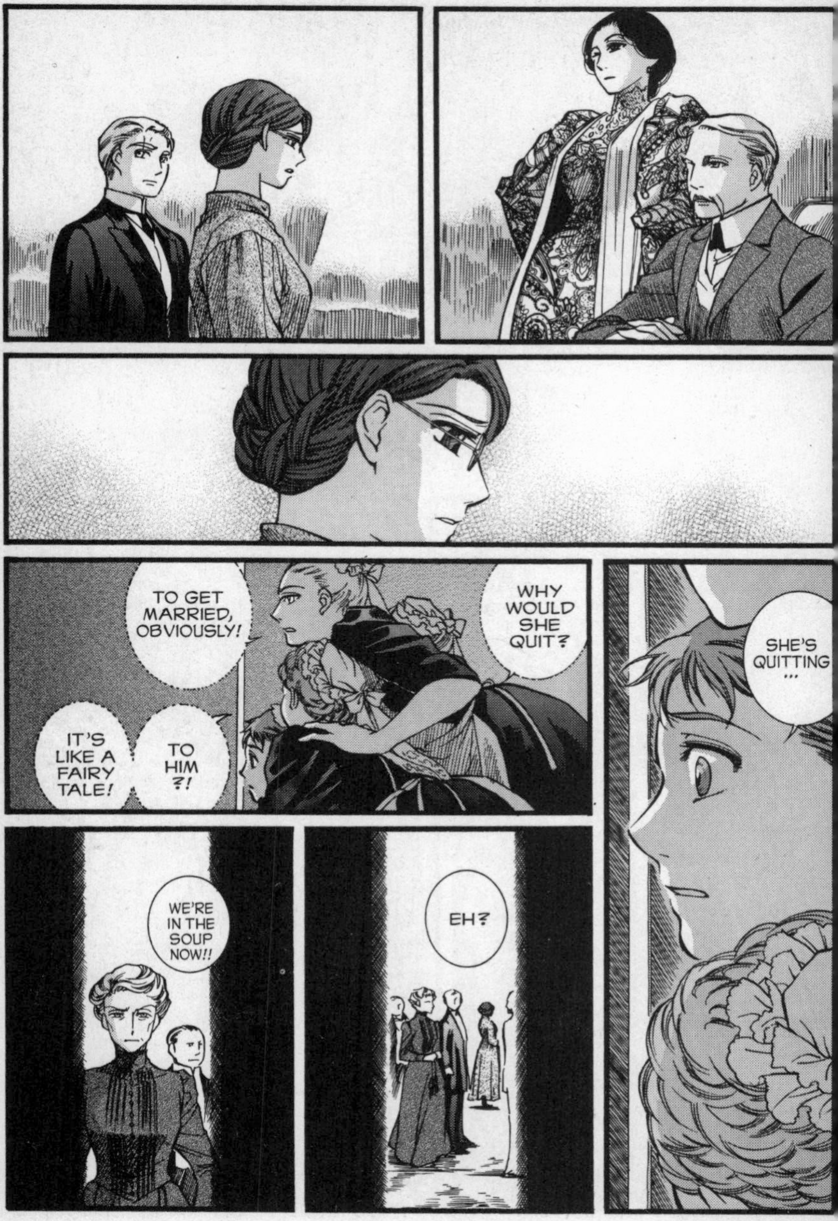
SHE'S QUITTING ...
WHY WOULD SHE QUIT?
TO GET MARRIED, OBVIOUSLY!
TO HIM ?!
IT'S LIKE A FAIRY TALE!
EH?
WE'RE IN THE SOUP NOW!!

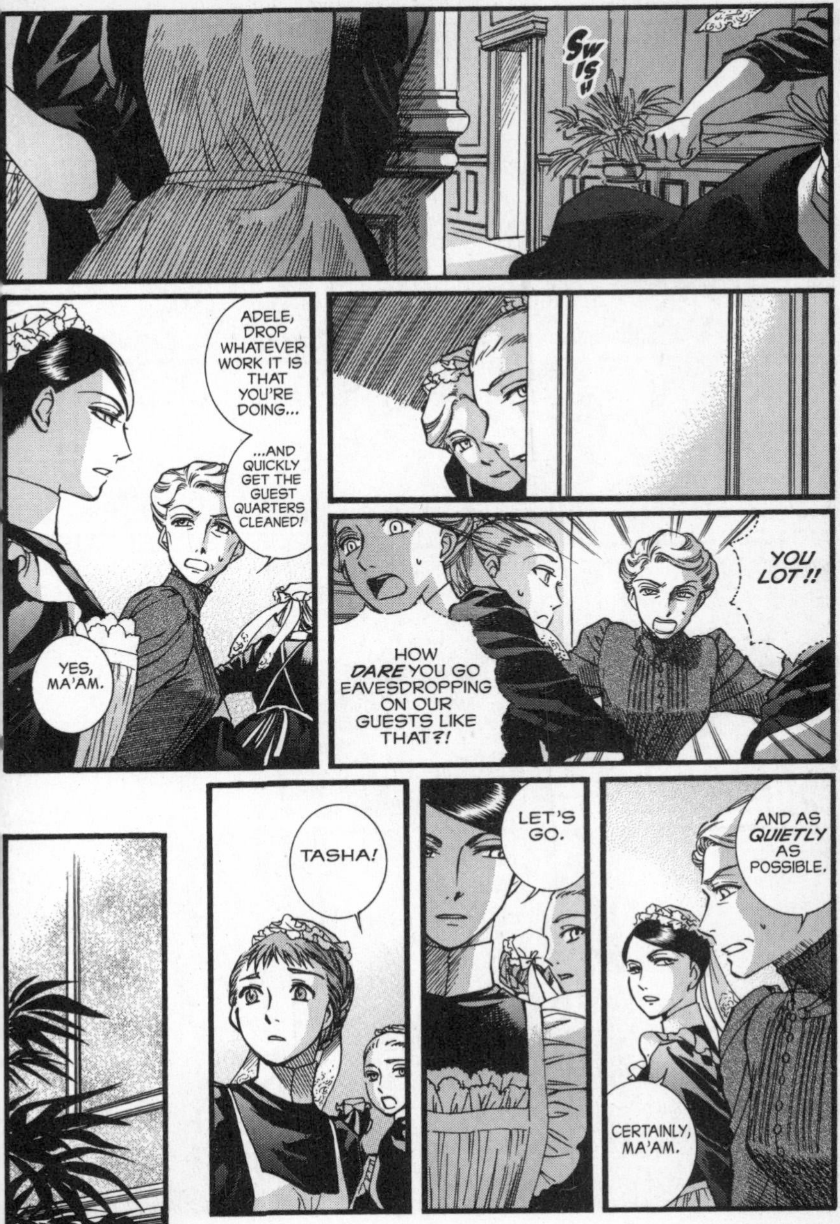
SWISH
YOU LOT!!
HOW DARE YOU GO EAVESDROPPING ON OUR GUESTS LIKE THAT?!
ADELE, DROP WHATEVER WORK IT IS THAT YOU'RE DOING...
...AND QUICKLY GET THE GUEST QUARTERS CLEANED!
YES, MA'AM.
AND AS QUIETLY AS POSSIBLE.
CERTAINLY, MA'AM.
LET'S GO.
TASHA!

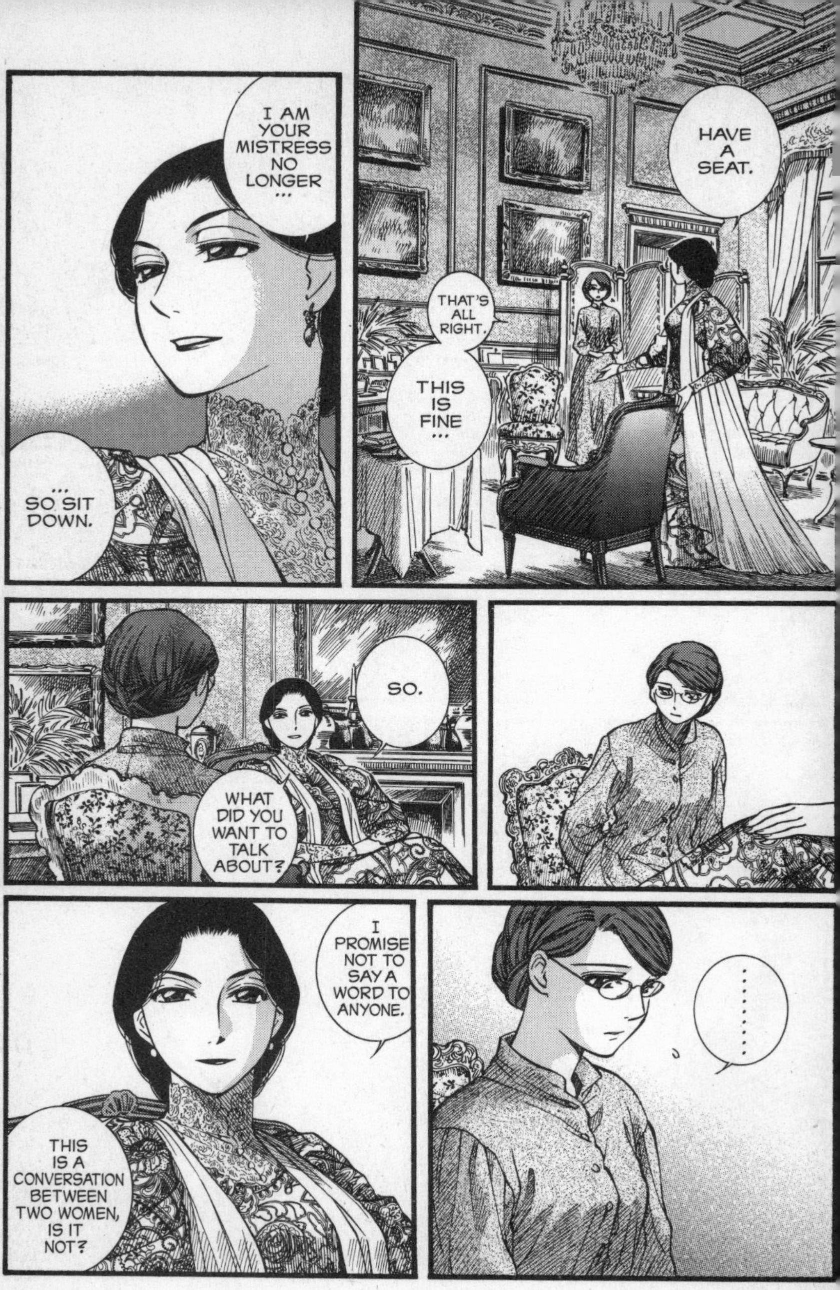
HAVE A SEAT.
THAT'S ALL RIGHT.
THIS IS FINE ...
I AM YOUR MISTRESS NO LONGER ...
... SO SIT DOWN.
SO.
WHAT DID YOU WANT TO TALK ABOUT?
....
I PROMISE NOT TO SAY A WORD TO ANYONE.
THIS IS A CONVERSATION BETWEEN TWO WOMEN, IS IT NOT?

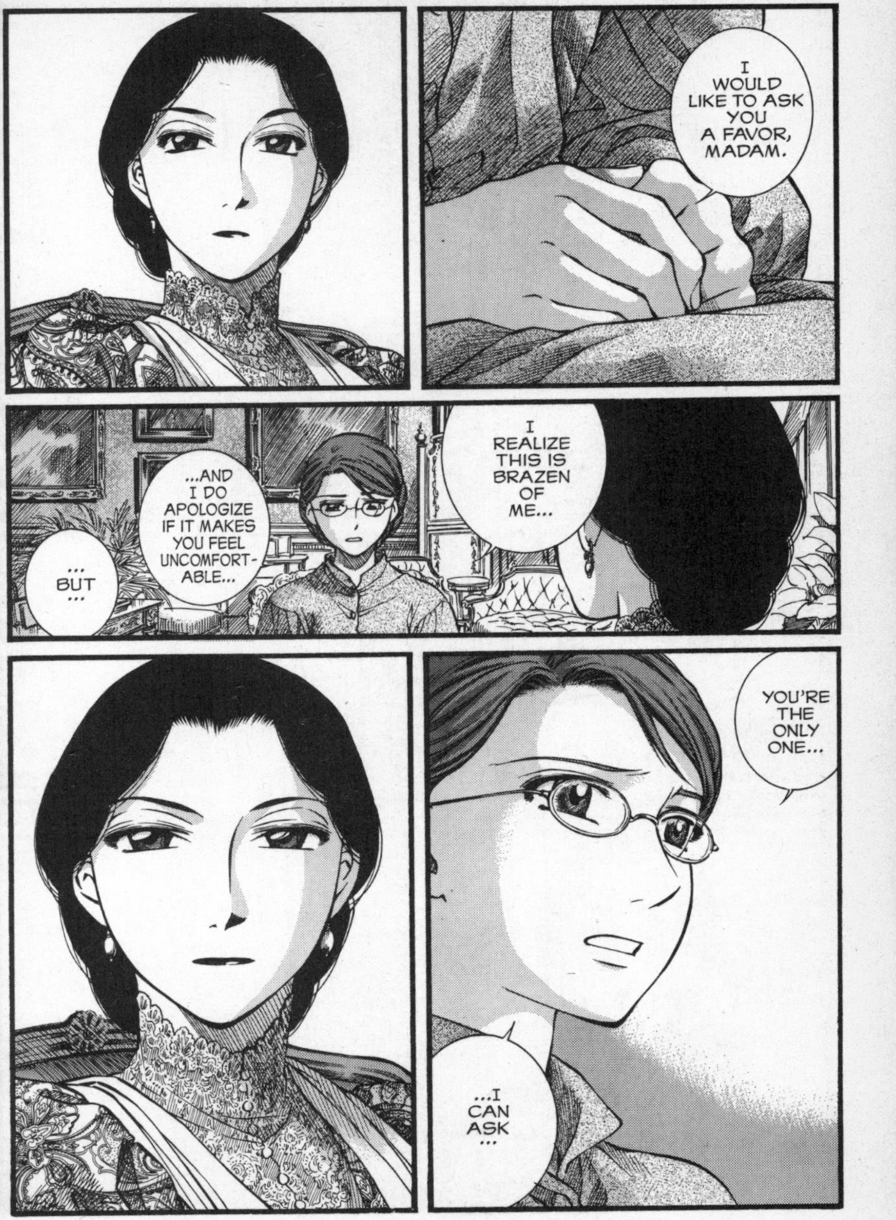
I WOULD LIKE TO ASK YOU A FAVOR, MADAM.
I REALIZE THIS IS BRAZEN OF ME...
...AND I DO APOLOGIZE IF IT MAKES YOU FEEL UNCOMFORT-ABLE...
...BUT...
YOU'RE THE ONLY ONE...
...I CAN ASK...

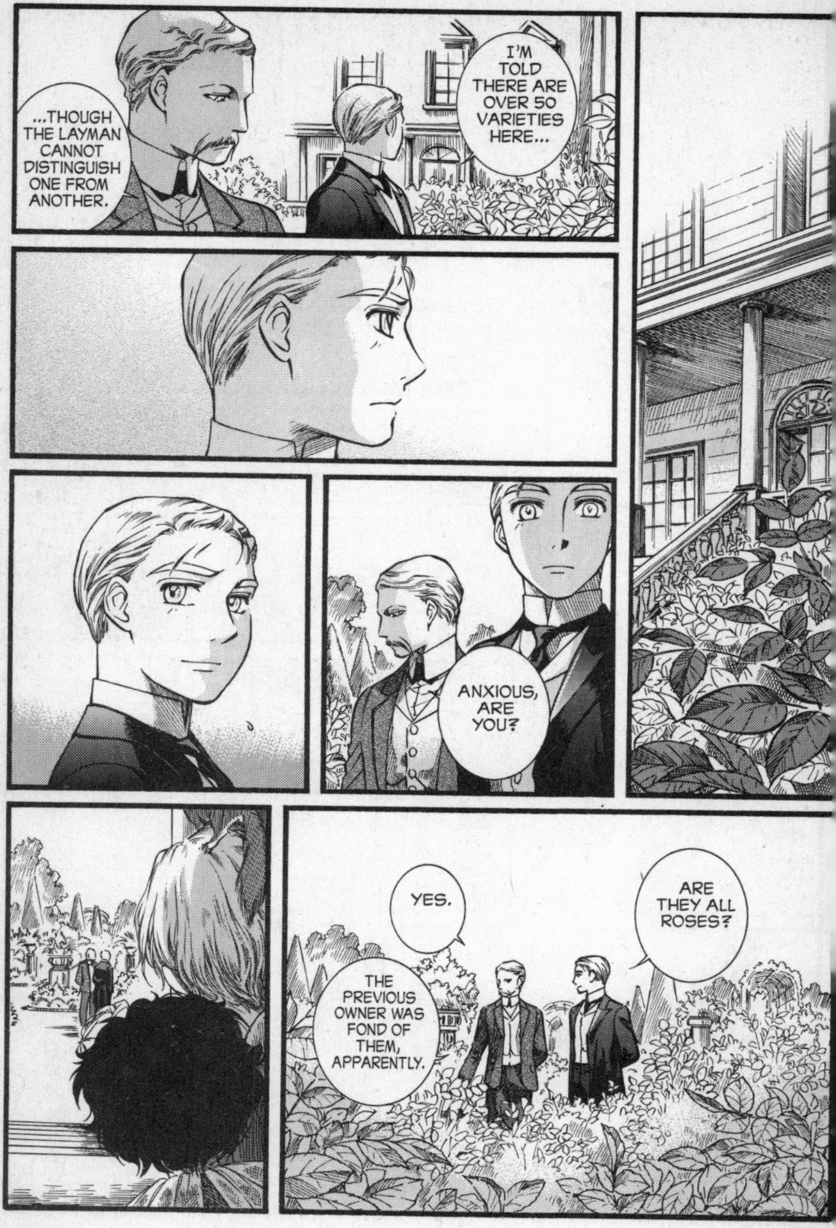
I'M TOLD THERE ARE OVER 50 VARIETIES HERE...
...THOUGH THE LAYMAN CANNOT DISTINGUISH ONE FROM ANOTHER.
ANXIOUS, ARE YOU?
ARE THEY ALL ROSES?
YES.
THE PREVIOUS OWNER WAS FOND OF THEM, APPARENTLY.

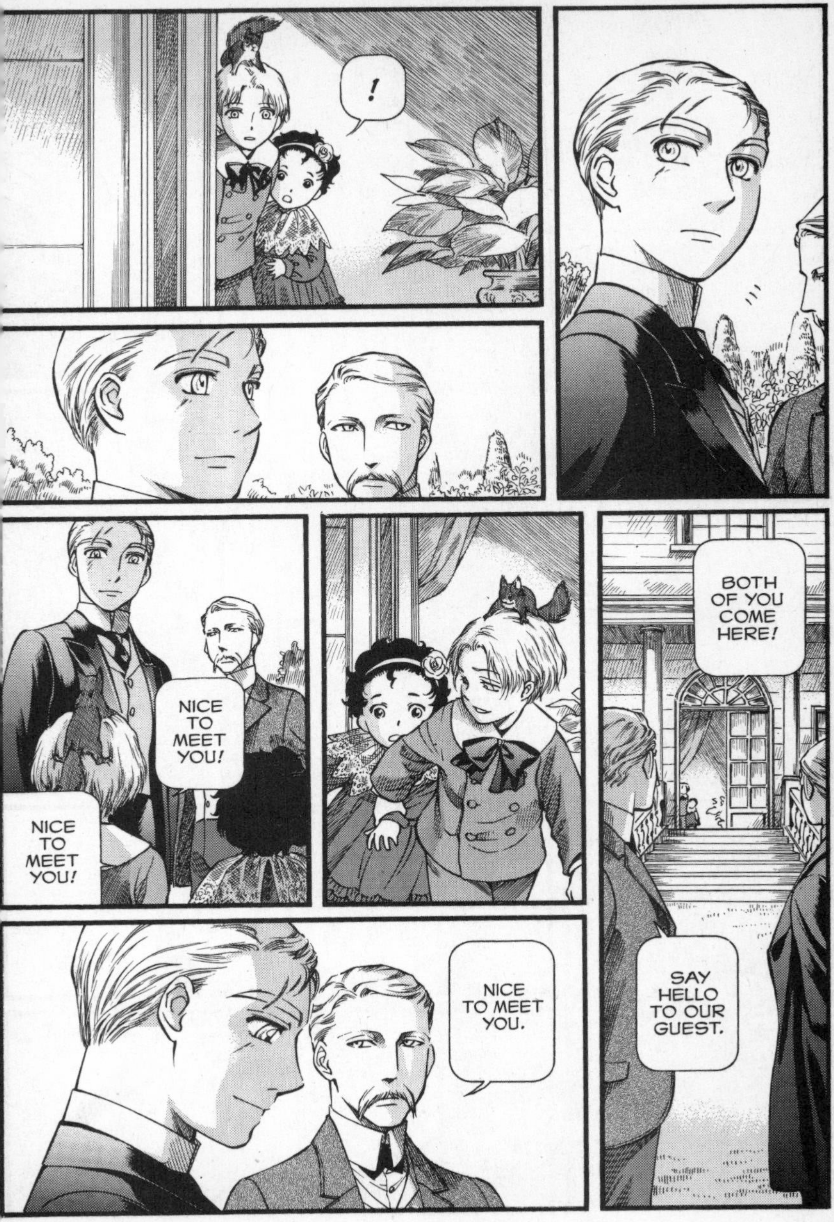

!
BOTH OF YOU COME HERE!
SAY HELLO TO OUR GUEST.
NICE TO MEET YOU!
NICE TO MEET YOU!
NICE TO MEET YOU.

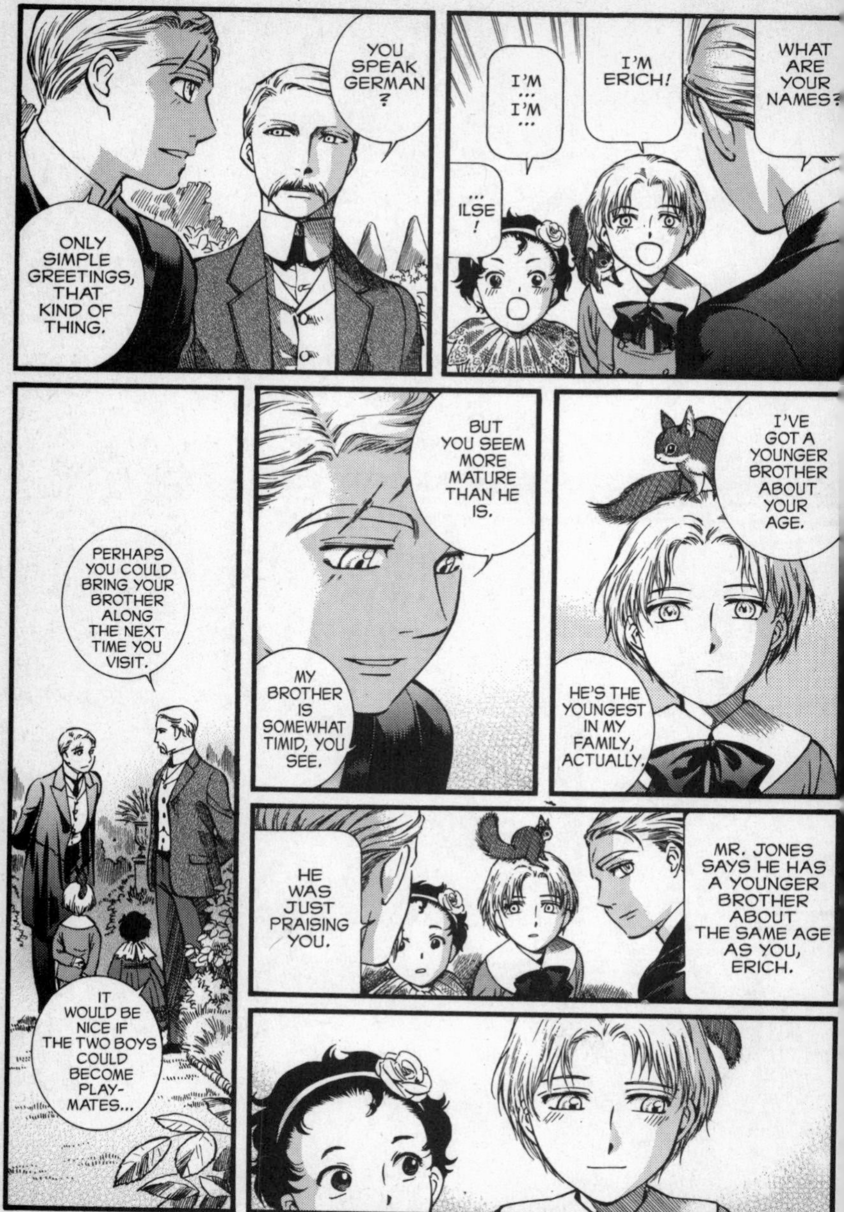
WHAT ARE YOUR NAMES?
I'M ERICH!
I'M... I'M...
...ILSE!
YOU SPEAK GERMAN?
ONLY SIMPLE GREETINGS, THAT KIND OF THING.
I'VE GOT A YOUNGER BROTHER ABOUT YOUR AGE.
HE'S THE YOUNGEST IN MY FAMILY, ACTUALLY.
BUT YOU SEEM MORE MATURE THAN HE IS.
MY BROTHER IS SOMEWHAT TIMID, YOU SEE.
MR. JONES SAYS HE HAS A YOUNGER BROTHER ABOUT THE SAME AGE AS YOU, ERICH.
HE WAS JUST PRAISING YOU.
PERHAPS YOU COULD BRING YOUR BROTHER ALONG THE NEXT TIME YOU VISIT.
IT WOULD BE NICE IF THE TWO BOYS COULD BECOME PLAY-MATES...

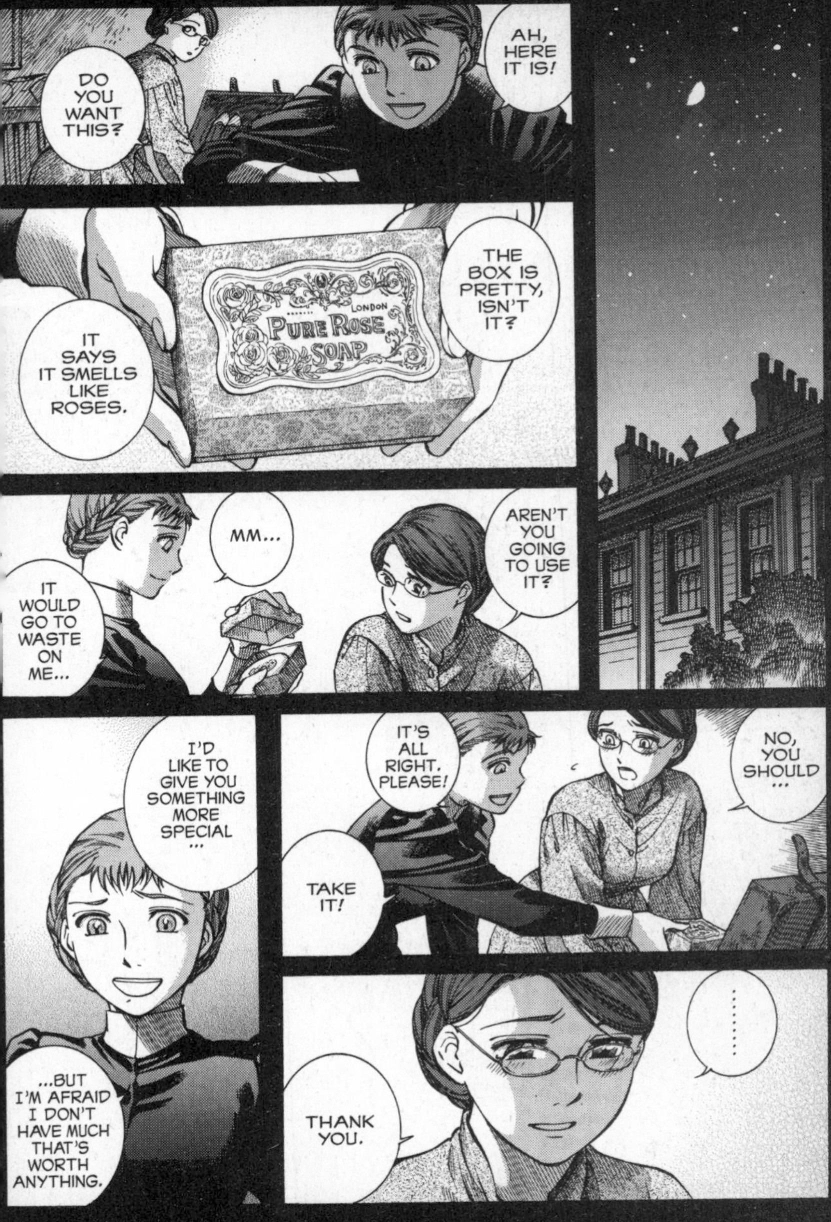
AH, HERE IT IS!
DO YOU WANT THIS?
THE BOX IS PRETTY, ISN'T IT?
LONDON
PURE ROSE SOAP
IT SAYS IT SMELLS LIKE ROSES.
AREN'T YOU GOING TO USE IT?
MM...
IT WOULD GO TO WASTE ON ME...
NO, YOU SHOULD ...
IT'S ALL RIGHT. PLEASE!
TAKE IT!
I'D LIKE TO GIVE YOU SOMETHING MORE SPECIAL ...
...BUT I'M AFRAID I DON'T HAVE MUCH THAT'S WORTH ANYTHING.
....
THANK YOU.

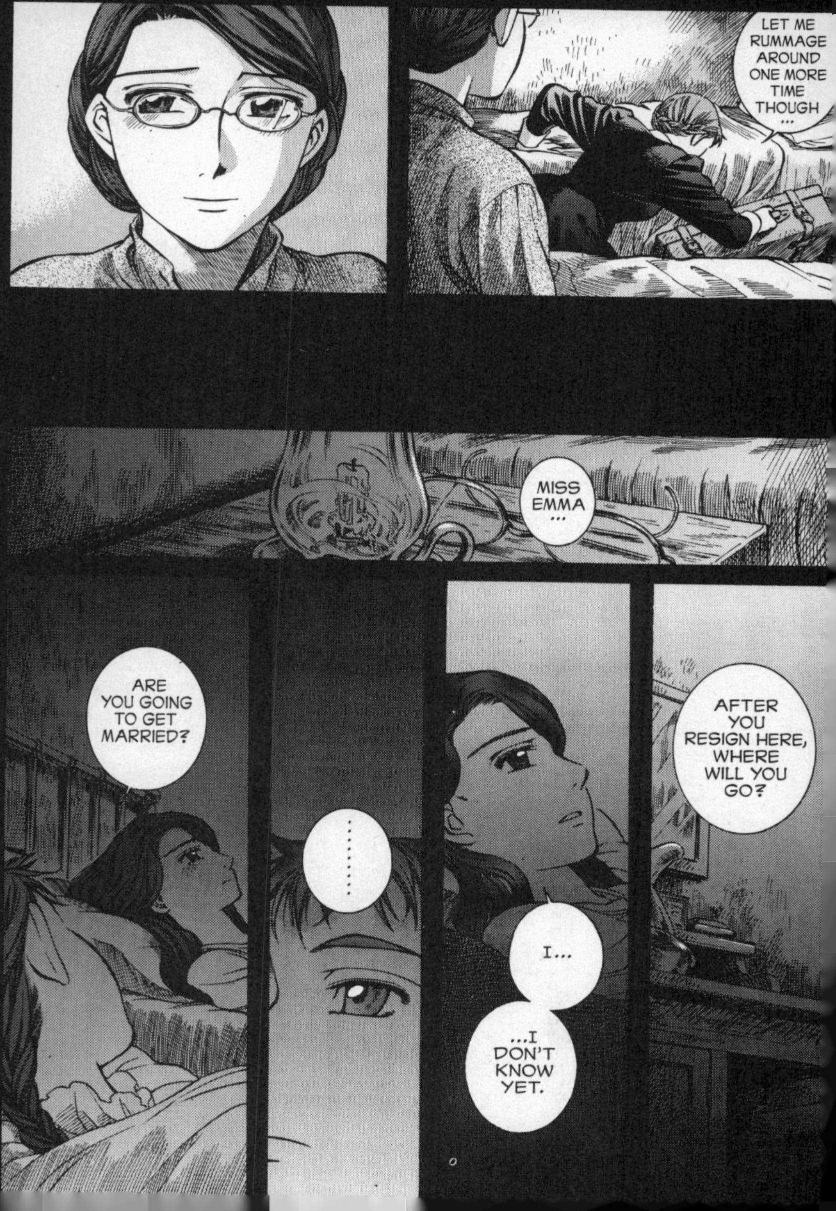
LET ME RUMMAGE AROUND ONE MORE TIME THOUGH ...
MISS EMMA ...
AFTER YOU RESIGN HERE, WHERE WILL YOU GO?
I...
...I DON'T KNOW YET.
....
ARE YOU GOING TO GET MARRIED?

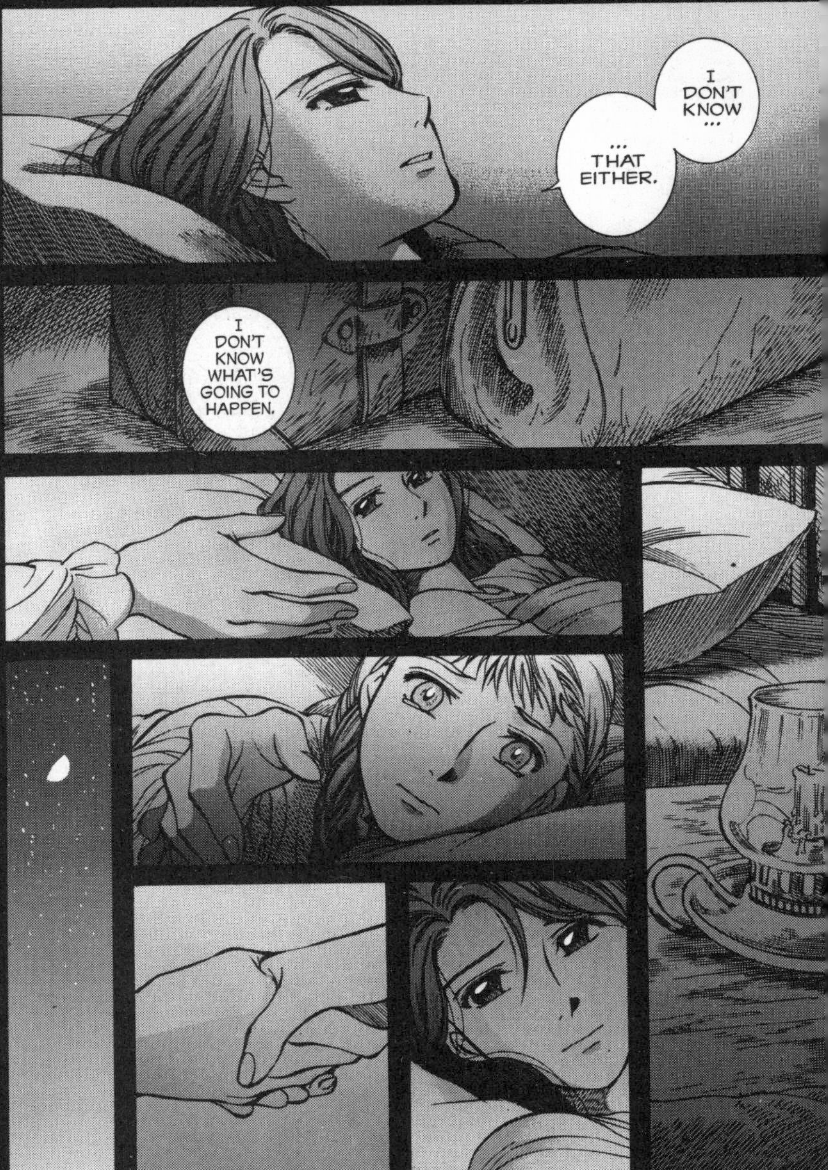
I DON'T KNOW ...
... THAT EITHER.
I DON'T KNOW WHAT'S GOING TO HAPPEN.

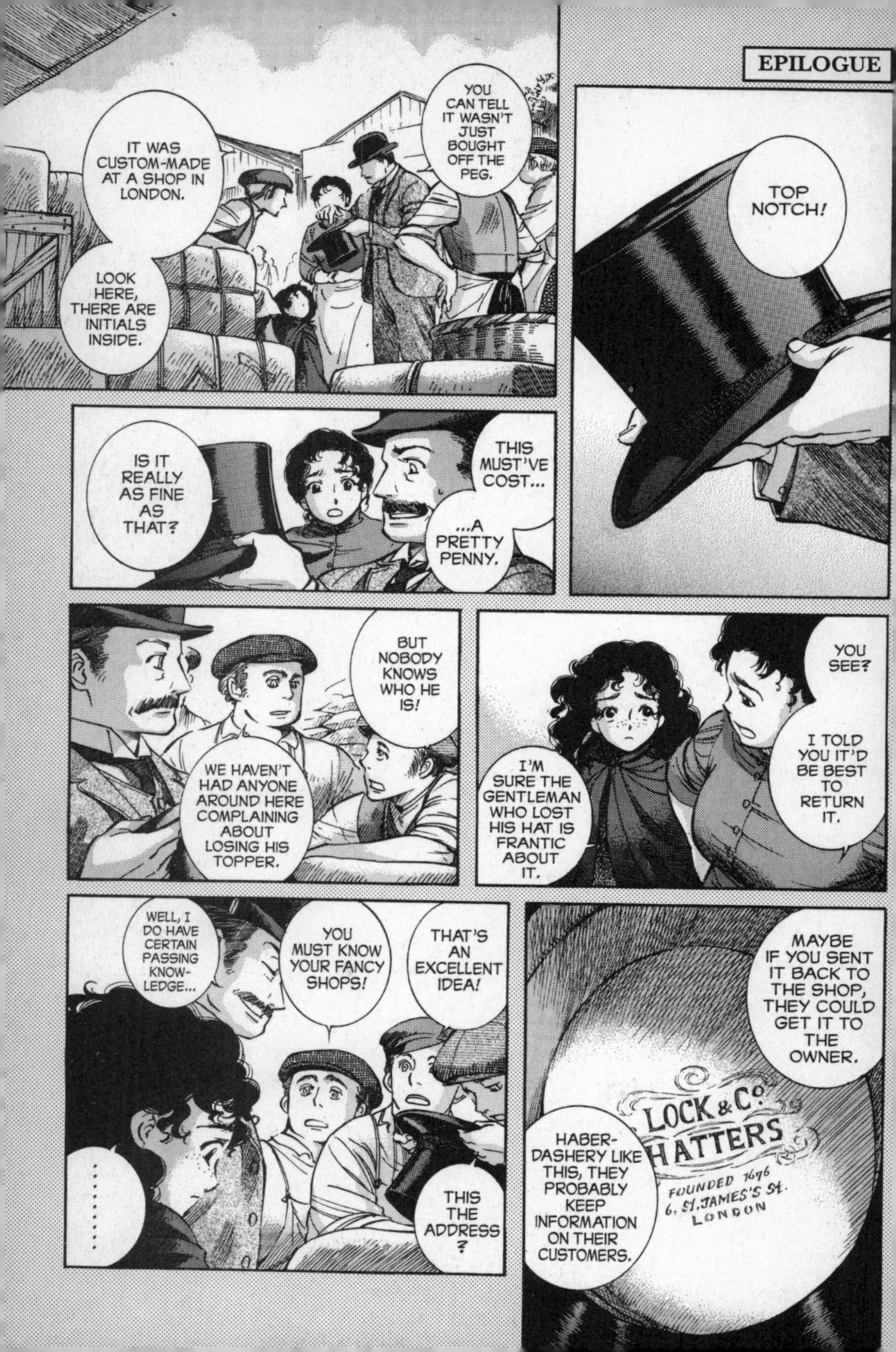
TOP NOTCH!
YOU CAN TELL IT WASN'T JUST BOUGHT OFF THE PEG.
IT WAS CUSTOM-MADE AT A SHOP IN LONDON.
LOOK HERE, THERE ARE INITIALS INSIDE.
THIS MUST'VE COST...
...A PRETTY PENNY.
IS IT REALLY AS FINE AS THAT?
YOU SEE?
I TOLD YOU IT'D BE BEST TO RETURN IT.
I'M SURE THE GENTLEMAN WHO LOST HIS HAT IS FRANTIC ABOUT IT.
BUT NOBODY KNOWS WHO HE IS!
WE HAVEN'T HAD ANYONE AROUND HERE COMPLAINING ABOUT LOSING HIS TOPPER.
MAYBE IF YOU SENT IT BACK TO THE SHOP, THEY COULD GET IT TO THE OWNER.
LOCK & Co.
HATTERS
FOUNDED 1676
6, St. JAMES'S St.
LONDON
HABER-DASHERY LIKE THIS, THEY PROBABLY KEEP INFORMATION ON THEIR CUSTOMERS.
THAT'S AN EXCELLENT IDEA!
YOU MUST KNOW YOUR FANCY SHOPS!
WELL, I DO HAVE CERTAIN PASSING KNOW-LEDGE...
THIS THE ADDRESS?
....

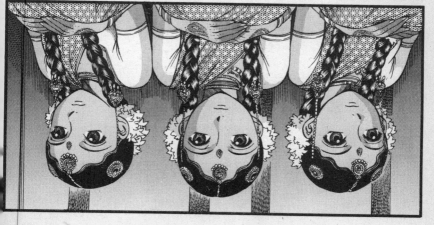

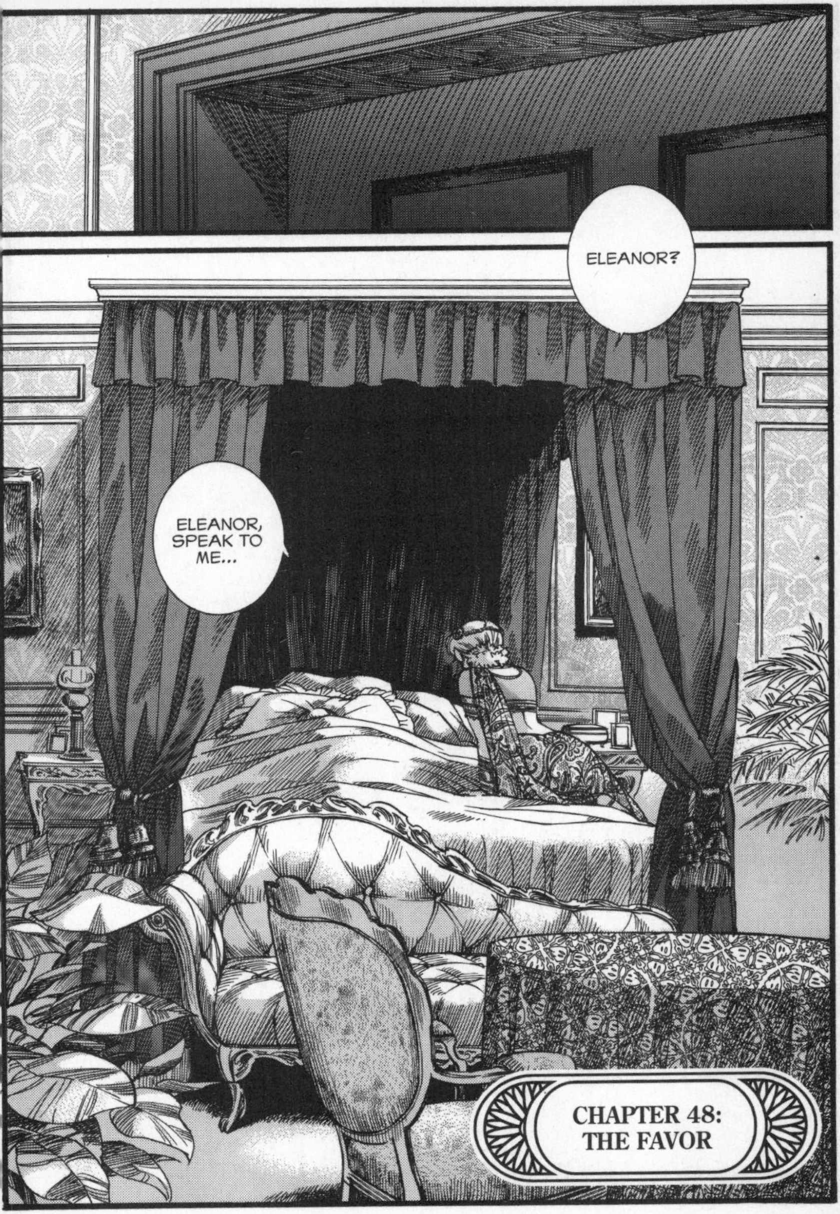
ELEANOR?
ELEANOR, SPEAK TO ME...
CHAPTER 48: THE FAVOR

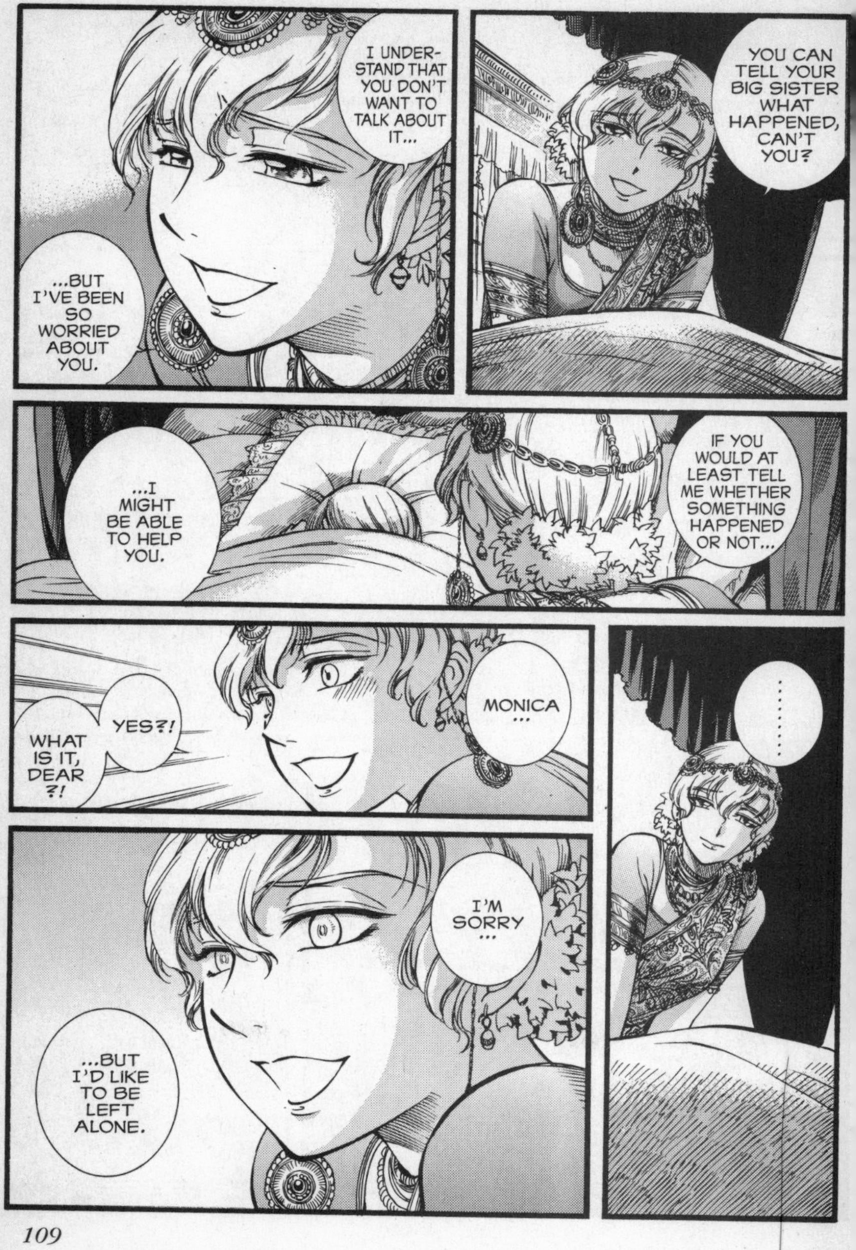
YOU CAN TELL YOUR BIG SISTER WHAT HAPPENED, CAN'T YOU?
I UNDER-STAND THAT YOU DON'T WANT TO TALK ABOUT IT...
...BUT I'VE BEEN SO WORRIED ABOUT YOU.
IF YOU WOULD AT LEAST TELL ME WHETHER SOMETHING HAPPENED OR NOT...
...I MIGHT BE ABLE TO HELP YOU.
......
MONICA...
YES?!
WHAT IS IT, DEAR?!
I'M SORRY...
...BUT I'D LIKE TO BE LEFT ALONE.

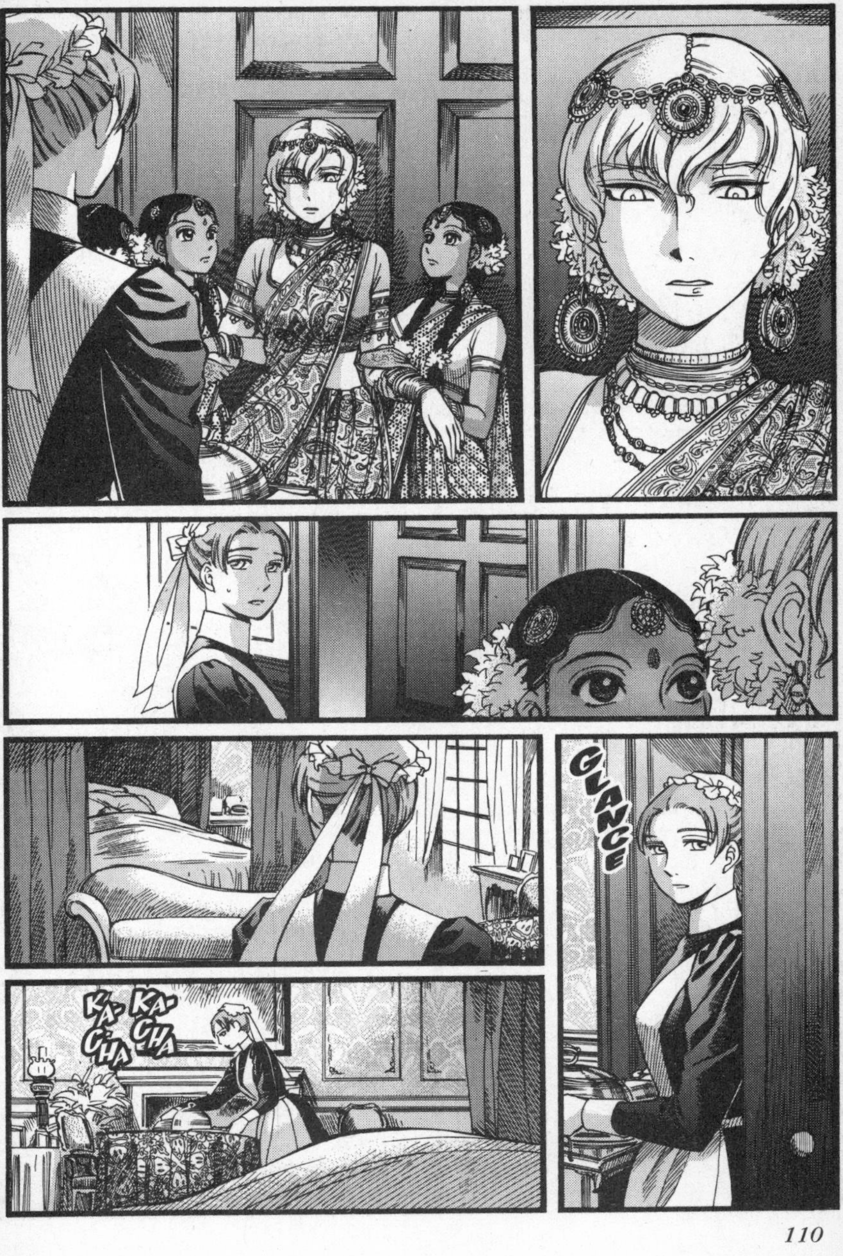
GLANCE
KA-CHA
KA-CHA

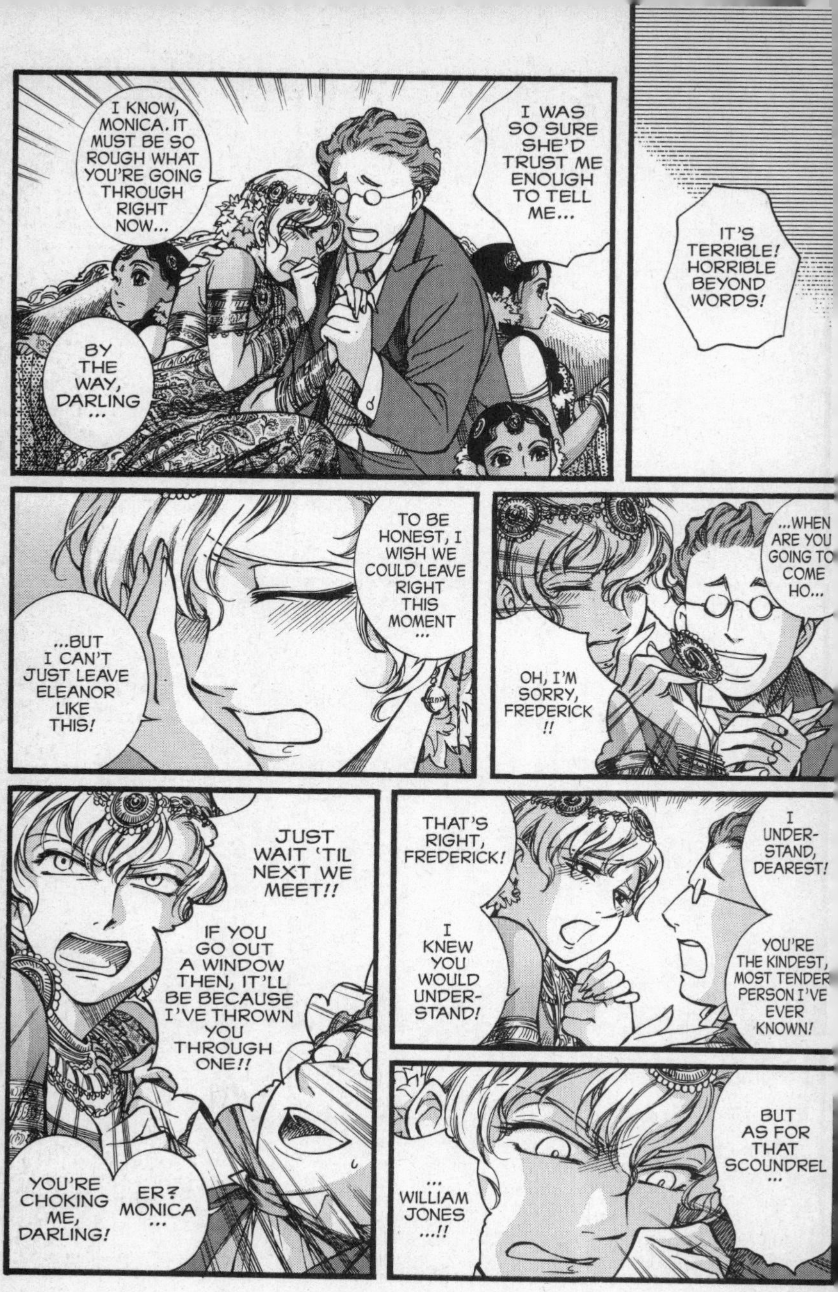
IT'S TERRIBLE! HORRIBLE BEYOND WORDS!
I WAS SO SURE SHE'D TRUST ME ENOUGH TO TELL ME...
I KNOW, MONICA. IT MUST BE SO ROUGH WHAT YOU'RE GOING THROUGH RIGHT NOW...
BY THE WAY, DARLING...
...WHEN ARE YOU GOING TO COME HO...
OH, I'M SORRY, FREDERICK!!
TO BE HONEST, I WISH WE COULD LEAVE RIGHT THIS MOMENT...
...BUT I CAN'T JUST LEAVE ELEANOR LIKE THIS!
I UNDER-STAND, DEAREST!
YOU'RE THE KINDEST, MOST TENDER PERSON I'VE EVER KNOWN!
THAT'S RIGHT, FREDERICK!
I KNEW YOU WOULD UNDER-STAND!
BUT AS FOR THAT SCOUNDREL...
...WILLIAM JONES...!!
JUST WAIT 'TIL NEXT WE MEET!!
IF YOU GO OUT A WINDOW THEN, IT'LL BE BECAUSE I'VE THROWN YOU THROUGH ONE!!
ER? MONICA...
YOU'RE CHOKING ME, DARLING!

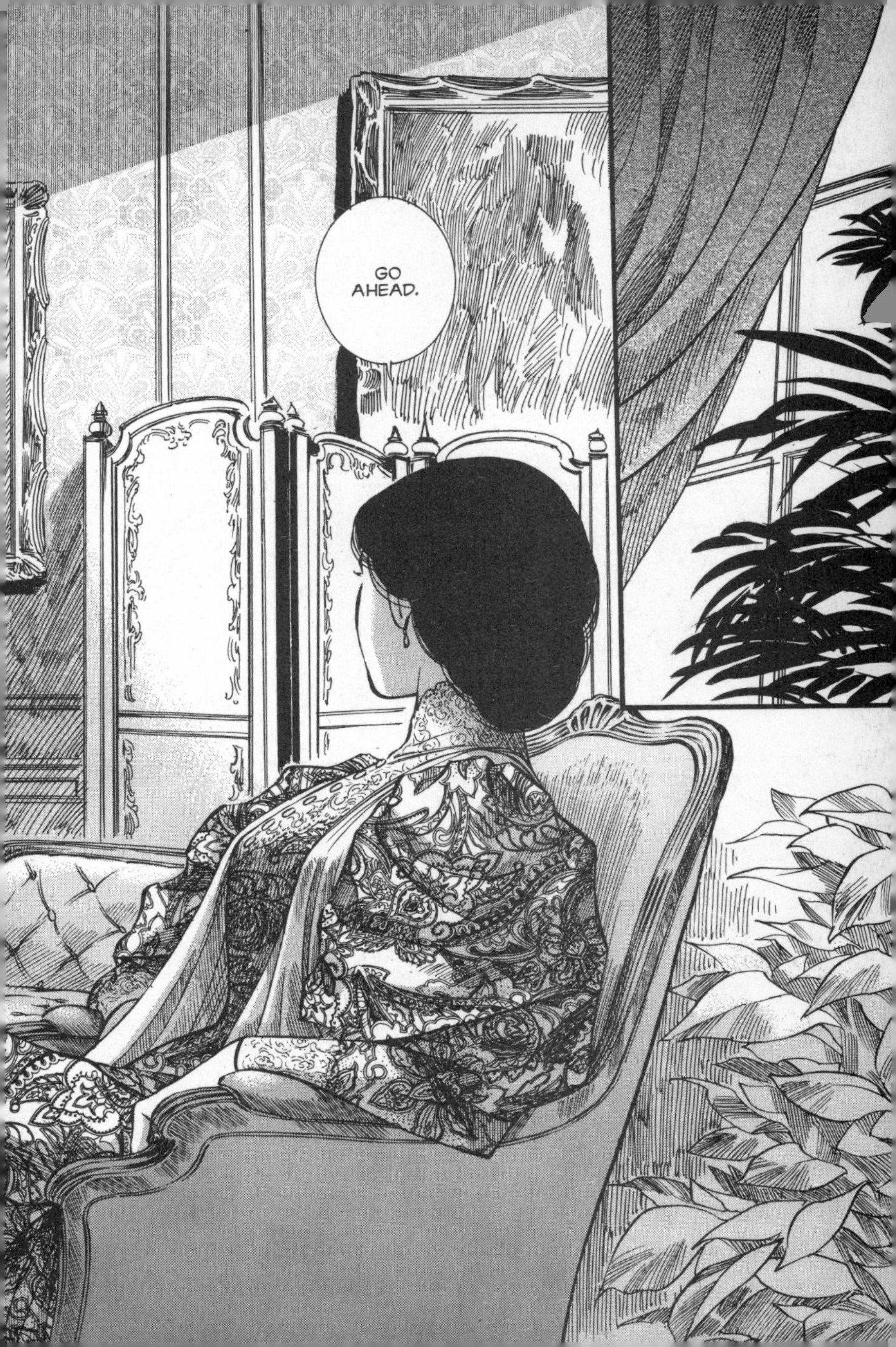
GO AHEAD.

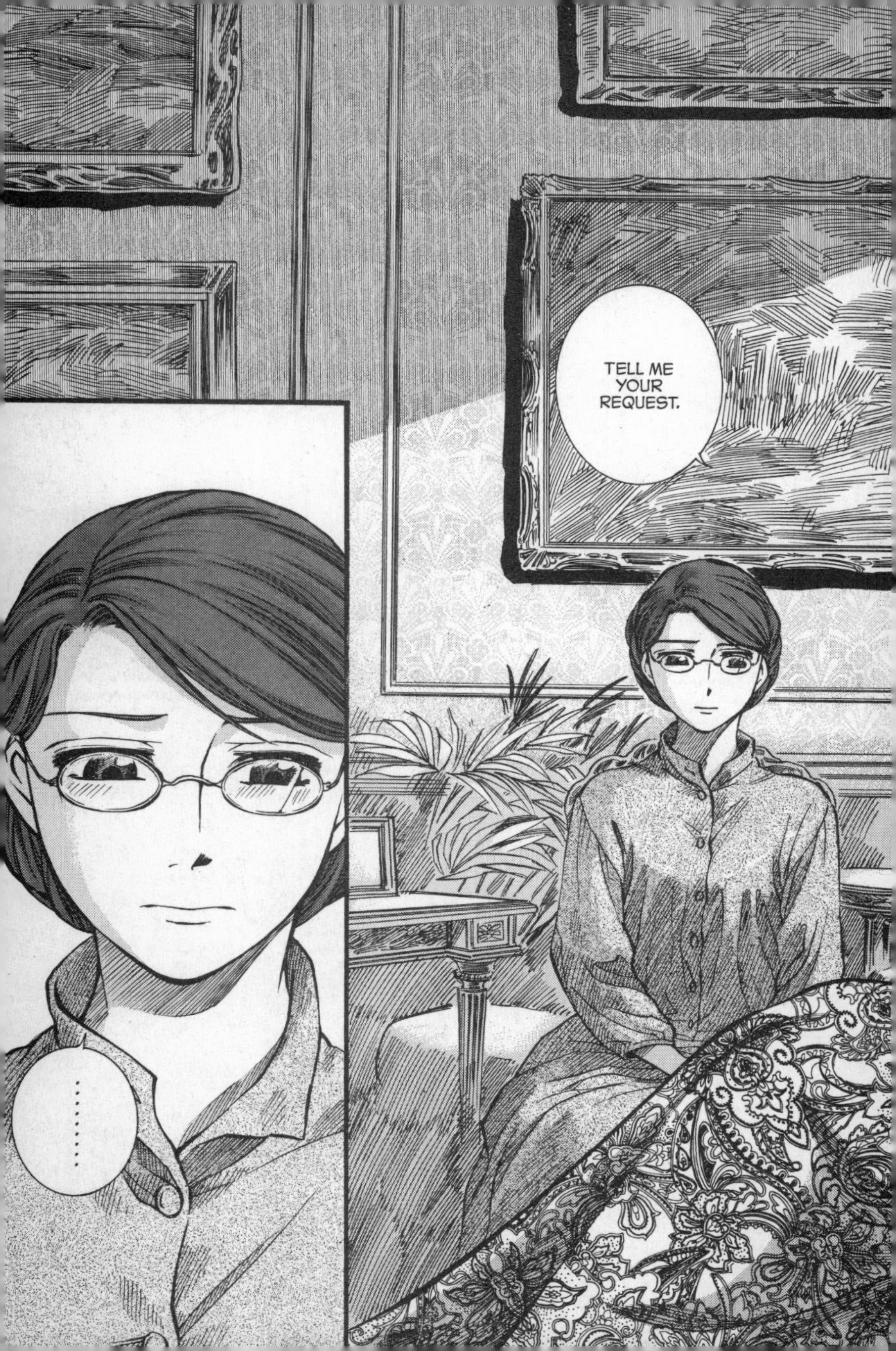
TELL ME YOUR REQUEST.
......

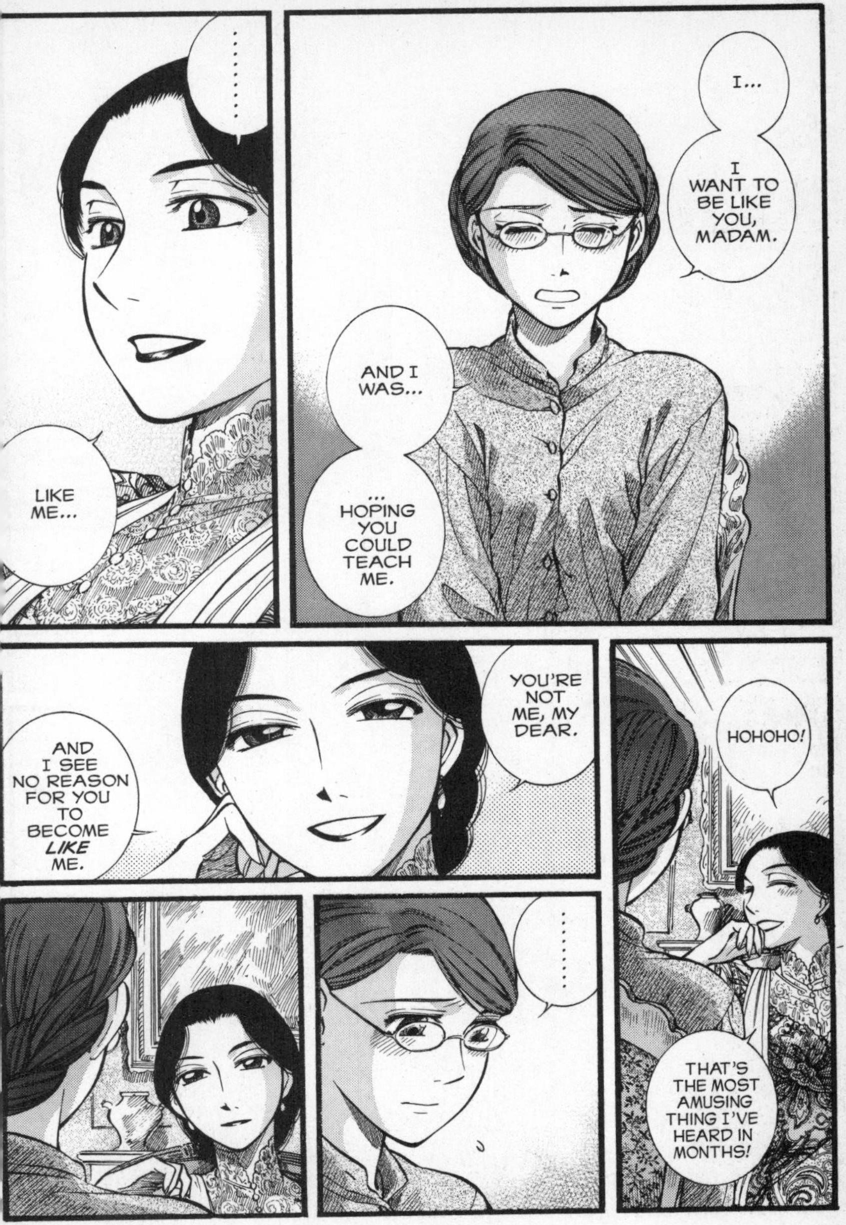
I...
I WANT TO BE LIKE YOU, MADAM.
AND I WAS...
... HOPING YOU COULD TEACH ME.
......
LIKE ME...
HOHOHO!
THAT'S THE MOST AMUSING THING I'VE HEARD IN MONTHS!
YOU'RE NOT ME, MY DEAR.
AND I SEE NO REASON FOR YOU TO BECOME *LIKE* ME.
......

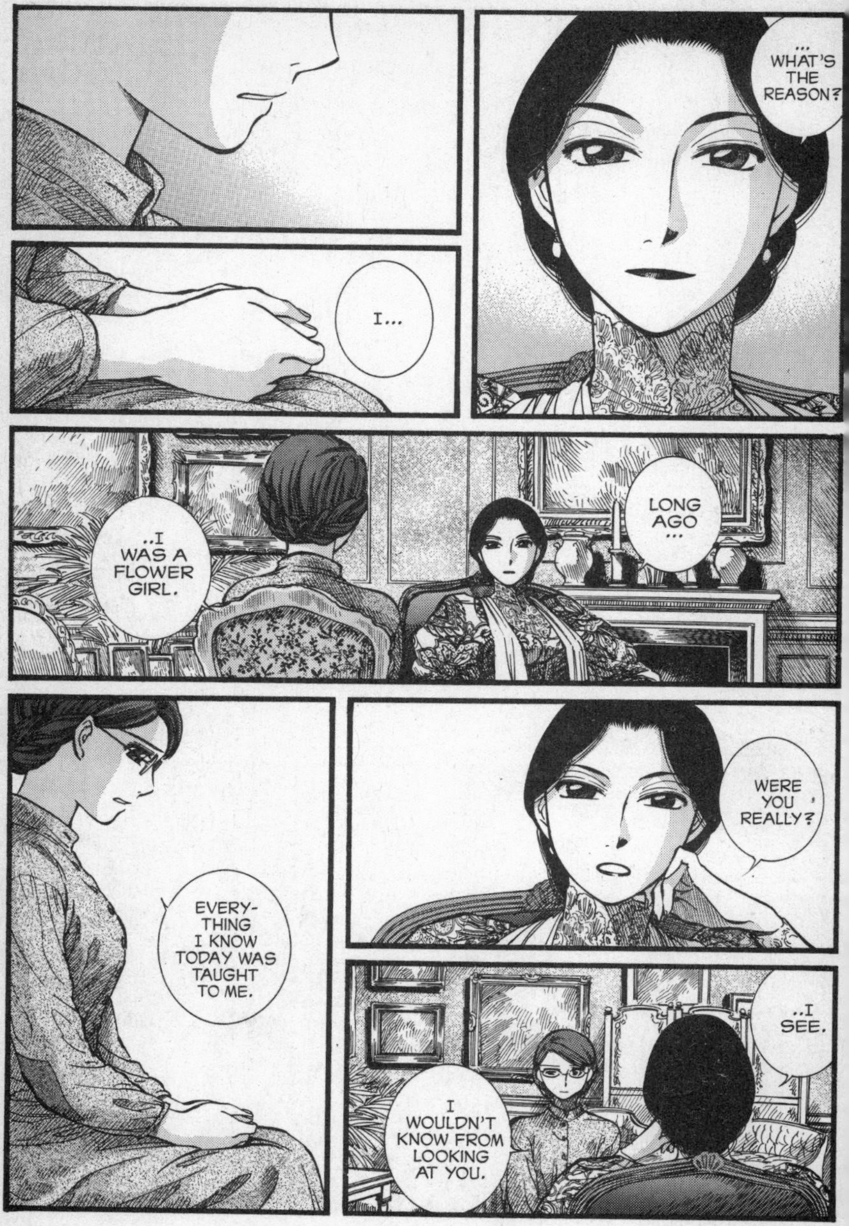
...WHAT'S THE REASON?
I...
LONG AGO...
..I WAS A FLOWER GIRL.
WERE YOU, REALLY?
..I SEE.
I WOULDN'T KNOW FROM LOOKING AT YOU.
EVERYTHING I KNOW TODAY WAS TAUGHT TO ME.

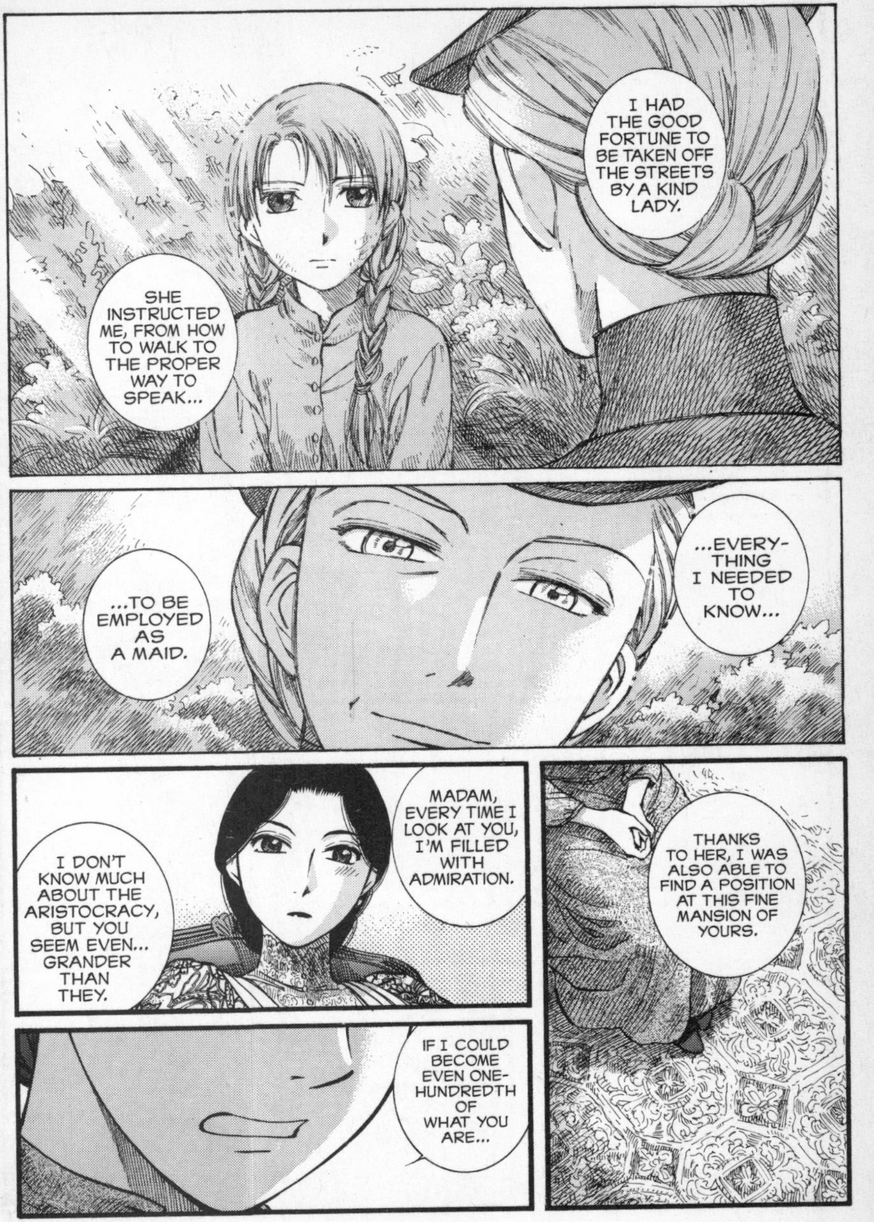
I HAD THE GOOD FORTUNE TO BE TAKEN OFF THE STREETS BY A KIND LADY.
SHE INSTRUCTED ME, FROM HOW TO WALK TO THE PROPER WAY TO SPEAK...
...EVERY-THING I NEEDED TO KNOW...
...TO BE EMPLOYED AS A MAID.
THANKS TO HER, I WAS ALSO ABLE TO FIND A POSITION AT THIS FINE MANSION OF YOURS.
MADAM, EVERY TIME I LOOK AT YOU, I'M FILLED WITH ADMIRATION.
I DON'T KNOW MUCH ABOUT THE ARISTOCRACY, BUT YOU SEEM EVEN... GRANDER THAN THEY.
IF I COULD BECOME EVEN ONE-HUNDREDTH OF WHAT YOU ARE...

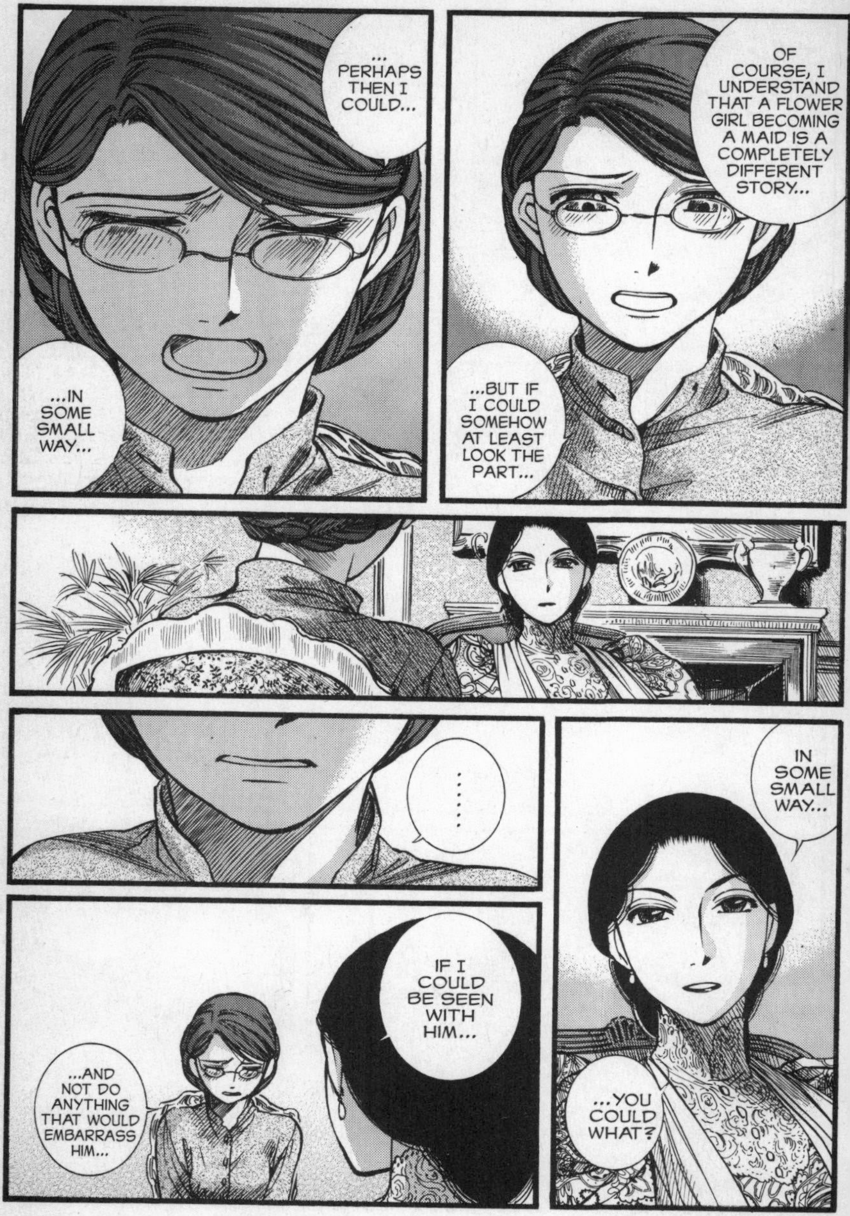
OF COURSE, I UNDERSTAND THAT A FLOWER GIRL BECOMING A MAID IS A COMPLETELY DIFFERENT STORY...
...BUT IF I COULD SOMEHOW AT LEAST LOOK THE PART...
...PERHAPS THEN I COULD...
...IN SOME SMALL WAY...
......
IN SOME SMALL WAY...
...YOU COULD WHAT?
IF I COULD BE SEEN WITH HIM...
...AND NOT DO ANYTHING THAT WOULD EMBARRASS HIM...

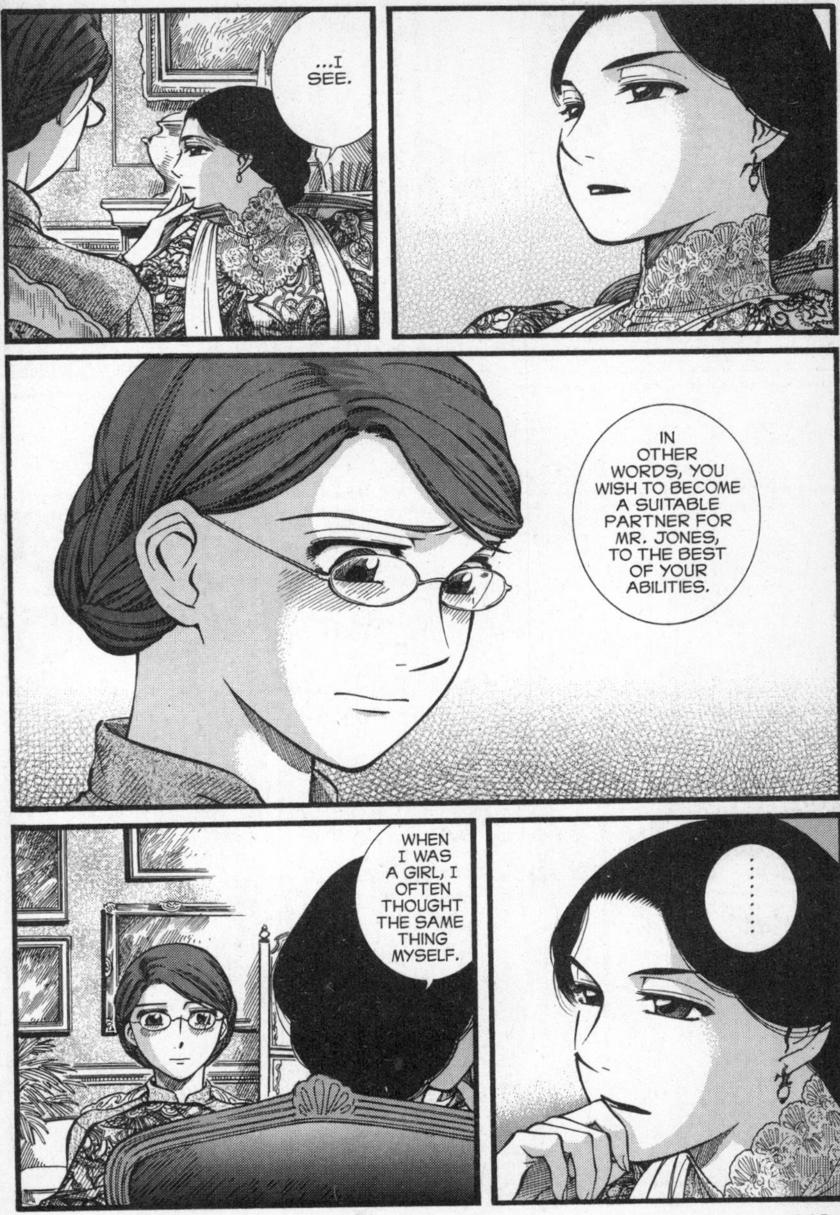
...I SEE.
IN OTHER WORDS, YOU WISH TO BECOME A SUITABLE PARTNER FOR MR. JONES, TO THE BEST OF YOUR ABILITIES.
......
WHEN I WAS A GIRL, I OFTEN THOUGHT THE SAME THING MYSELF.

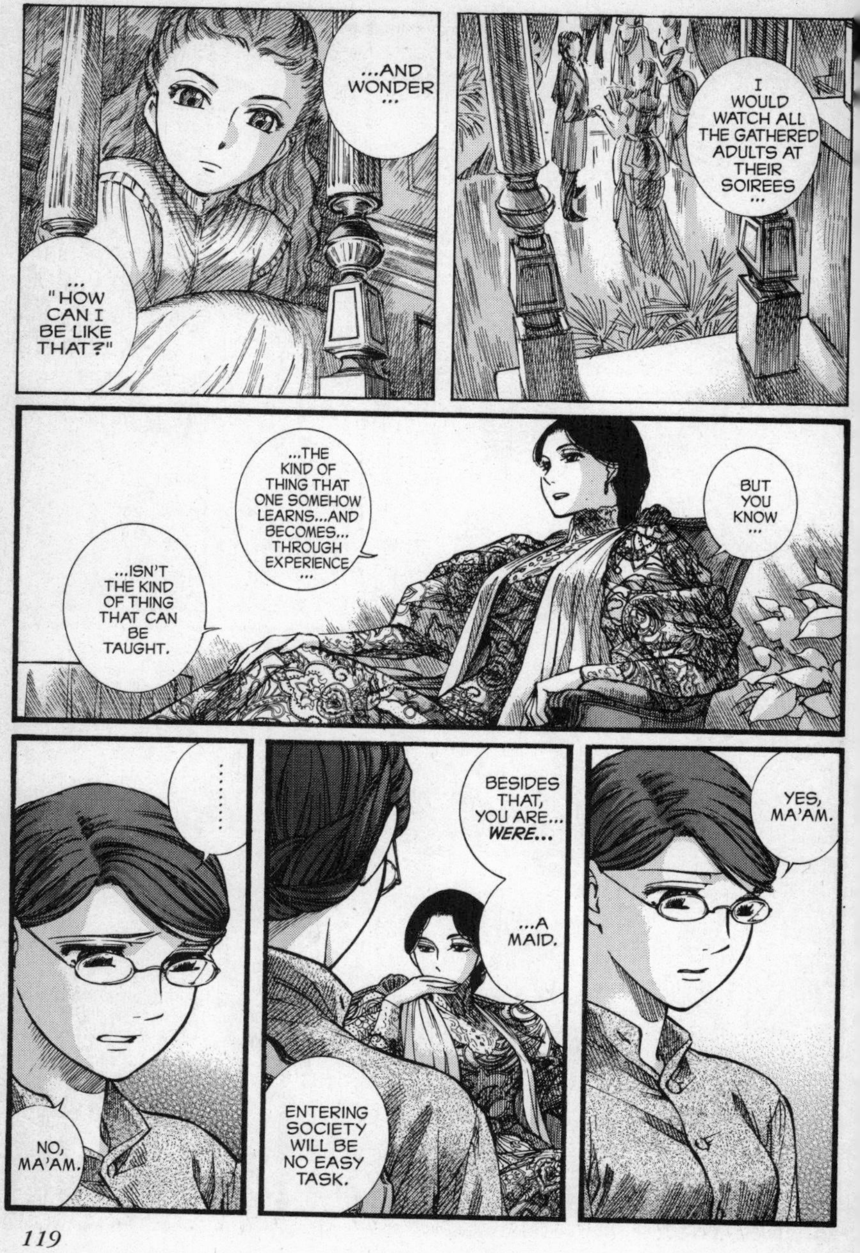
I WOULD WATCH ALL THE GATHERED ADULTS AT THEIR SOIREES ...
...AND WONDER ...
... "HOW CAN I BE LIKE THAT?"
BUT YOU KNOW ...
...THE KIND OF THING THAT ONE SOMEHOW LEARNS...AND BECOMES... THROUGH EXPERIENCE ...
...ISN'T THE KIND OF THING THAT CAN BE TAUGHT.
YES, MA'AM.
BESIDES THAT, YOU ARE... ***WERE...***
...A MAID.
ENTERING SOCIETY WILL BE NO EASY TASK.
......
NO, MA'AM.

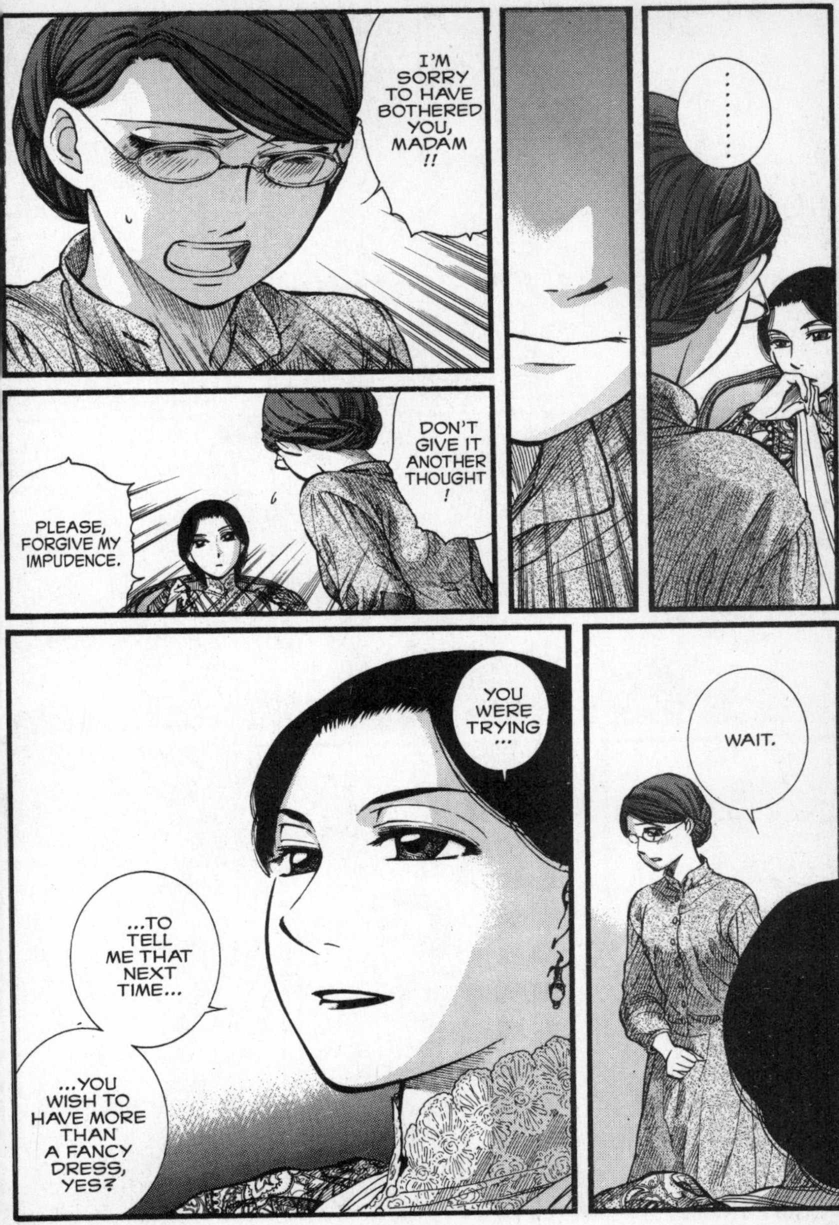
....
I'M SORRY TO HAVE BOTHERED YOU, MADAM !!
DON'T GIVE IT ANOTHER THOUGHT !
PLEASE, FORGIVE MY IMPUDENCE.
WAIT.
YOU WERE TRYING ...
...TO TELL ME THAT NEXT TIME...
...YOU WISH TO HAVE MORE THAN A FANCY DRESS, YES?

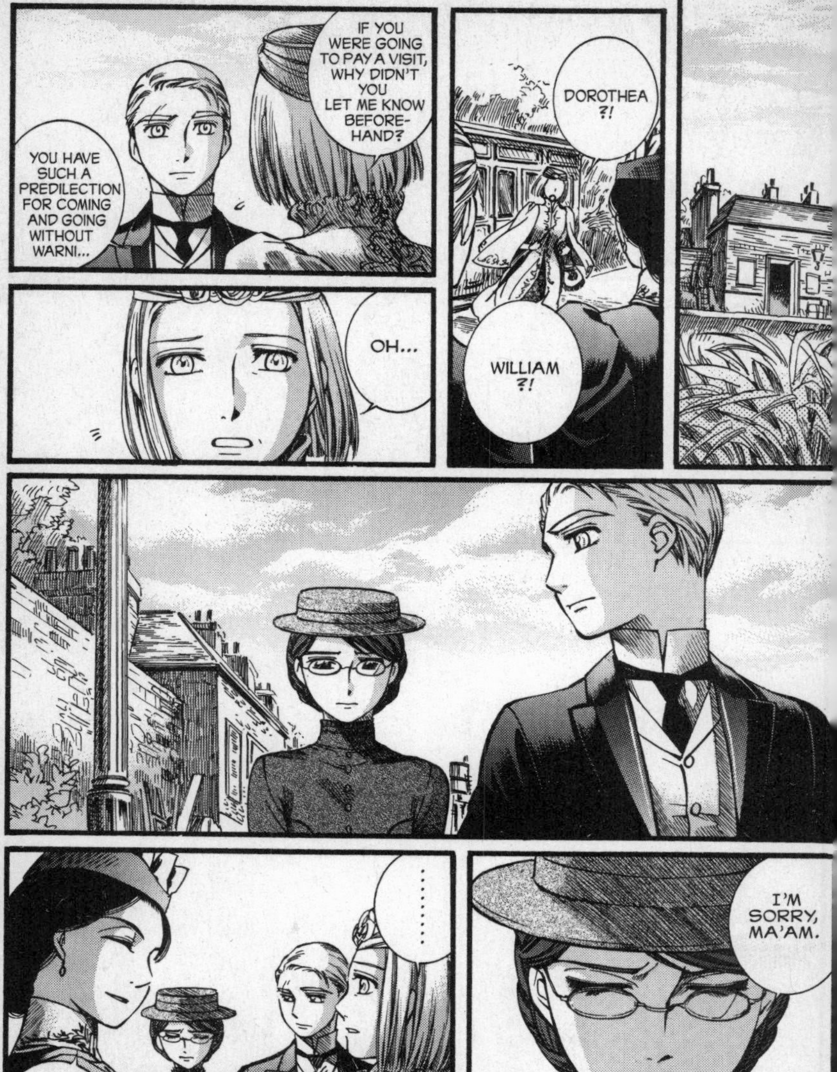
DOROTHEA ?!
WILLIAM ?!
IF YOU WERE GOING TO PAY A VISIT, WHY DIDN'T YOU LET ME KNOW BEFORE-HAND?
YOU HAVE SUCH A PREDILECTION FOR COMING AND GOING WITHOUT WARNI...
OH...
I'M SORRY, MA'AM.
......
WE'VE COME FOR A LITTLE CONSULTATION.

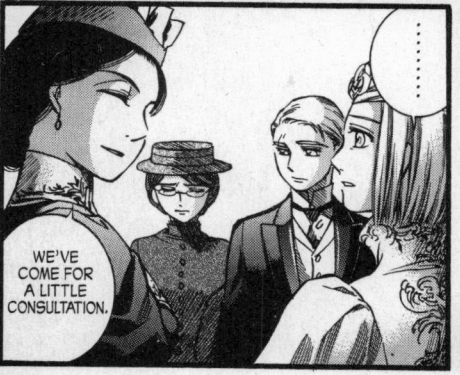

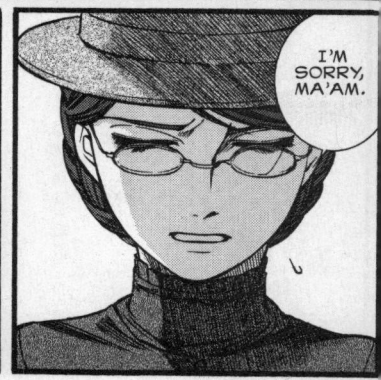

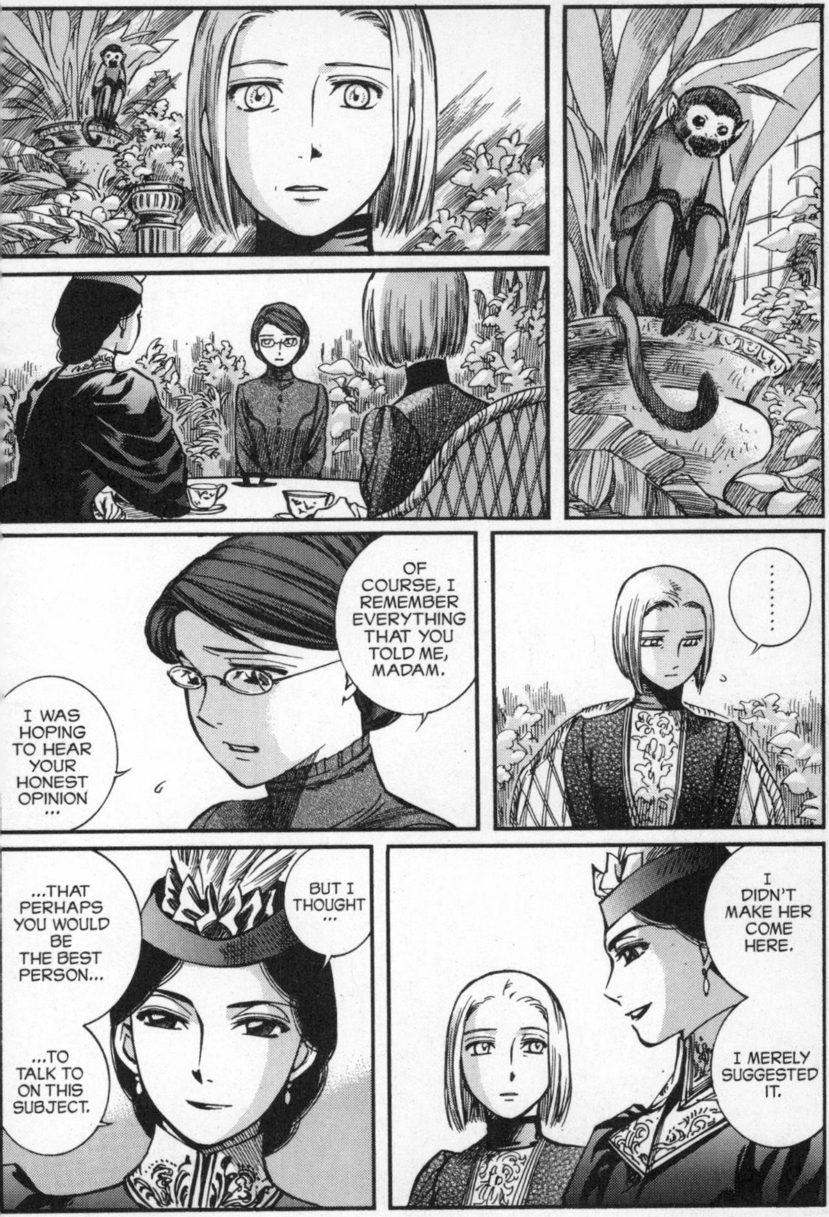

......
OF COURSE, I REMEMBER EVERYTHING THAT YOU TOLD ME, MADAM.
I WAS HOPING TO HEAR YOUR HONEST OPINION ...
I DIDN'T MAKE HER COME HERE.
I MERELY SUGGESTED IT.
BUT I THOUGHT ...
...THAT PERHAPS YOU WOULD BE THE BEST PERSON...
...TO TALK TO ON THIS SUBJECT.

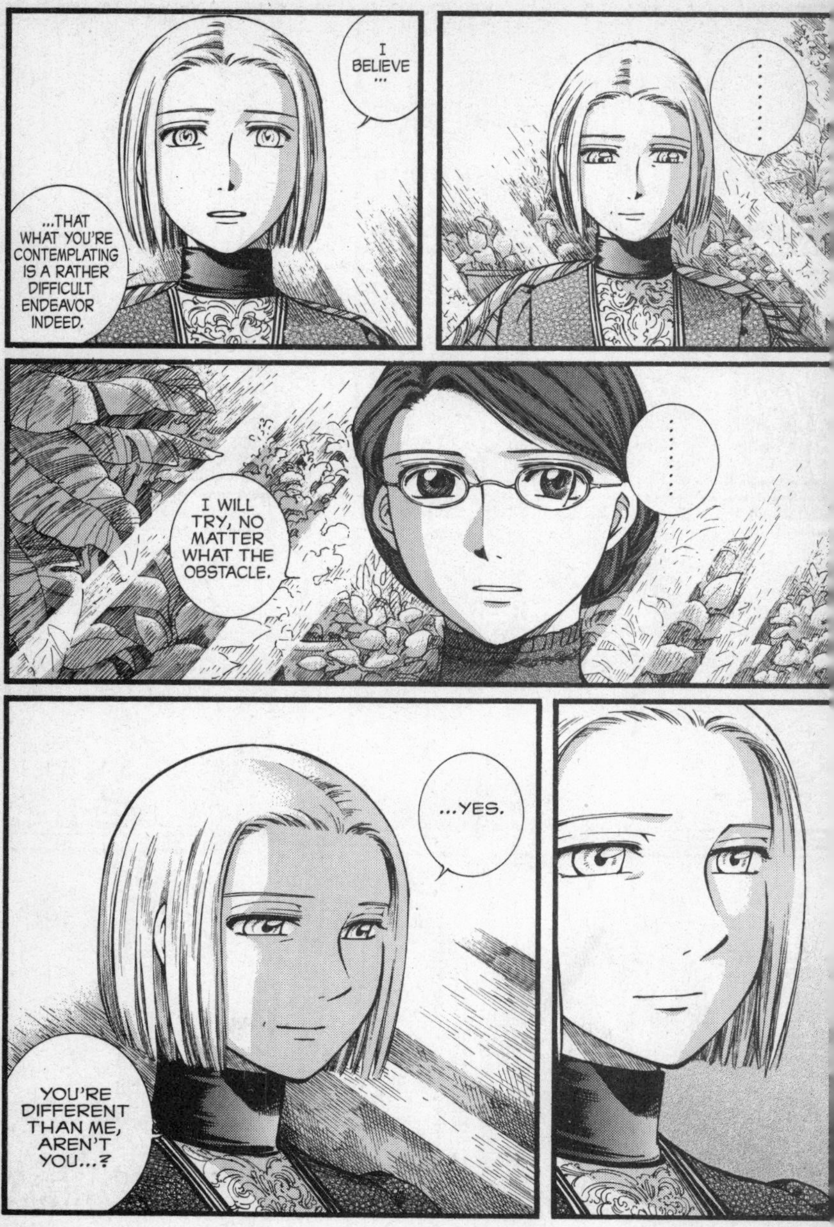
......
I BELIEVE ...
...THAT WHAT YOU'RE CONTEMPLATING IS A RATHER DIFFICULT ENDEAVOR INDEED.
......
I WILL TRY, NO MATTER WHAT THE OBSTACLE.
...YES.
YOU'RE DIFFERENT THAN ME, AREN'T YOU...?

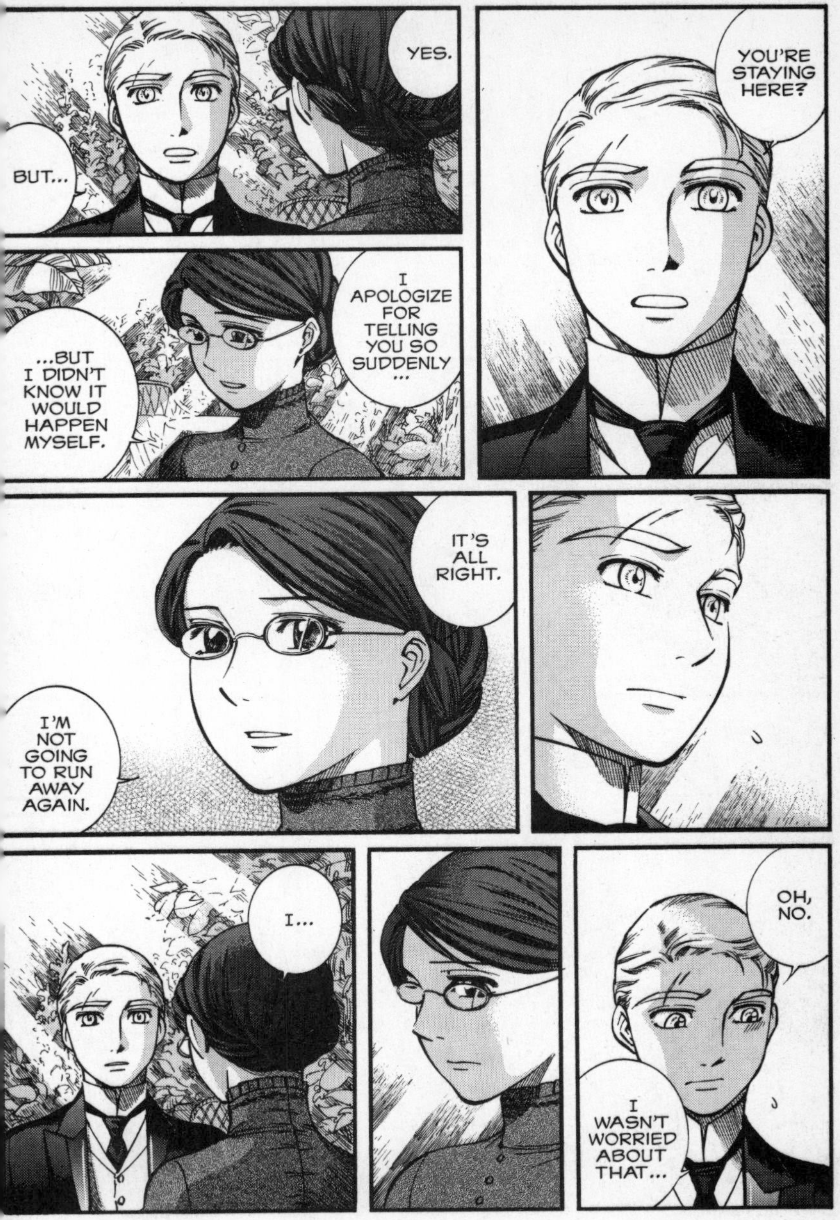
YOU'RE STAYING HERE?
YES.
BUT...
I APOLOGIZE FOR TELLING YOU SO SUDDENLY ...
...BUT I DIDN'T KNOW IT WOULD HAPPEN MYSELF.
IT'S ALL RIGHT.
I'M NOT GOING TO RUN AWAY AGAIN.
OH, NO.
I WASN'T WORRIED ABOUT THAT...
I...

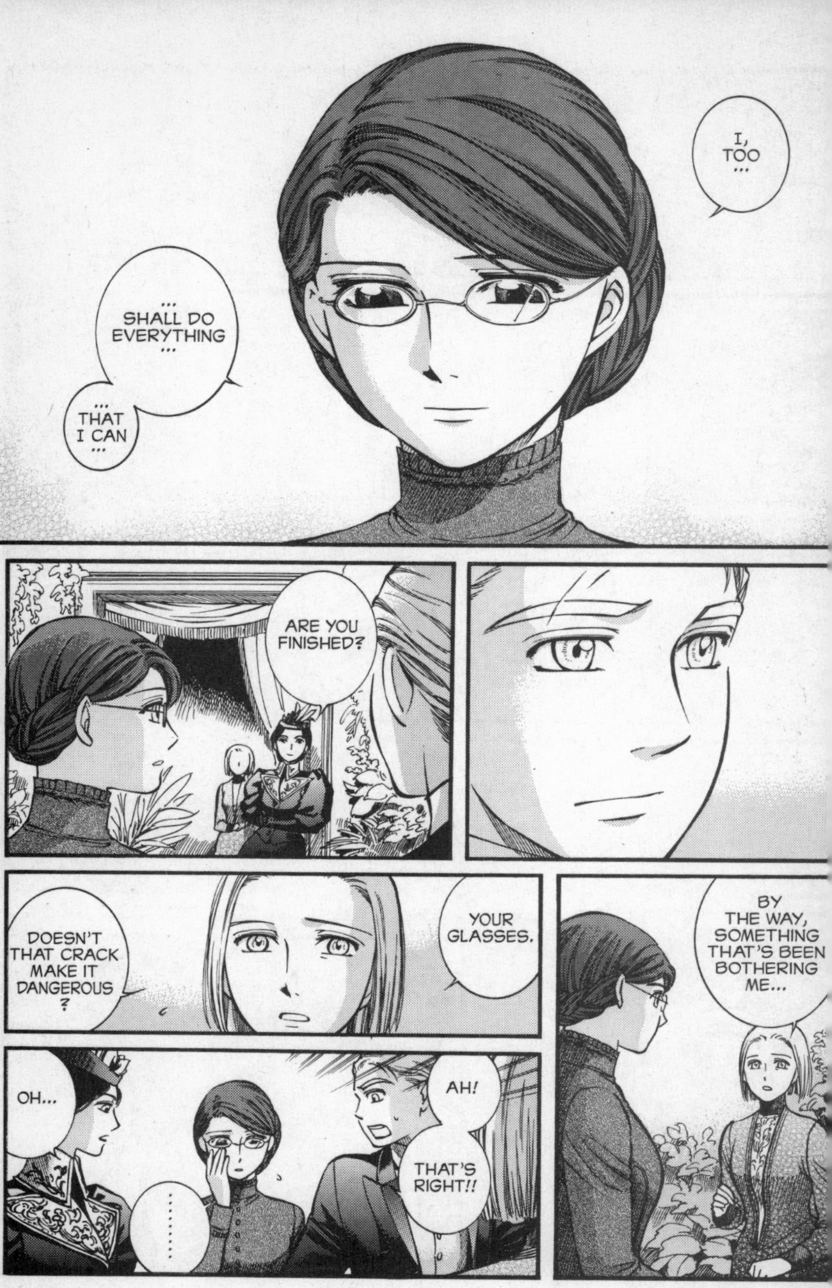
I, TOO ...
... SHALL DO EVERYTHING ...
... THAT I CAN ...
ARE YOU FINISHED?
BY THE WAY, SOMETHING THAT'S BEEN BOTHERING ME...
YOUR GLASSES.
DOESN'T THAT CRACK MAKE IT DANGEROUS ?
AH!
THAT'S RIGHT!!
....
OH...

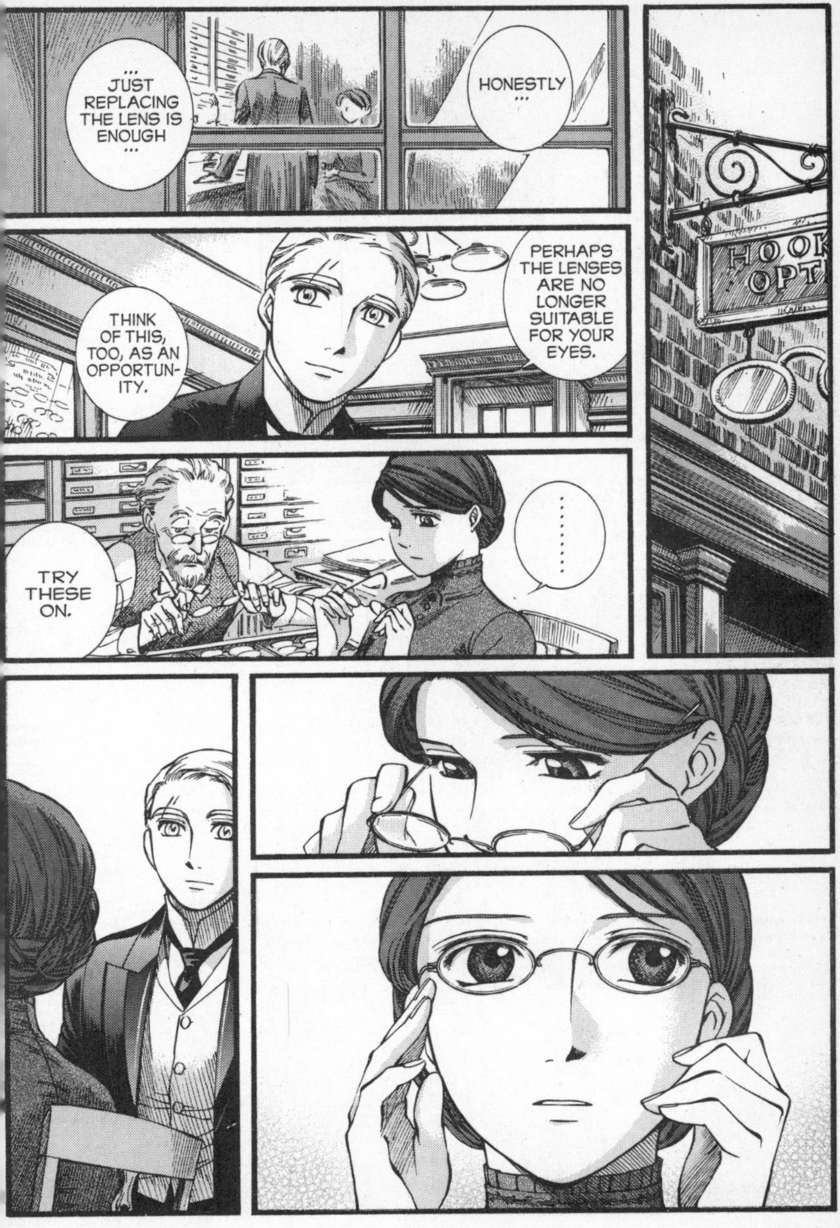
HONESTLY ...
... JUST REPLACING THE LENS IS ENOUGH ...
PERHAPS THE LENSES ARE NO LONGER SUITABLE FOR YOUR EYES.
THINK OF THIS, TOO, AS AN OPPORTUN-ITY.
......
TRY THESE ON.

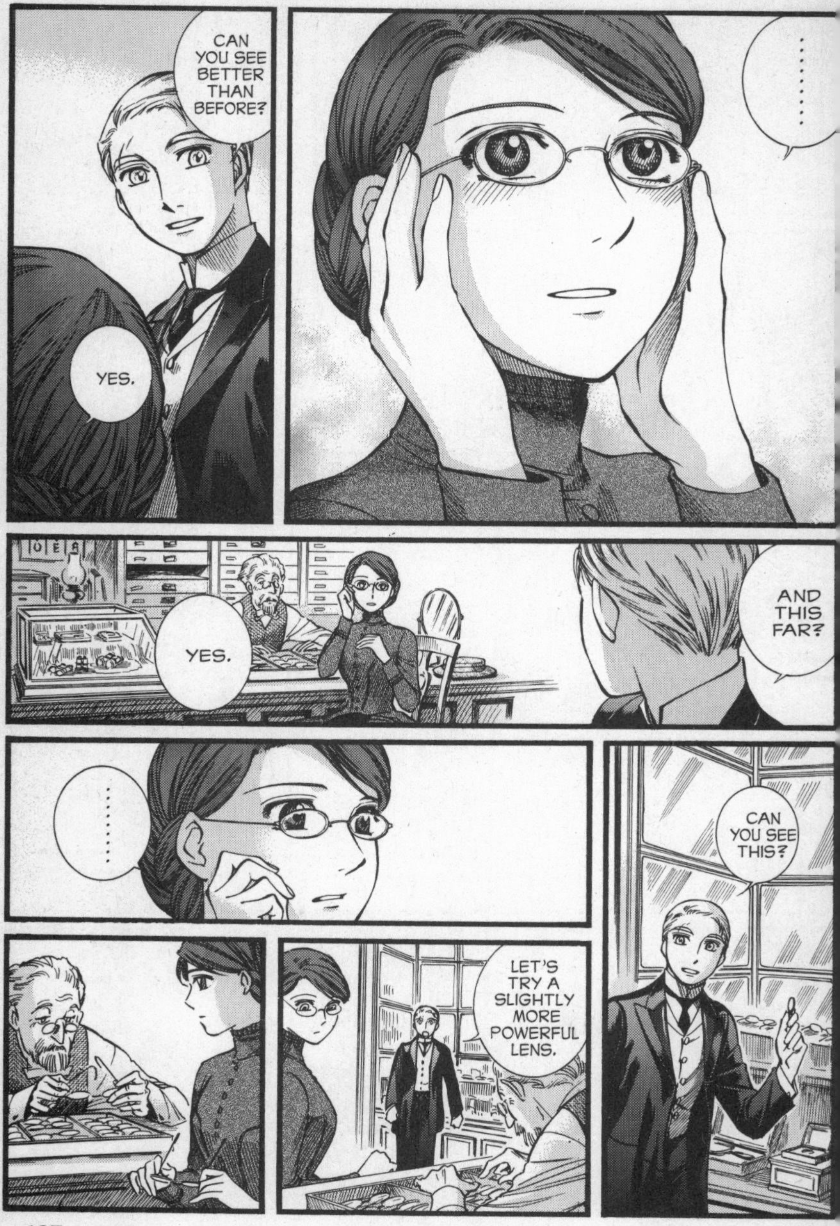
......
CAN YOU SEE BETTER THAN BEFORE?
YES.
AND THIS FAR?
YES.
CAN YOU SEE THIS?
......
LET'S TRY A SLIGHTLY MORE POWERFUL LENS.

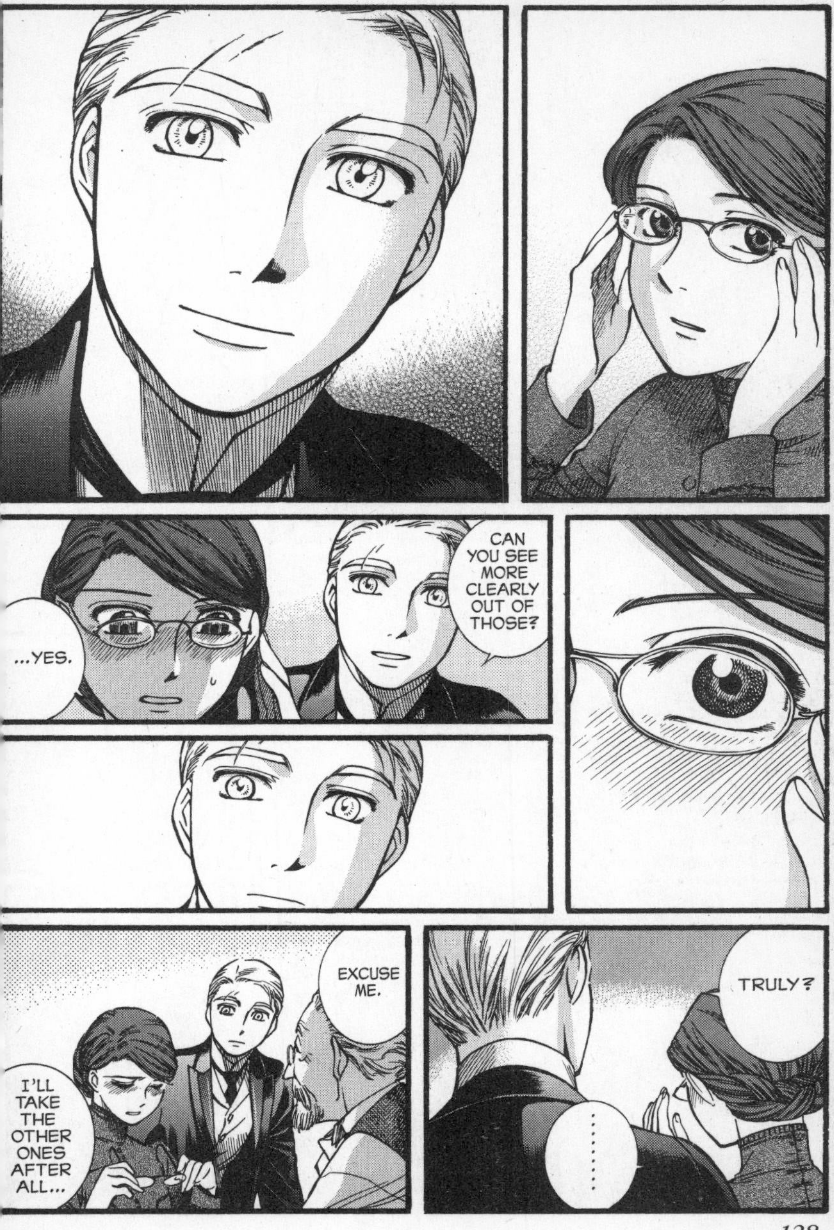
CAN YOU SEE MORE CLEARLY OUT OF THOSE?
...YES.
TRULY?
......
EXCUSE ME.
I'LL TAKE THE OTHER ONES AFTER ALL...

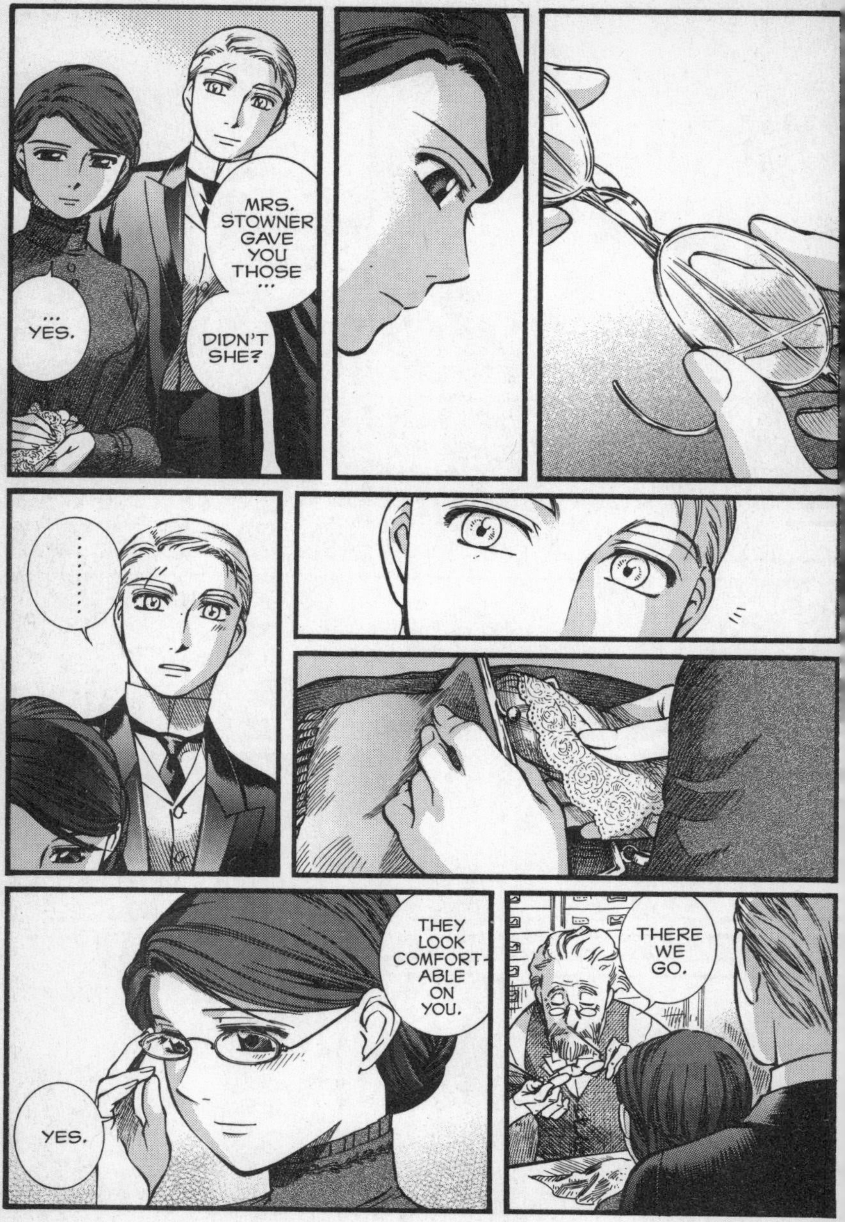
THERE WE GO.
THEY LOOK COMFORT-ABLE ON YOU.
YES.
MRS. STOWNER GAVE YOU THOSE ...
DIDN'T SHE?
... YES.
......

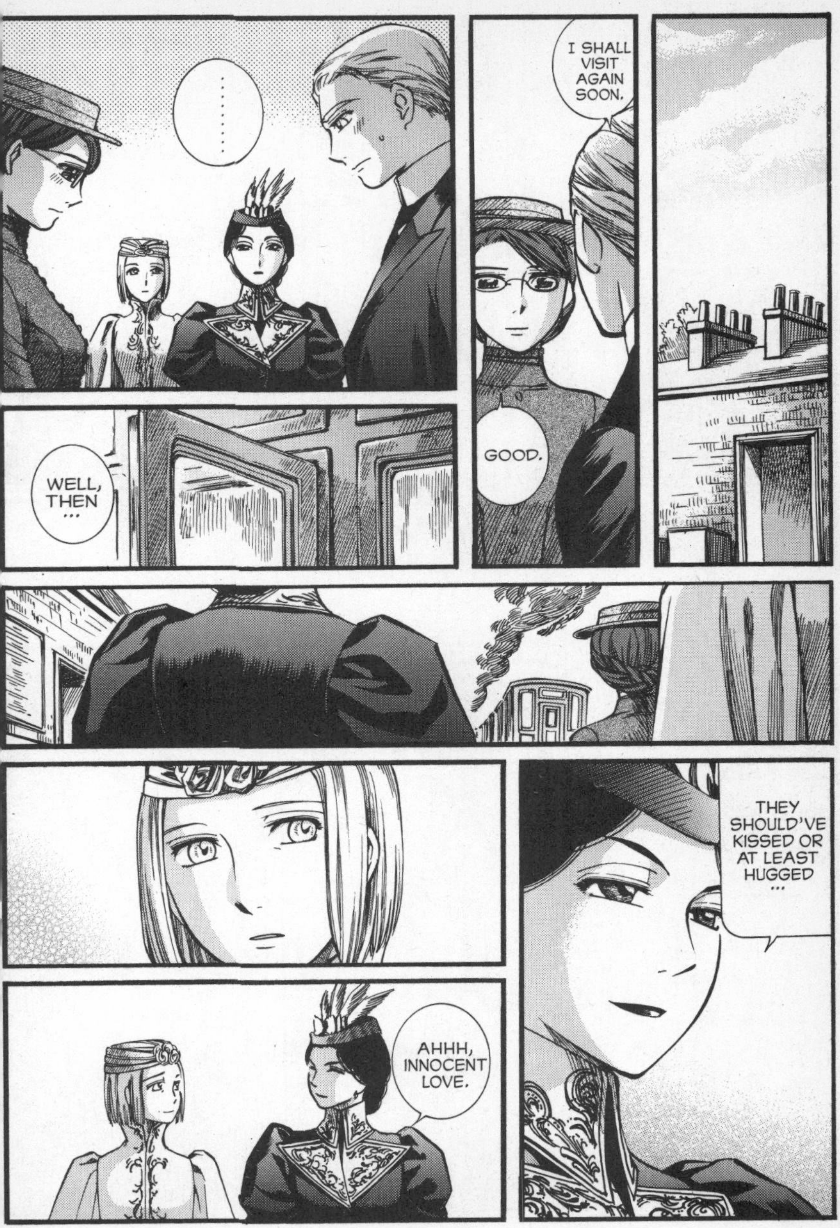
I SHALL VISIT AGAIN SOON.
GOOD.
......
WELL, THEN ...
THEY SHOULD'VE KISSED OR AT LEAST HUGGED ...
AHHH, INNOCENT LOVE.

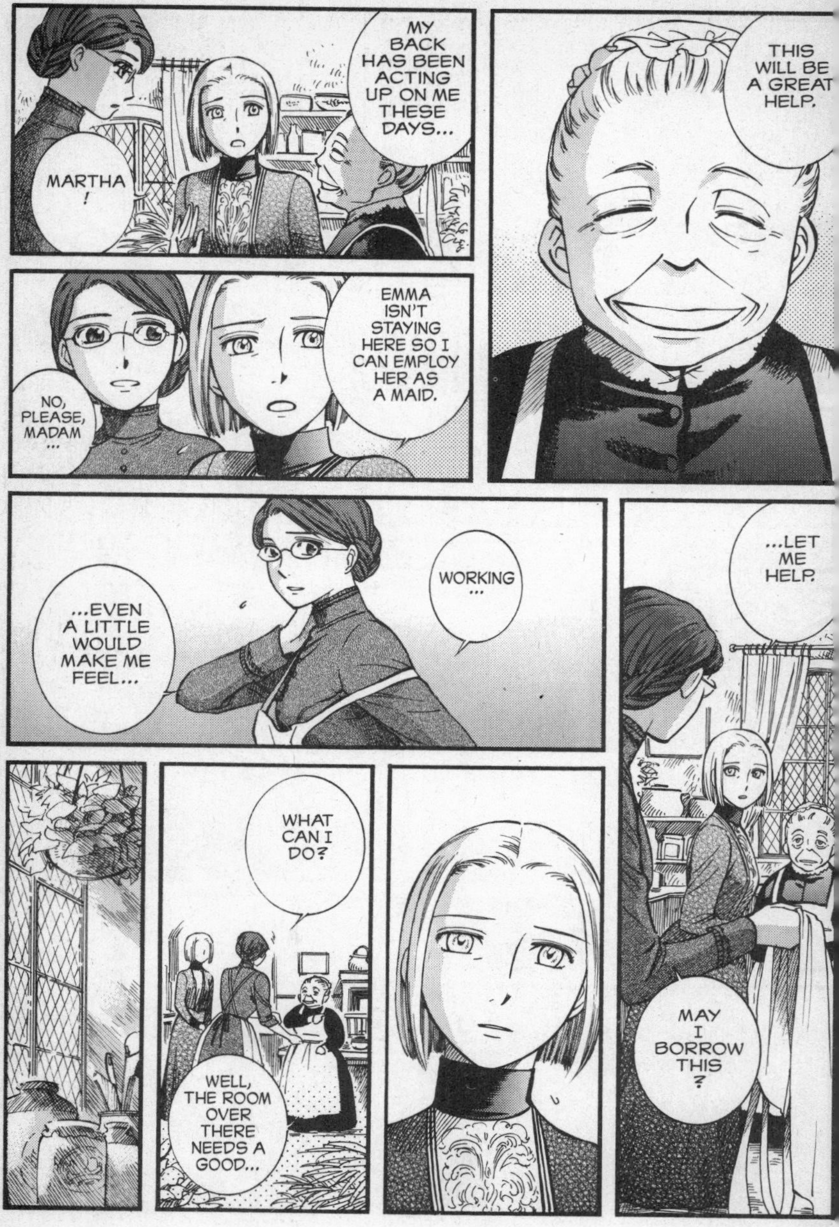
THIS WILL BE A GREAT HELP.
MY BACK HAS BEEN ACTING UP ON ME THESE DAYS...
MARTHA!
EMMA ISN'T STAYING HERE SO I CAN EMPLOY HER AS A MAID.
NO, PLEASE, MADAM...
WORKING...
...EVEN A LITTLE WOULD MAKE ME FEEL...
...LET ME HELP.
MAY I BORROW THIS?
WHAT CAN I DO?
WELL, THE ROOM OVER THERE NEEDS A GOOD...

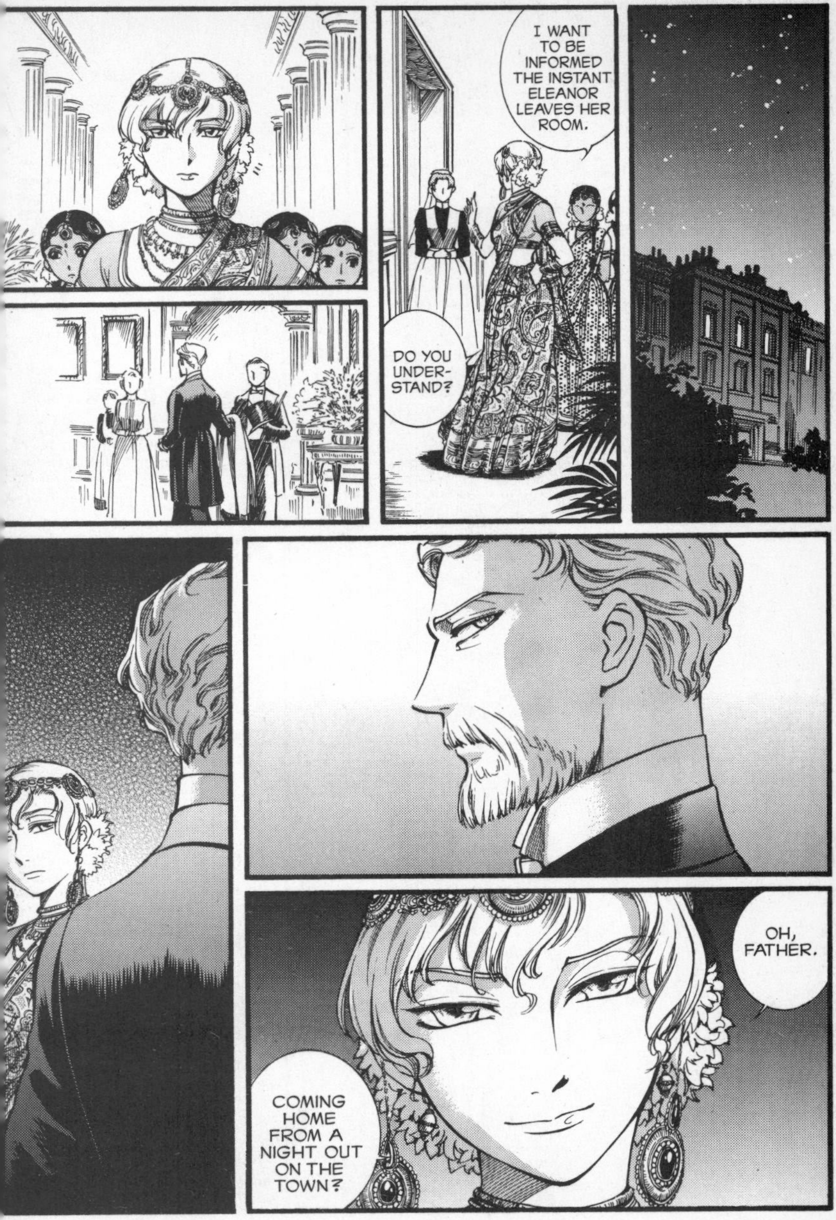
I WANT TO BE INFORMED THE INSTANT ELEANOR LEAVES HER ROOM.
DO YOU UNDER-STAND?
OH, FATHER.
COMING HOME FROM A NIGHT OUT ON THE TOWN?

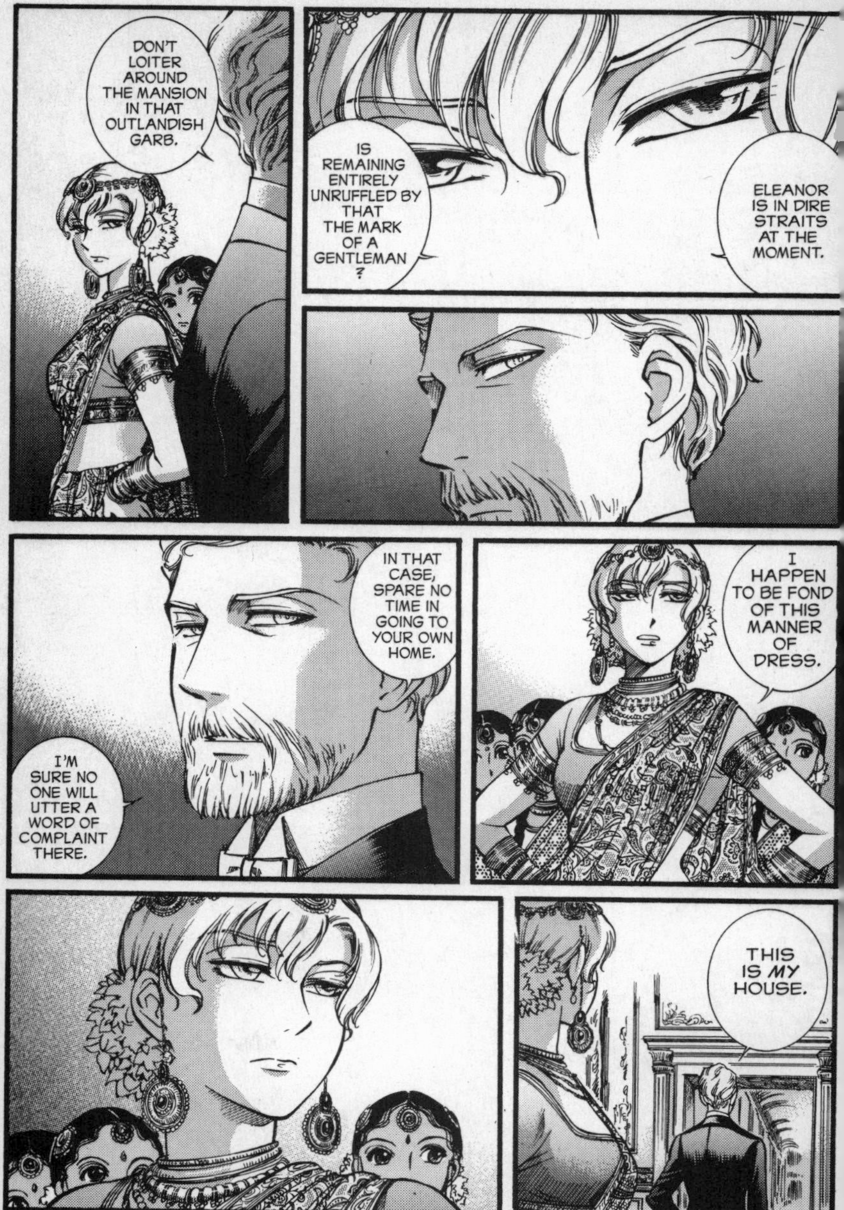
ELEANOR IS IN DIRE STRAITS AT THE MOMENT.
IS REMAINING ENTIRELY UNRUFFLED BY THAT THE MARK OF A GENTLEMAN?
DON'T LOITER AROUND THE MANSION IN THAT OUTLANDISH GARB.
I HAPPEN TO BE FOND OF THIS MANNER OF DRESS.
IN THAT CASE, SPARE NO TIME IN GOING TO YOUR OWN HOME.
I'M SURE NO ONE WILL UTTER A WORD OF COMPLAINT THERE.
THIS IS *MY* HOUSE.

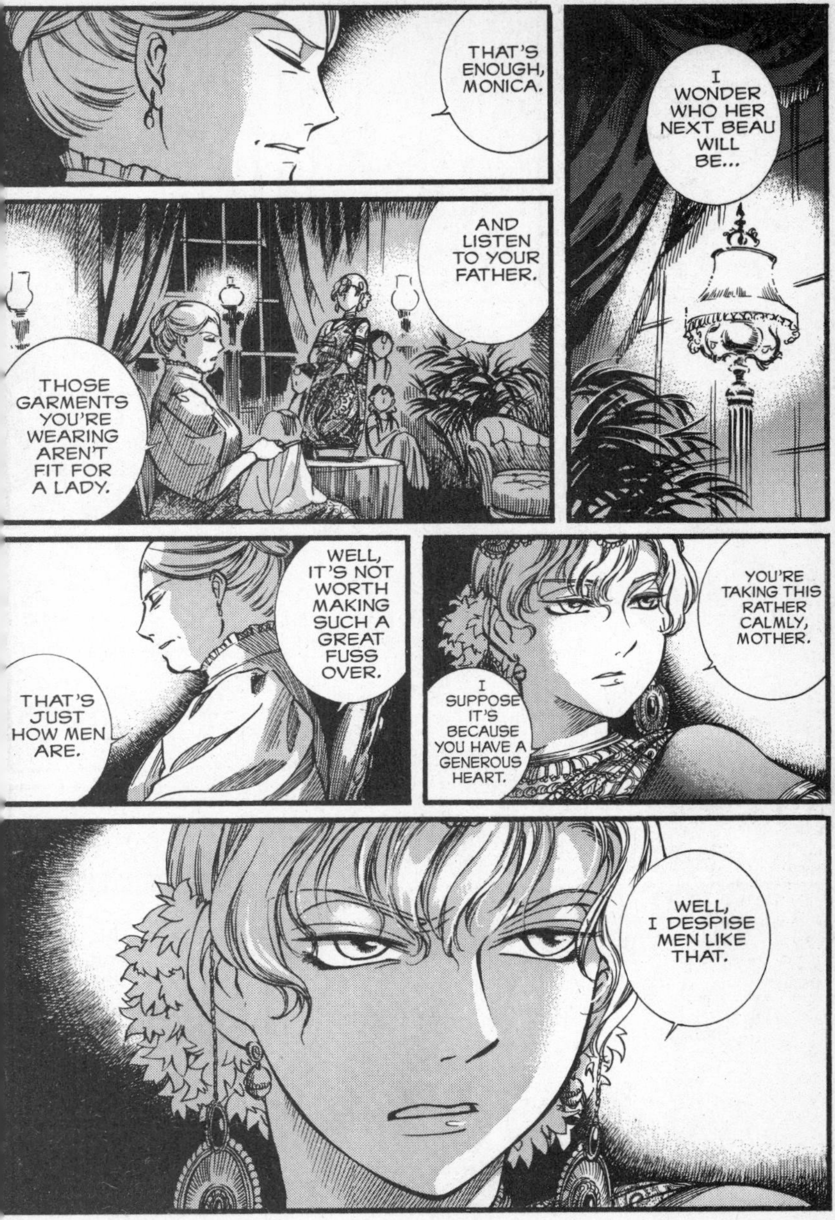
I WONDER WHO HER NEXT BEAU WILL BE...
THAT'S ENOUGH, MONICA.
AND LISTEN TO YOUR FATHER.
THOSE GARMENTS YOU'RE WEARING AREN'T FIT FOR A LADY.
YOU'RE TAKING THIS RATHER CALMLY, MOTHER.
I SUPPOSE IT'S BECAUSE YOU HAVE A GENEROUS HEART.
WELL, IT'S NOT WORTH MAKING SUCH A GREAT FUSS OVER.
THAT'S JUST HOW MEN ARE.
WELL, I DESPISE MEN LIKE THAT.

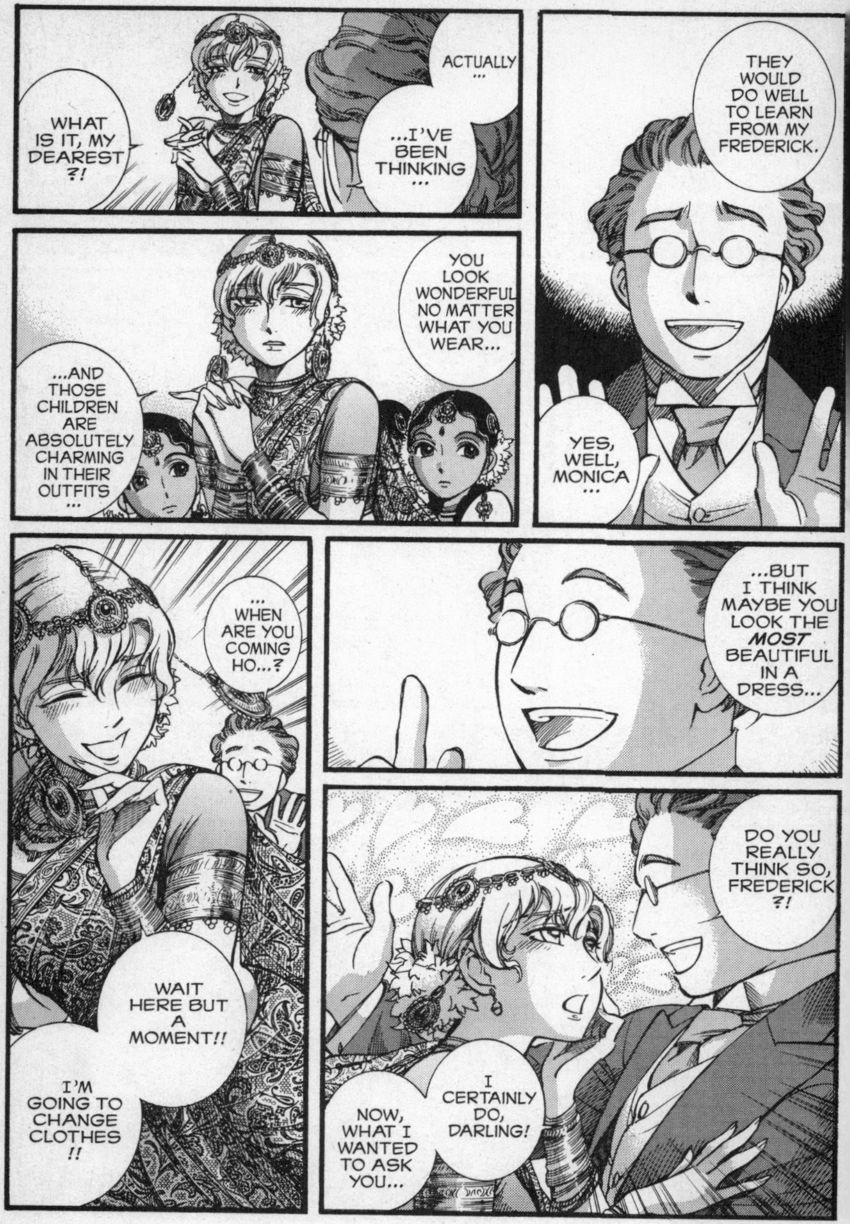
THEY WOULD DO WELL TO LEARN FROM MY FREDERICK.
YES, WELL, MONICA ...
ACTUALLY ...
...I'VE BEEN THINKING ...
WHAT IS IT, MY DEAREST ?!
YOU LOOK WONDERFUL NO MATTER WHAT YOU WEAR...
...AND THOSE CHILDREN ARE ABSOLUTELY CHARMING IN THEIR OUTFITS ...
...BUT I THINK MAYBE YOU LOOK THE *MOST* BEAUTIFUL IN A DRESS...
DO YOU REALLY THINK SO, FREDERICK ?!
I CERTAINLY DO, DARLING!
NOW, WHAT I WANTED TO ASK YOU...
... WHEN ARE YOU COMING HO...?
WAIT HERE BUT A MOMENT!!
I'M GOING TO CHANGE CLOTHES !!

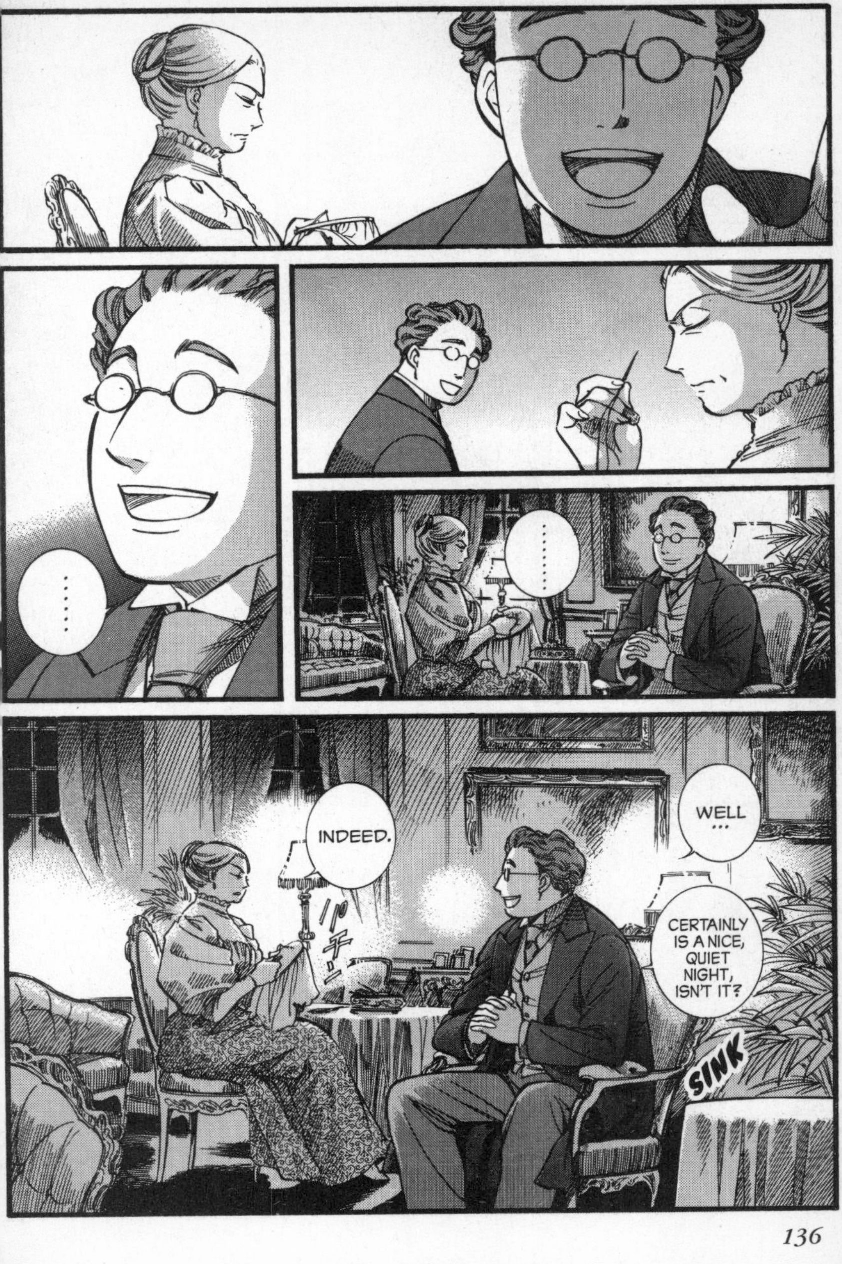
……
……
WELL …
CERTAINLY IS A NICE, QUIET NIGHT, ISN'T IT?
SINK
INDEED.
パチ

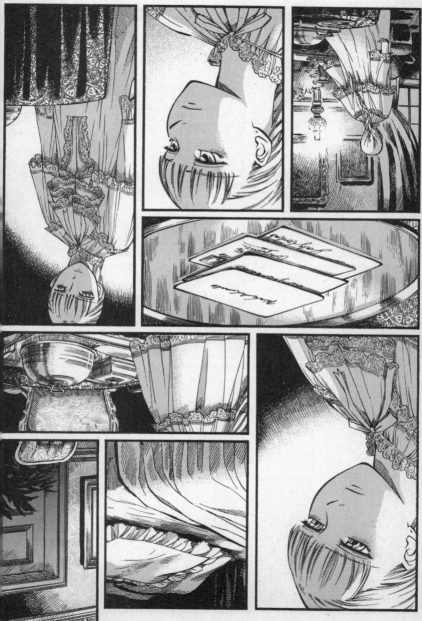

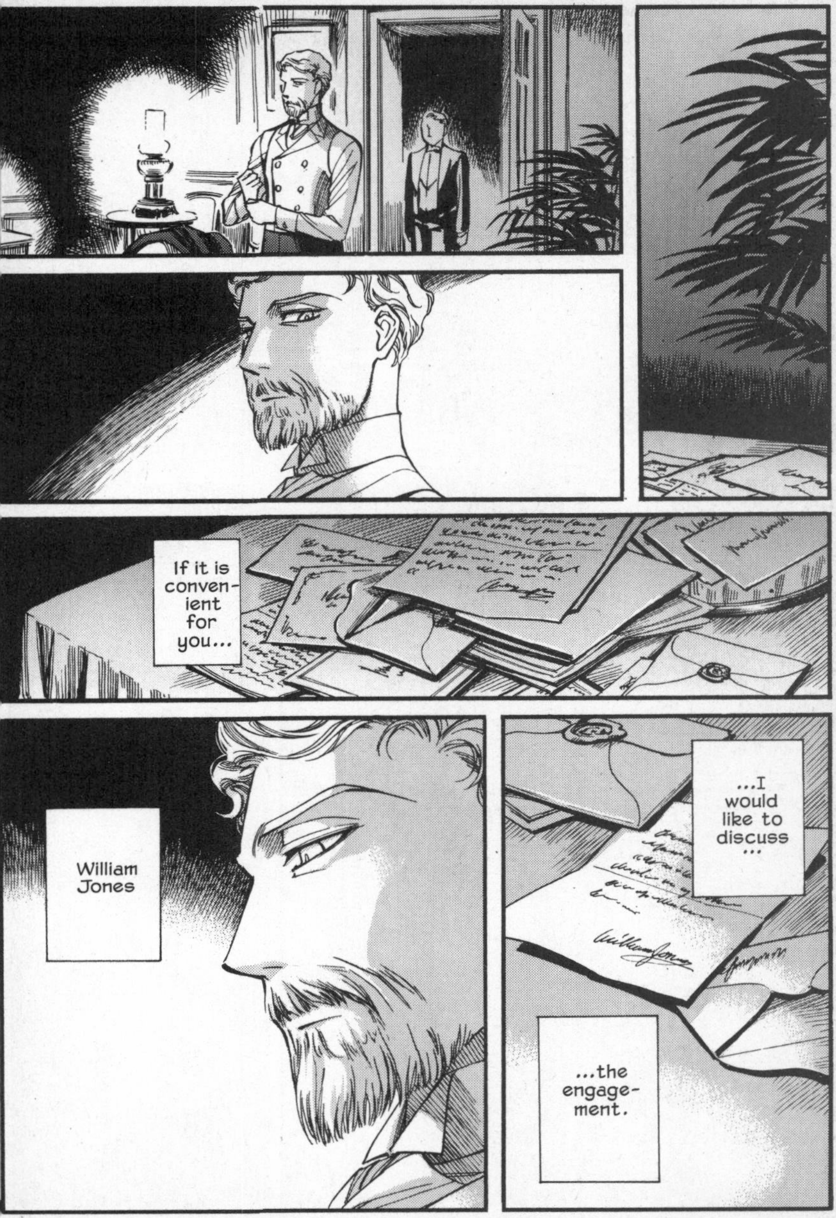
If it is conven-ient for you...
...I would like to discuss ...
...the engage-ment.
William Jones

Chapter Forty Eight:
The End

EPILOGUE

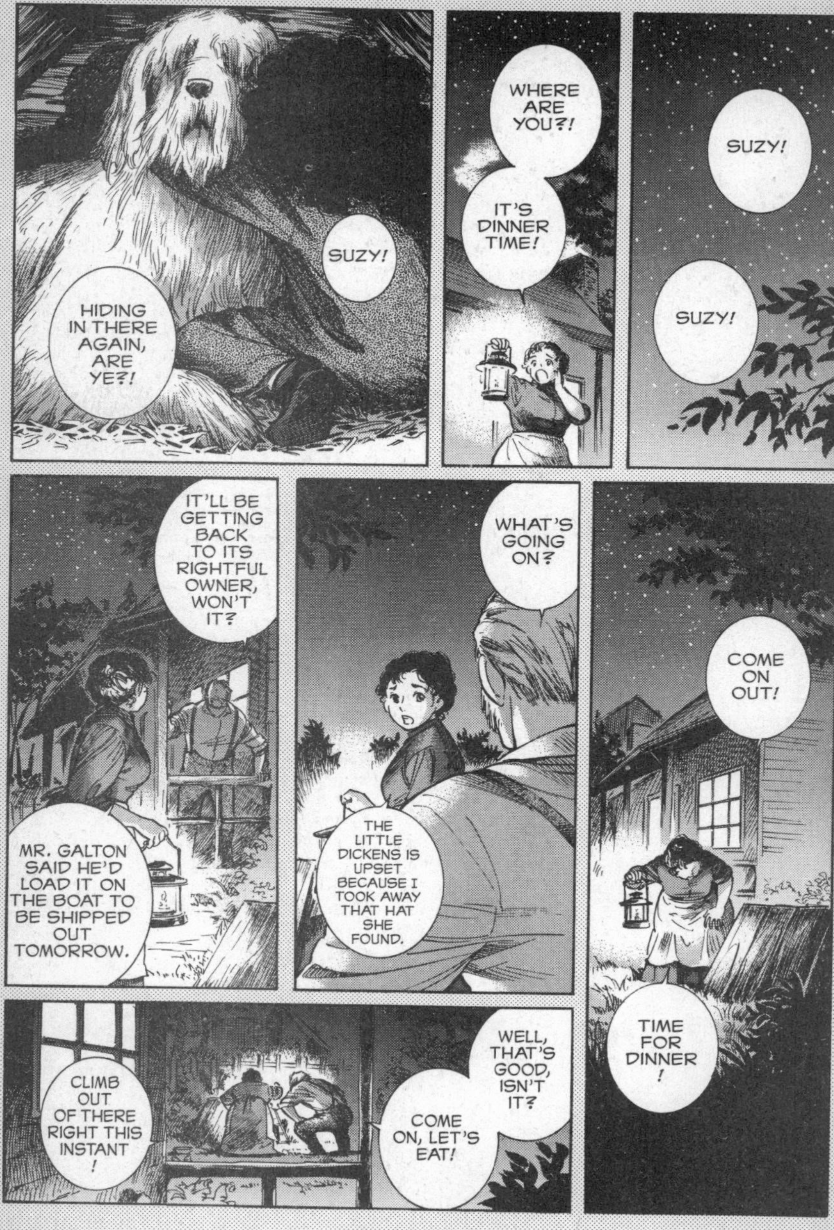
SUZY!
SUZY!
WHERE ARE YOU?!
IT'S DINNER TIME!
SUZY!
HIDING IN THERE AGAIN, ARE YE?!
COME ON OUT!
TIME FOR DINNER!
WHAT'S GOING ON?
THE LITTLE DICKENS IS UPSET BECAUSE I TOOK AWAY THAT HAT SHE FOUND.
MR. GALTON SAID HE'D LOAD IT ON THE BOAT TO BE SHIPPED OUT TOMORROW.
IT'LL BE GETTING BACK TO ITS RIGHTFUL OWNER, WON'T IT?
WELL, THAT'S GOOD, ISN'T IT?
COME ON, LET'S EAT!
CLIMB OUT OF THERE RIGHT THIS INSTANT!

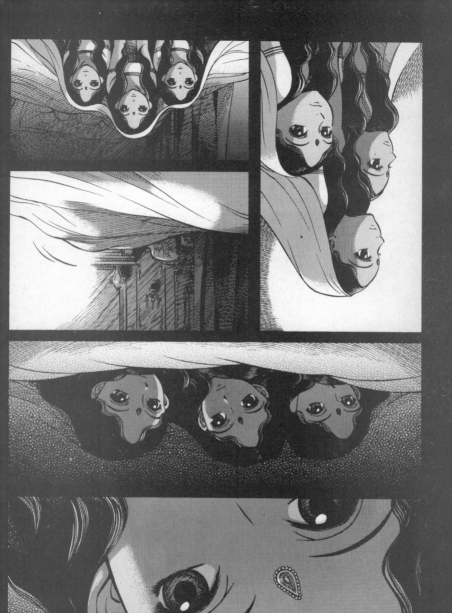

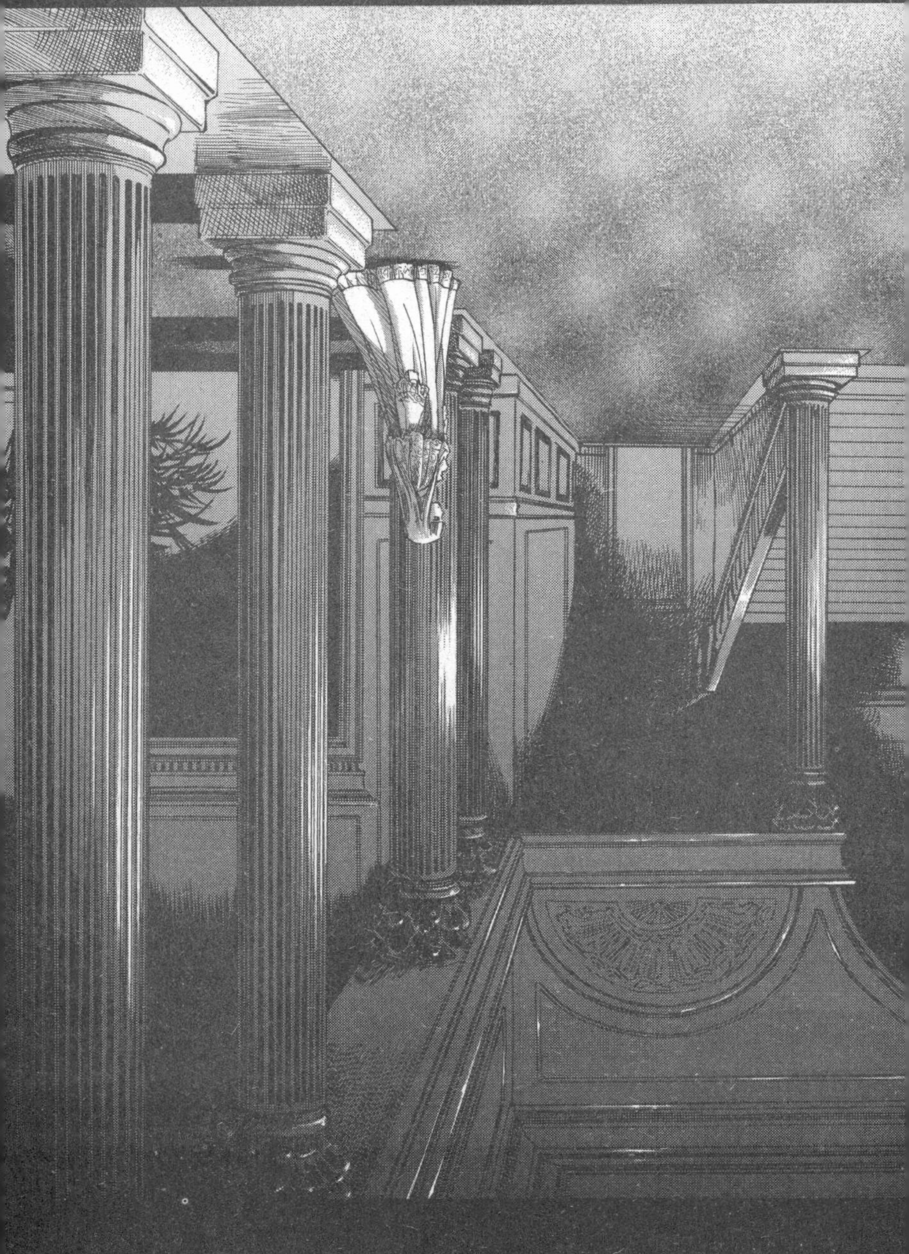

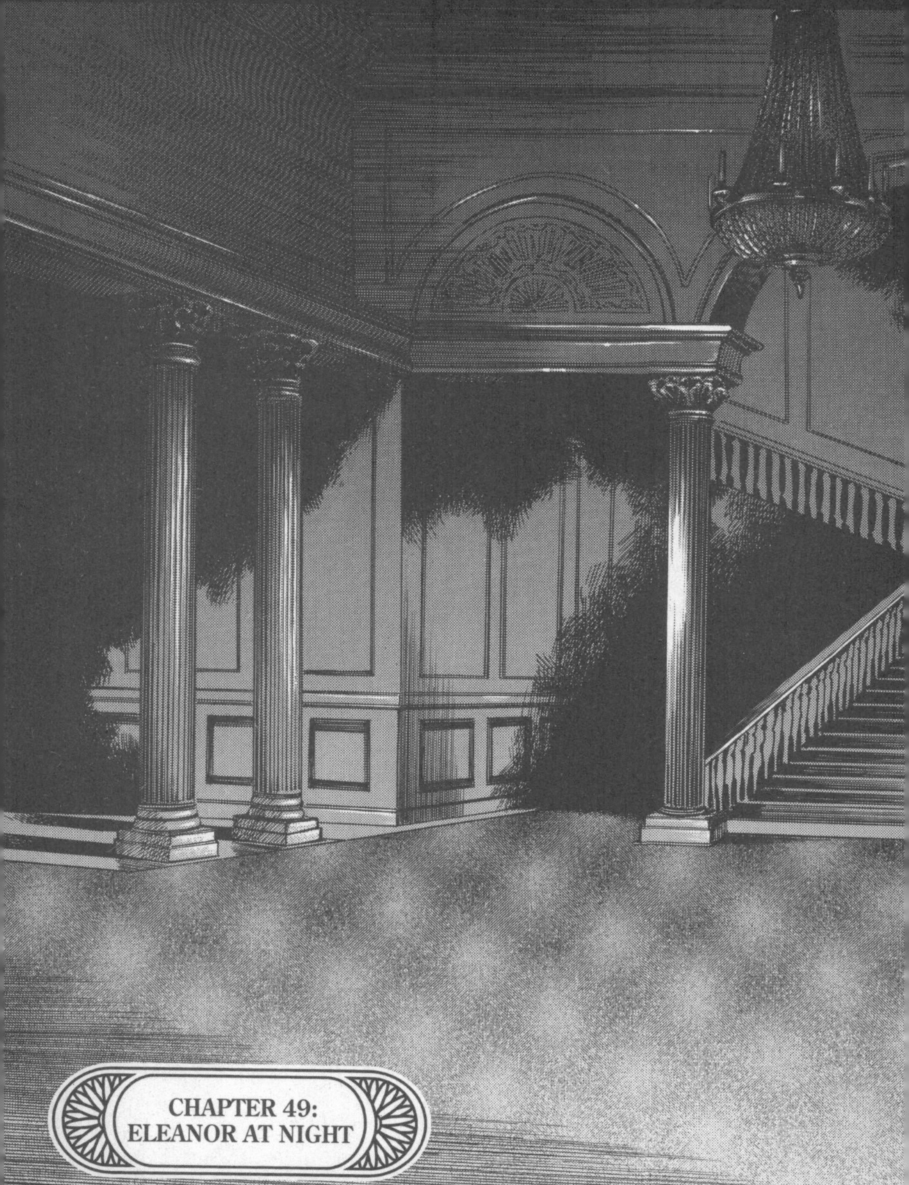
CHAPTER 49:
ELEANOR AT NIGHT

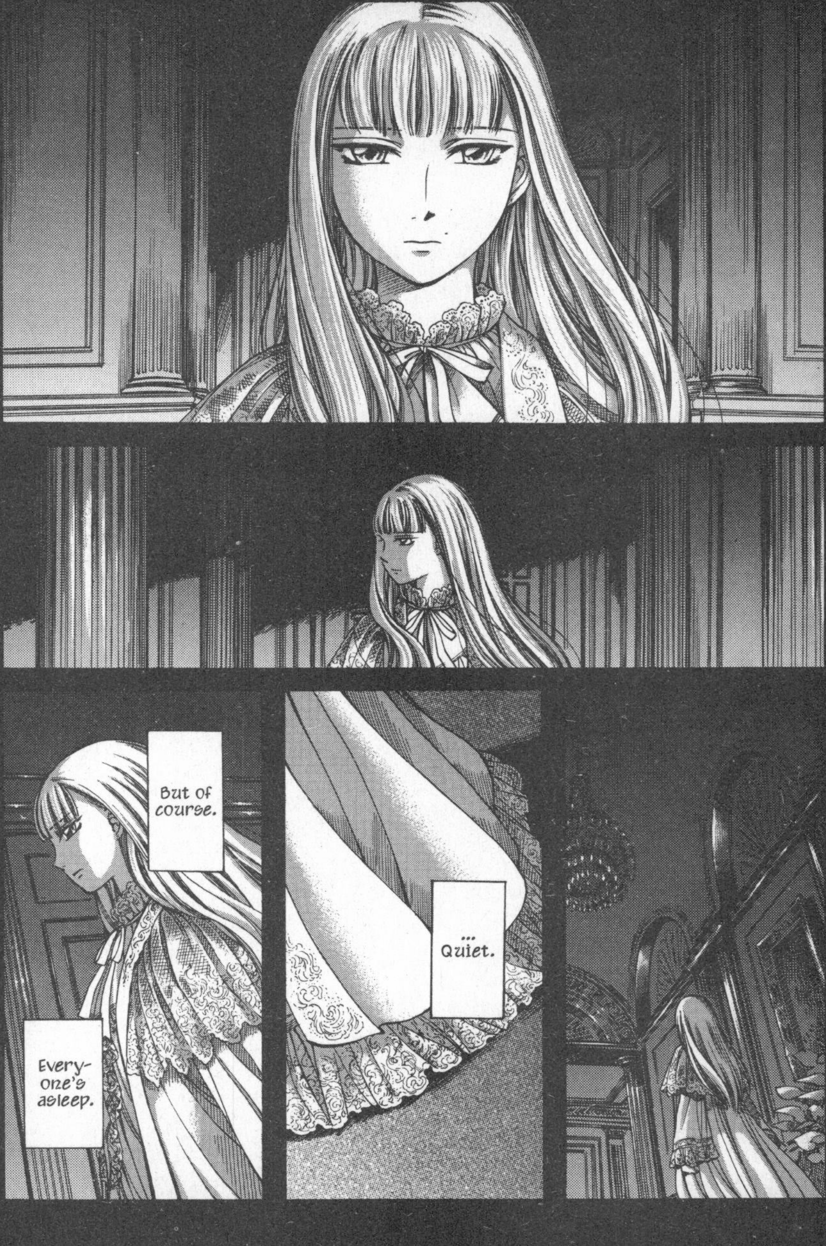
... Quiet.
But of course.
Every-one's asleep.

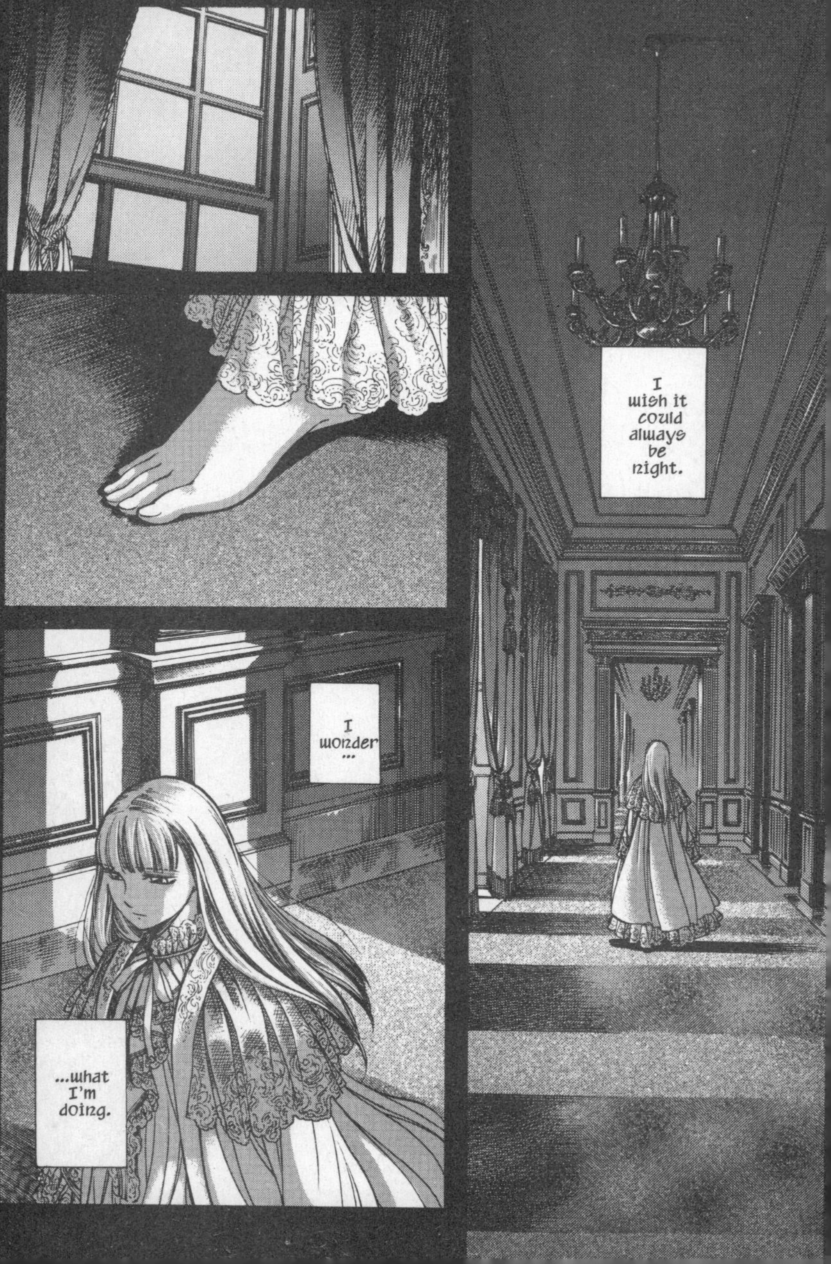
I wish it could always be night.
I wonder...
...what I'm doing.

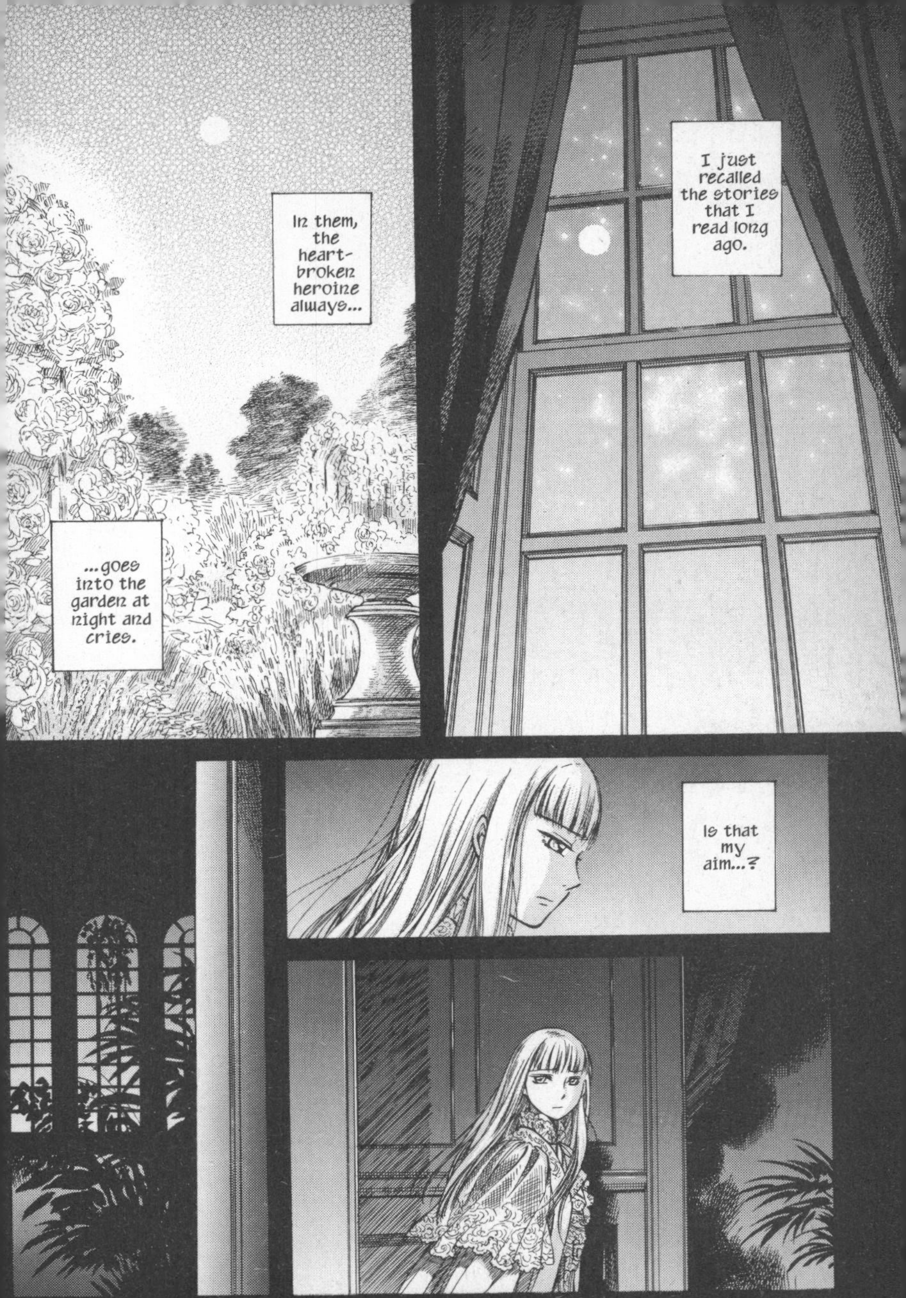
I just recalled the stories that I read long ago.
In them, the heart-broken heroine always...
...goes into the garden at night and cries.
Is that my aim...?

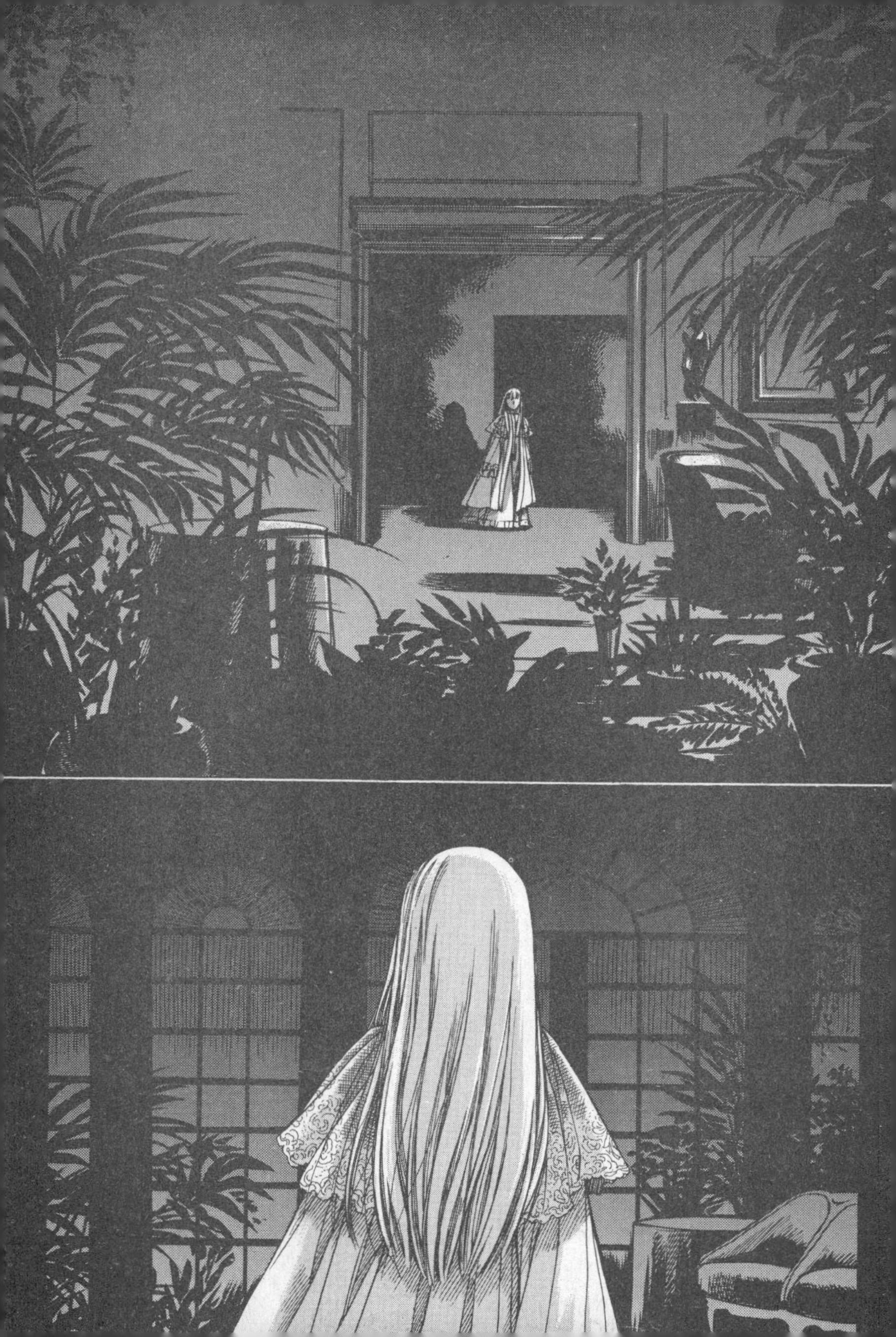

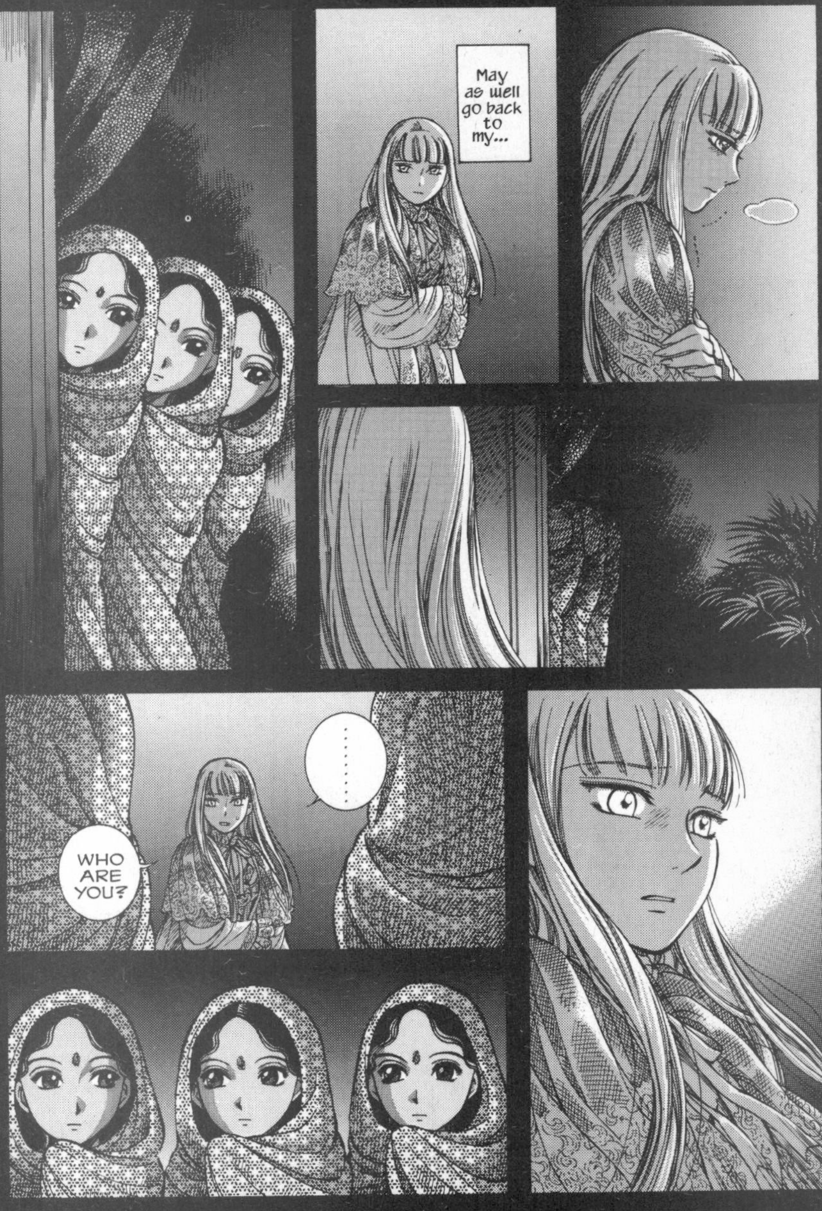
May as well go back to my...
......
WHO ARE YOU?

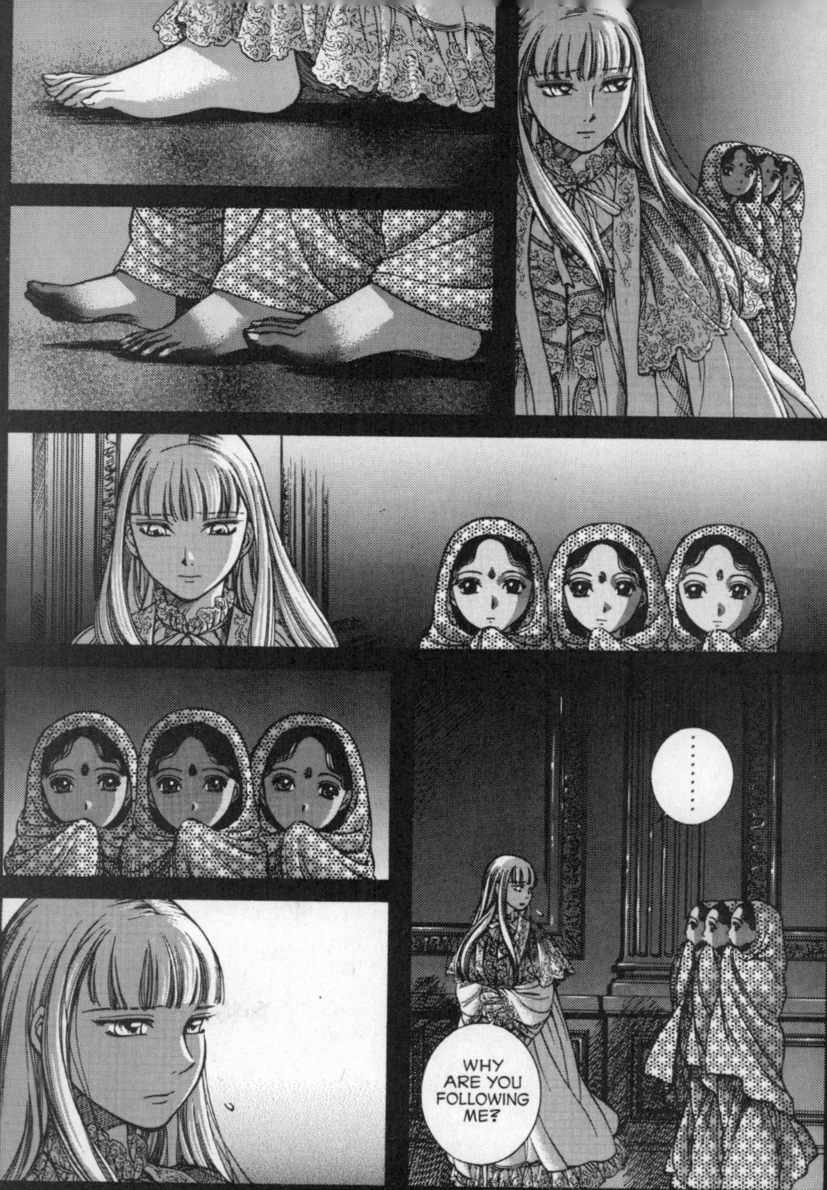
WHY ARE YOU FOLLOWING ME?
......

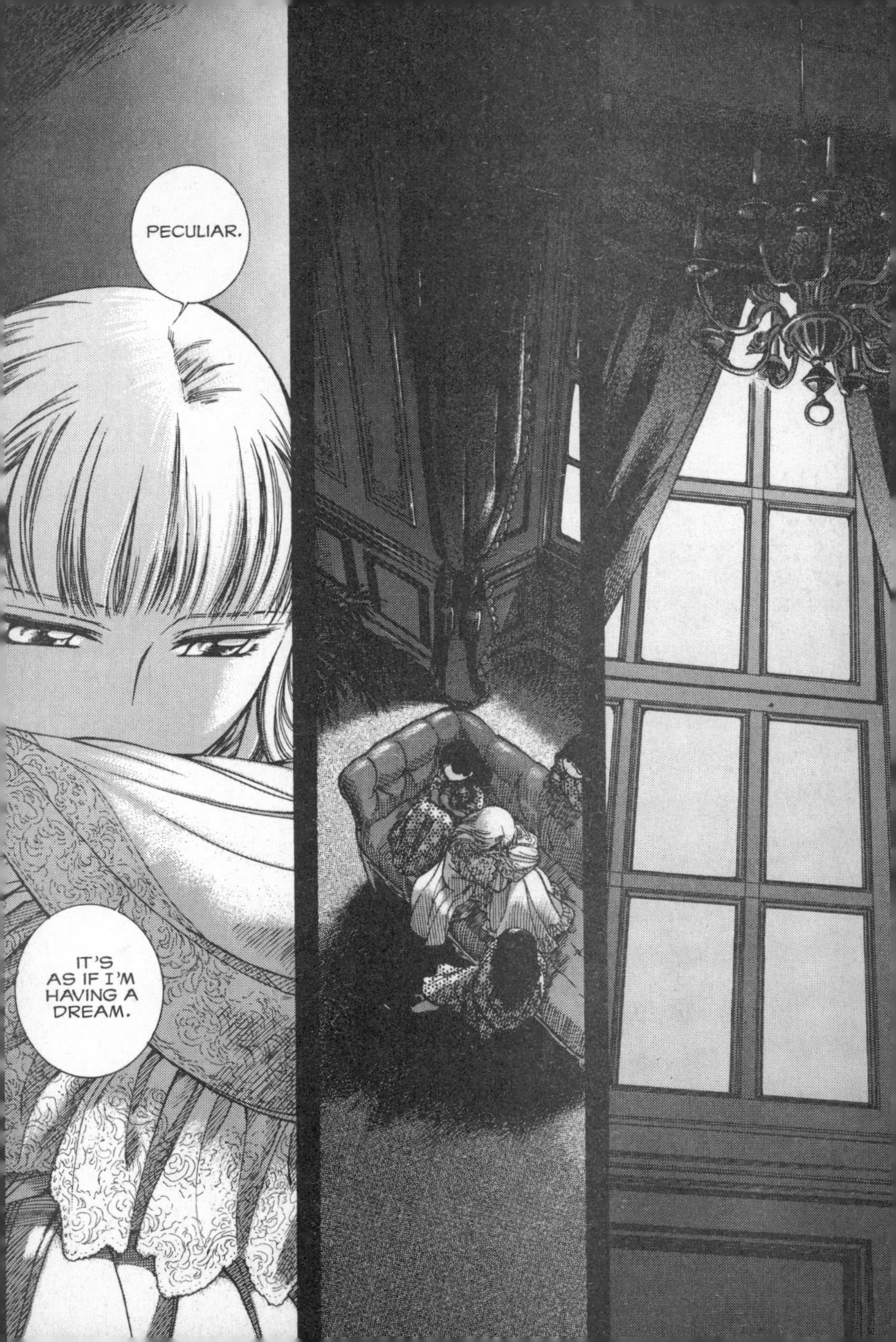
PECULIAR.
IT'S AS IF I'M HAVING A DREAM.

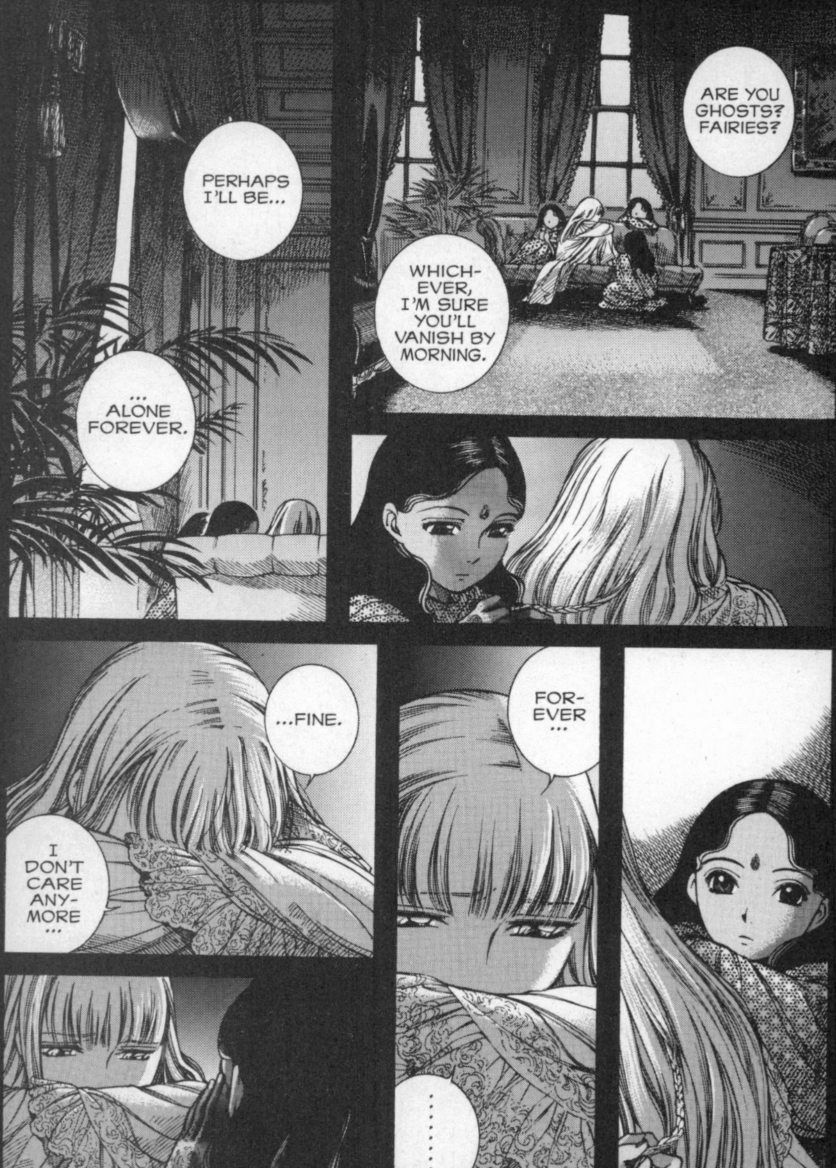
ARE YOU GHOSTS? FAIRIES?
WHICH-EVER, I'M SURE YOU'LL VANISH BY MORNING.
PERHAPS I'LL BE...
...ALONE FOREVER.
FOR-EVER...
...FINE.
I DON'T CARE ANY-MORE...
......

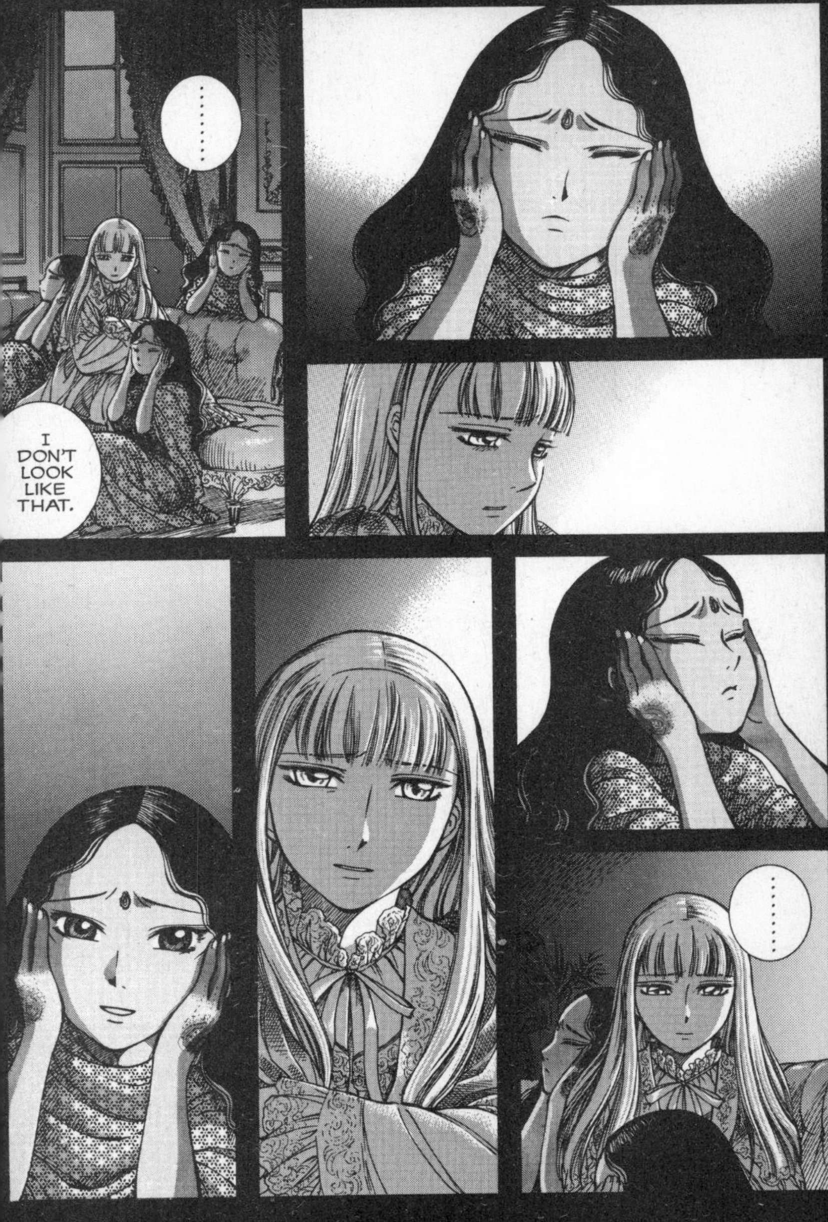
......
I DON'T LOOK LIKE THAT.
......

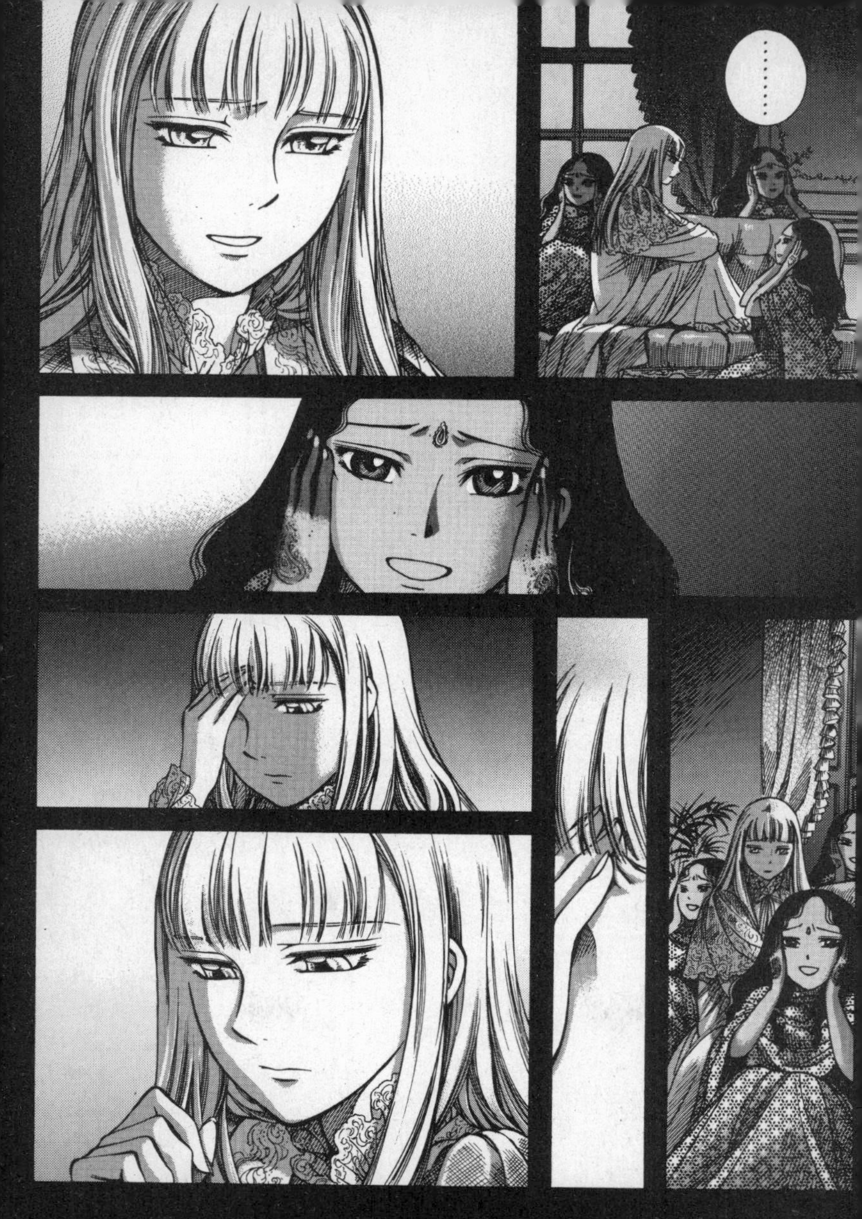
......

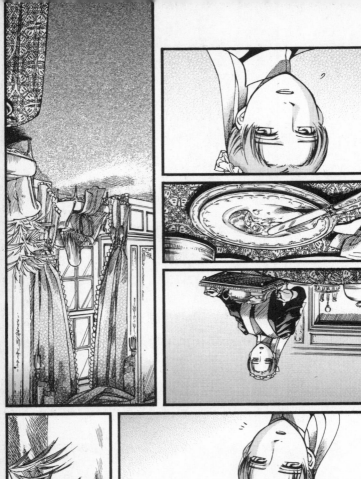

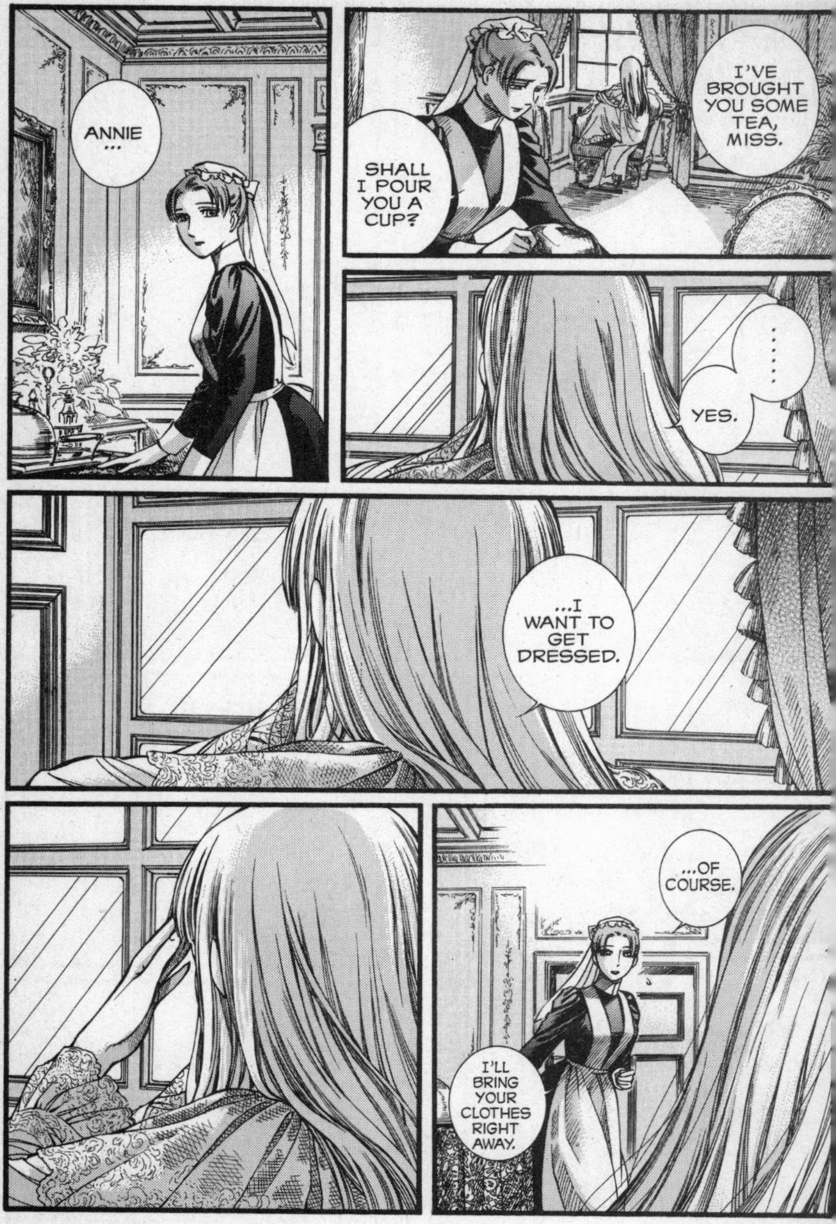
I'VE BROUGHT YOU SOME TEA, MISS.
SHALL I POUR YOU A CUP?
ANNIE ...
......
YES.
...I WANT TO GET DRESSED.
...OF COURSE.
I'LL BRING YOUR CLOTHES RIGHT AWAY.

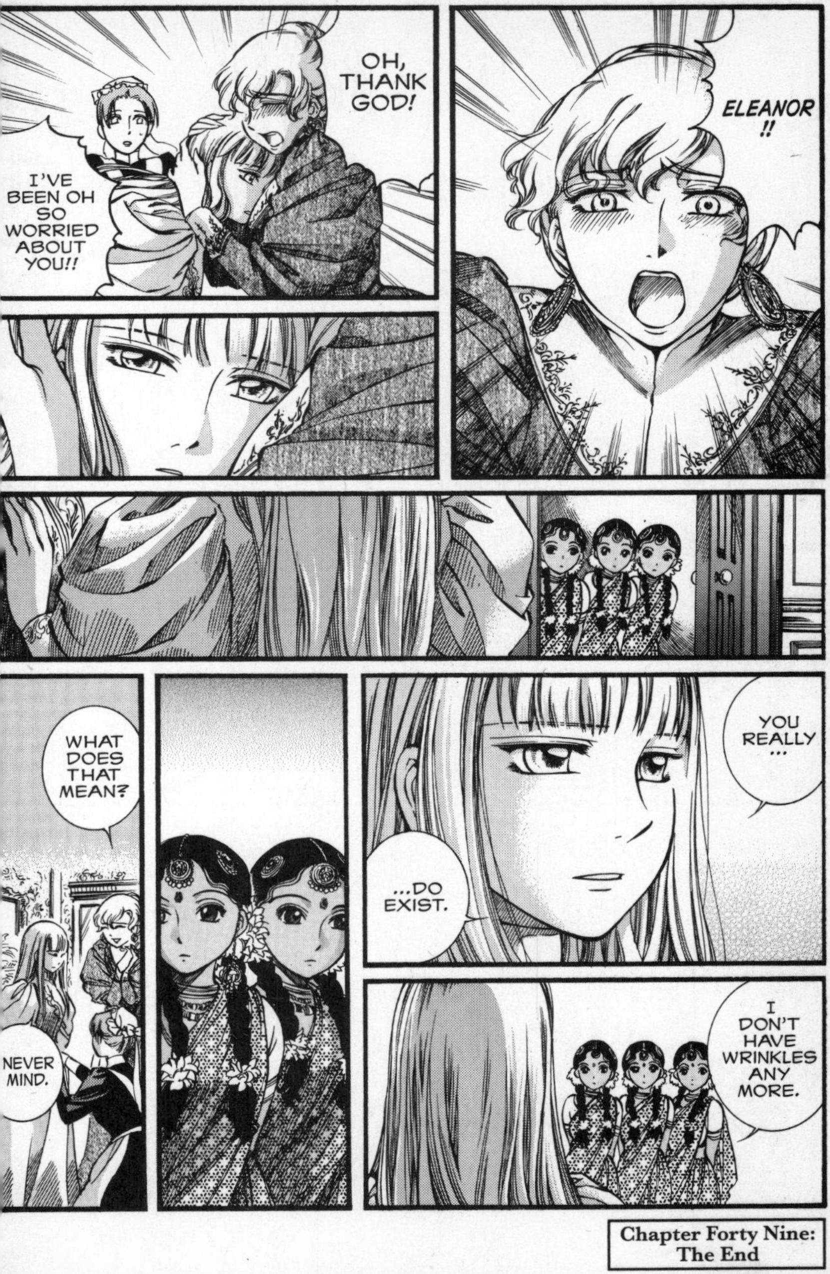
ELEANOR !!
OH, THANK GOD!
I'VE BEEN OH SO WORRIED ABOUT YOU!!
YOU REALLY ...
...DO EXIST.
I DON'T HAVE WRINKLES ANY MORE.
WHAT DOES THAT MEAN?
NEVER MIND.

Chapter Forty Nine:
The End

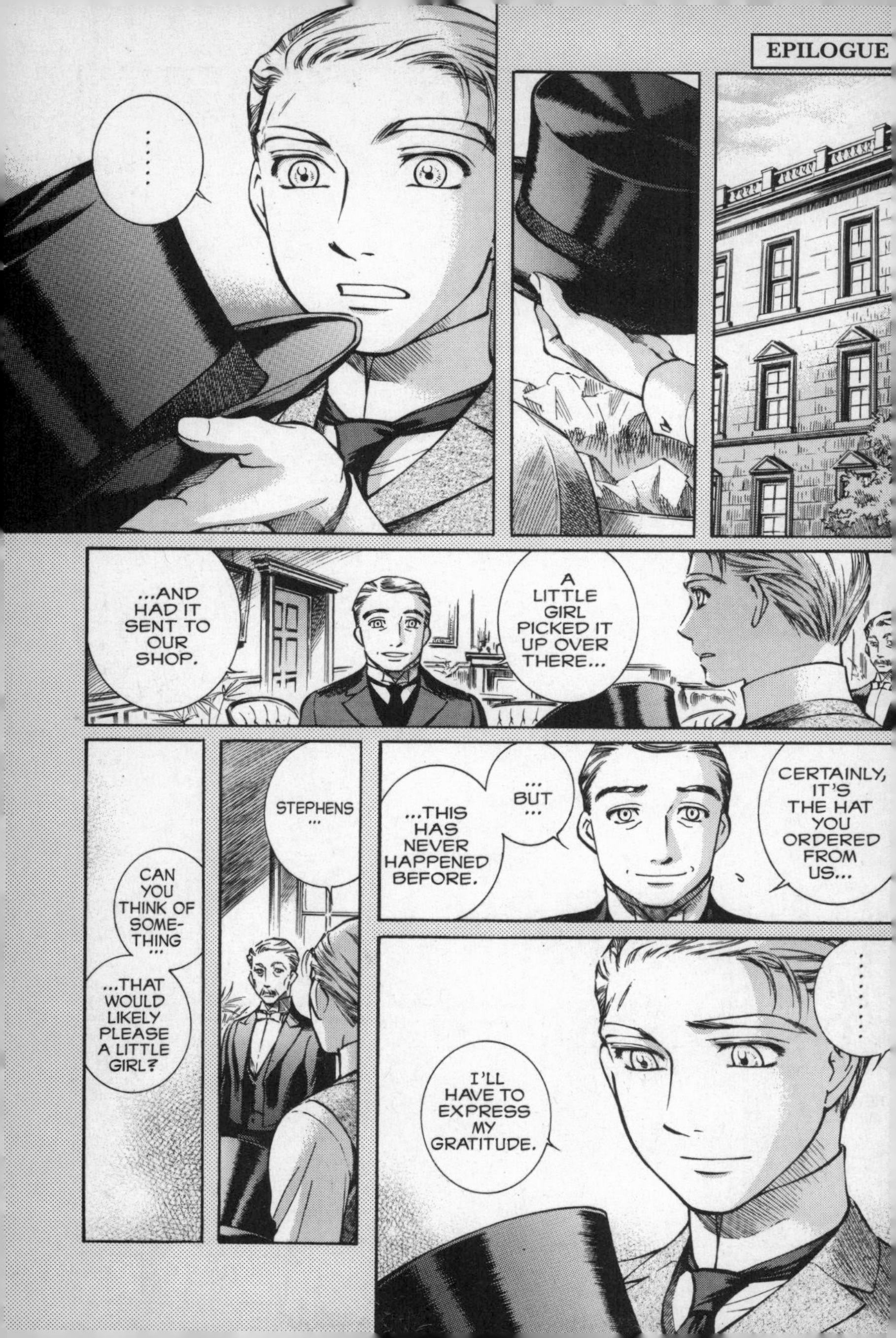
......
A LITTLE GIRL PICKED IT UP OVER THERE...
...AND HAD IT SENT TO OUR SHOP.
CERTAINLY, IT'S THE HAT YOU ORDERED FROM US...
...BUT...
...THIS HAS NEVER HAPPENED BEFORE.
......
I'LL HAVE TO EXPRESS MY GRATITUDE.
STEPHENS...
CAN YOU THINK OF SOME-THING...
...THAT WOULD LIKELY PLEASE A LITTLE GIRL?

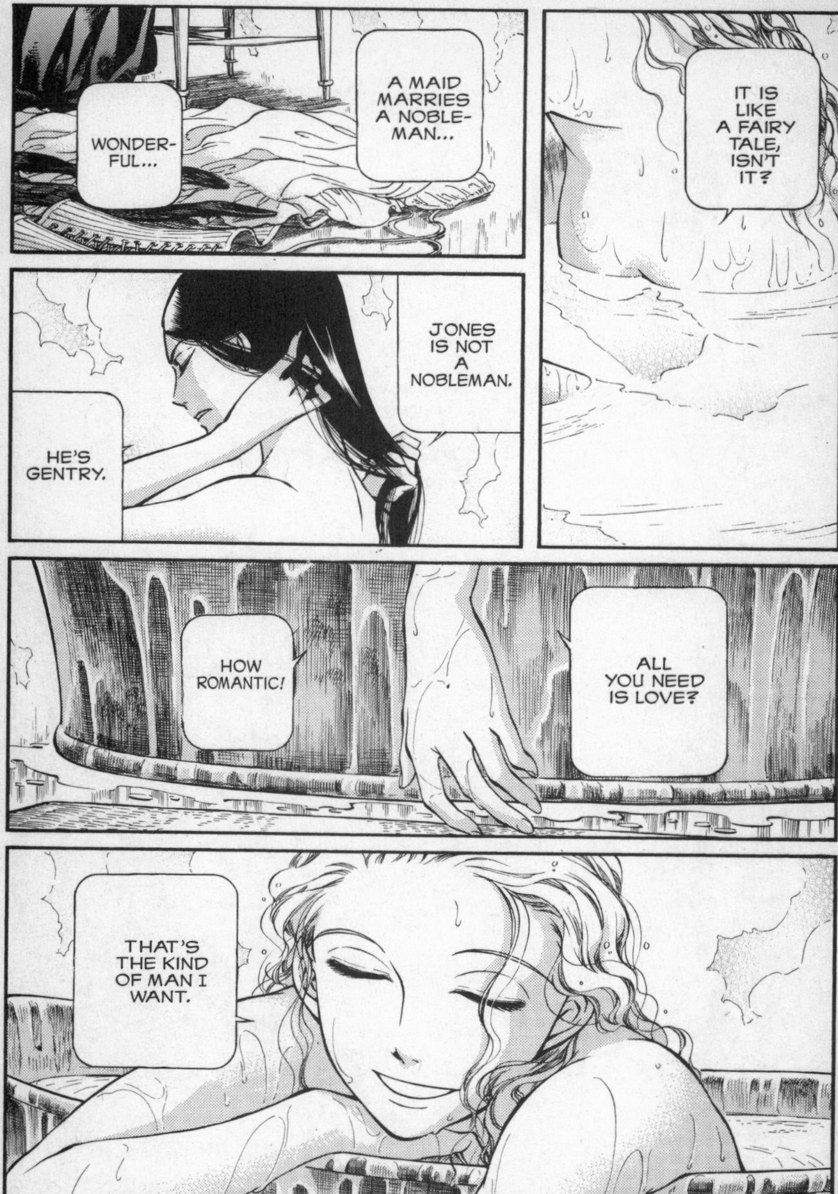
IT IS LIKE A FAIRY TALE, ISN'T IT?
A MAID MARRIES A NOBLE-MAN...
WONDER-FUL...
JONES IS NOT A NOBLEMAN.
HE'S GENTRY.
ALL YOU NEED IS LOVE?
HOW ROMANTIC!
THAT'S THE KIND OF MAN I WANT.

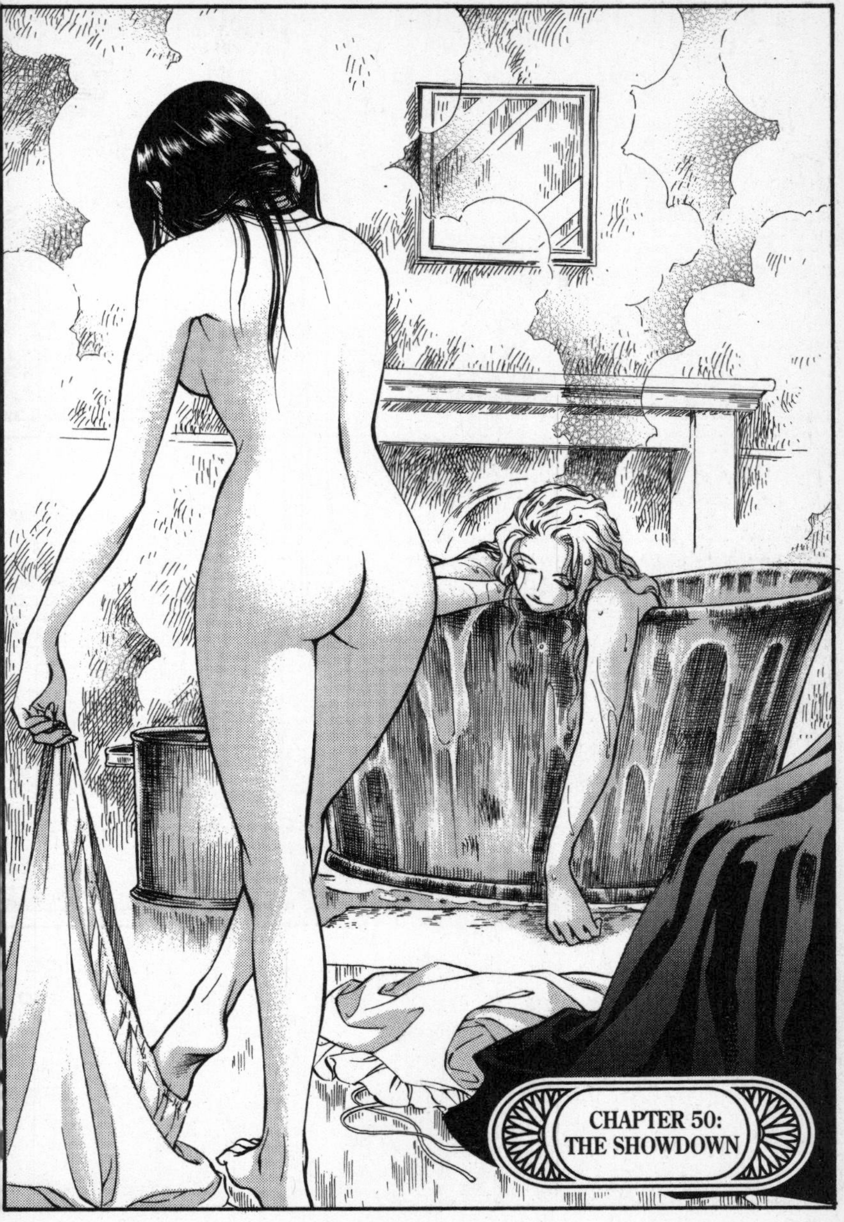
CHAPTER 50:
THE SHOWDOWN

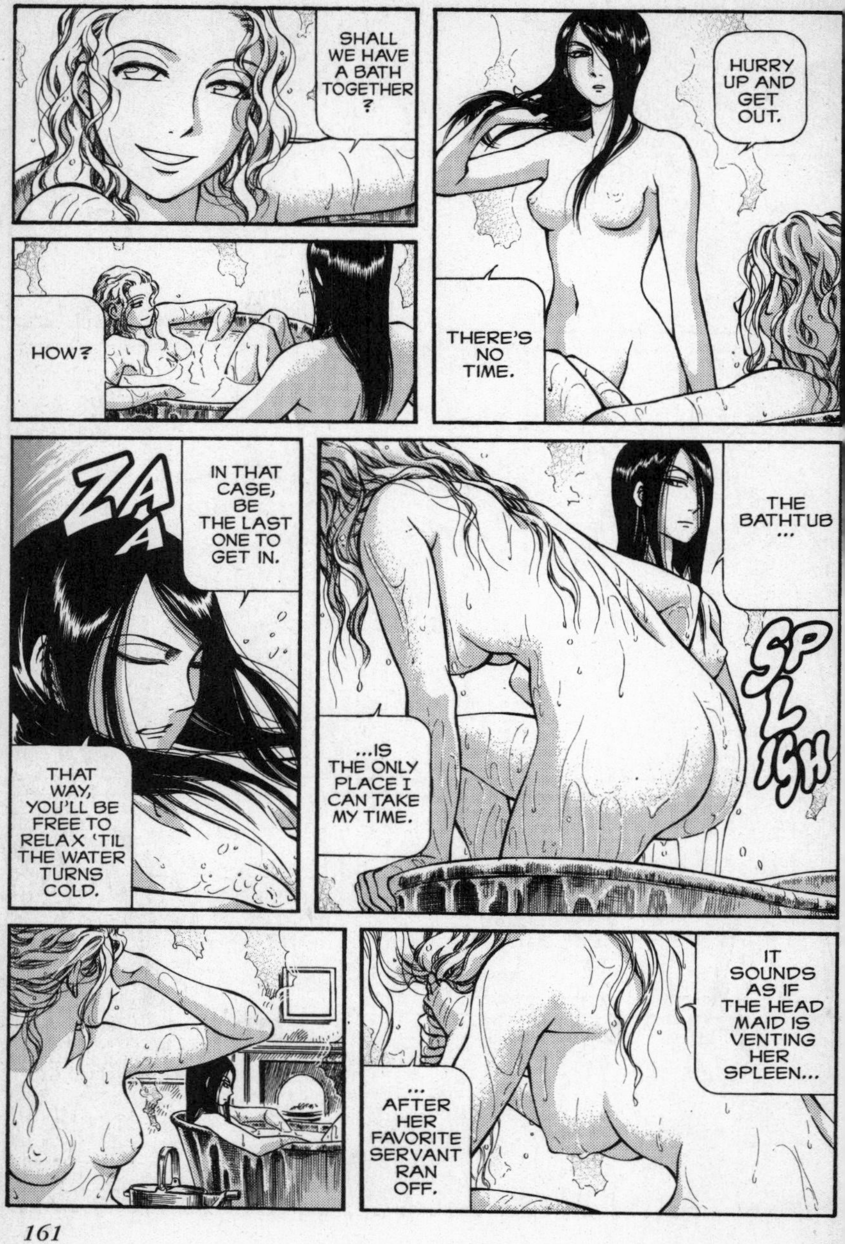
HURRY UP AND GET OUT.
THERE'S NO TIME.
SHALL WE HAVE A BATH TOGETHER?
HOW?
THE BATHTUB...
SPLISH
...IS THE ONLY PLACE I CAN TAKE MY TIME.
ZAA
IN THAT CASE, BE THE LAST ONE TO GET IN.
THAT WAY, YOU'LL BE FREE TO RELAX 'TIL THE WATER TURNS COLD.
IT SOUNDS AS IF THE HEAD MAID IS VENTING HER SPLEEN...
...AFTER HER FAVORITE SERVANT RAN OFF.

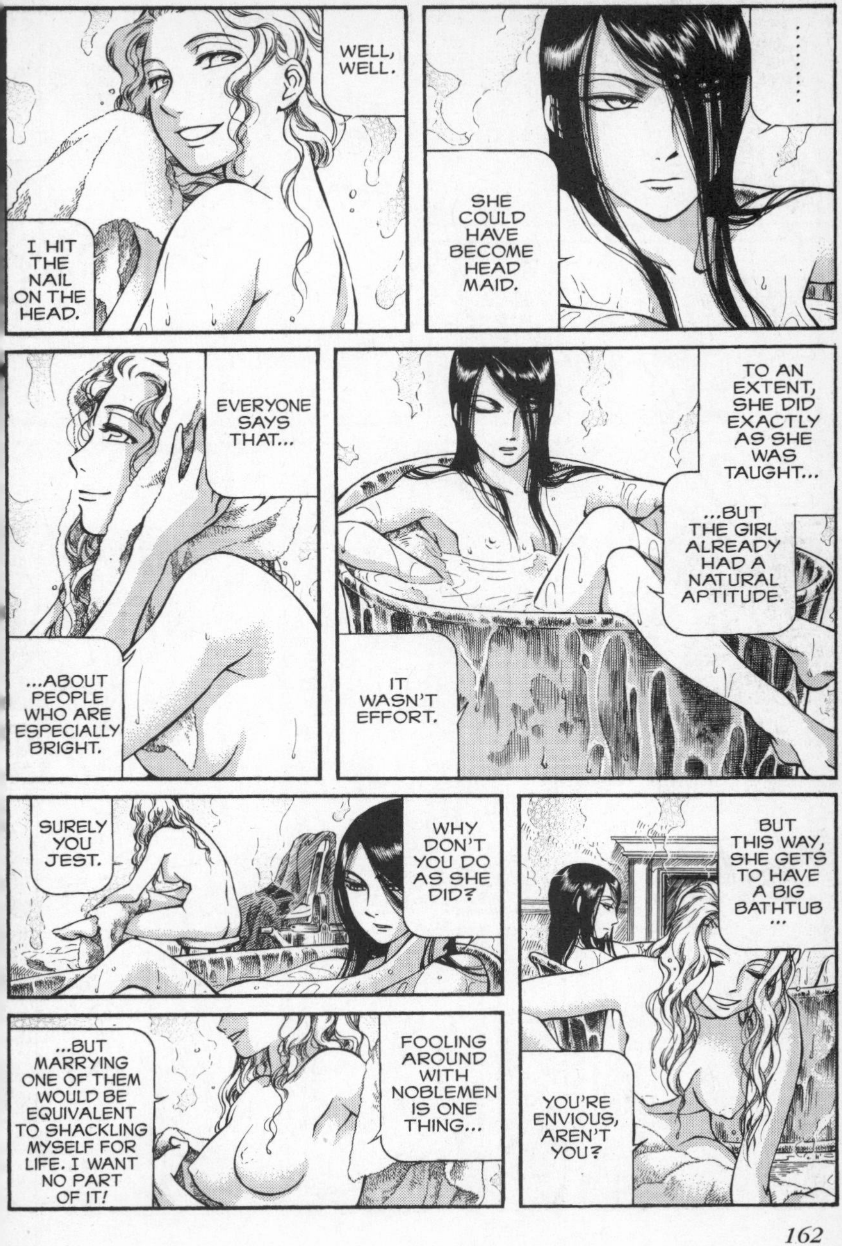
......
SHE COULD HAVE BECOME HEAD MAID.
WELL, WELL.
I HIT THE NAIL ON THE HEAD.
TO AN EXTENT, SHE DID EXACTLY AS SHE WAS TAUGHT...
...BUT THE GIRL ALREADY HAD A NATURAL APTITUDE.
IT WASN'T EFFORT.
EVERYONE SAYS THAT...
...ABOUT PEOPLE WHO ARE ESPECIALLY BRIGHT.
BUT THIS WAY, SHE GETS TO HAVE A BIG BATHTUB ...
YOU'RE ENVIOUS, AREN'T YOU?
WHY DON'T YOU DO AS SHE DID?
SURELY YOU JEST.
FOOLING AROUND WITH NOBLEMEN IS ONE THING...
...BUT MARRYING ONE OF THEM WOULD BE EQUIVALENT TO SHACKLING MYSELF FOR LIFE. I WANT NO PART OF IT!

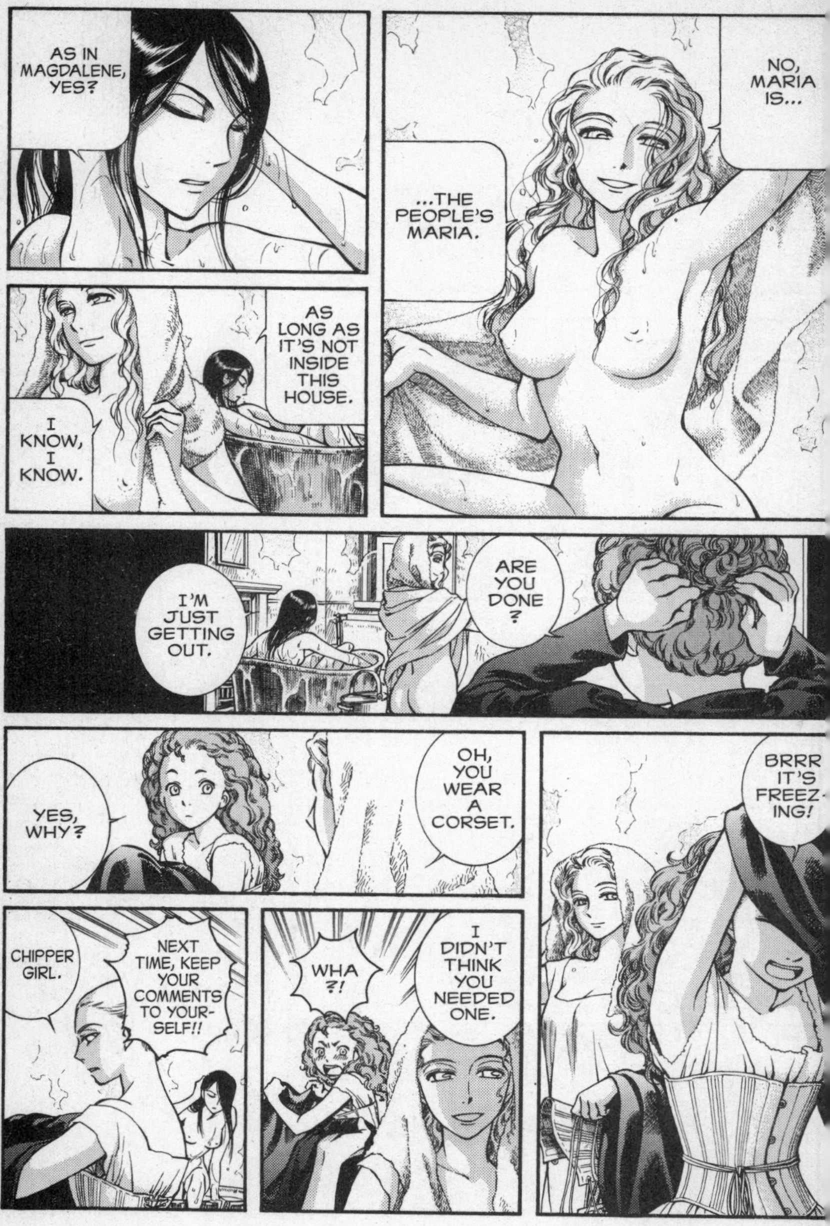
NO, MARIA IS...
...THE PEOPLE'S MARIA.
AS IN MAGDALENE, YES?
AS LONG AS IT'S NOT INSIDE THIS HOUSE.
I KNOW, I KNOW.
ARE YOU DONE?
I'M JUST GETTING OUT.
BRRR IT'S FREEZ-ING!
OH, YOU WEAR A CORSET.
YES, WHY?
I DIDN'T THINK YOU NEEDED ONE.
WHA?!
NEXT TIME, KEEP YOUR COMMENTS TO YOUR-SELF!!
CHIPPER GIRL.

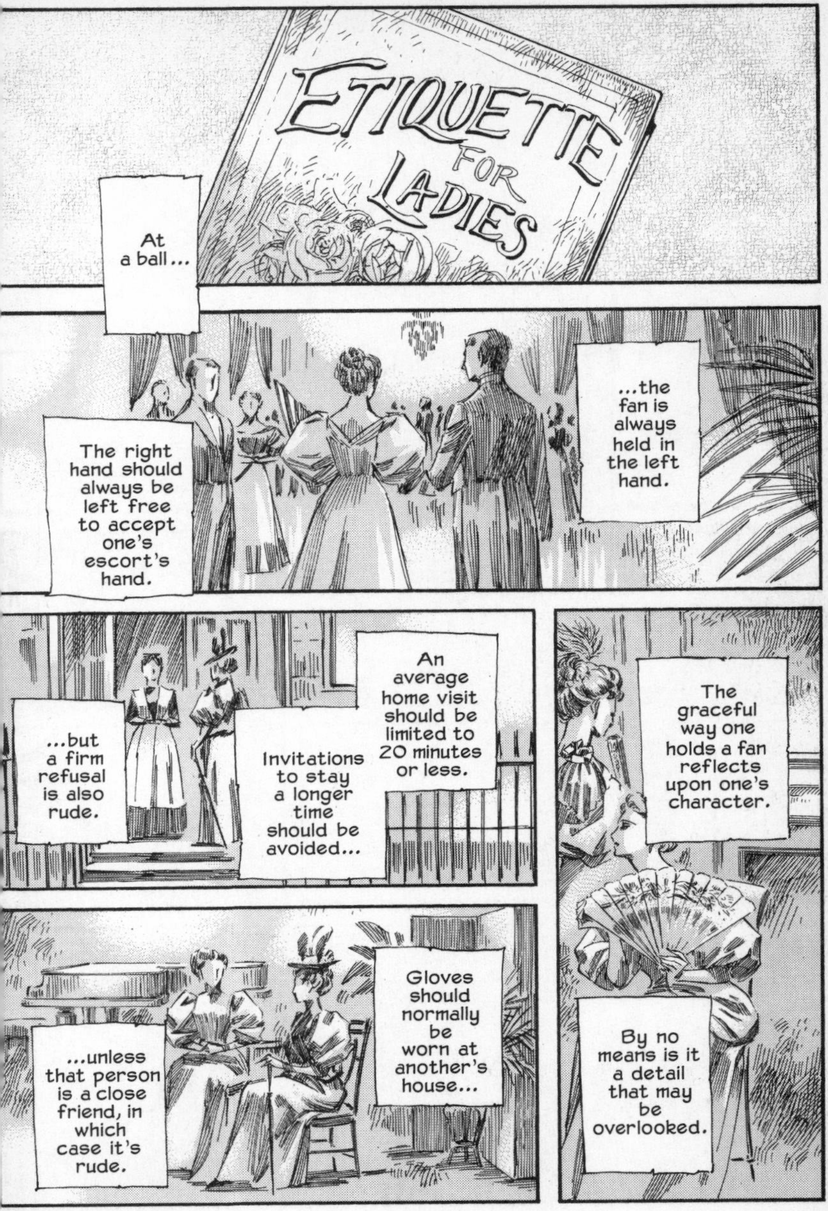

ETIQUETTE FOR LADIES
At a ball...
...the fan is always held in the left hand.
The right hand should always be left free to accept one's escort's hand.
The graceful way one holds a fan reflects upon one's character.
By no means is it a detail that may be overlooked.
An average home visit should be limited to 20 minutes or less.
Invitations to stay a longer time should be avoided...
...but a firm refusal is also rude.
Gloves should normally be worn at another's house...
...unless that person is a close friend, in which case it's rude.

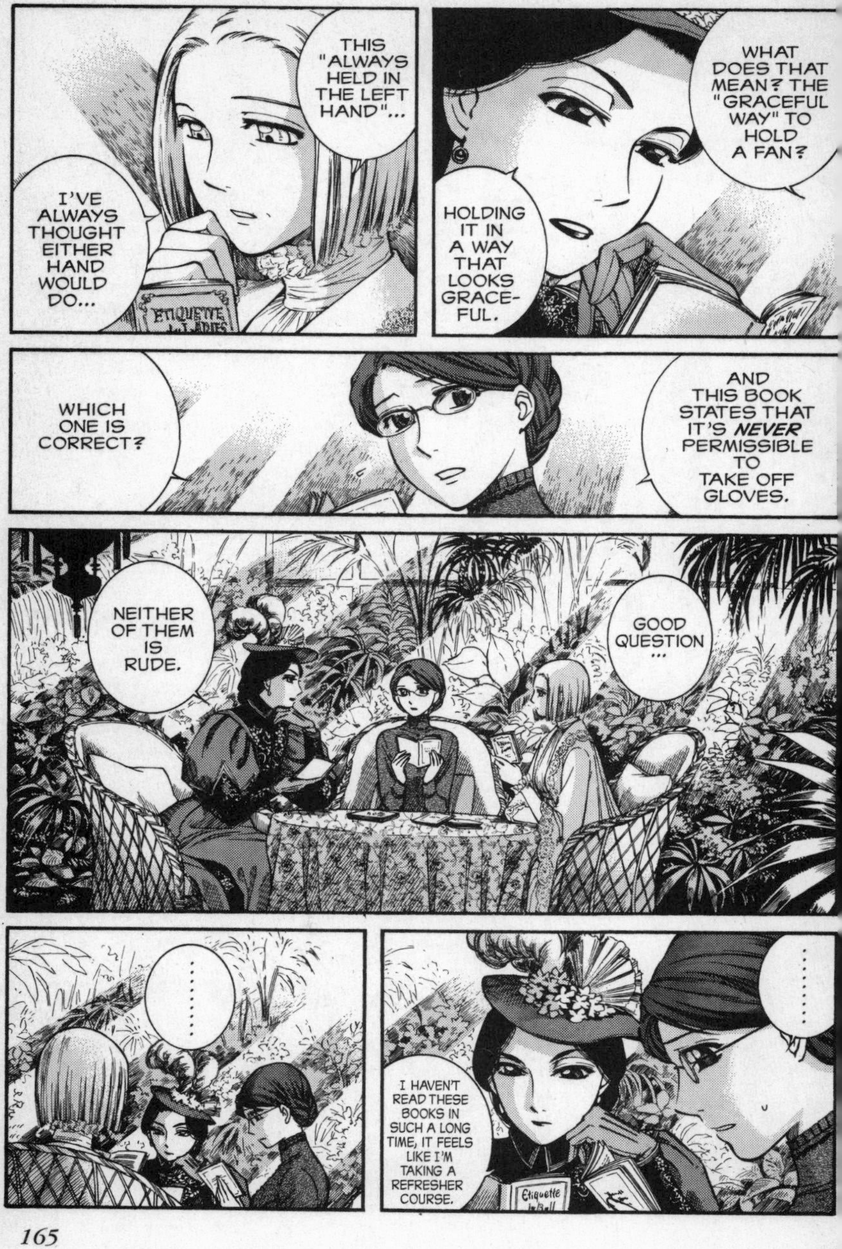
WHAT DOES THAT MEAN? THE "GRACEFUL WAY" TO HOLD A FAN?
HOLDING IT IN A WAY THAT LOOKS GRACE-FUL.
THIS "ALWAYS HELD IN THE LEFT HAND"...
I'VE ALWAYS THOUGHT EITHER HAND WOULD DO...
ETIQUETTE for LADIES
AND THIS BOOK STATES THAT IT'S *NEVER* PERMISSIBLE TO TAKE OFF GLOVES.
WHICH ONE IS CORRECT?
GOOD QUESTION ...
NEITHER OF THEM IS RUDE.
......
I HAVEN'T READ THESE BOOKS IN SUCH A LONG TIME, IT FEELS LIKE I'M TAKING A REFRESHER COURSE.
Etiquette in Ball
......

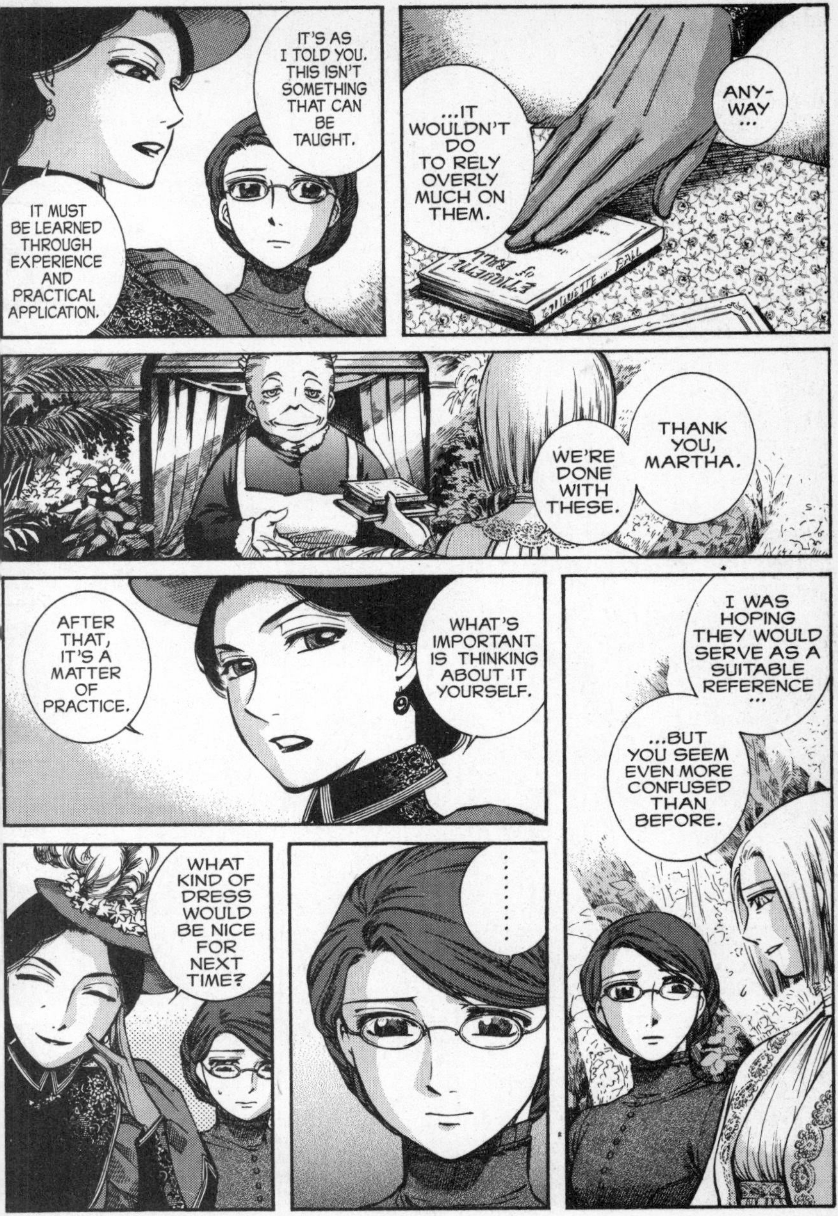
ANY-WAY ...
...IT WOULDN'T DO TO RELY OVERLY MUCH ON THEM.
IT'S AS I TOLD YOU. THIS ISN'T SOMETHING THAT CAN BE TAUGHT.
IT MUST BE LEARNED THROUGH EXPERIENCE AND PRACTICAL APPLICATION.
THANK YOU, MARTHA.
WE'RE DONE WITH THESE.
I WAS HOPING THEY WOULD SERVE AS A SUITABLE REFERENCE ...
...BUT YOU SEEM EVEN MORE CONFUSED THAN BEFORE.
WHAT'S IMPORTANT IS THINKING ABOUT IT YOURSELF.
AFTER THAT, IT'S A MATTER OF PRACTICE.
......
WHAT KIND OF DRESS WOULD BE NICE FOR NEXT TIME?

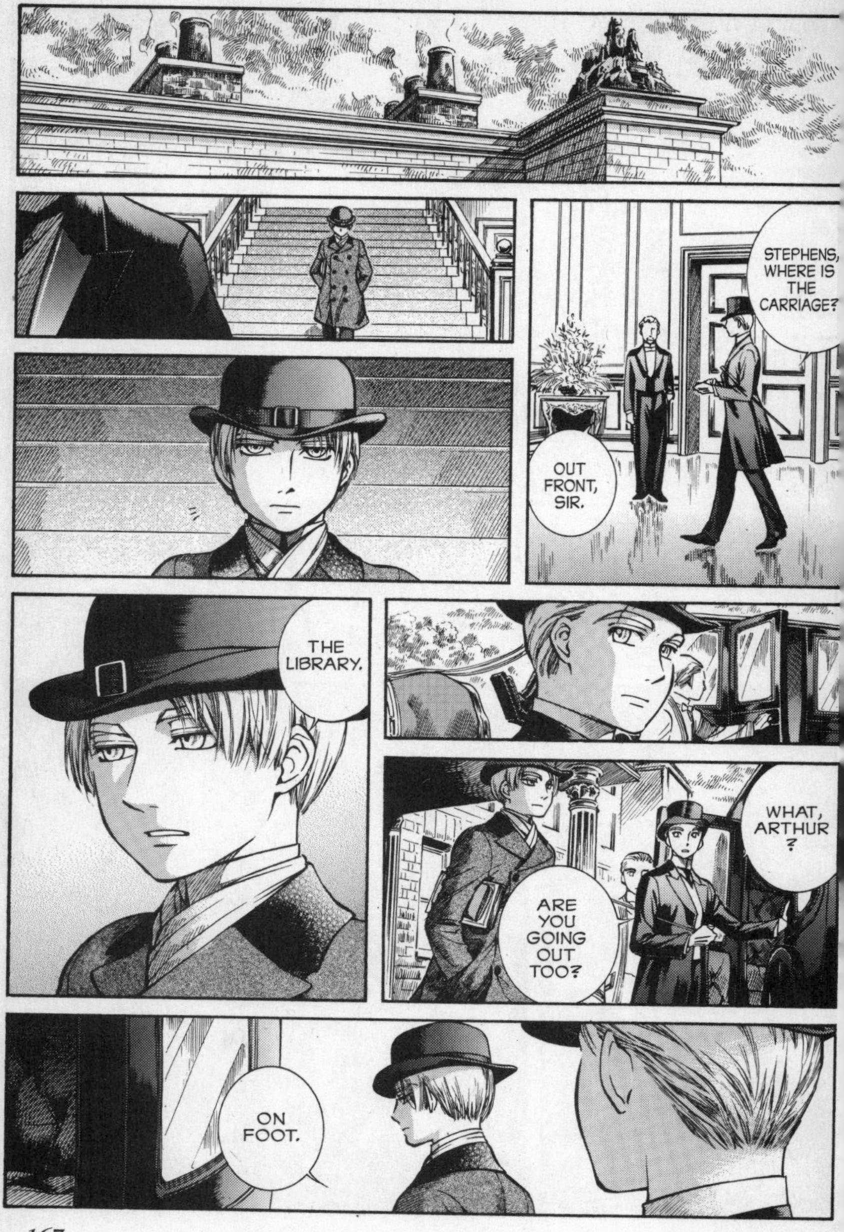
STEPHENS, WHERE IS THE CARRIAGE?
OUT FRONT, SIR.
WHAT, ARTHUR?
ARE YOU GOING OUT TOO?
THE LIBRARY.
ON FOOT.

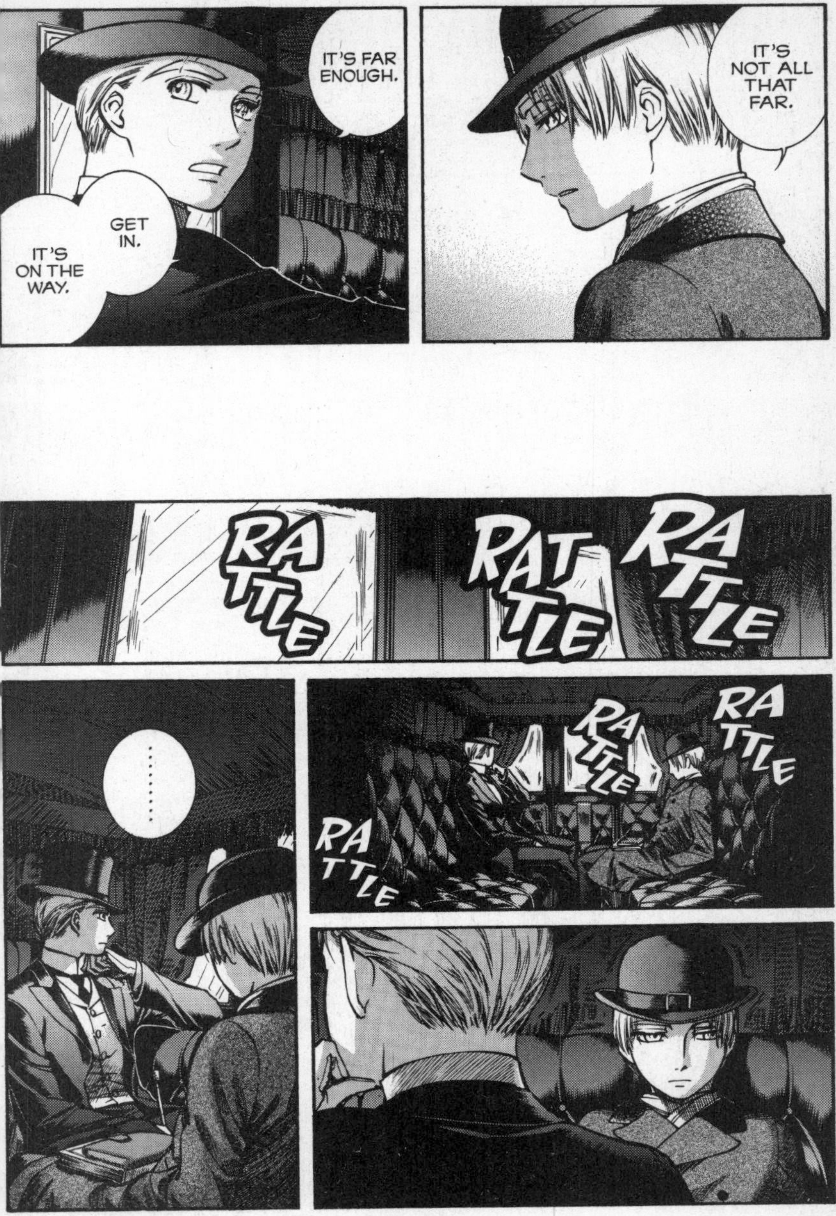
IT'S NOT ALL THAT FAR.
IT'S FAR ENOUGH.
GET IN.
IT'S ON THE WAY.
RATTLE
RATTLE
RATTLE
RATTLE
RATTLE
RATTLE
......

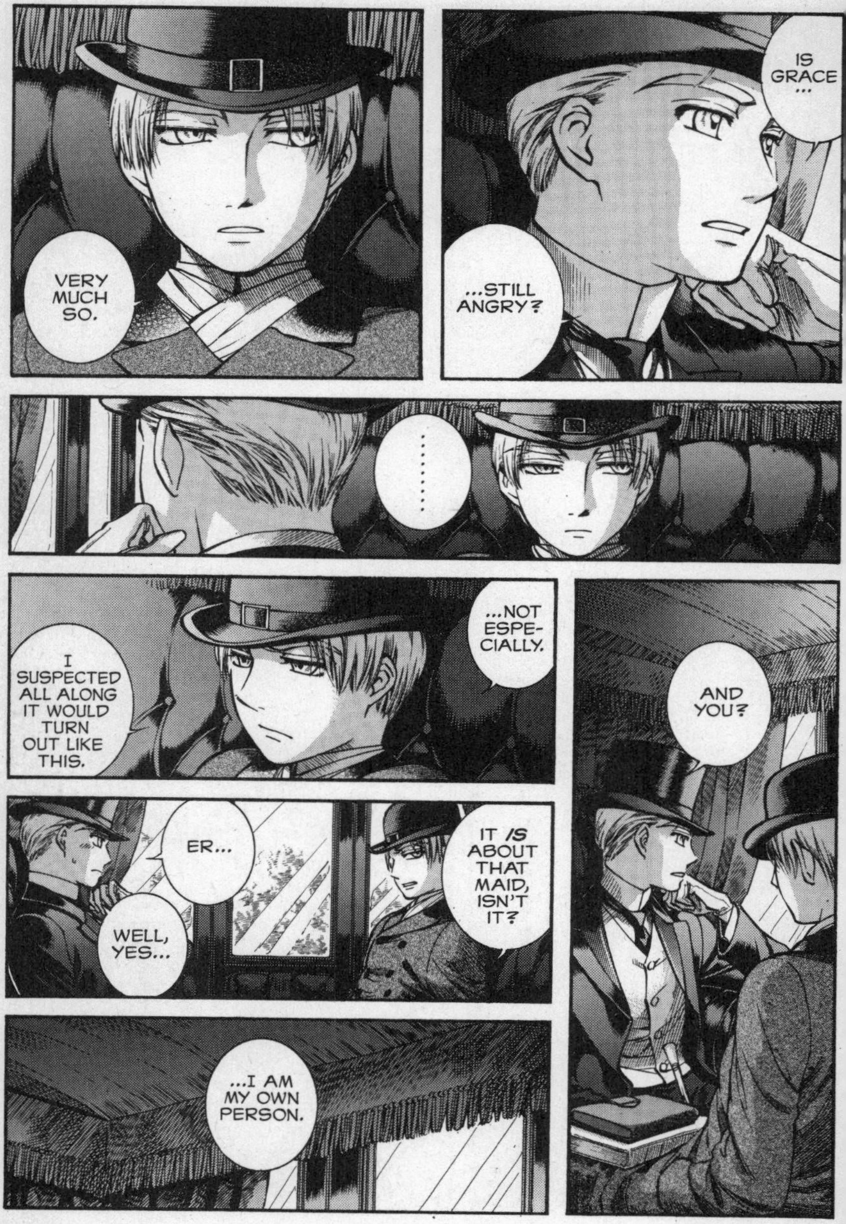
IS GRACE ...
...STILL ANGRY?
VERY MUCH SO.
......
AND YOU?
...NOT ESPECIALLY.
I SUSPECTED ALL ALONG IT WOULD TURN OUT LIKE THIS.
IT *IS* ABOUT THAT MAID, ISN'T IT?
ER...
WELL, YES...
...I AM MY OWN PERSON.

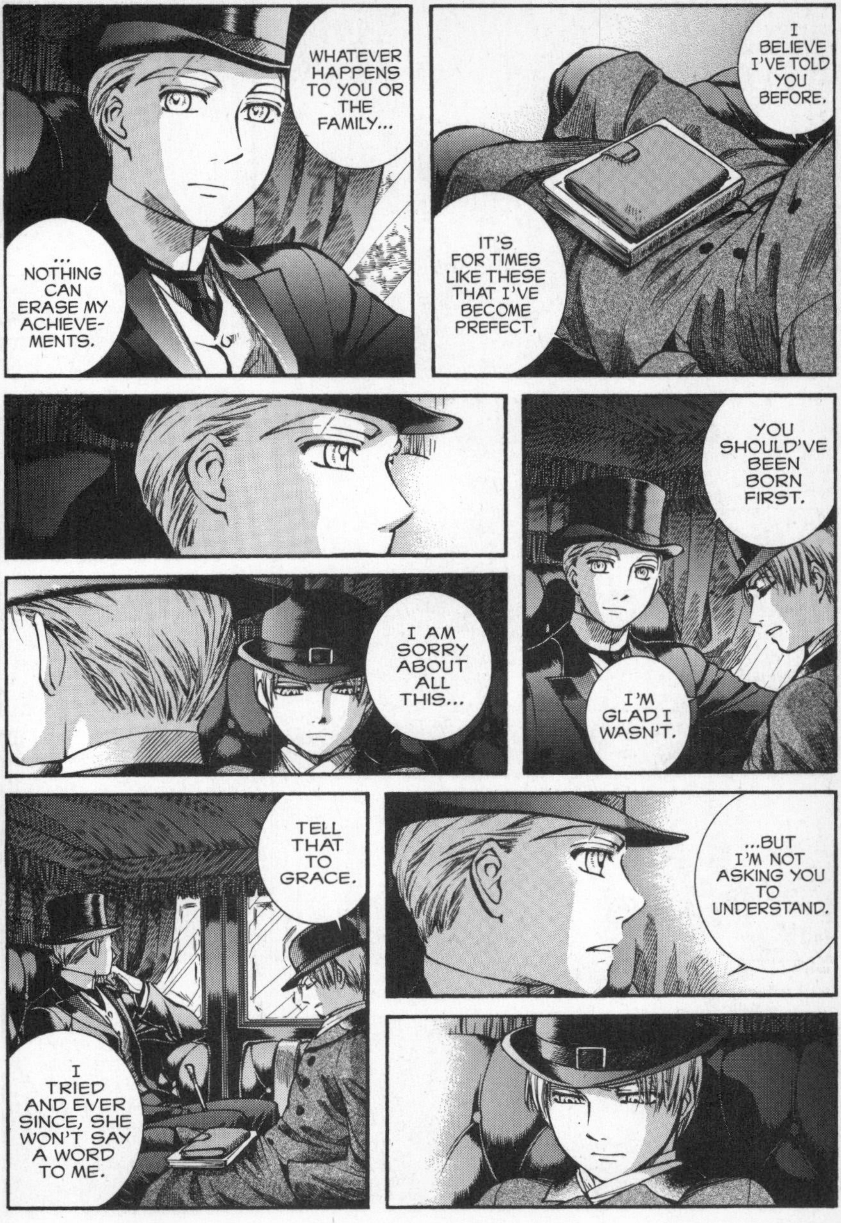
I BELIEVE I'VE TOLD YOU BEFORE.
IT'S FOR TIMES LIKE THESE THAT I'VE BECOME PREFECT.
WHATEVER HAPPENS TO YOU OR THE FAMILY...
...NOTHING CAN ERASE MY ACHIEVE-MENTS.
YOU SHOULD'VE BEEN BORN FIRST.
I'M GLAD I WASN'T.
I AM SORRY ABOUT ALL THIS...
...BUT I'M NOT ASKING YOU TO UNDERSTAND.
TELL THAT TO GRACE.
I TRIED AND EVER SINCE, SHE WON'T SAY A WORD TO ME.

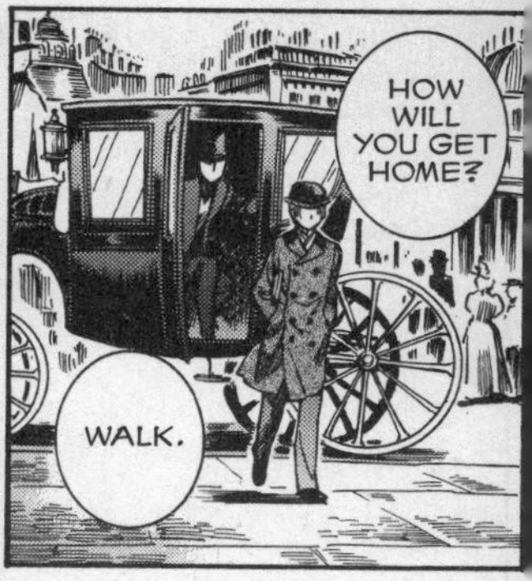
HOW WILL YOU GET HOME?
WALK.
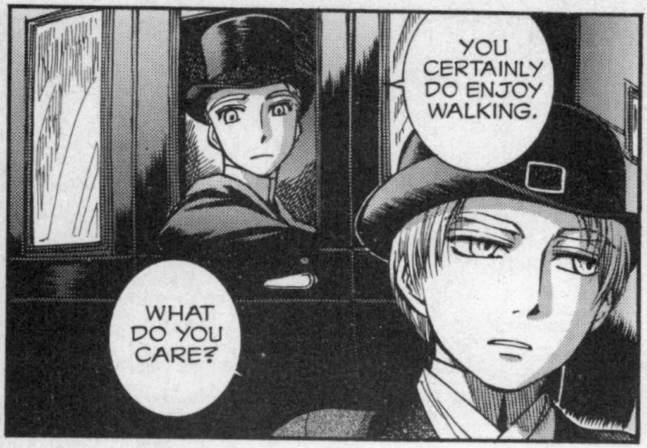
YOU CERTAINLY DO ENJOY WALKING.
WHAT DO YOU CARE?
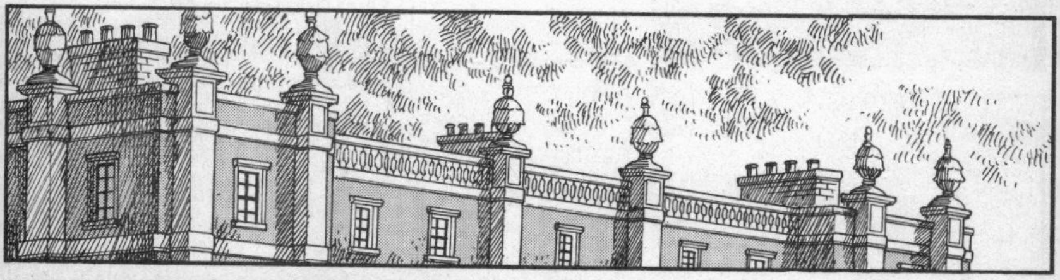
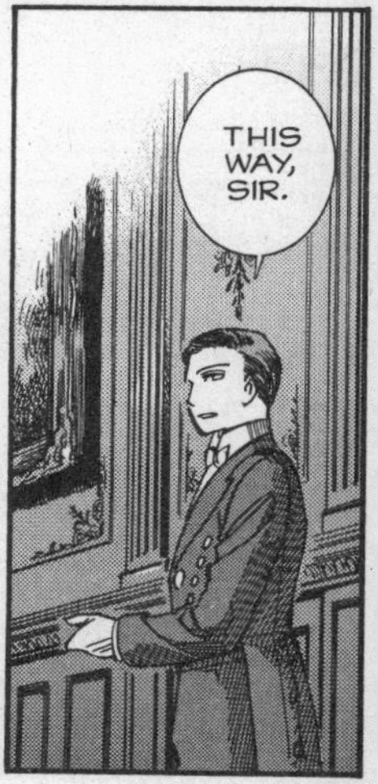
THIS WAY, SIR.
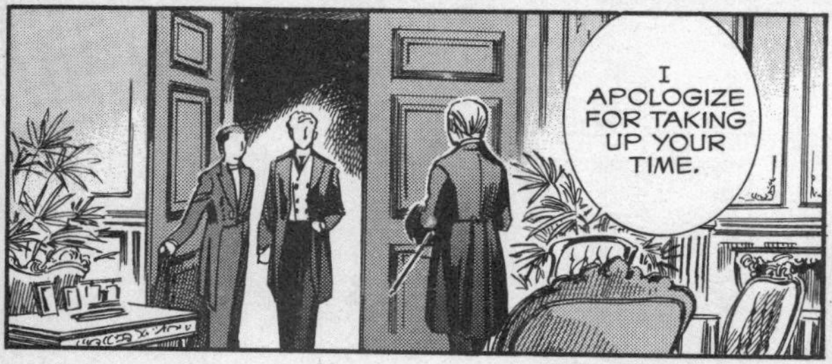
I APOLOGIZE FOR TAKING UP YOUR TIME.
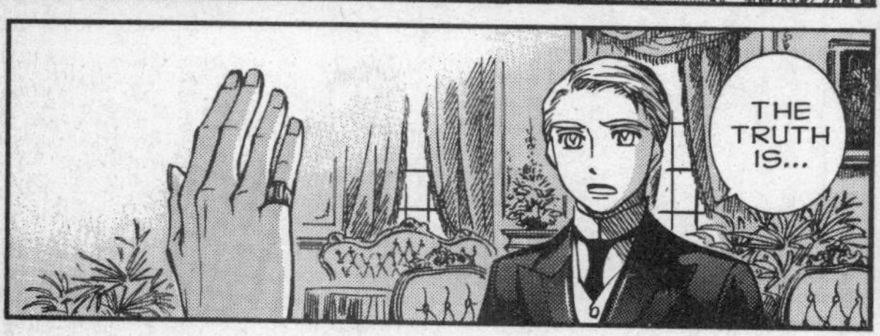
THE TRUTH IS...

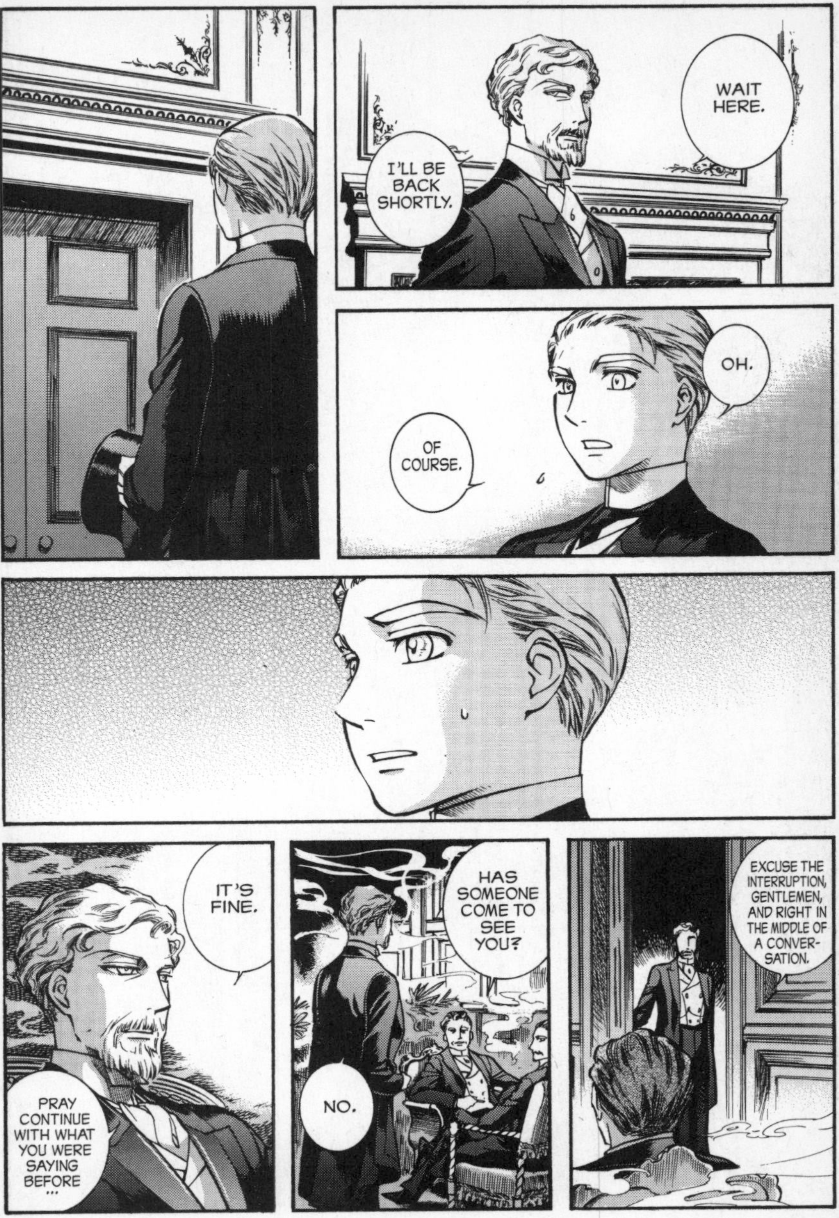
WAIT HERE.
I'LL BE BACK SHORTLY.
OH.
OF COURSE.
EXCUSE THE INTERRUPTION, GENTLEMEN, AND RIGHT IN THE MIDDLE OF A CONVER-SATION.
HAS SOMEONE COME TO SEE YOU?
NO.
IT'S FINE.
PRAY CONTINUE WITH WHAT YOU WERE SAYING BEFORE ...

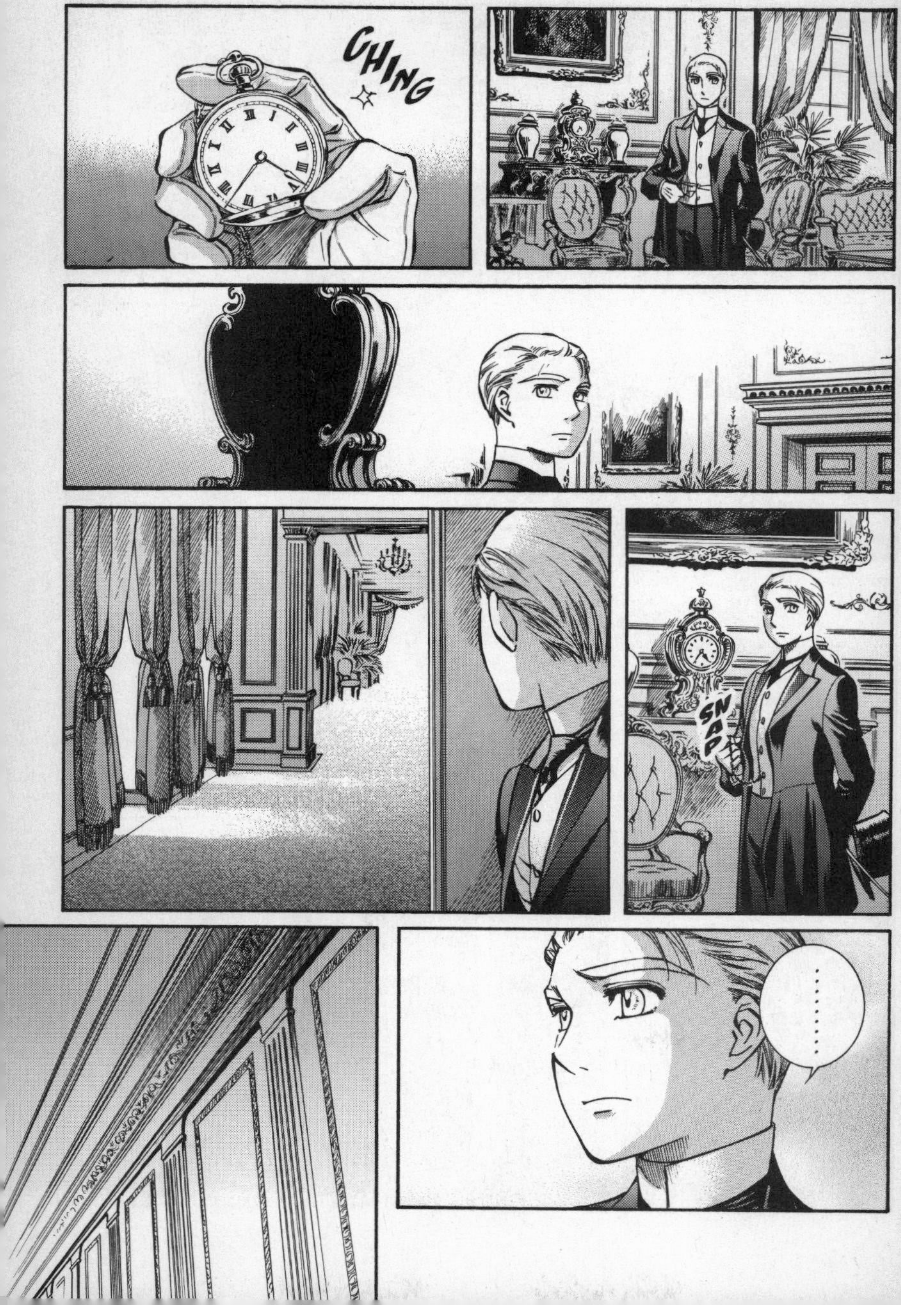
CHING
SNAP
......

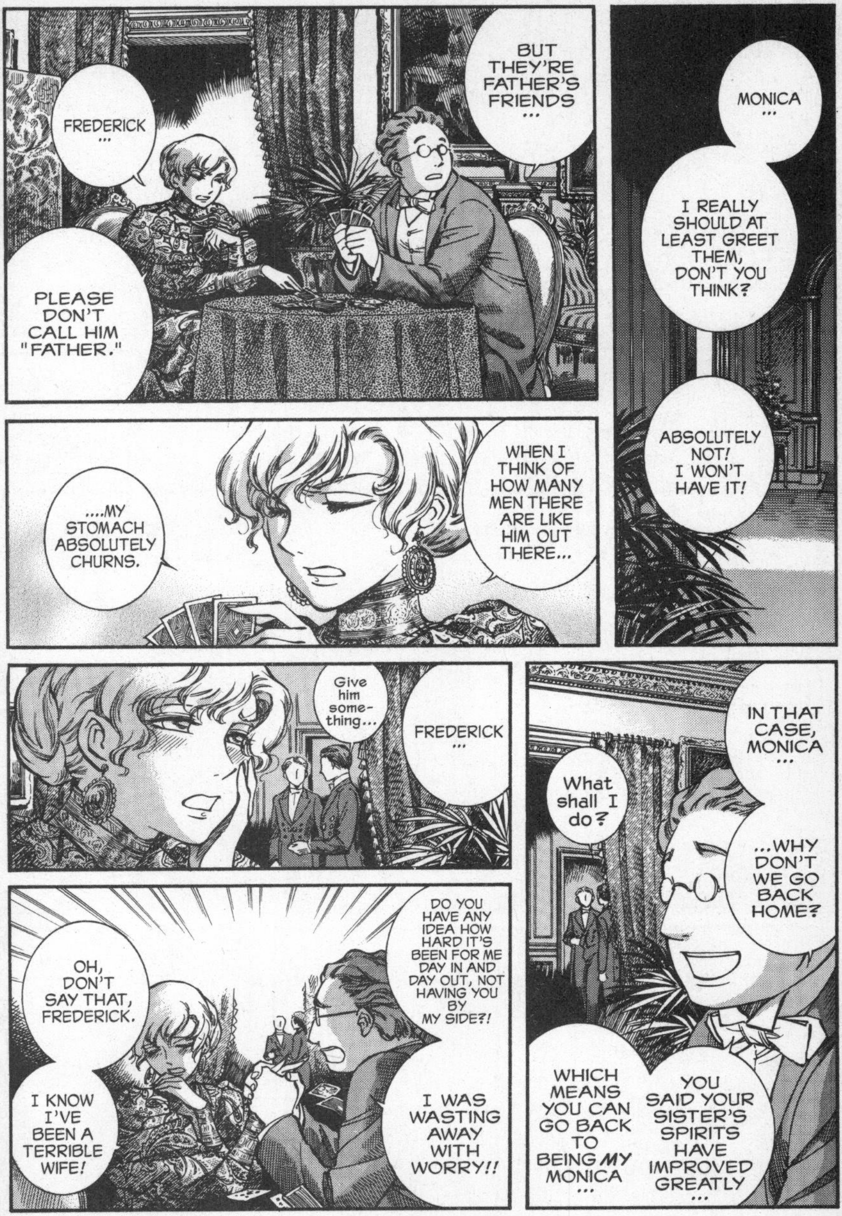
MONICA ...
I REALLY SHOULD AT LEAST GREET THEM, DON'T YOU THINK?
ABSOLUTELY NOT! I WON'T HAVE IT!
BUT THEY'RE FATHER'S FRIENDS ...
FREDERICK ...
PLEASE DON'T CALL HIM "FATHER."
WHEN I THINK OF HOW MANY MEN THERE ARE LIKE HIM OUT THERE...
....MY STOMACH ABSOLUTELY CHURNS.
IN THAT CASE, MONICA ...
What shall I do?
...WHY DON'T WE GO BACK HOME?
YOU SAID YOUR SISTER'S SPIRITS HAVE IMPROVED GREATLY ...
WHICH MEANS YOU CAN GO BACK TO BEING MY MONICA ...
FREDERICK ...
Give him some-thing...
DO YOU HAVE ANY IDEA HOW HARD IT'S BEEN FOR ME DAY IN AND DAY OUT, NOT HAVING YOU BY MY SIDE?!
I WAS WASTING AWAY WITH WORRY!!
OH, DON'T SAY THAT, FREDERICK.
I KNOW I'VE BEEN A TERRIBLE WIFE!

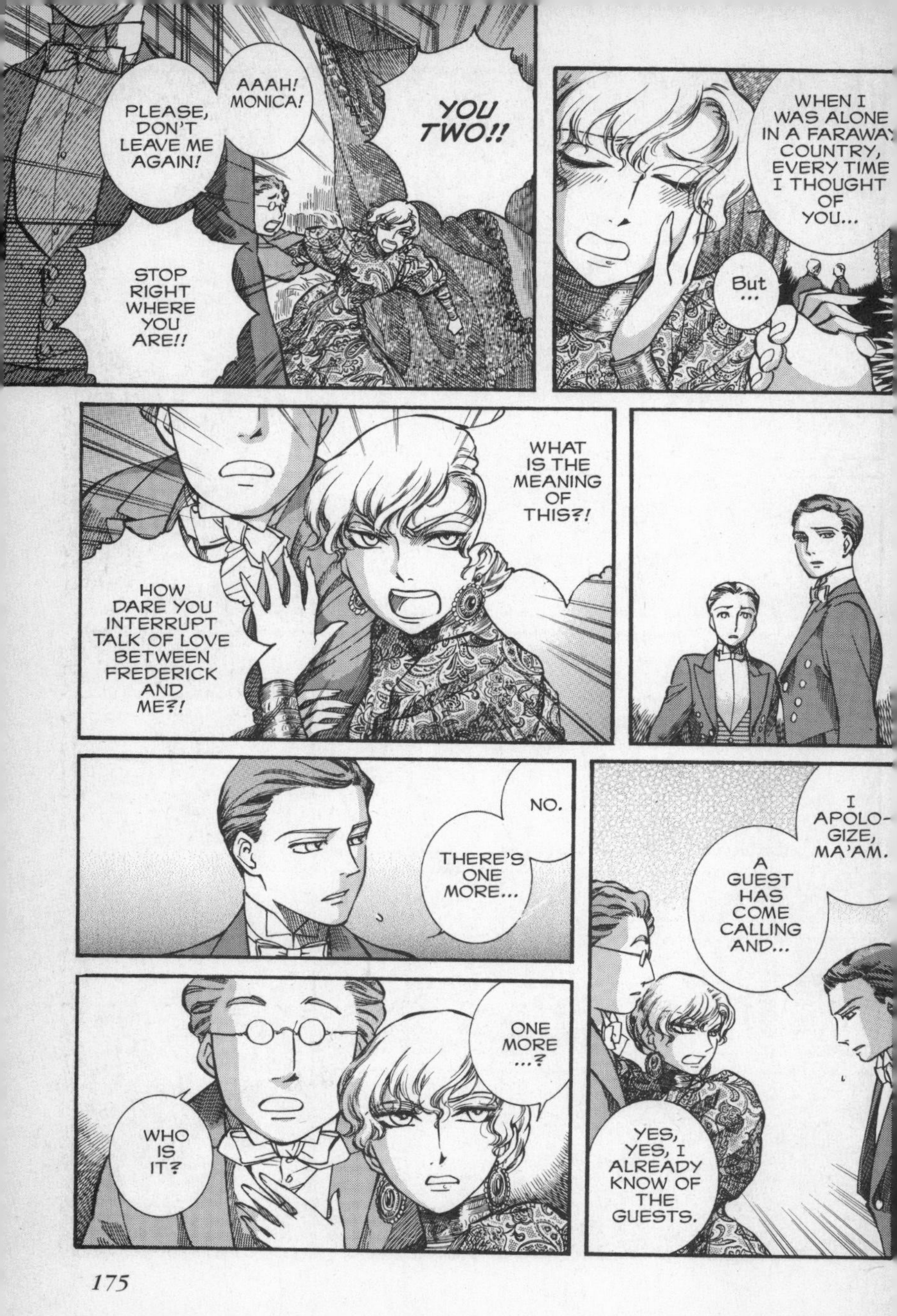
WHEN I WAS ALONE IN A FARAWAY COUNTRY, EVERY TIME I THOUGHT OF YOU...
But ...
YOU TWO!!
AAAH! MONICA!
PLEASE, DON'T LEAVE ME AGAIN!
STOP RIGHT WHERE YOU ARE!!
WHAT IS THE MEANING OF THIS?!
HOW DARE YOU INTERRUPT TALK OF LOVE BETWEEN FREDERICK AND ME?!
I APOLOGIZE, MA'AM.
A GUEST HAS COME CALLING AND...
YES, YES, I ALREADY KNOW OF THE GUESTS.
NO.
THERE'S ONE MORE...
ONE MORE ...?
WHO IS IT?

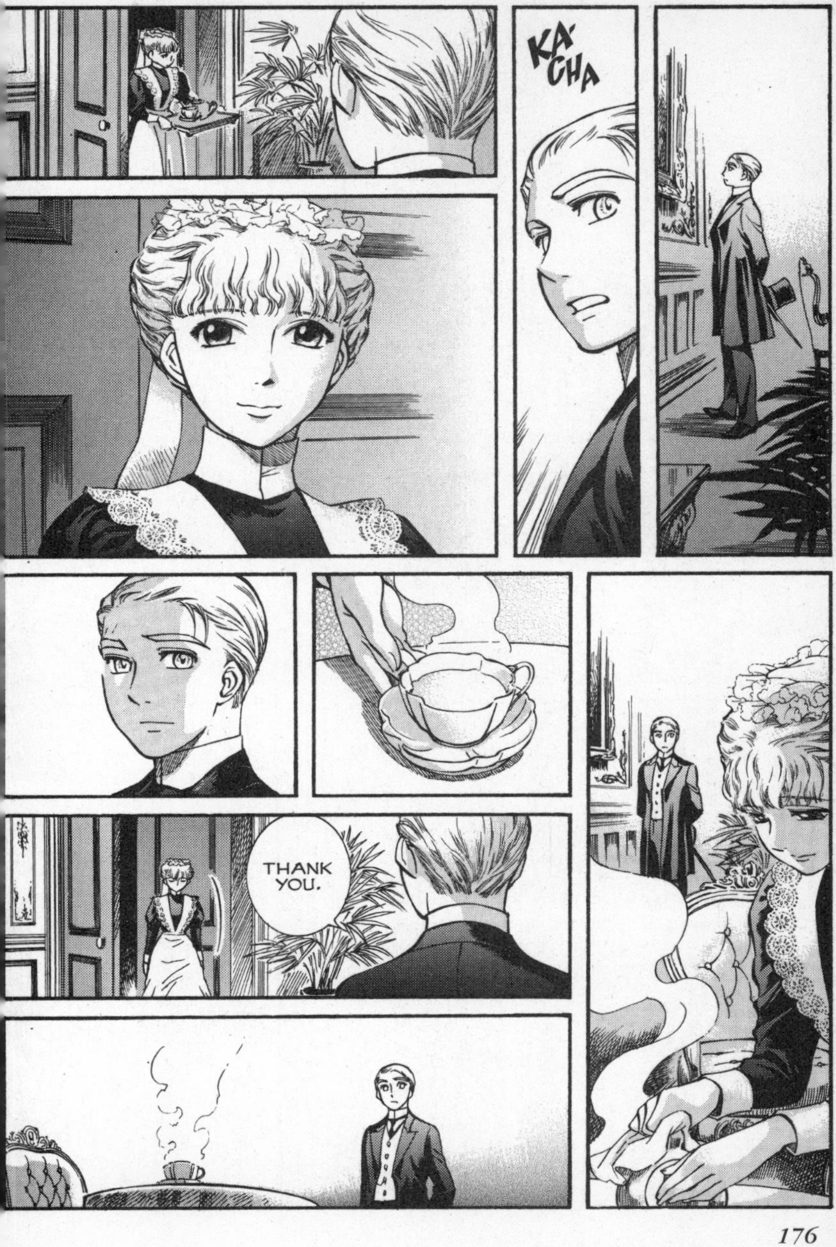
KA'CHA
THANK YOU.

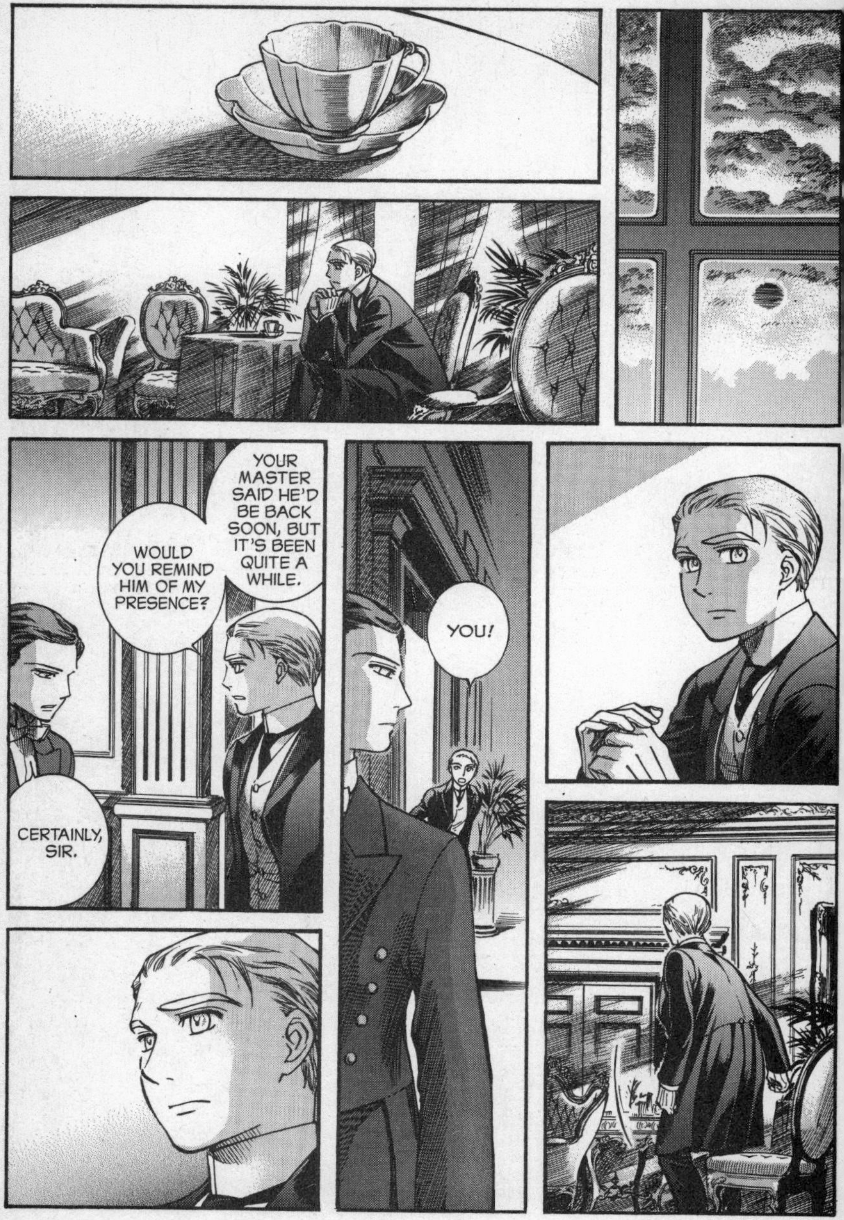
YOU!
YOUR MASTER SAID HE'D BE BACK SOON, BUT IT'S BEEN QUITE A WHILE.
WOULD YOU REMIND HIM OF MY PRESENCE?
CERTAINLY, SIR.

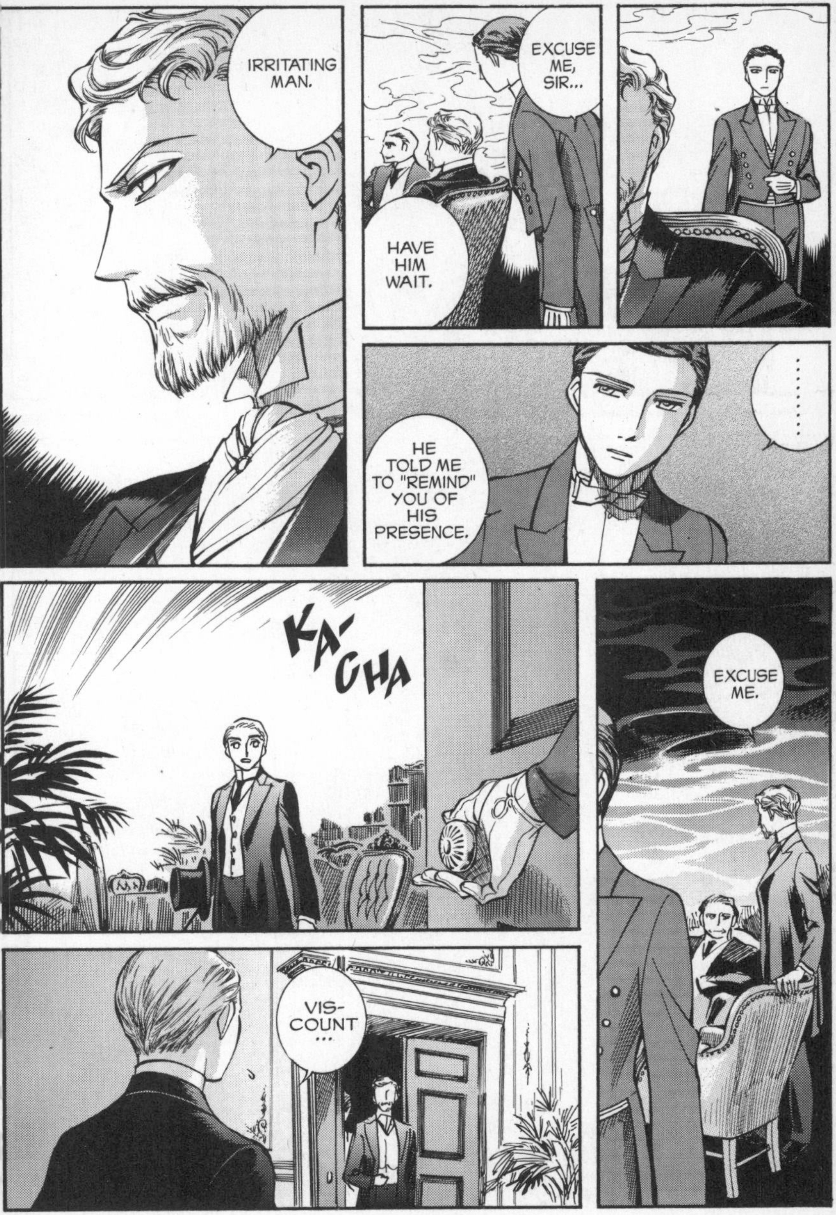
EXCUSE ME, SIR...
HAVE HIM WAIT.
......
HE TOLD ME TO "REMIND" YOU OF HIS PRESENCE.
IRRITATING MAN.
EXCUSE ME.
KA-CHA
VIS-COUNT...

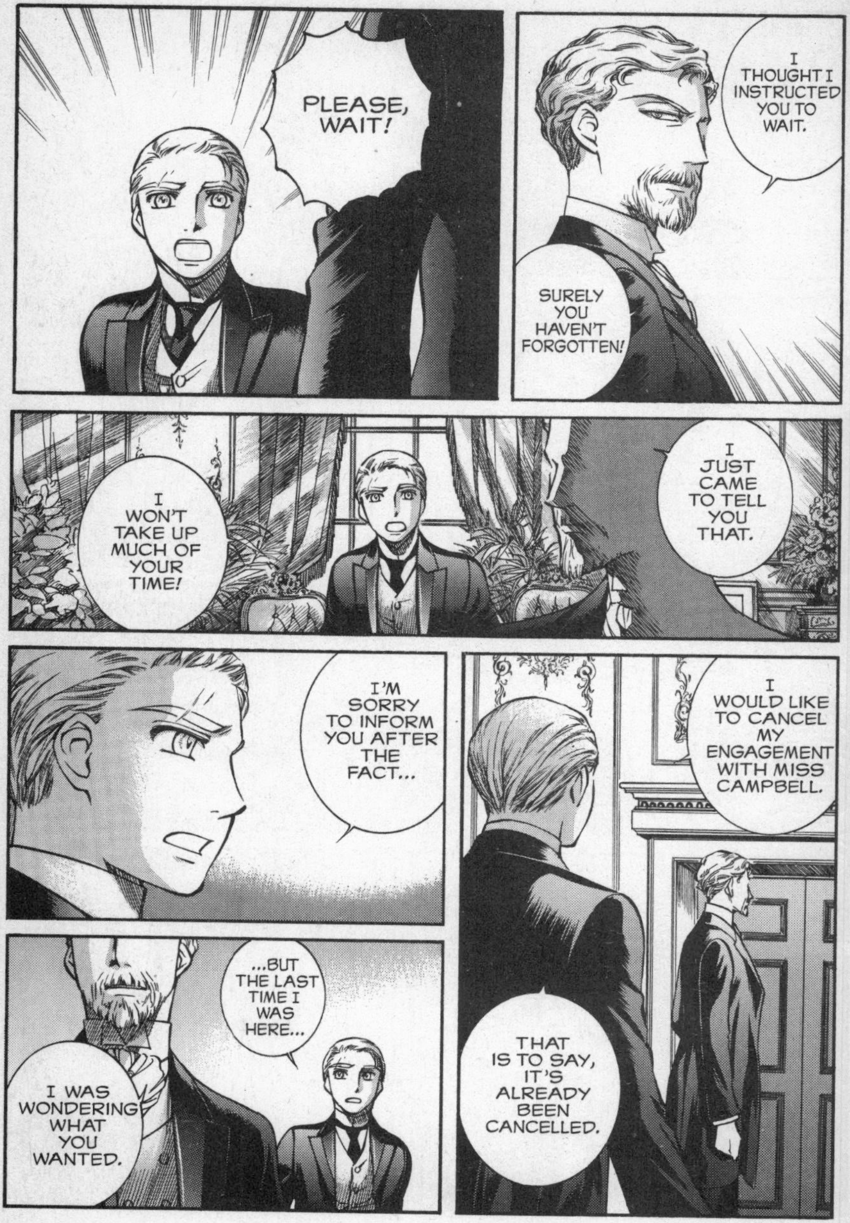
I THOUGHT I INSTRUCTED YOU TO WAIT.
SURELY YOU HAVEN'T FORGOTTEN!
PLEASE, WAIT!
I JUST CAME TO TELL YOU THAT.
I WON'T TAKE UP MUCH OF YOUR TIME!
I WOULD LIKE TO CANCEL MY ENGAGEMENT WITH MISS CAMPBELL.
THAT IS TO SAY, IT'S ALREADY BEEN CANCELLED.
I'M SORRY TO INFORM YOU AFTER THE FACT...
...BUT THE LAST TIME I WAS HERE...
I WAS WONDERING WHAT YOU WANTED.

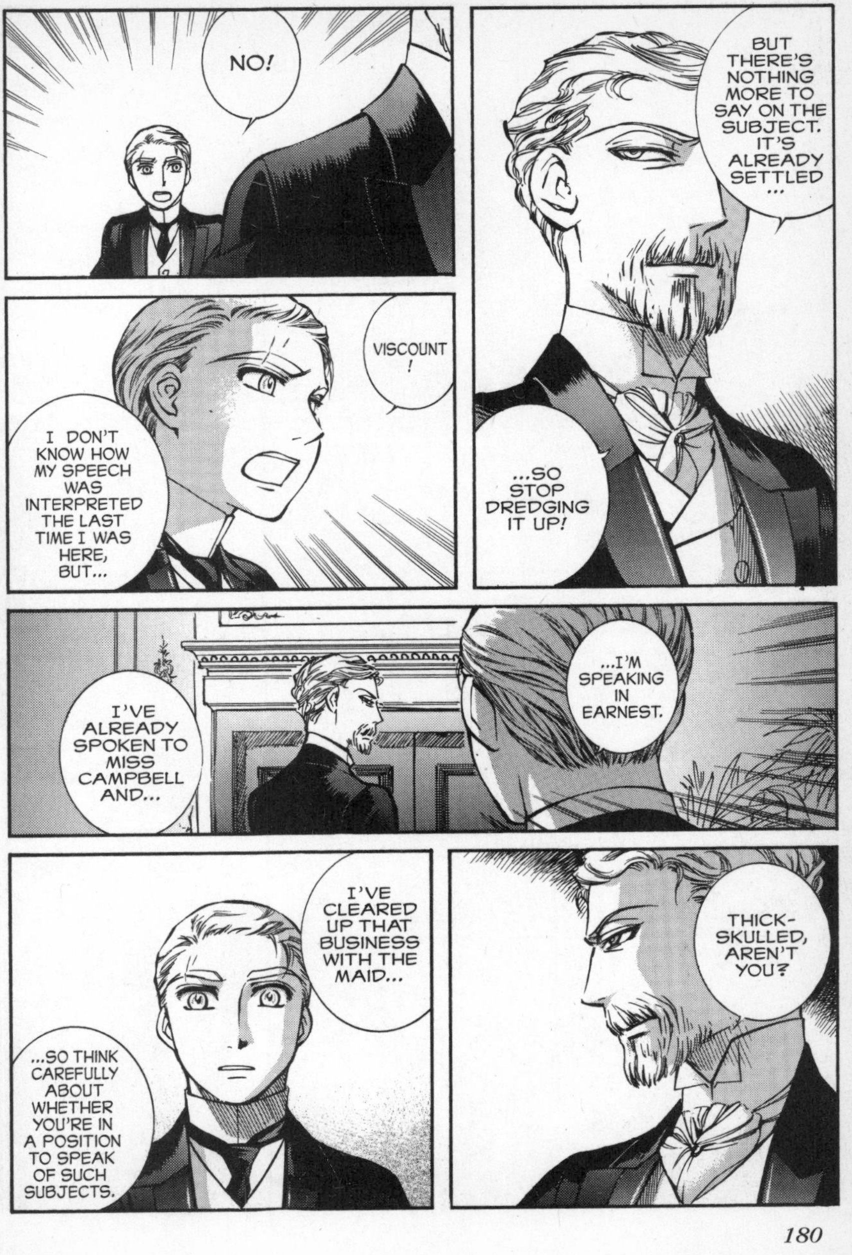
BUT THERE'S NOTHING MORE TO SAY ON THE SUBJECT. IT'S ALREADY SETTLED ...
...SO STOP DREDGING IT UP!
NO!
VISCOUNT!
I DON'T KNOW HOW MY SPEECH WAS INTERPRETED THE LAST TIME I WAS HERE, BUT...
...I'M SPEAKING IN EARNEST.
I'VE ALREADY SPOKEN TO MISS CAMPBELL AND...
THICK-SKULLED, AREN'T YOU?
I'VE CLEARED UP THAT BUSINESS WITH THE MAID...
...SO THINK CAREFULLY ABOUT WHETHER YOU'RE IN A POSITION TO SPEAK OF SUCH SUBJECTS.

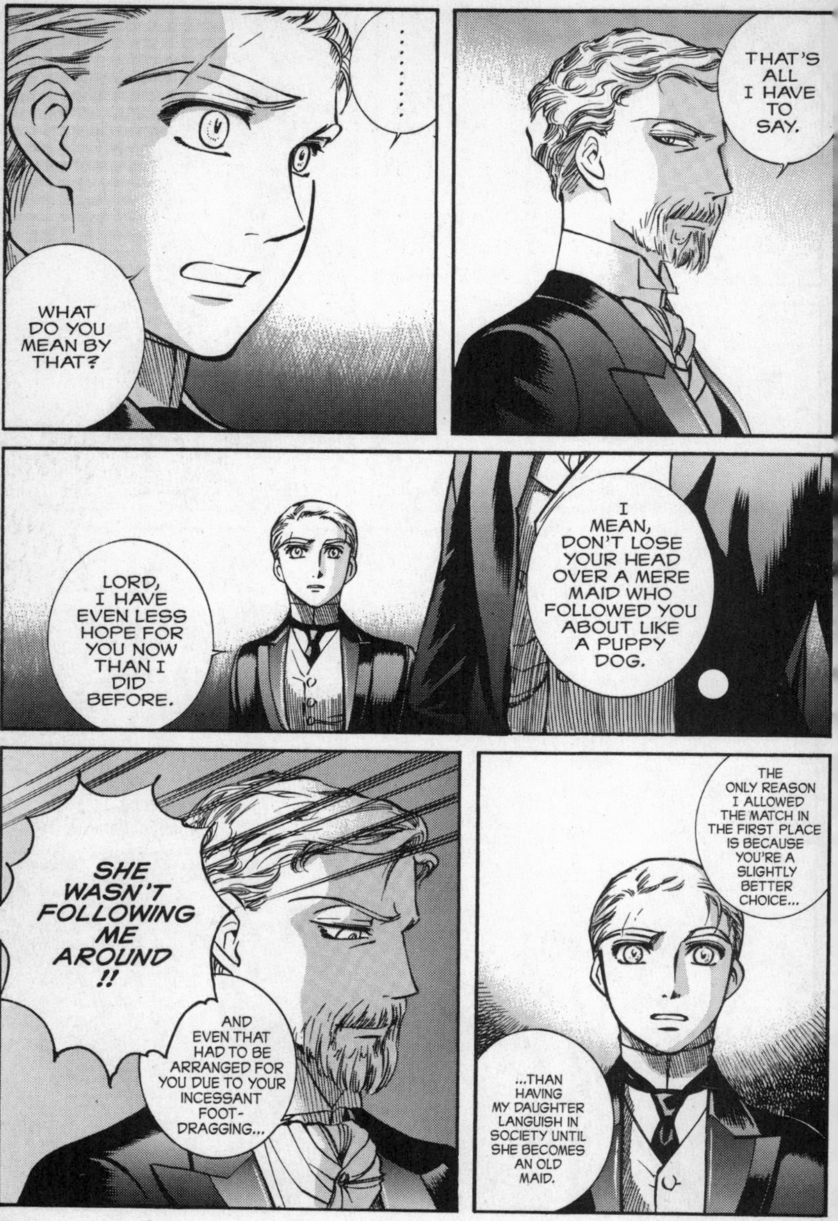
THAT'S ALL I HAVE TO SAY.
......
WHAT DO YOU MEAN BY THAT?
I MEAN, DON'T LOSE YOUR HEAD OVER A MERE MAID WHO FOLLOWED YOU ABOUT LIKE A PUPPY DOG.
LORD, I HAVE EVEN LESS HOPE FOR YOU NOW THAN I DID BEFORE.
THE ONLY REASON I ALLOWED THE MATCH IN THE FIRST PLACE IS BECAUSE YOU'RE A SLIGHTLY BETTER CHOICE...
...THAN HAVING MY DAUGHTER LANGUISH IN SOCIETY UNTIL SHE BECOMES AN OLD MAID.
AND EVEN THAT HAD TO BE ARRANGED FOR YOU DUE TO YOUR INCESSANT FOOT-DRAGGING...
SHE WASN'T FOLLOWING ME AROUND!!

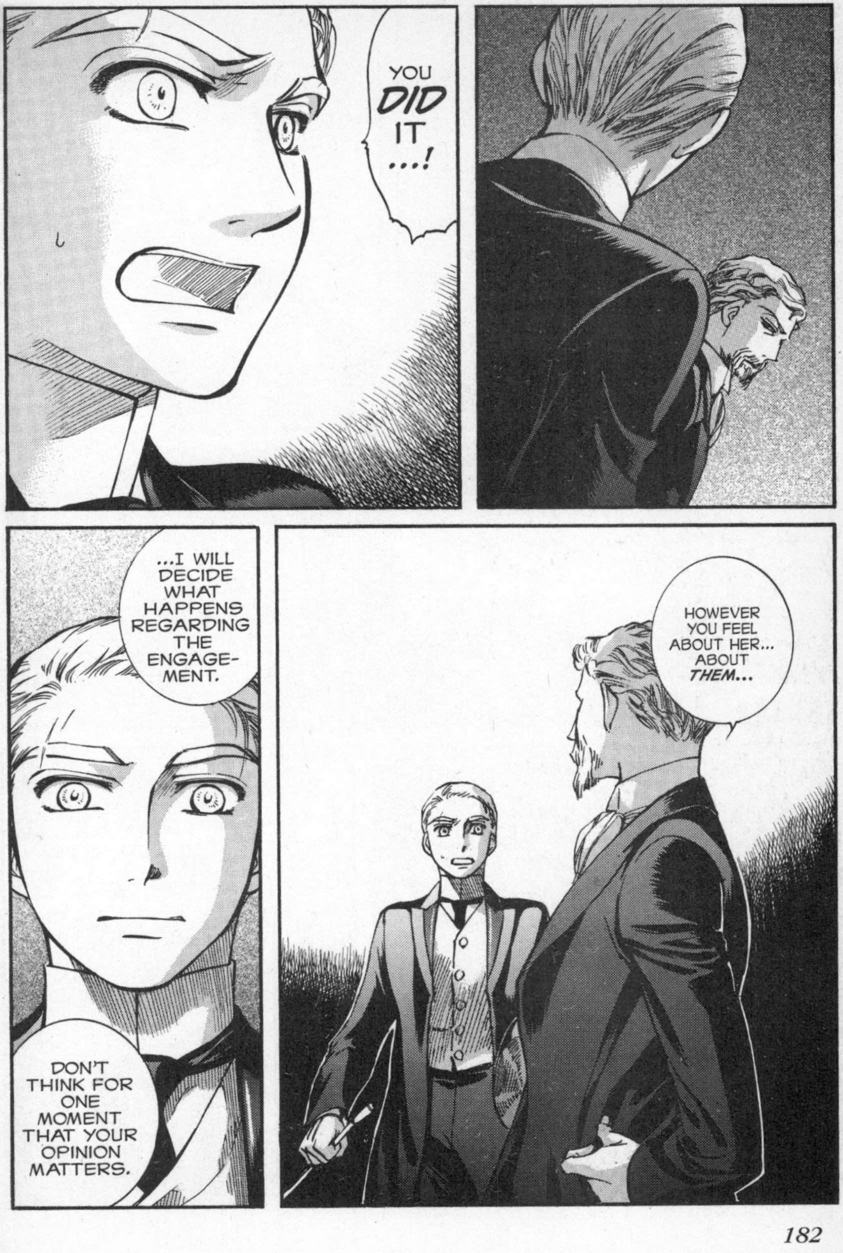
YOU *DID* IT ...!
HOWEVER YOU FEEL ABOUT HER... ABOUT *THEM*...
...I WILL DECIDE WHAT HAPPENS REGARDING THE ENGAGE-MENT.
DON'T THINK FOR ONE MOMENT THAT YOUR OPINION MATTERS.

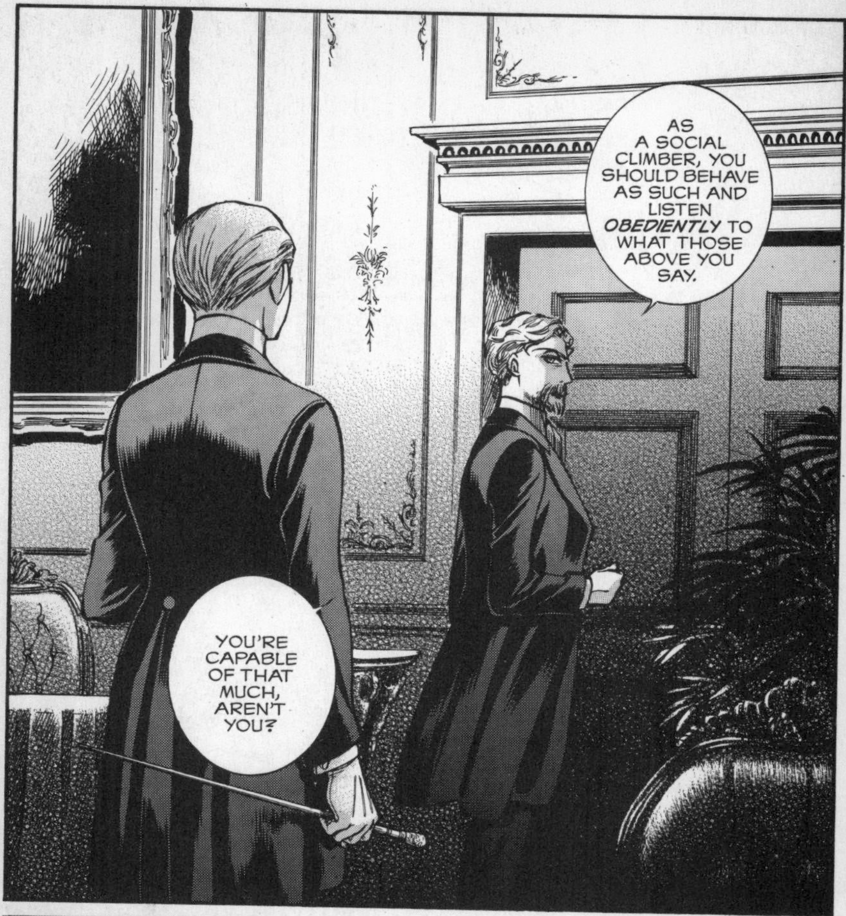
AS A SOCIAL CLIMBER, YOU SHOULD BEHAVE AS SUCH AND LISTEN **OBEDIENTLY** TO WHAT THOSE ABOVE YOU SAY.
YOU'RE CAPABLE OF THAT MUCH, AREN'T YOU?
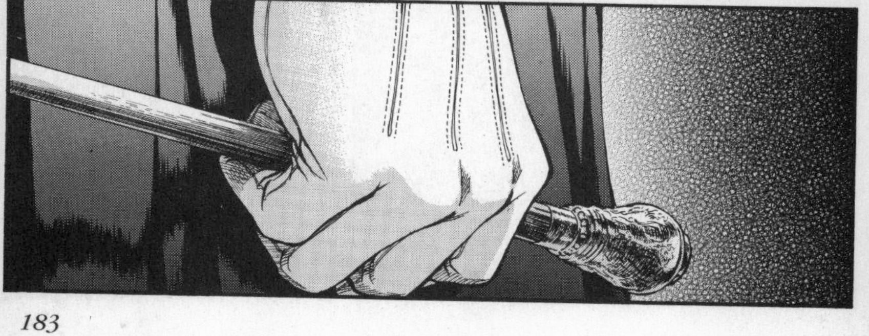

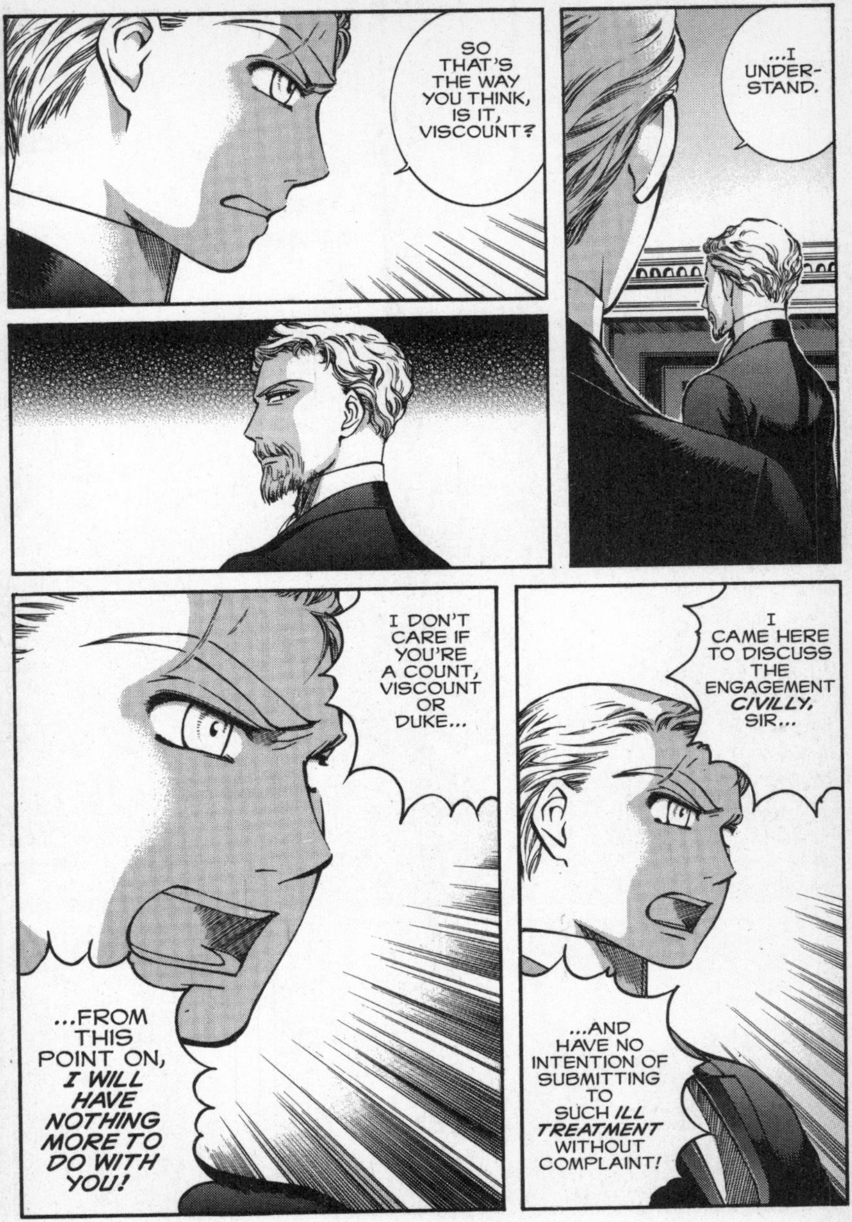
SO THAT'S THE WAY YOU THINK, IS IT, VISCOUNT?
...I UNDERSTAND.
I CAME HERE TO DISCUSS THE ENGAGEMENT *CIVILLY,* SIR...
...AND HAVE NO INTENTION OF SUBMITTING TO SUCH *ILL TREATMENT* WITHOUT COMPLAINT!
I DON'T CARE IF YOU'RE A COUNT, VISCOUNT OR DUKE...
...FROM THIS POINT ON, ***I WILL HAVE NOTHING MORE TO DO WITH YOU!***

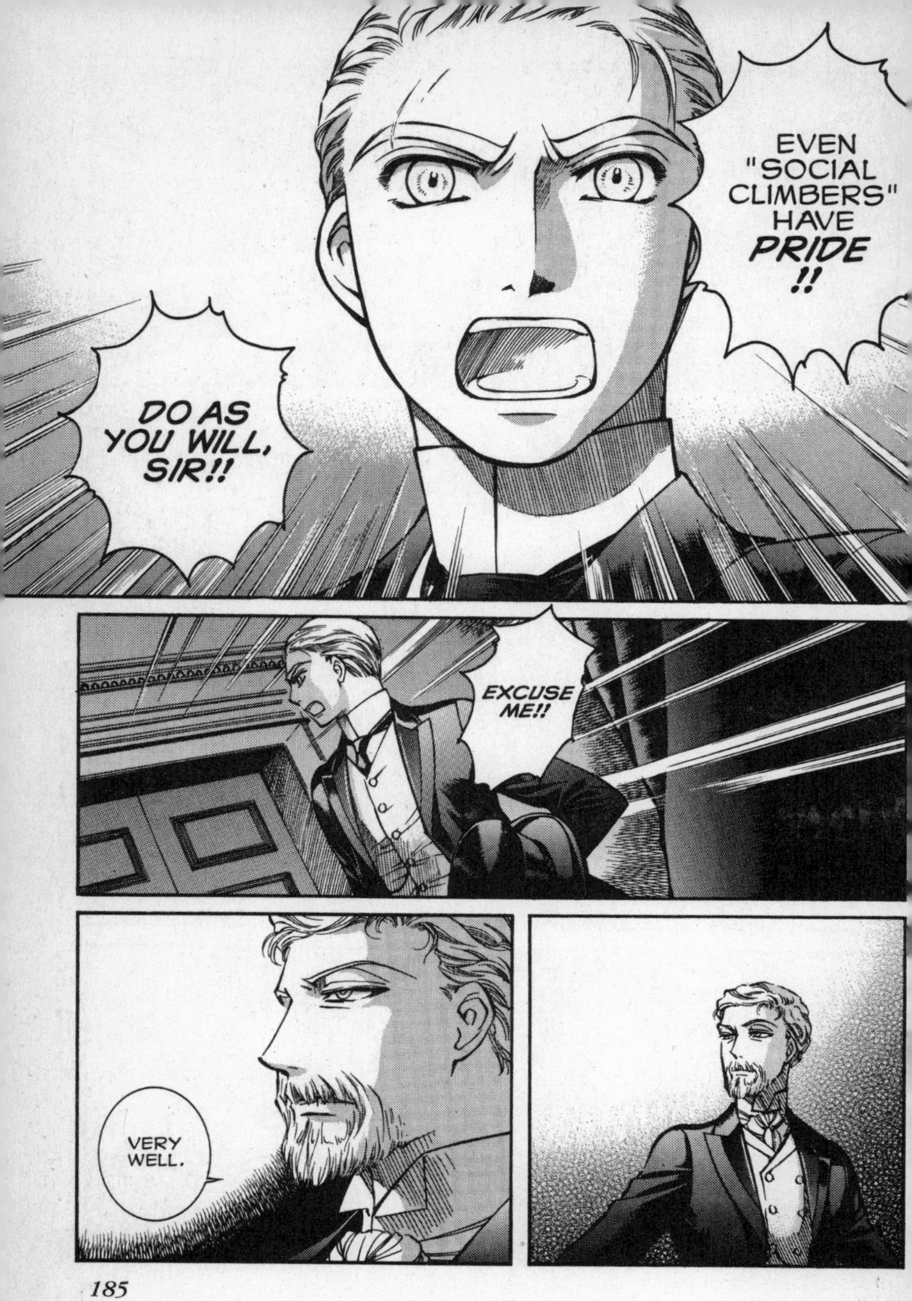
EVEN "SOCIAL CLIMBERS" HAVE PRIDE !!
DO AS YOU WILL, SIR!!
EXCUSE ME!!
VERY WELL.

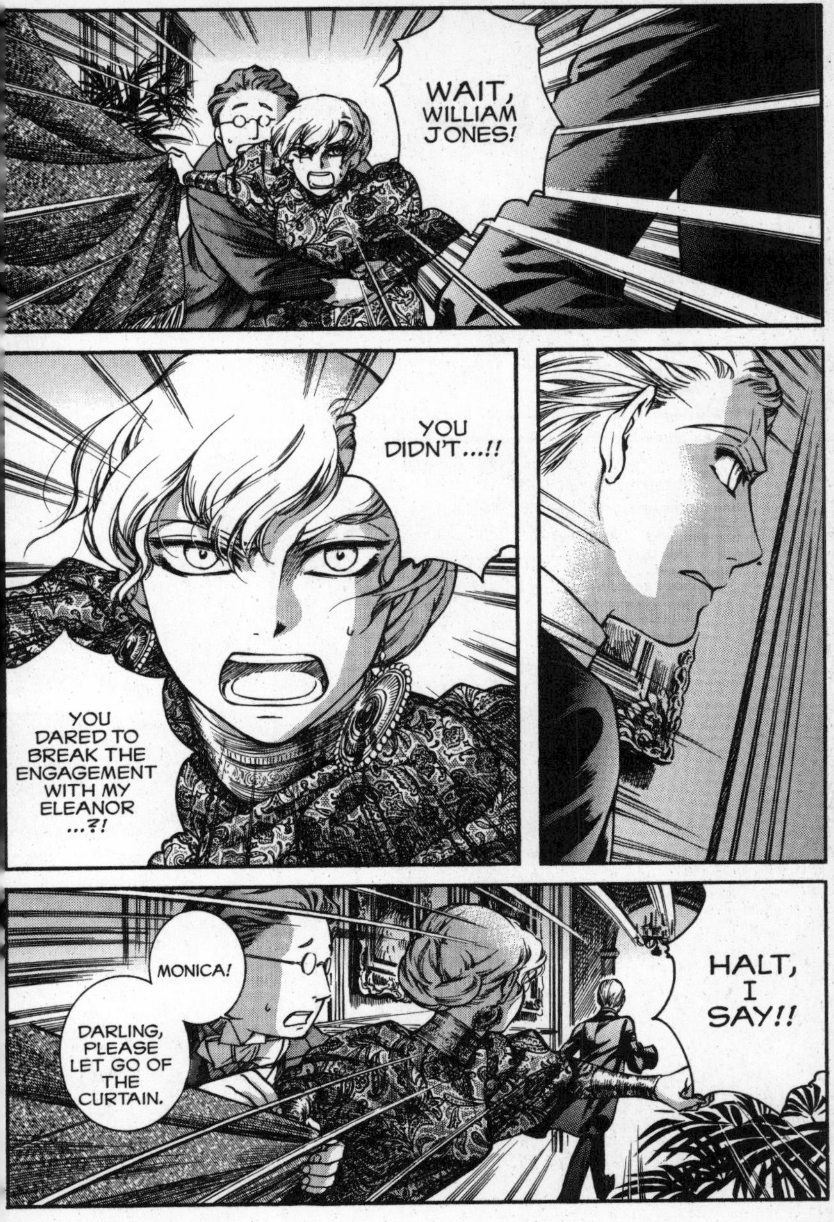
WAIT, WILLIAM JONES!
YOU DIDN'T...!!
YOU DARED TO BREAK THE ENGAGEMENT WITH MY ELEANOR ...?!
HALT, I SAY!!
MONICA!
DARLING, PLEASE LET GO OF THE CURTAIN.

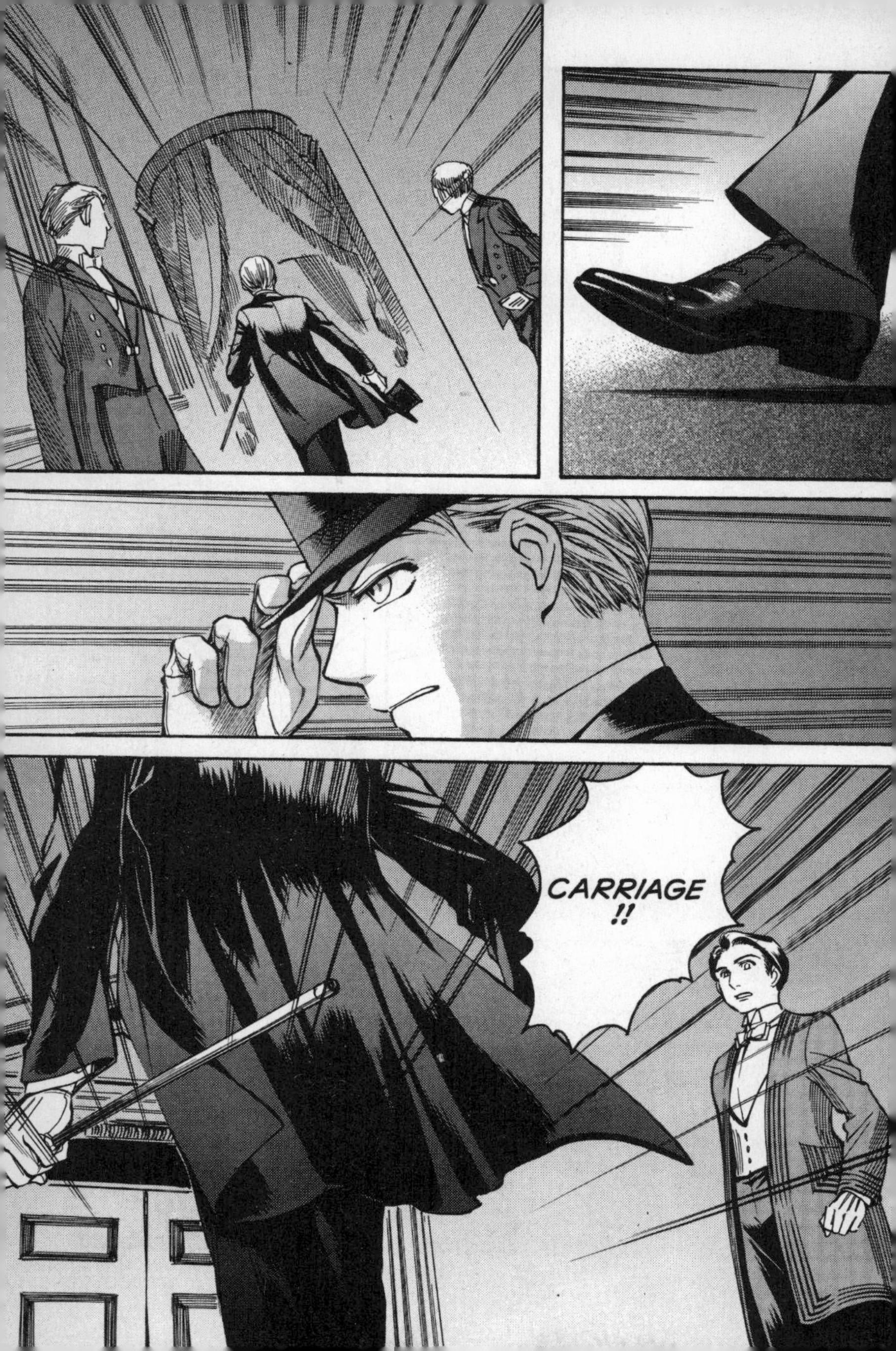
CARRIAGE !!

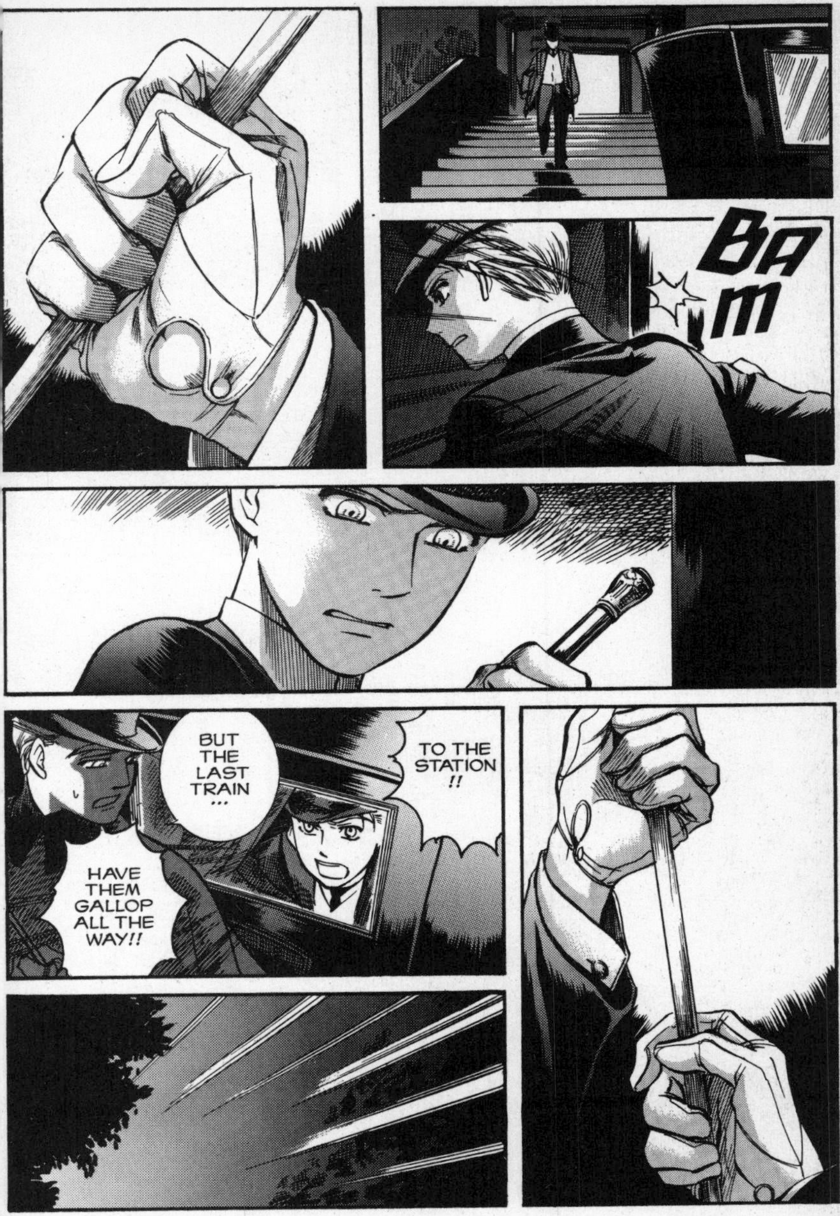
BAM
TO THE STATION !!
BUT THE LAST TRAIN ...
HAVE THEM GALLOP ALL THE WAY!!

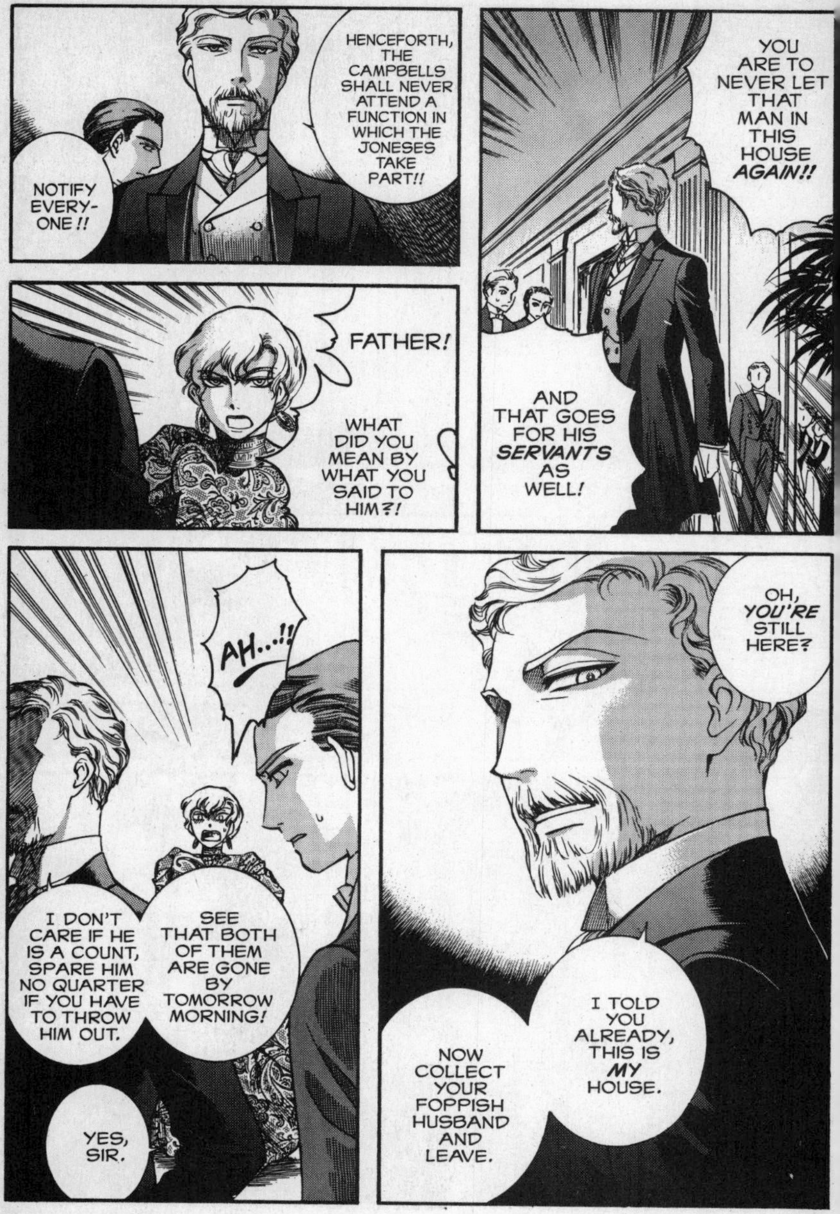
YOU ARE TO NEVER LET THAT MAN IN THIS HOUSE *AGAIN!!*
AND THAT GOES FOR HIS *SERVANTS* AS WELL!
HENCEFORTH, THE CAMPBELLS SHALL NEVER ATTEND A FUNCTION IN WHICH THE JONESES TAKE PART!!
NOTIFY EVERY-ONE!!
FATHER!
WHAT DID YOU MEAN BY WHAT YOU SAID TO HIM?!
OH, *YOU'RE* STILL HERE?
I TOLD YOU ALREADY, THIS IS *MY* HOUSE.
NOW COLLECT YOUR FOPPISH HUSBAND AND LEAVE.
AH...!!
SEE THAT BOTH OF THEM ARE GONE BY TOMORROW MORNING!
I DON'T CARE IF HE IS A COUNT, SPARE HIM NO QUARTER IF YOU HAVE TO THROW HIM OUT.
YES, SIR.

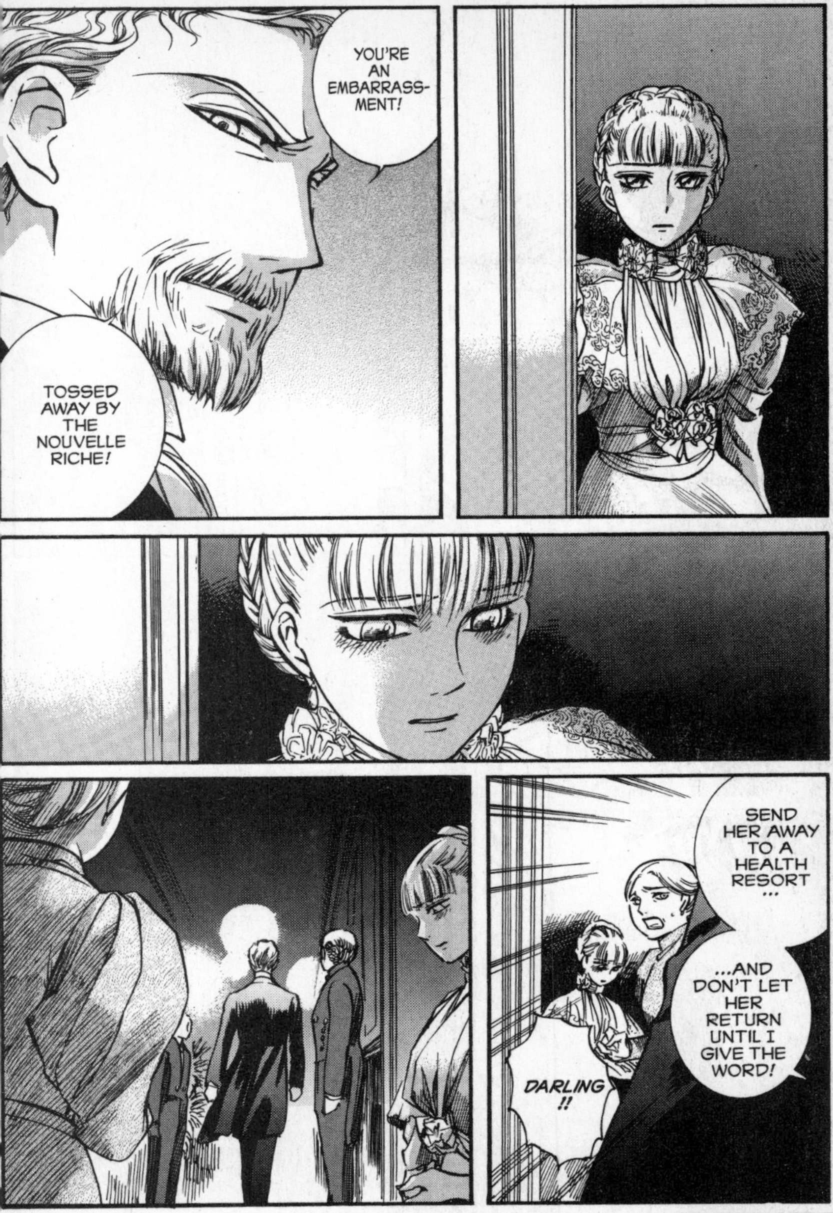
YOU'RE AN EMBARRASS-MENT!
TOSSED AWAY BY THE NOUVELLE RICHE!
SEND HER AWAY TO A HEALTH RESORT ...
...AND DON'T LET HER RETURN UNTIL I GIVE THE WORD!
DARLING !!

Chapter Fifty:
The End

EPILOGUE

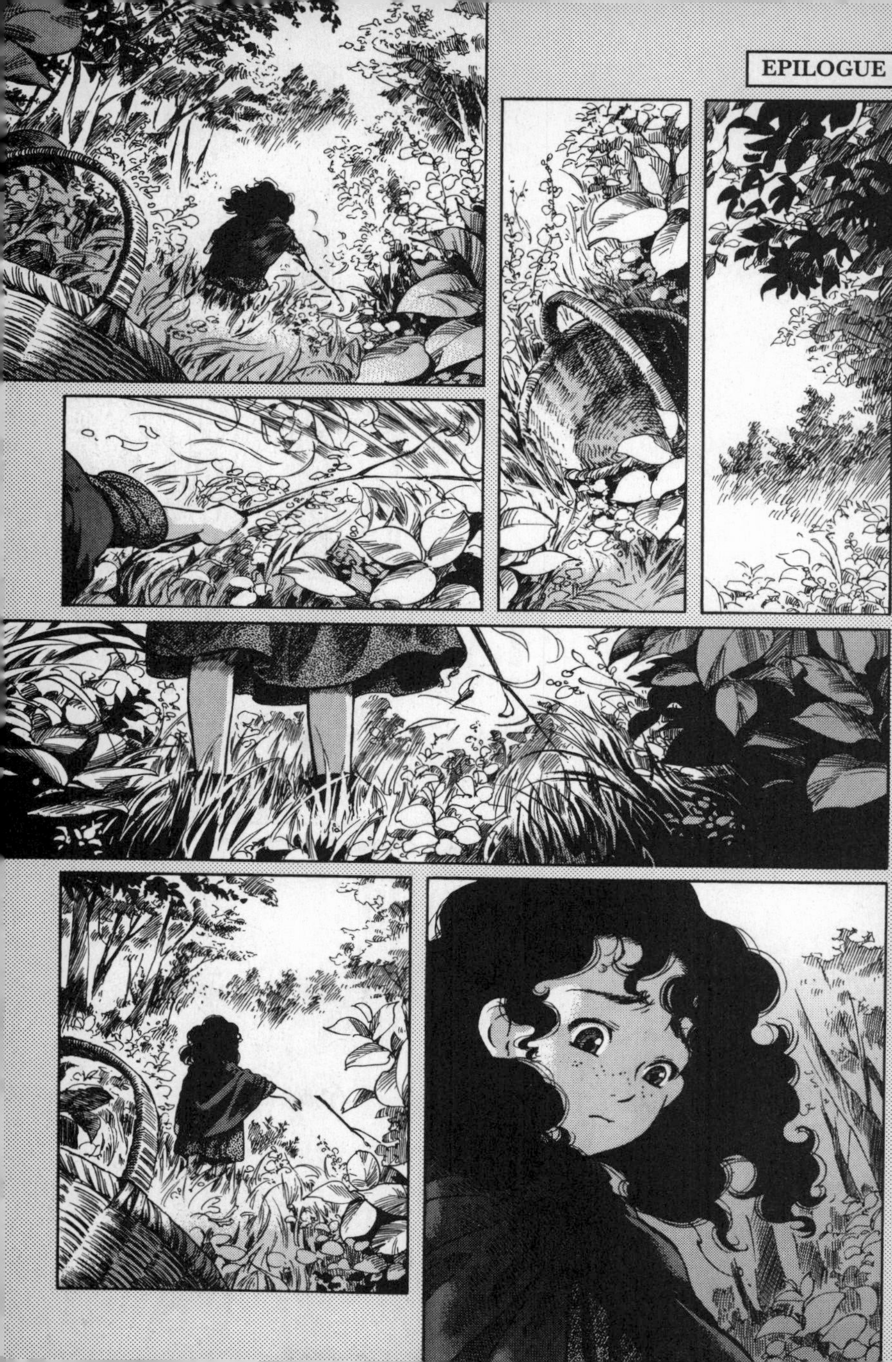

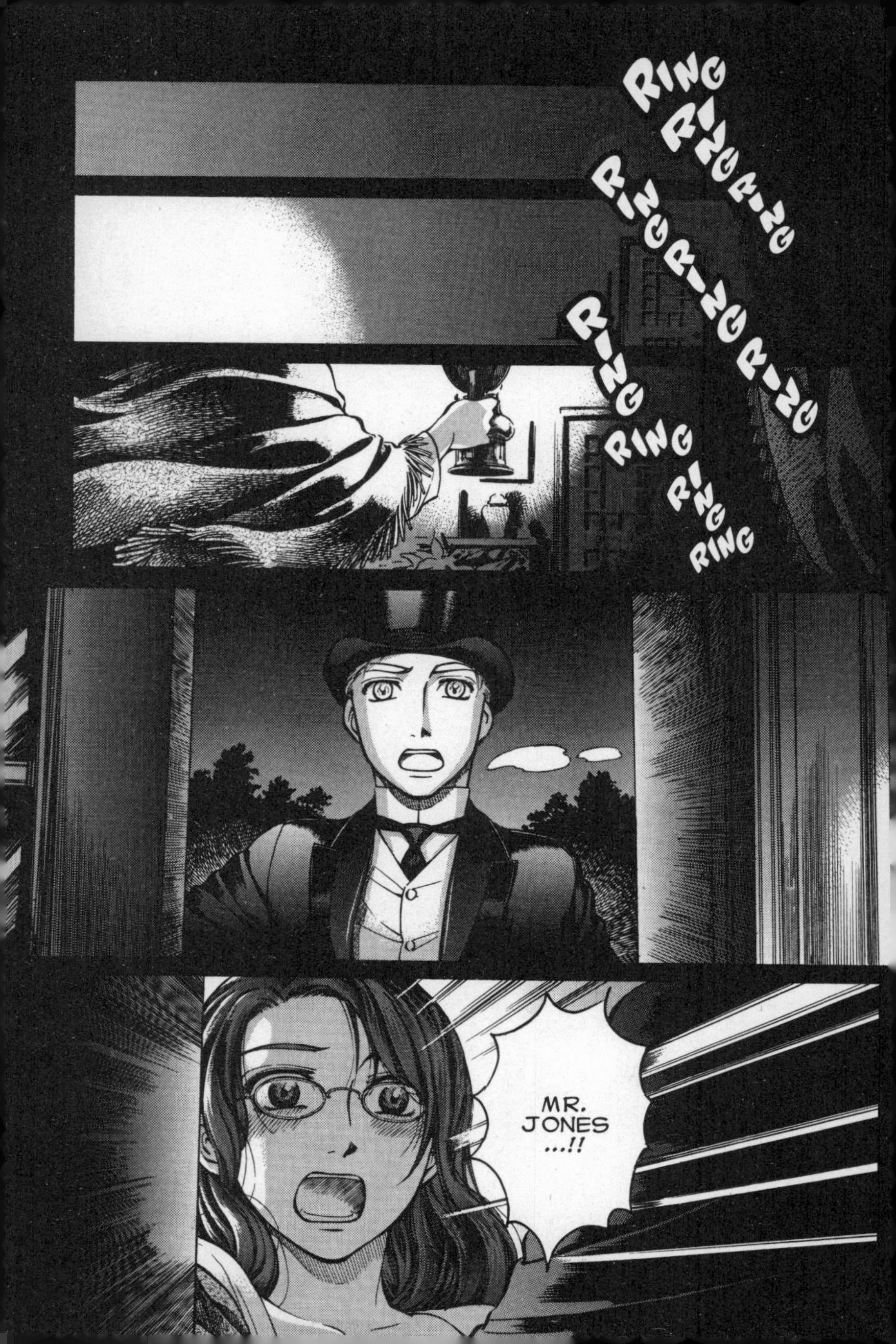
RING RING-RING-R-RING-R-RING-R-RING
RING RING RING RING
MR. JONES ...!!

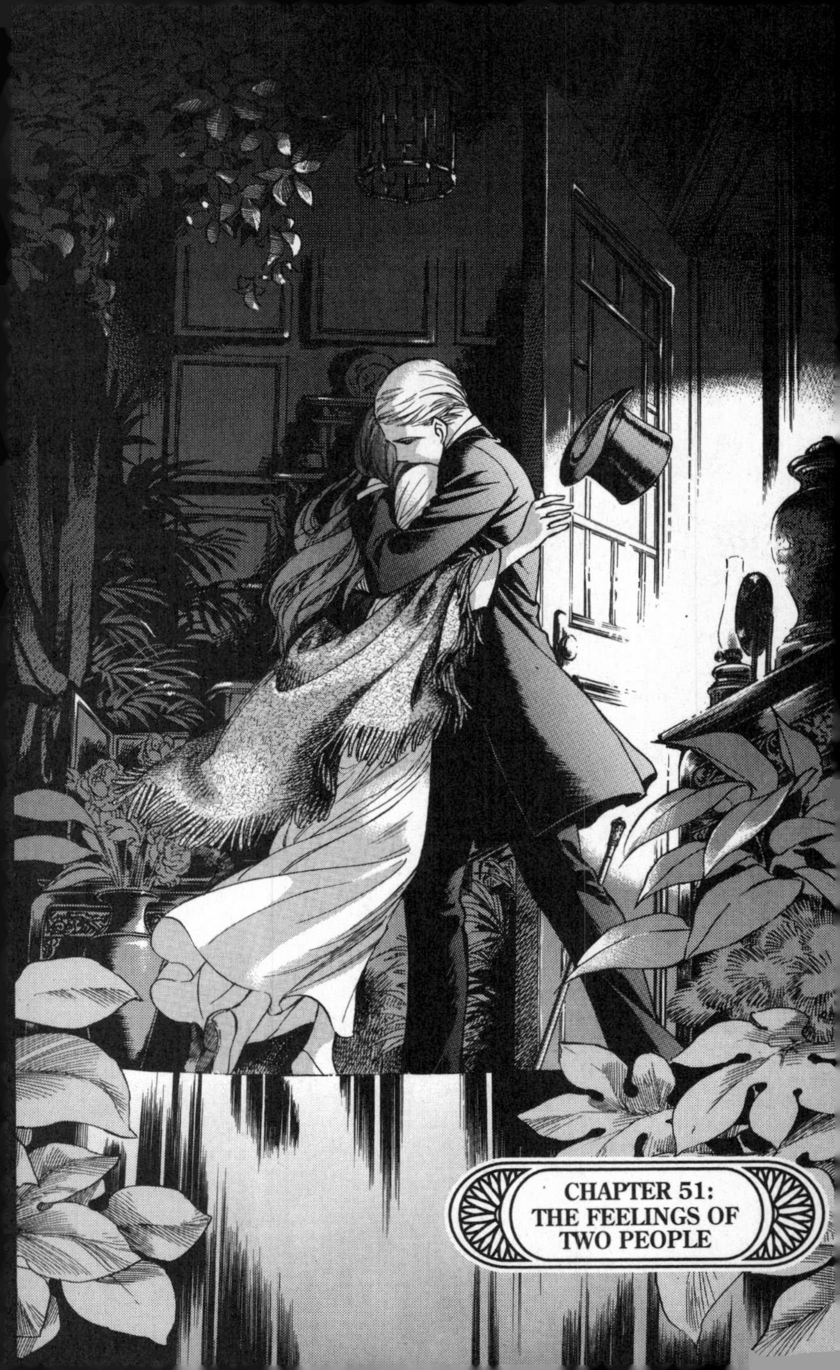
CHAPTER 51:
THE FEELINGS OF
TWO PEOPLE

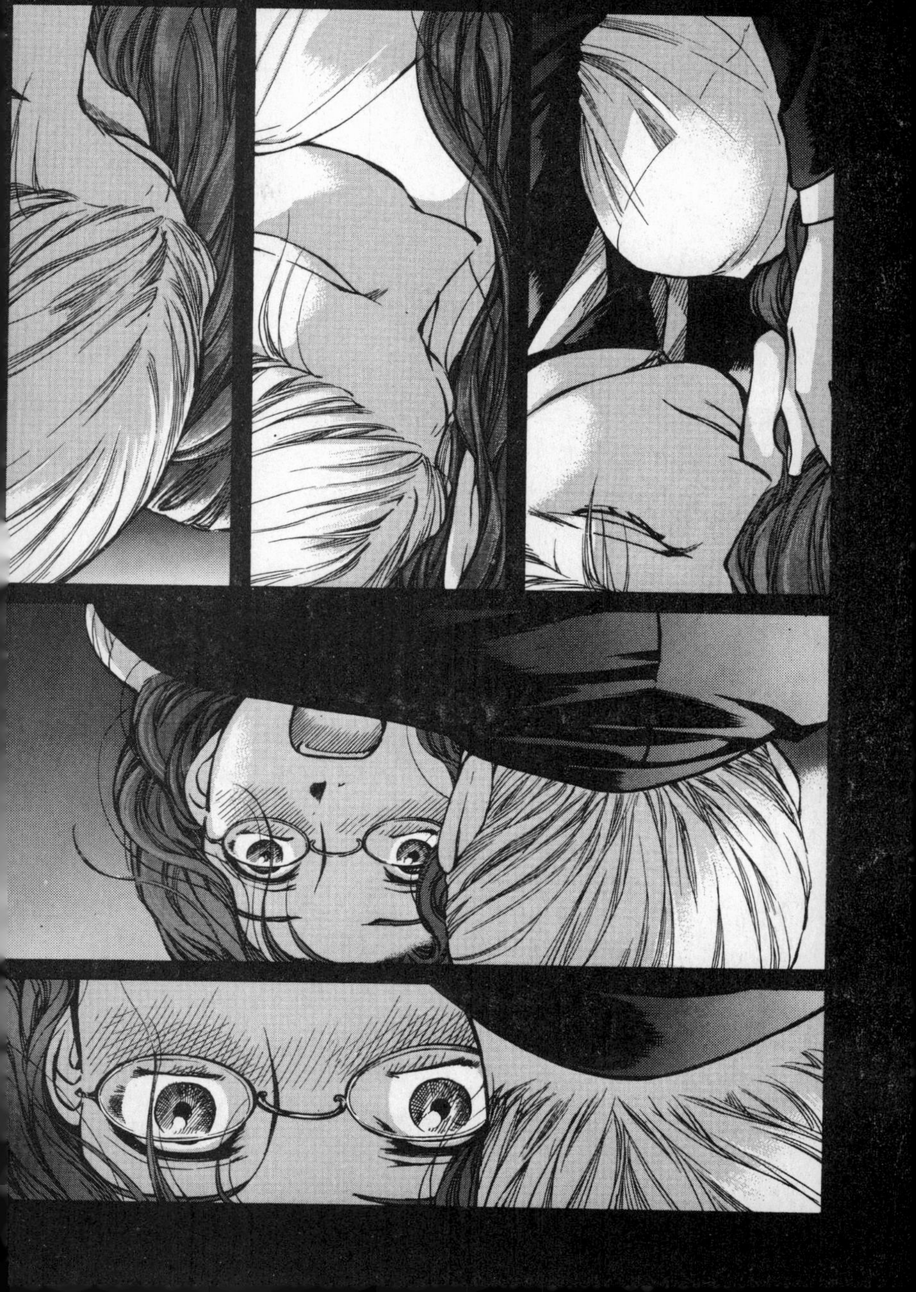

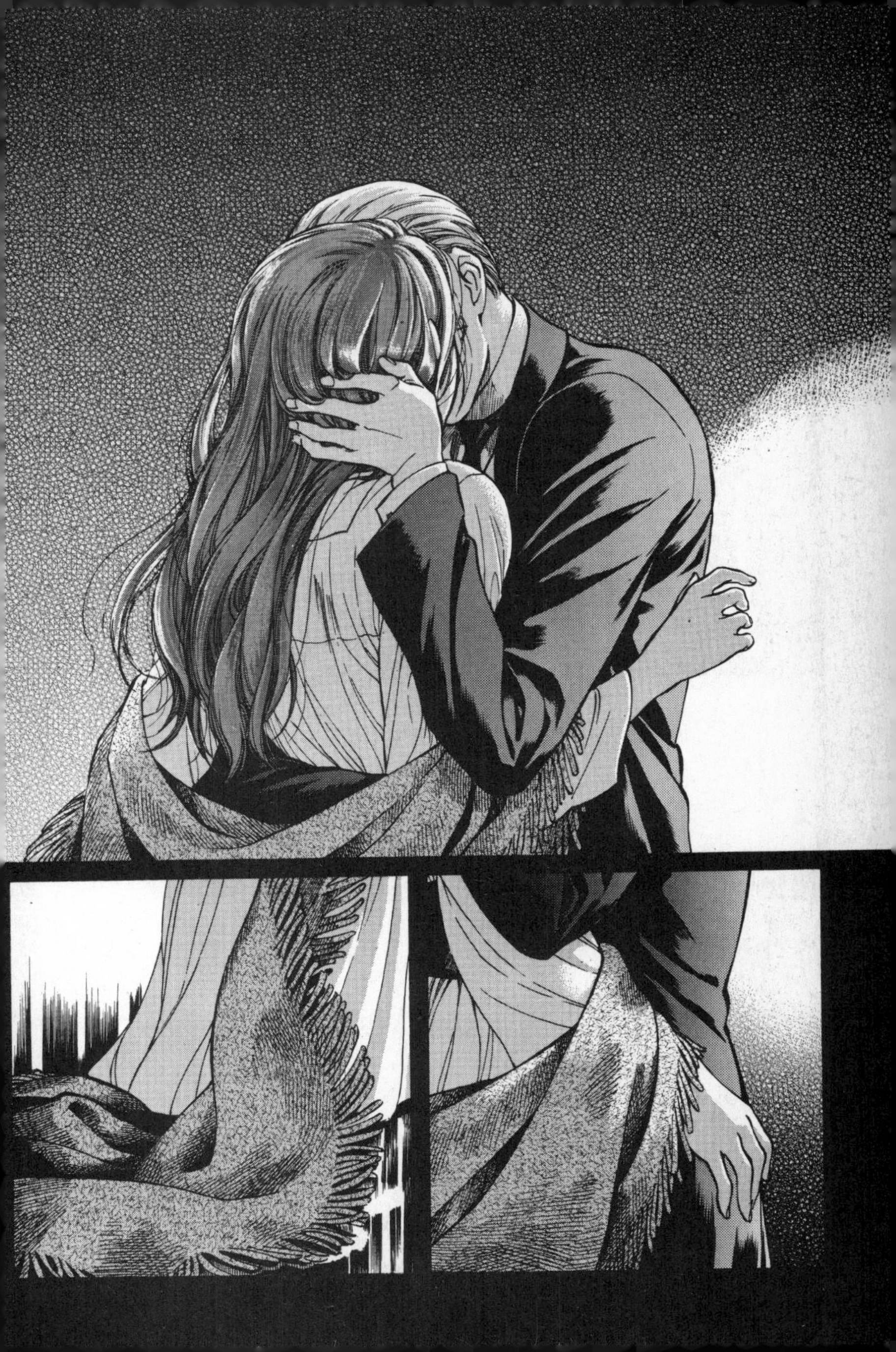

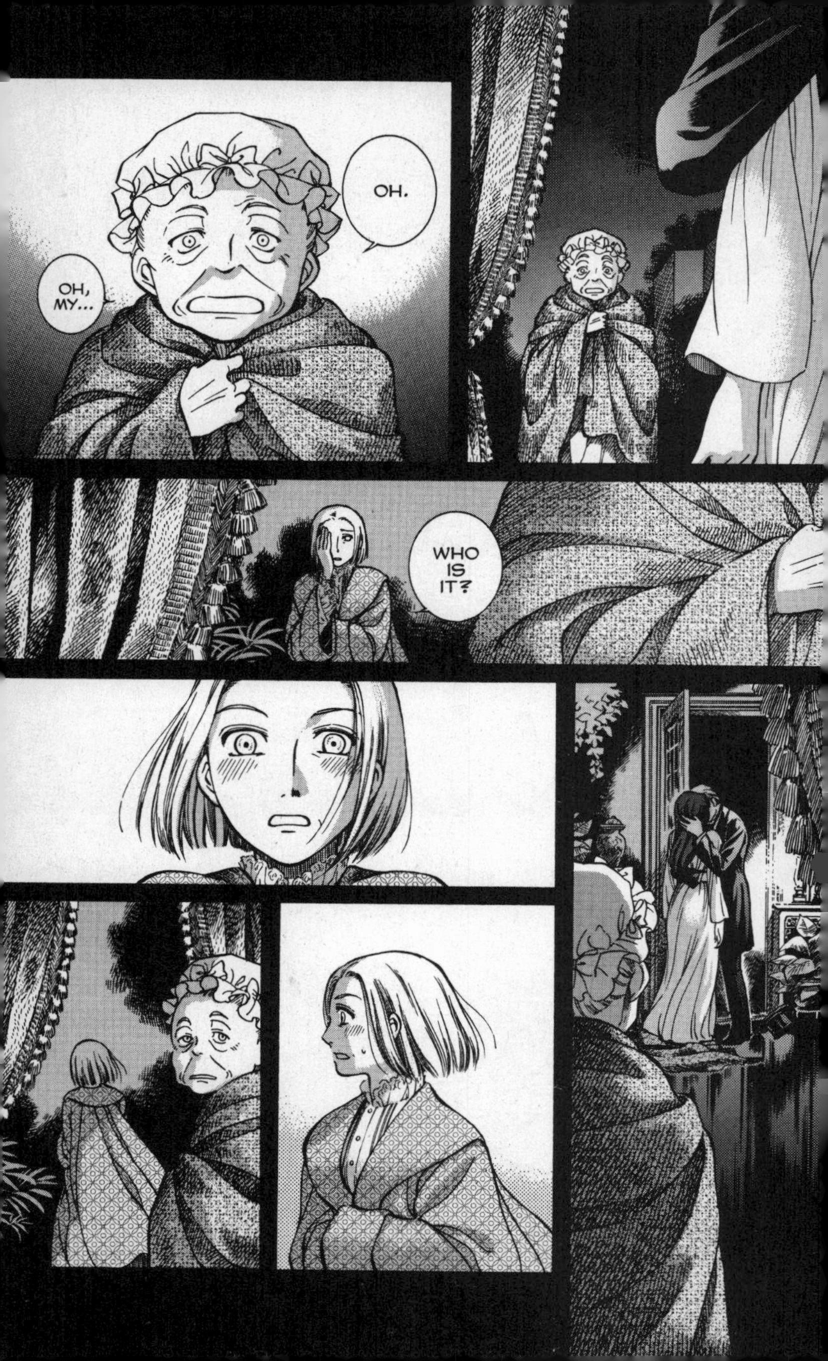
OH.
OH, MY...
WHO IS IT?

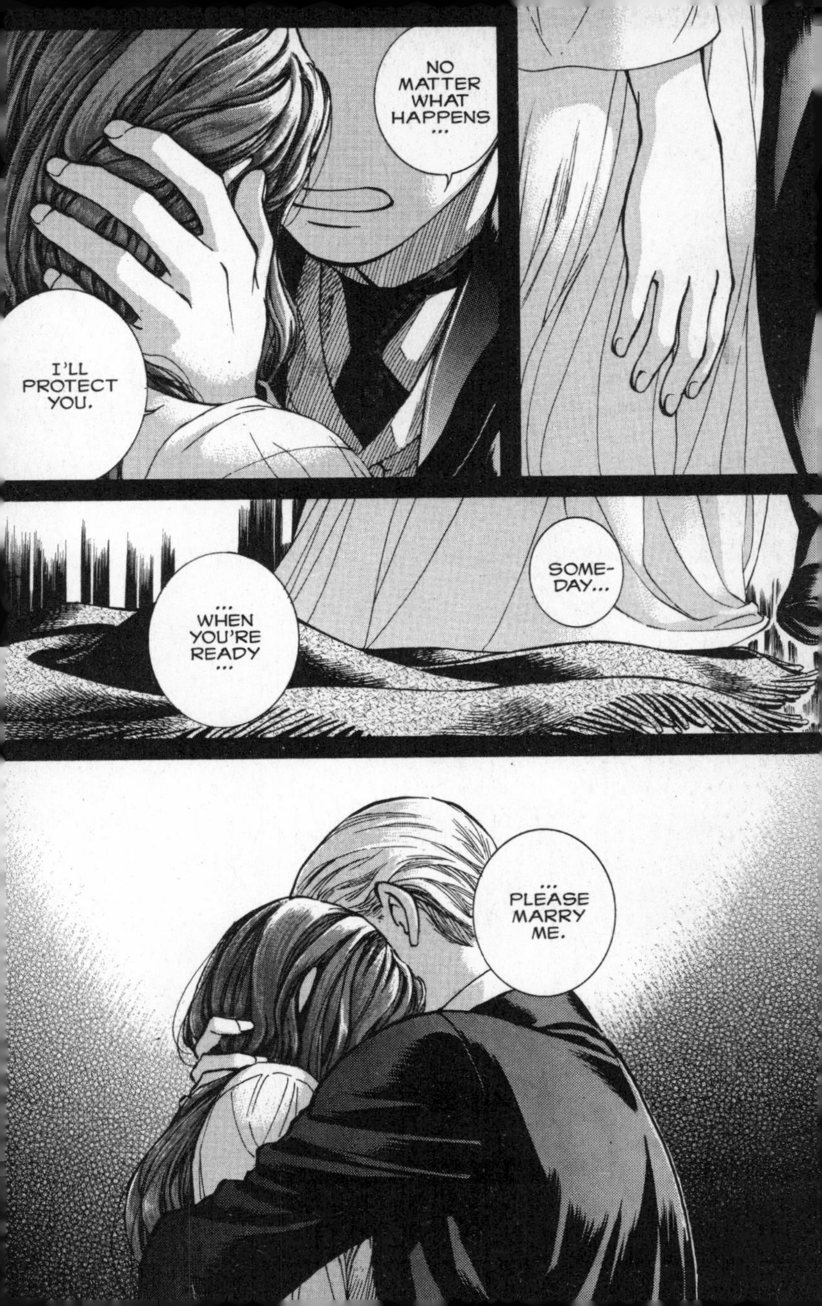
NO MATTER WHAT HAPPENS ...
I'LL PROTECT YOU.
SOME-DAY...
... WHEN YOU'RE READY ...
... PLEASE MARRY ME.

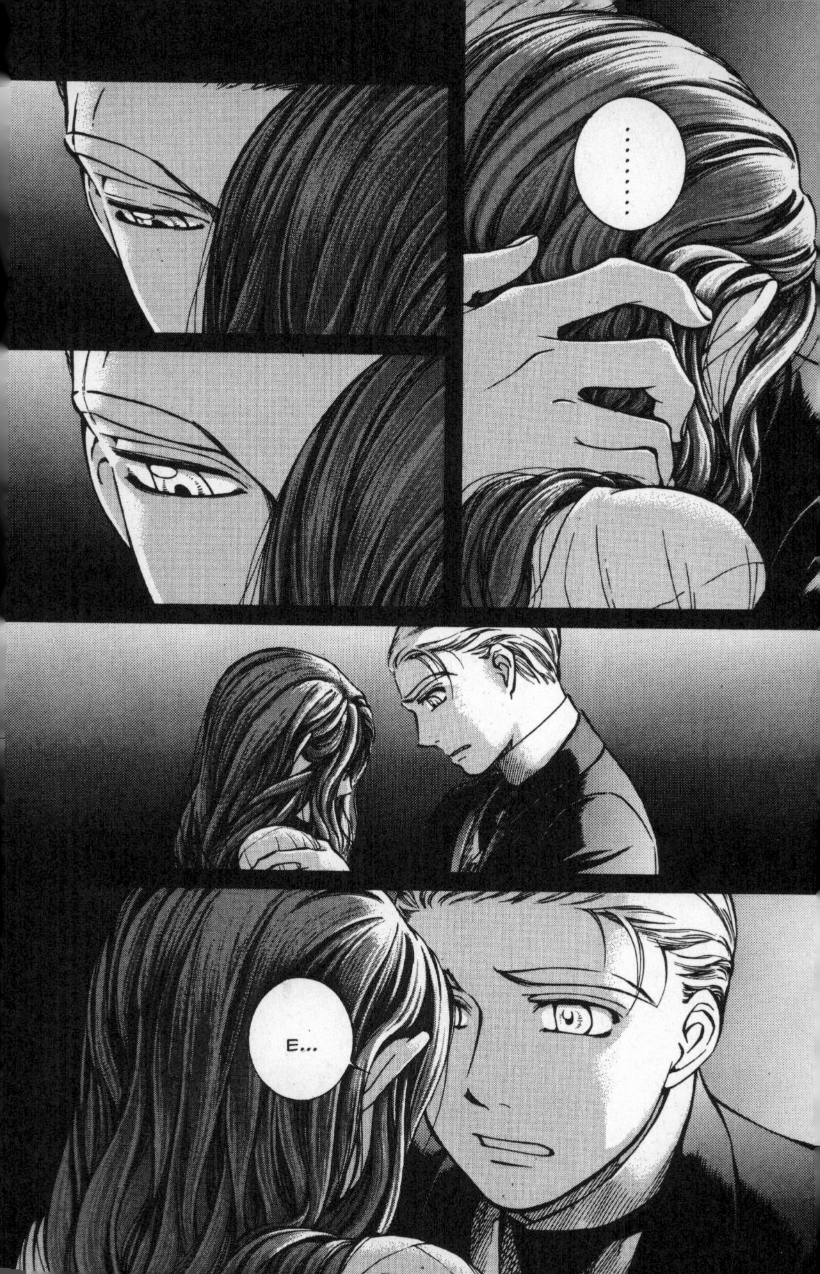
......
E...

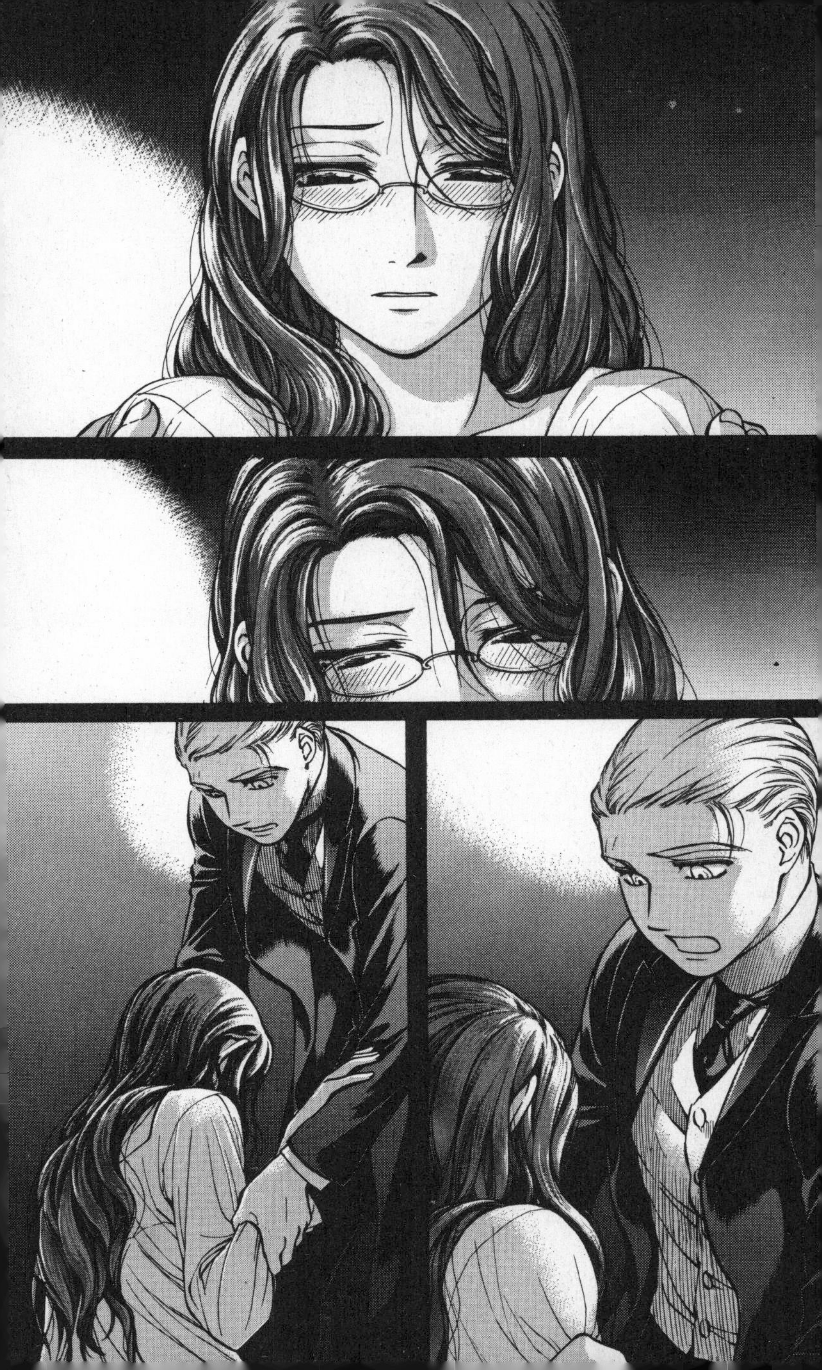

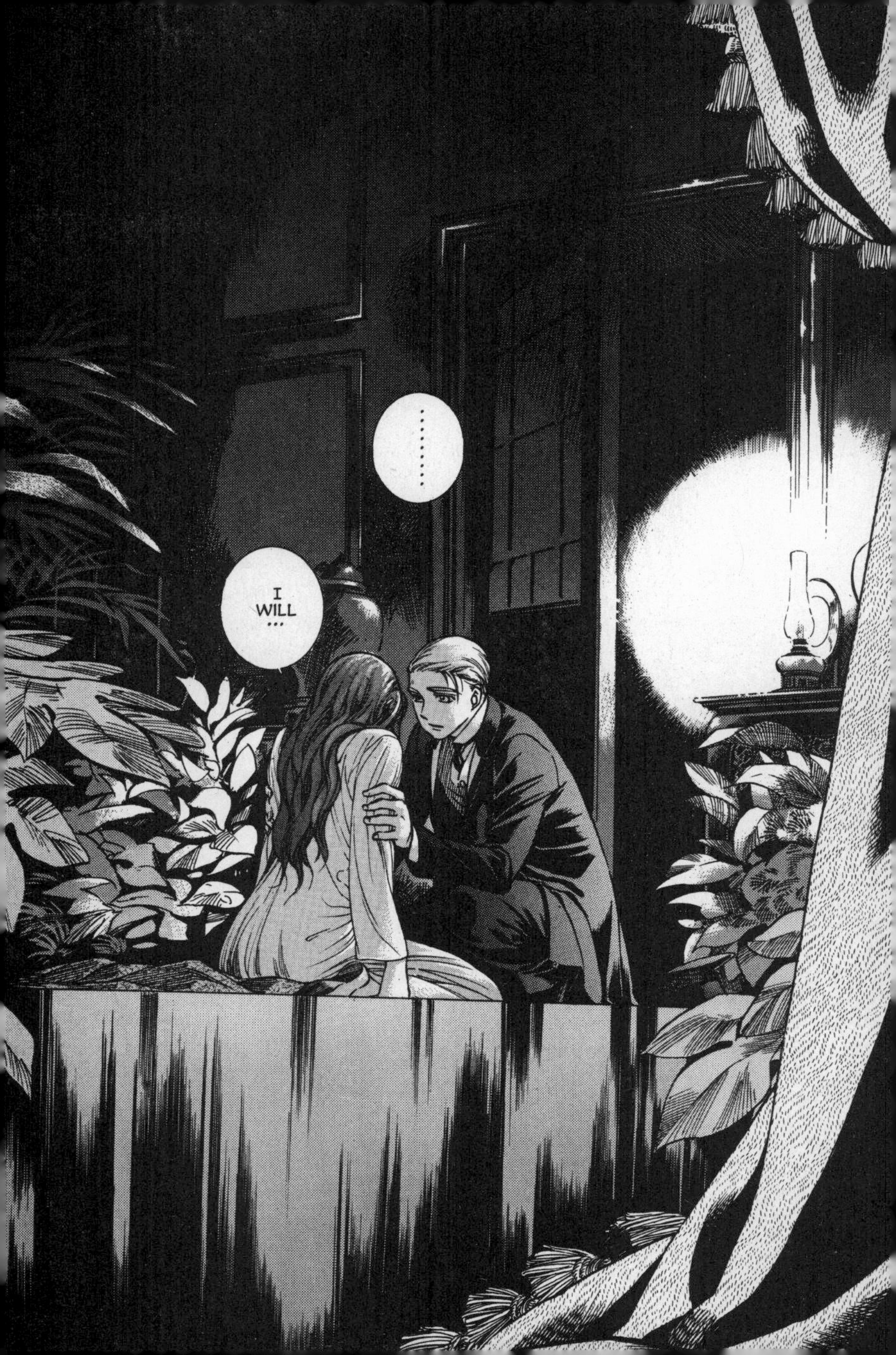
......
I WILL...

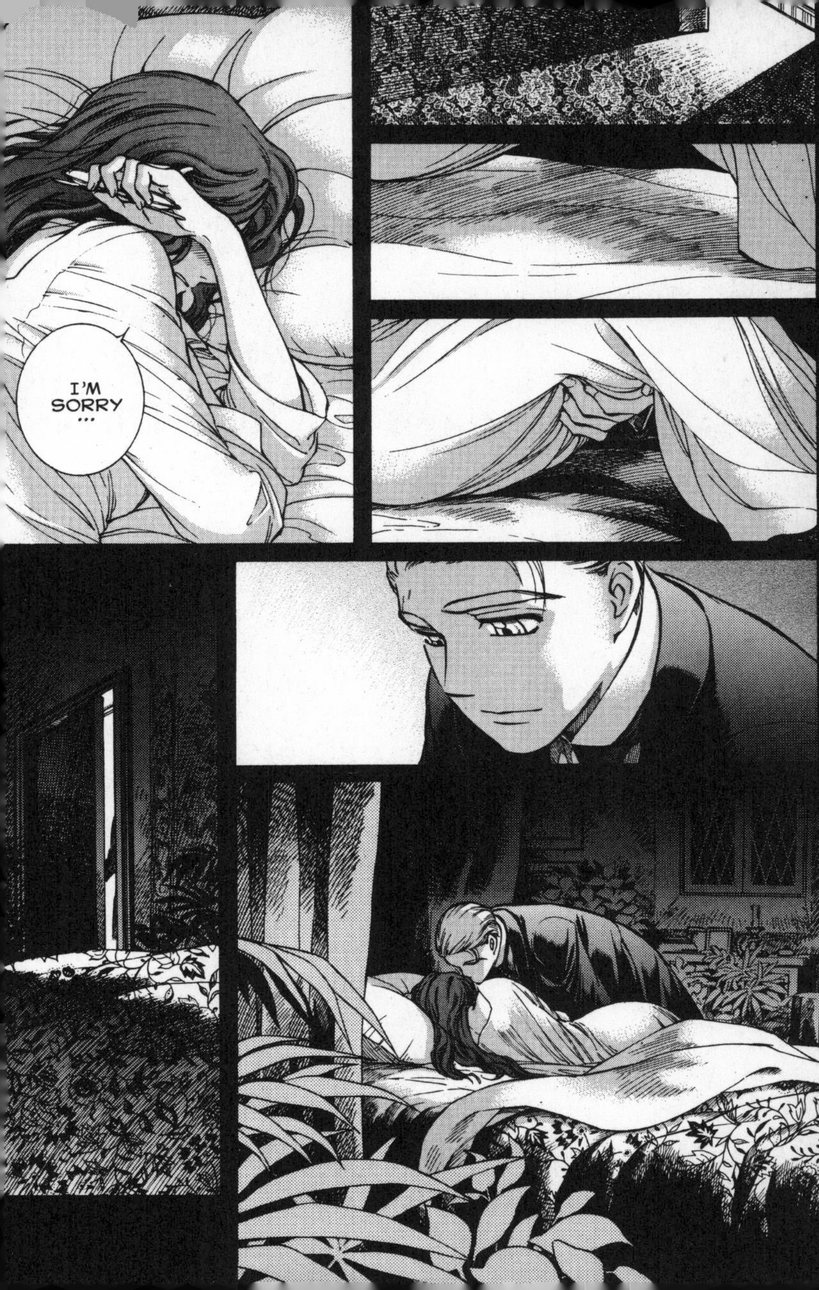
I'M SORRY ...

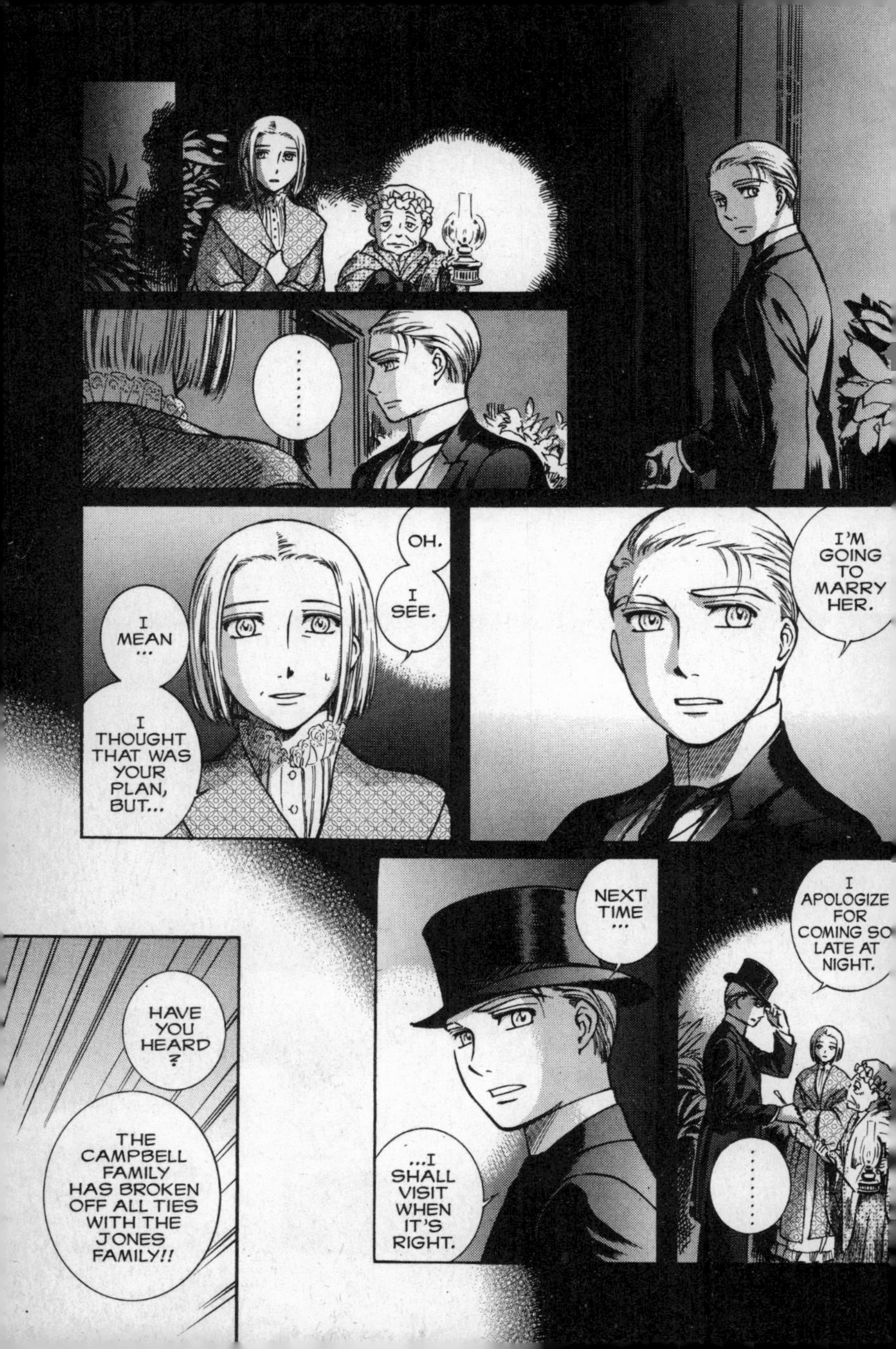
......
I'M GOING TO MARRY HER.
OH.
I SEE.
I MEAN...
I THOUGHT THAT WAS YOUR PLAN, BUT...
I APOLOGIZE FOR COMING SO LATE AT NIGHT.
......
NEXT TIME...
...I SHALL VISIT WHEN IT'S RIGHT.
HAVE YOU HEARD?
THE CAMPBELL FAMILY HAS BROKEN OFF ALL TIES WITH THE JONES FAMILY!!

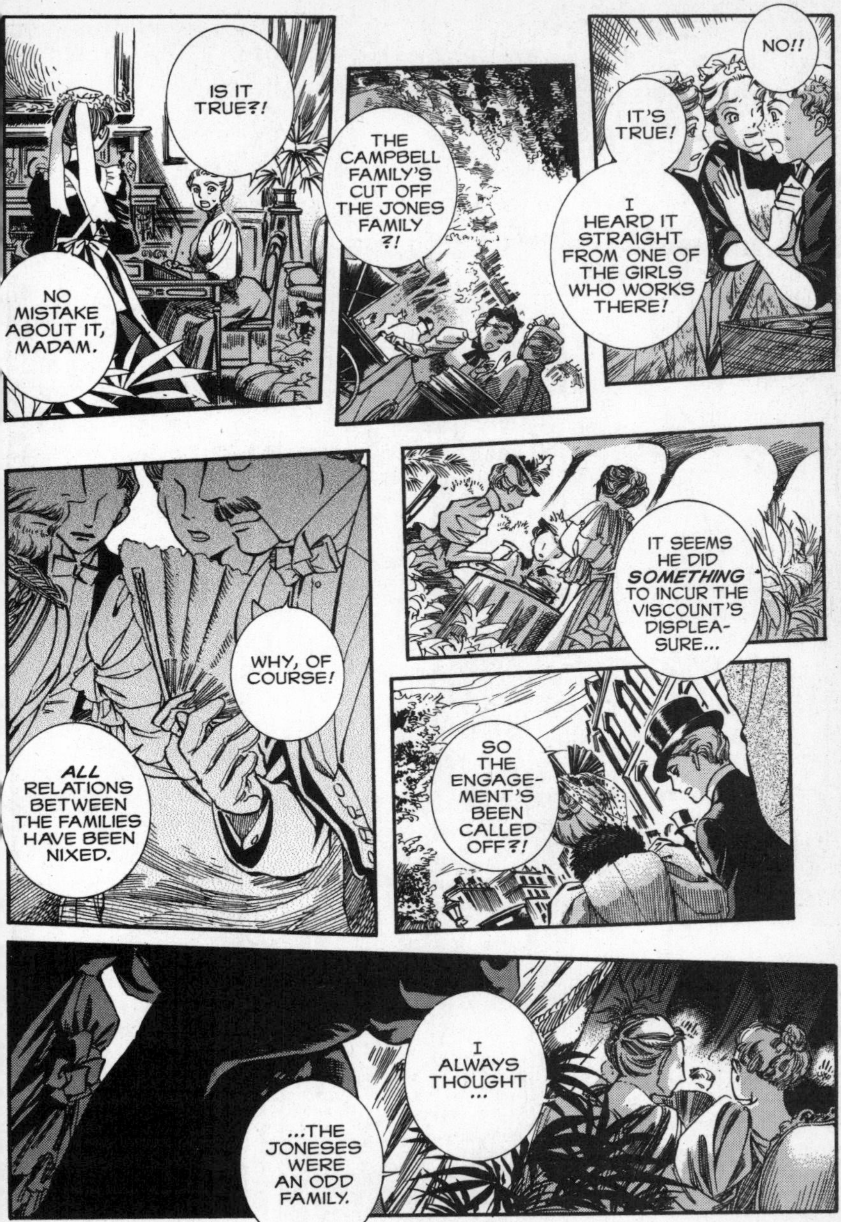
NO!!
IT'S TRUE!
I HEARD IT STRAIGHT FROM ONE OF THE GIRLS WHO WORKS THERE!
THE CAMPBELL FAMILY'S CUT OFF THE JONES FAMILY ?!
IS IT TRUE?!
NO MISTAKE ABOUT IT, MADAM.
IT SEEMS HE DID ***SOMETHING*** TO INCUR THE VISCOUNT'S DISPLEA-SURE...
SO THE ENGAGE-MENT'S BEEN CALLED OFF?!
WHY, OF COURSE!
ALL RELATIONS BETWEEN THE FAMILIES HAVE BEEN NIXED.
I ALWAYS THOUGHT ...
...THE JONESES WERE AN ODD FAMILY.

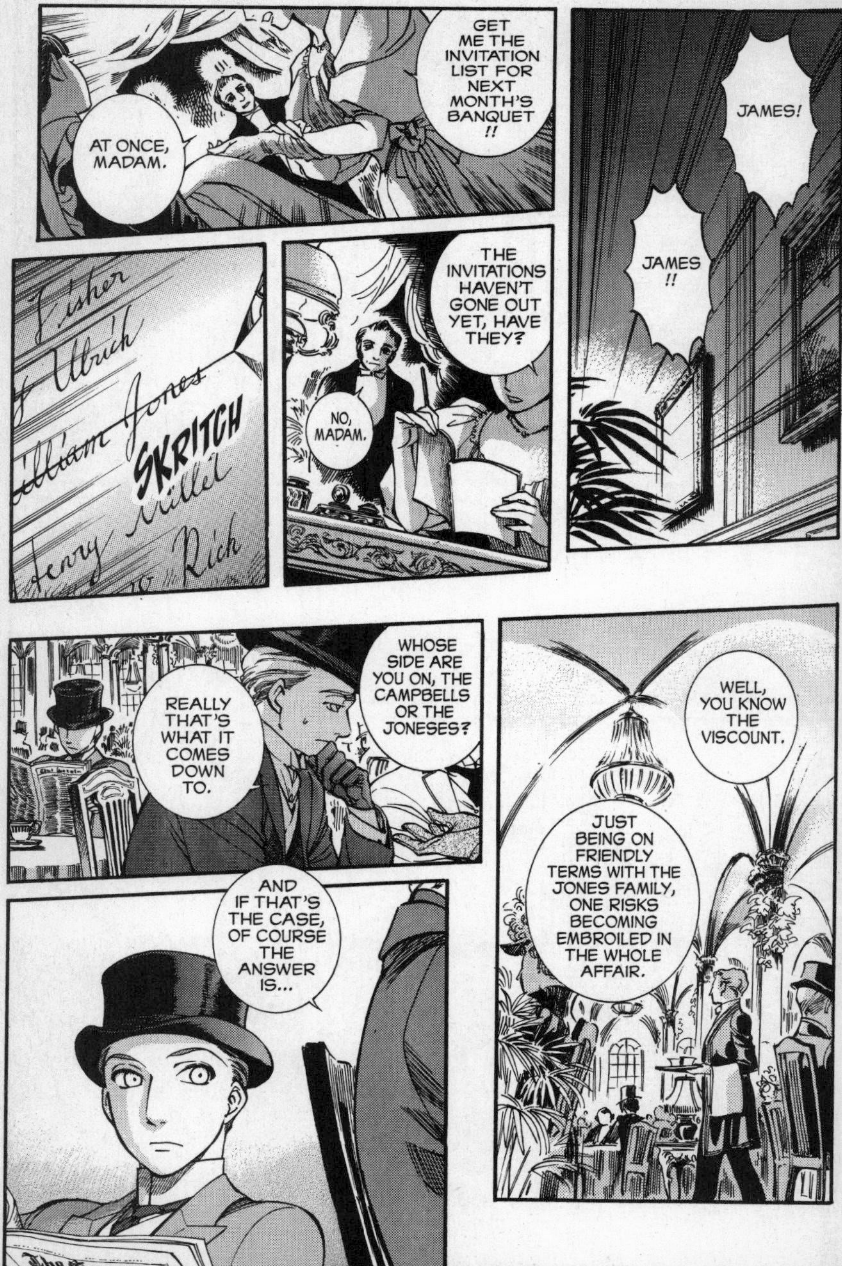
JAMES!
JAMES !!
GET ME THE INVITATION LIST FOR NEXT MONTH'S BANQUET !!
AT ONCE, MADAM.
THE INVITATIONS HAVEN'T GONE OUT YET, HAVE THEY?
NO, MADAM.
Fisher
Ulrich
William Jones
SKRITCH
Henry Miller
Rich
WELL, YOU KNOW THE VISCOUNT.
JUST BEING ON FRIENDLY TERMS WITH THE JONES FAMILY, ONE RISKS BECOMING EMBROILED IN THE WHOLE AFFAIR.
WHOSE SIDE ARE YOU ON, THE CAMPBELLS OR THE JONESES?
REALLY THAT'S WHAT IT COMES DOWN TO.
AND IF THAT'S THE CASE, OF COURSE THE ANSWER IS...

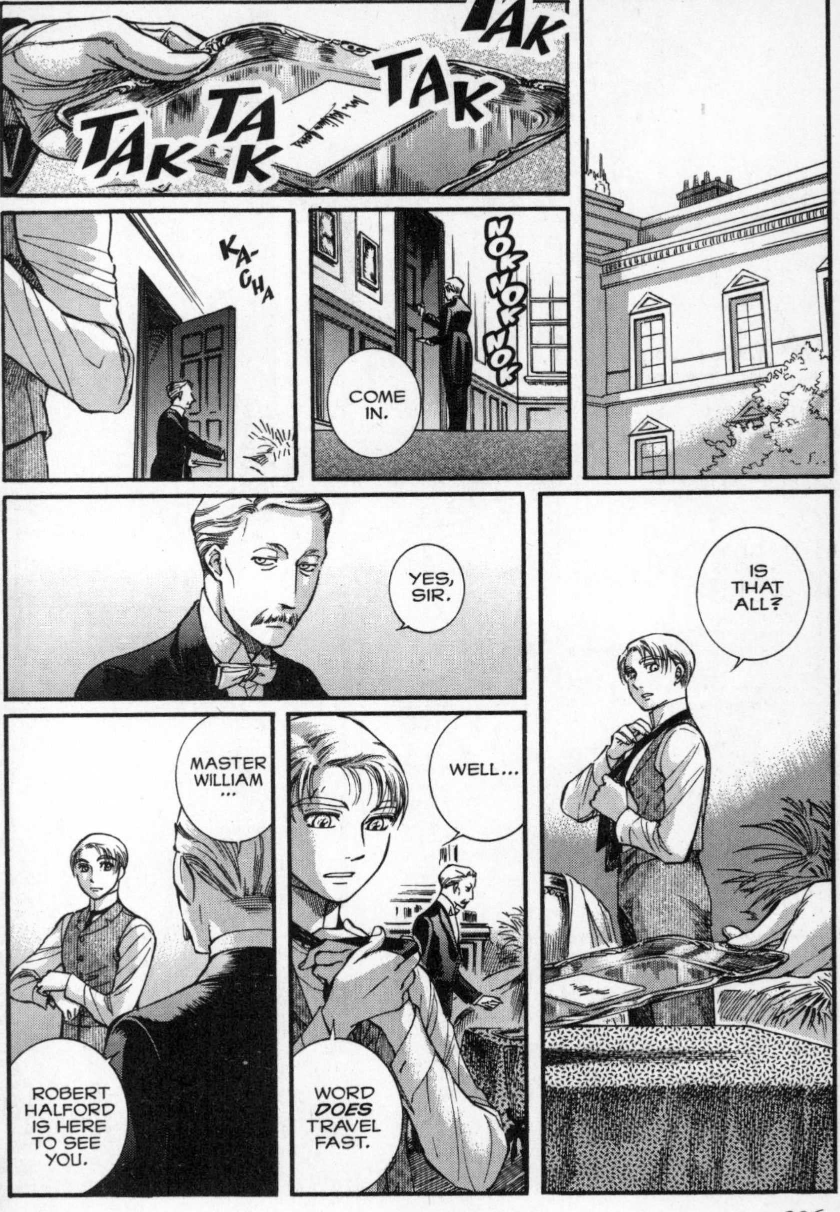
TAK TAK TA K TAK
NOK NOK NOK
COME IN.
KA-CHA
YES, SIR.
IS THAT ALL?
WELL...
WORD DOES TRAVEL FAST.
MASTER WILLIAM ...
ROBERT HALFORD IS HERE TO SEE YOU.

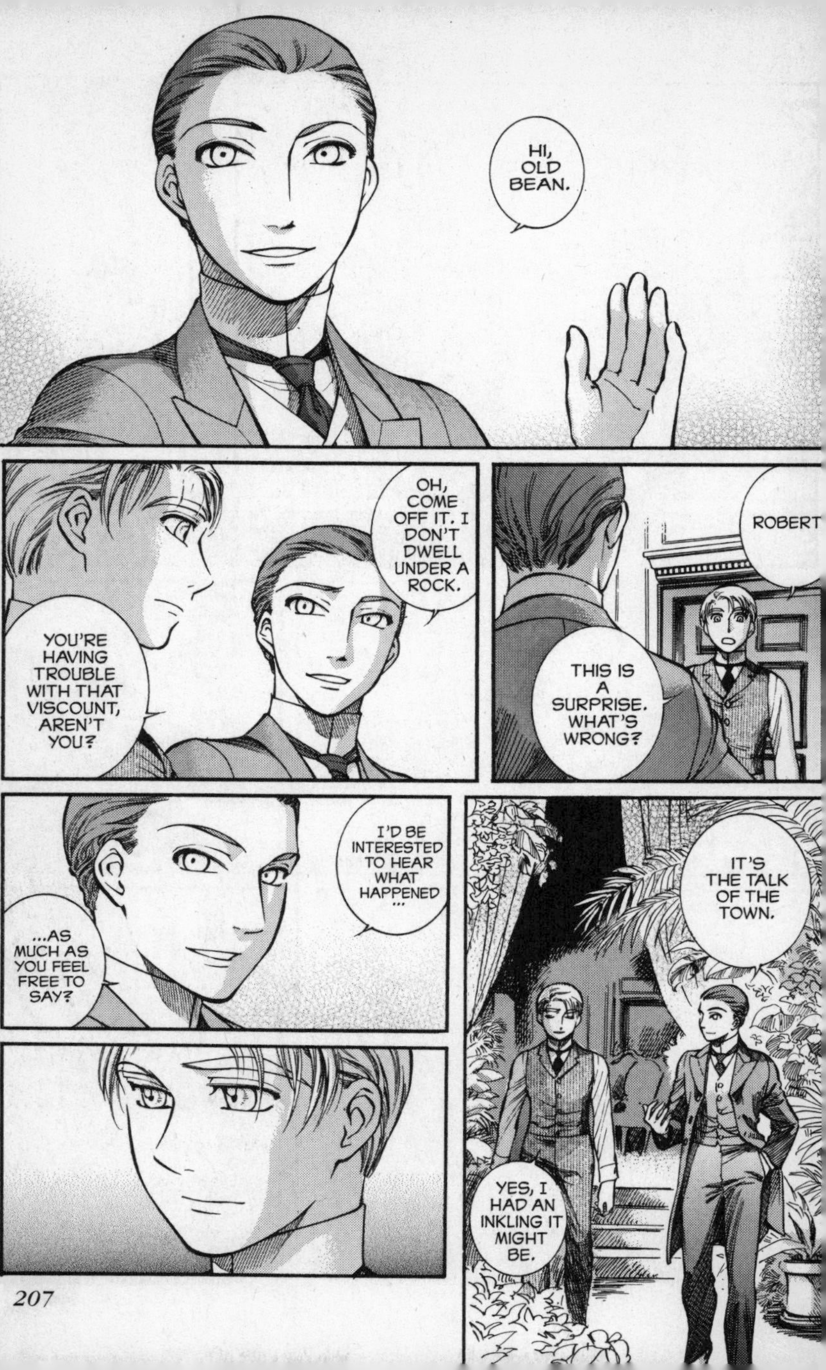
HI, OLD BEAN.
ROBERT
THIS IS A SURPRISE. WHAT'S WRONG?
YOU'RE HAVING TROUBLE WITH THAT VISCOUNT, AREN'T YOU?
OH, COME OFF IT. I DON'T DWELL UNDER A ROCK.
IT'S THE TALK OF THE TOWN.
YES, I HAD AN INKLING IT MIGHT BE.
I'D BE INTERESTED TO HEAR WHAT HAPPENED ...
...AS MUCH AS YOU FEEL FREE TO SAY?

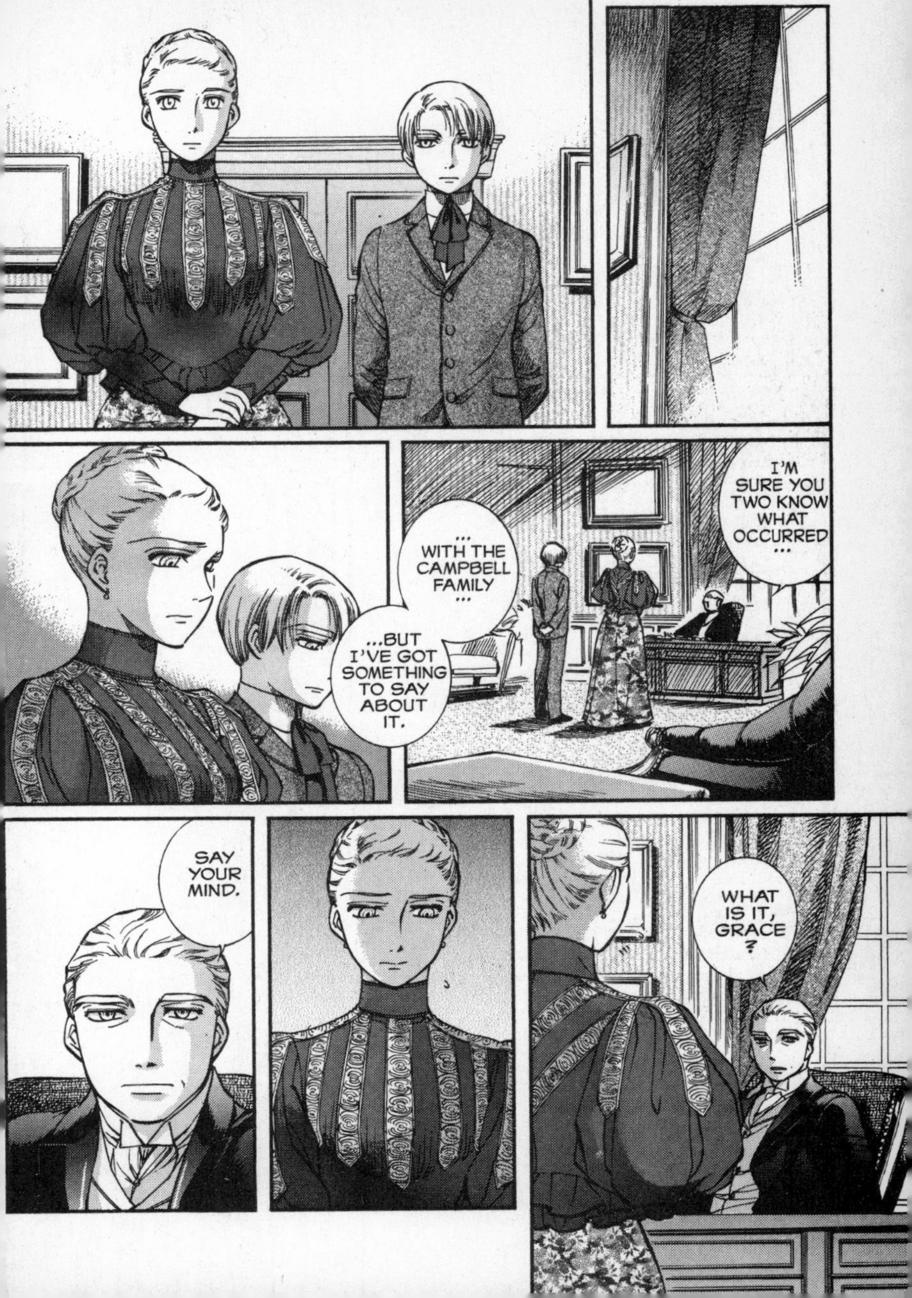
I'M SURE YOU TWO KNOW WHAT OCCURRED ...
... WITH THE CAMPBELL FAMILY ...
...BUT I'VE GOT SOMETHING TO SAY ABOUT IT.
WHAT IS IT, GRACE ?
SAY YOUR MIND.

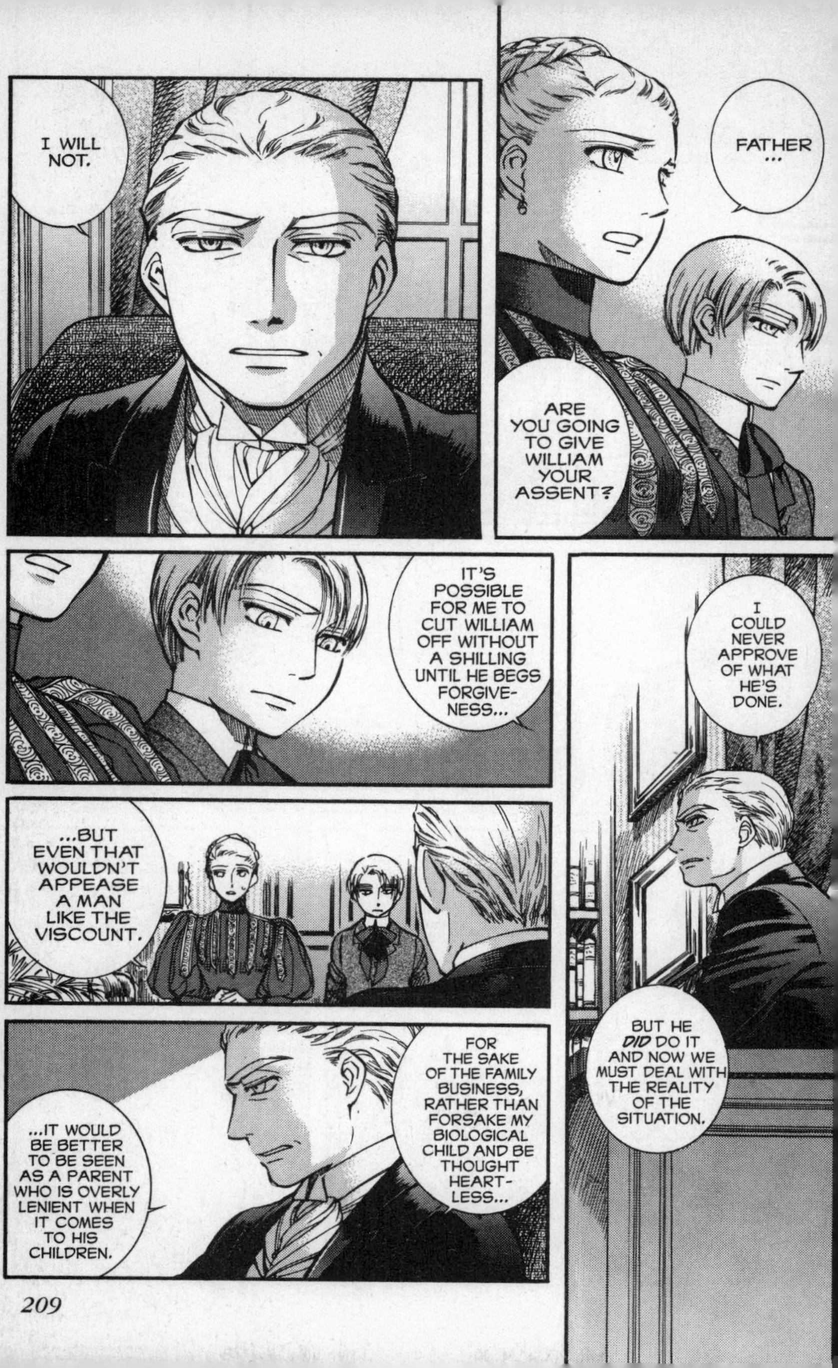
FATHER ...
ARE YOU GOING TO GIVE WILLIAM YOUR ASSENT?
I WILL NOT.
I COULD NEVER APPROVE OF WHAT HE'S DONE.
BUT HE *DID* DO IT AND NOW WE MUST DEAL WITH THE REALITY OF THE SITUATION.
IT'S POSSIBLE FOR ME TO CUT WILLIAM OFF WITHOUT A SHILLING UNTIL HE BEGS FORGIVE-NESS...
...BUT EVEN THAT WOULDN'T APPEASE A MAN LIKE THE VISCOUNT.
FOR THE SAKE OF THE FAMILY BUSINESS, RATHER THAN FORSAKE MY BIOLOGICAL CHILD AND BE THOUGHT HEART-LESS...
...IT WOULD BE BETTER TO BE SEEN AS A PARENT WHO IS OVERLY LENIENT WHEN IT COMES TO HIS CHILDREN.

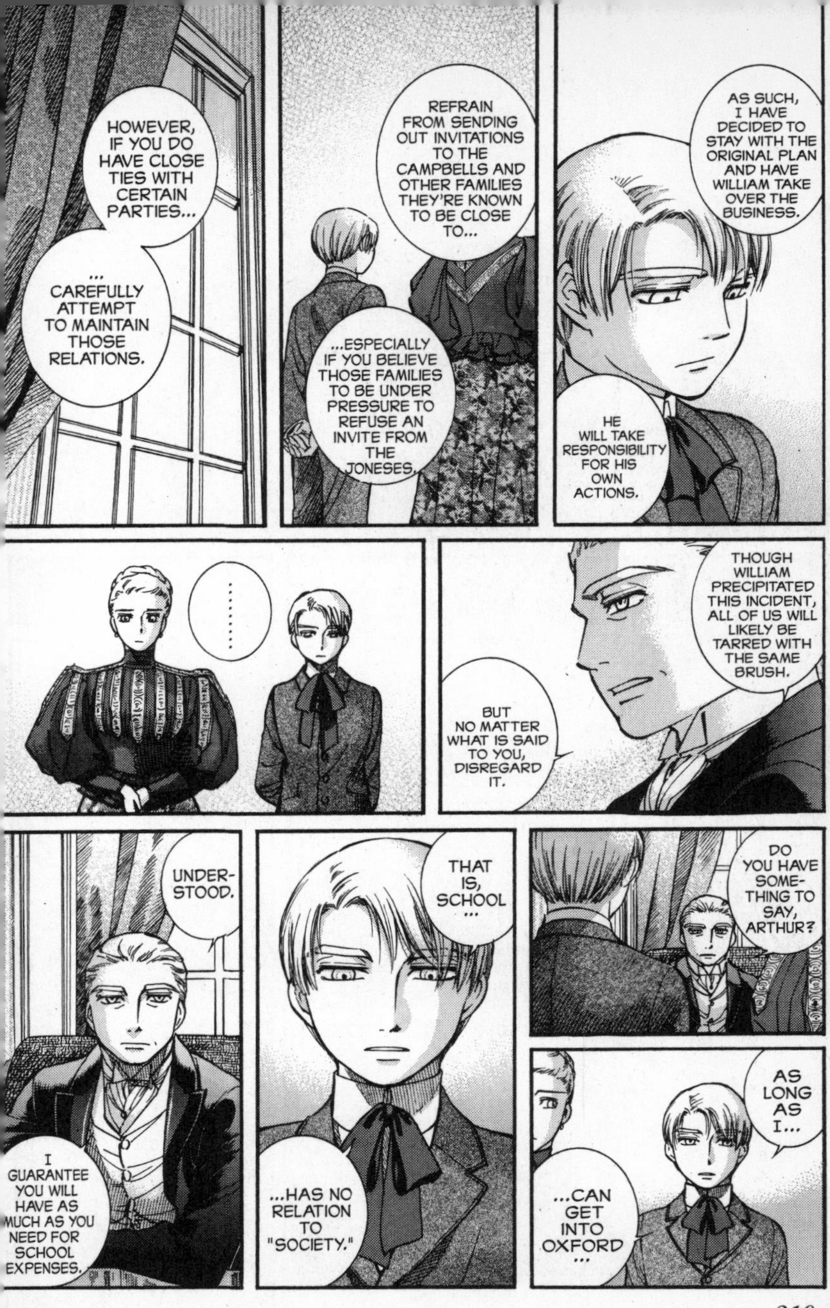
AS SUCH, I HAVE DECIDED TO STAY WITH THE ORIGINAL PLAN AND HAVE WILLIAM TAKE OVER THE BUSINESS.
HE WILL TAKE RESPONSIBILITY FOR HIS OWN ACTIONS.
REFRAIN FROM SENDING OUT INVITATIONS TO THE CAMPBELLS AND OTHER FAMILIES THEY'RE KNOWN TO BE CLOSE TO...
...ESPECIALLY IF YOU BELIEVE THOSE FAMILIES TO BE UNDER PRESSURE TO REFUSE AN INVITE FROM THE JONESES.
HOWEVER, IF YOU DO HAVE CLOSE TIES WITH CERTAIN PARTIES...
... CAREFULLY ATTEMPT TO MAINTAIN THOSE RELATIONS.
THOUGH WILLIAM PRECIPITATED THIS INCIDENT, ALL OF US WILL LIKELY BE TARRED WITH THE SAME BRUSH.
BUT NO MATTER WHAT IS SAID TO YOU, DISREGARD IT.
....
DO YOU HAVE SOME-THING TO SAY, ARTHUR?
AS LONG AS I...
...CAN GET INTO OXFORD ...
THAT IS, SCHOOL ...
...HAS NO RELATION TO "SOCIETY."
UNDER-STOOD.
I GUARANTEE YOU WILL HAVE AS MUCH AS YOU NEED FOR SCHOOL EXPENSES.

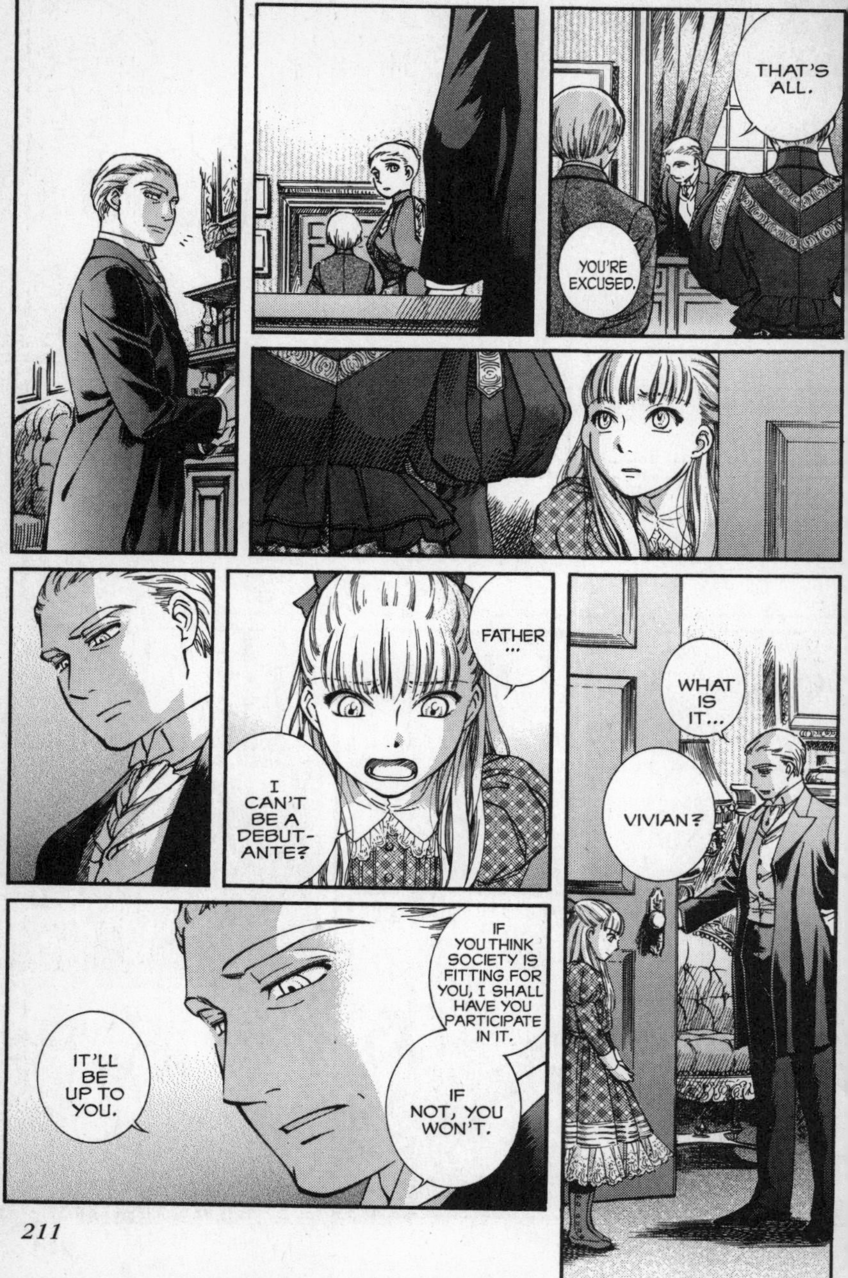
THAT'S ALL.
YOU'RE EXCUSED.
WHAT IS IT...
VIVIAN?
FATHER ...
I CAN'T BE A DEBUT-ANTE?
IF YOU THINK SOCIETY IS FITTING FOR YOU, I SHALL HAVE YOU PARTICIPATE IN IT.
IF NOT, YOU WON'T.
IT'LL BE UP TO YOU.

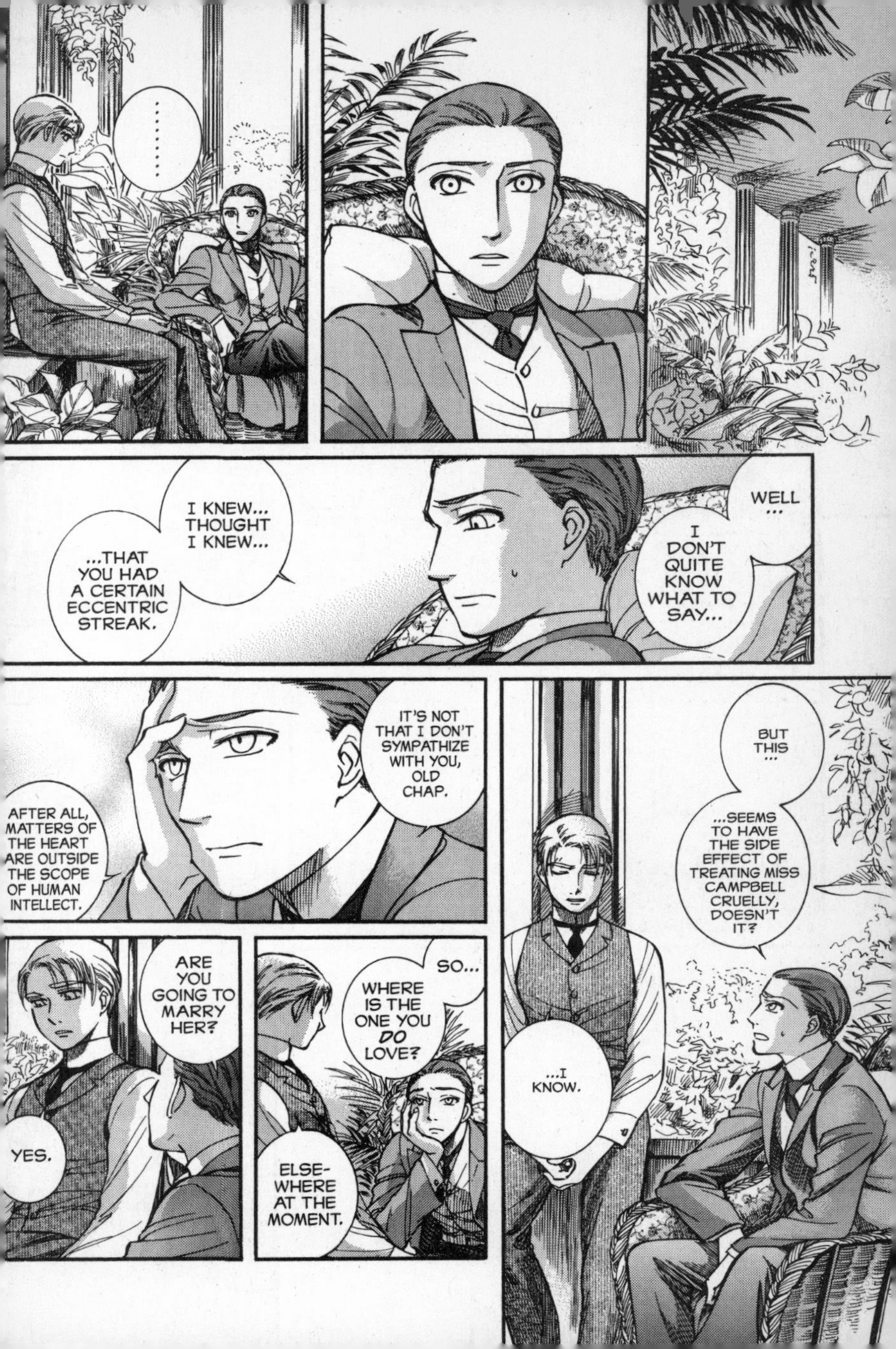
......
WELL... I DON'T QUITE KNOW WHAT TO SAY...
I KNEW... THOUGHT I KNEW...
...THAT YOU HAD A CERTAIN ECCENTRIC STREAK.
IT'S NOT THAT I DON'T SYMPATHIZE WITH YOU, OLD CHAP.
AFTER ALL, MATTERS OF THE HEART ARE OUTSIDE THE SCOPE OF HUMAN INTELLECT.
BUT THIS...
...SEEMS TO HAVE THE SIDE EFFECT OF TREATING MISS CAMPBELL CRUELLY, DOESN'T IT?
...I KNOW.
SO...
WHERE IS THE ONE YOU *DO* LOVE?
ELSE-WHERE AT THE MOMENT.
ARE YOU GOING TO MARRY HER?
YES.

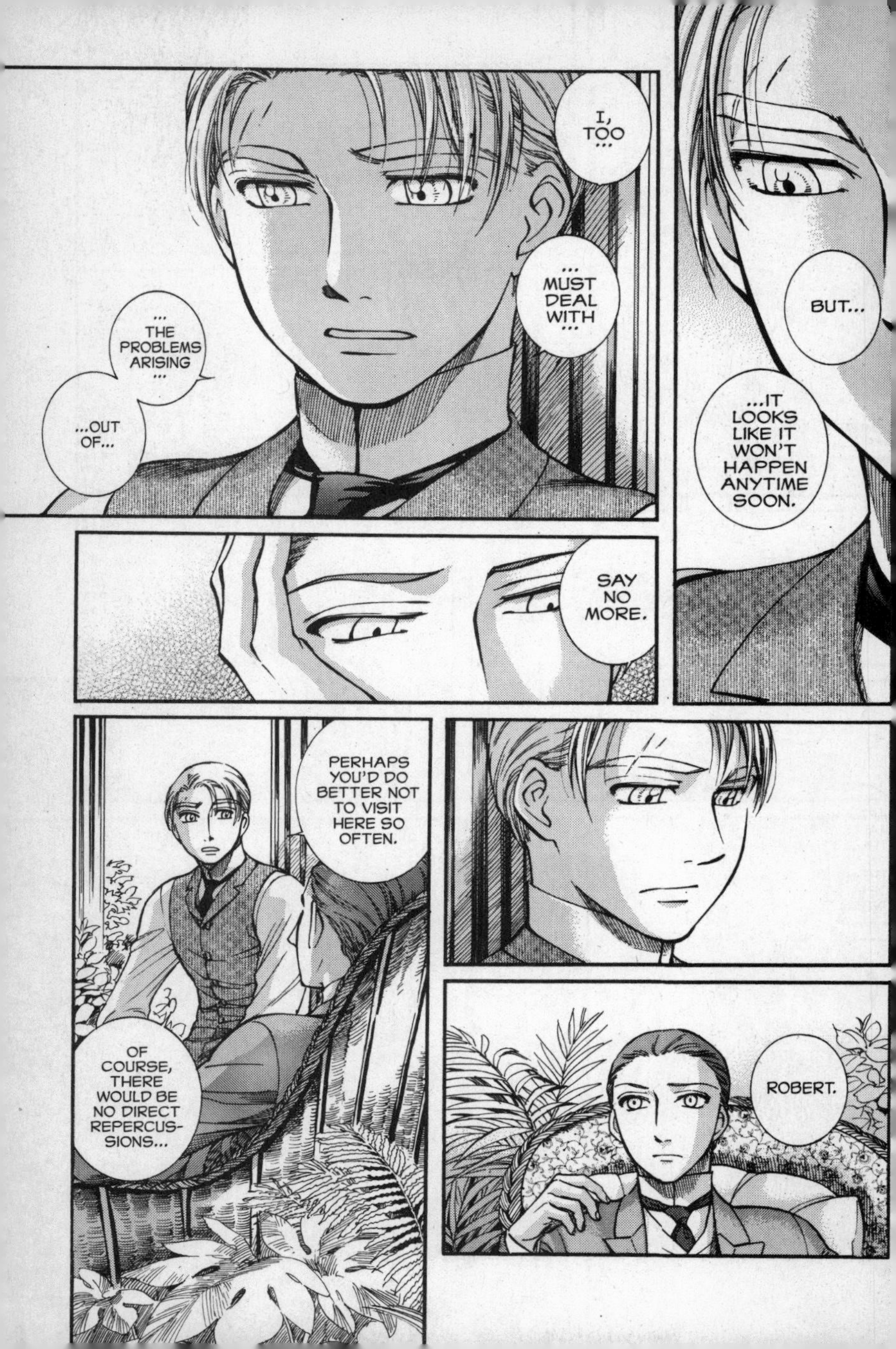
I, TOO ...
... MUST DEAL WITH ...
... THE PROBLEMS ARISING ...
...OUT OF...
BUT...
...IT LOOKS LIKE IT WON'T HAPPEN ANYTIME SOON.
SAY NO MORE.
PERHAPS YOU'D DO BETTER NOT TO VISIT HERE SO OFTEN.
OF COURSE, THERE WOULD BE NO DIRECT REPERCUS-SIONS...
ROBERT.

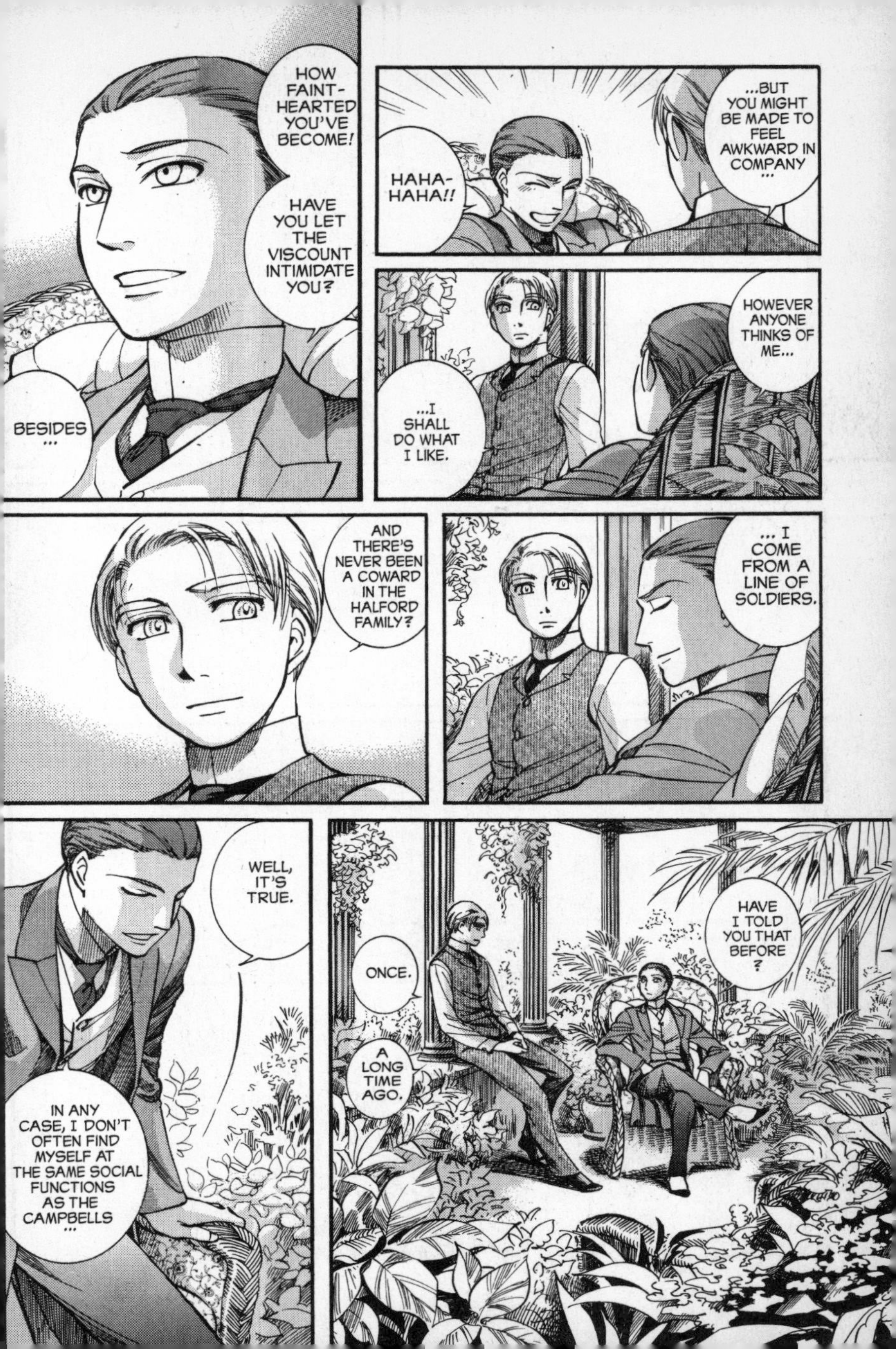
...BUT YOU MIGHT BE MADE TO FEEL AWKWARD IN COMPANY ...
HAHA-HAHA!!
HOWEVER ANYONE THINKS OF ME...
...I SHALL DO WHAT I LIKE.
HOW FAINT-HEARTED YOU'VE BECOME!
HAVE YOU LET THE VISCOUNT INTIMIDATE YOU?
BESIDES ...
... I COME FROM A LINE OF SOLDIERS.
AND THERE'S NEVER BEEN A COWARD IN THE HALFORD FAMILY?
HAVE I TOLD YOU THAT BEFORE ?
ONCE.
A LONG TIME AGO.
WELL, IT'S TRUE.
IN ANY CASE, I DON'T OFTEN FIND MYSELF AT THE SAME SOCIAL FUNCTIONS AS THE CAMPBELLS ...

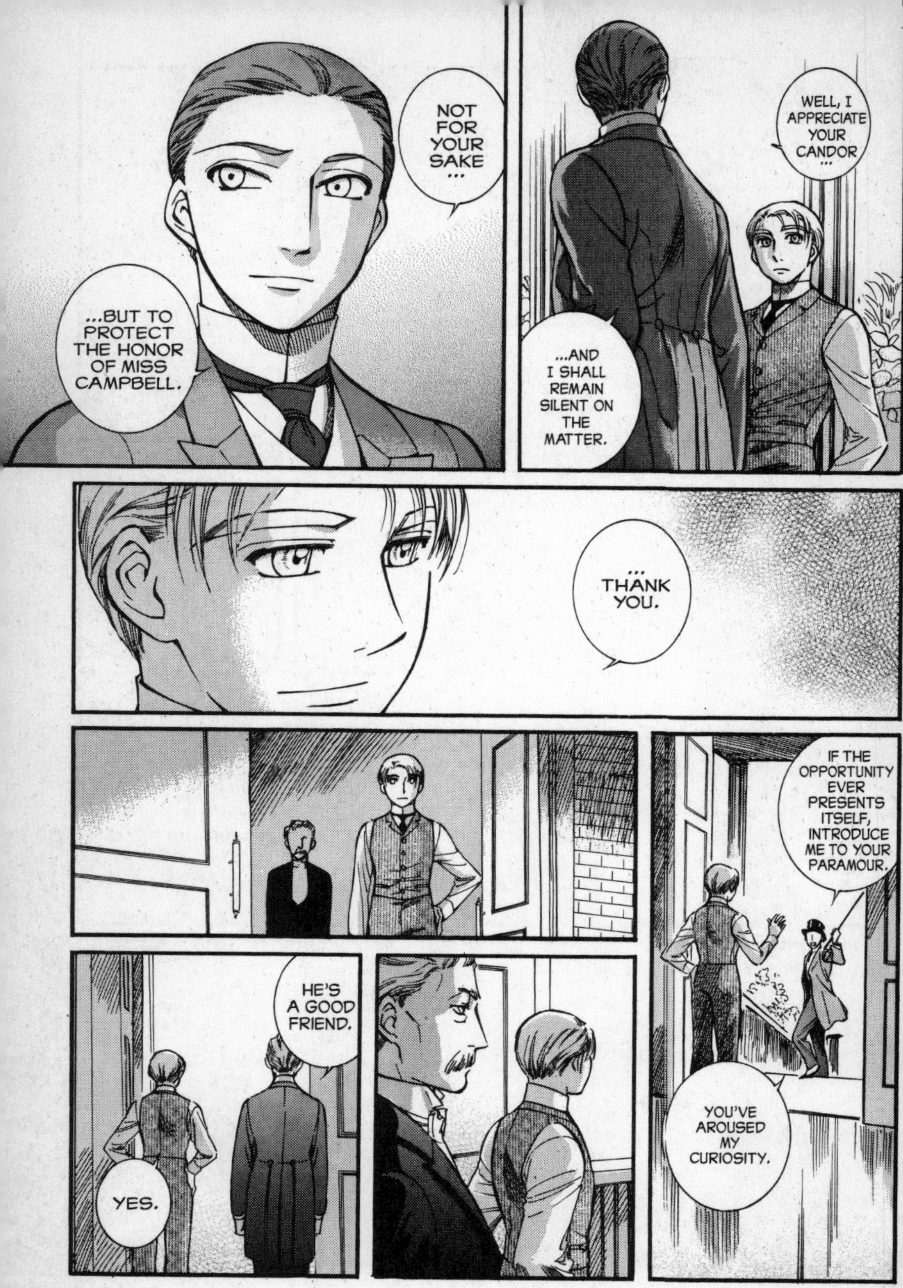
WELL, I APPRECIATE YOUR CANDOR ...
...AND I SHALL REMAIN SILENT ON THE MATTER.
NOT FOR YOUR SAKE ...
...BUT TO PROTECT THE HONOR OF MISS CAMPBELL.
... THANK YOU.
IF THE OPPORTUNITY EVER PRESENTS ITSELF, INTRODUCE ME TO YOUR PARAMOUR.
YOU'VE AROUSED MY CURIOSITY.
HE'S A GOOD FRIEND.
YES.

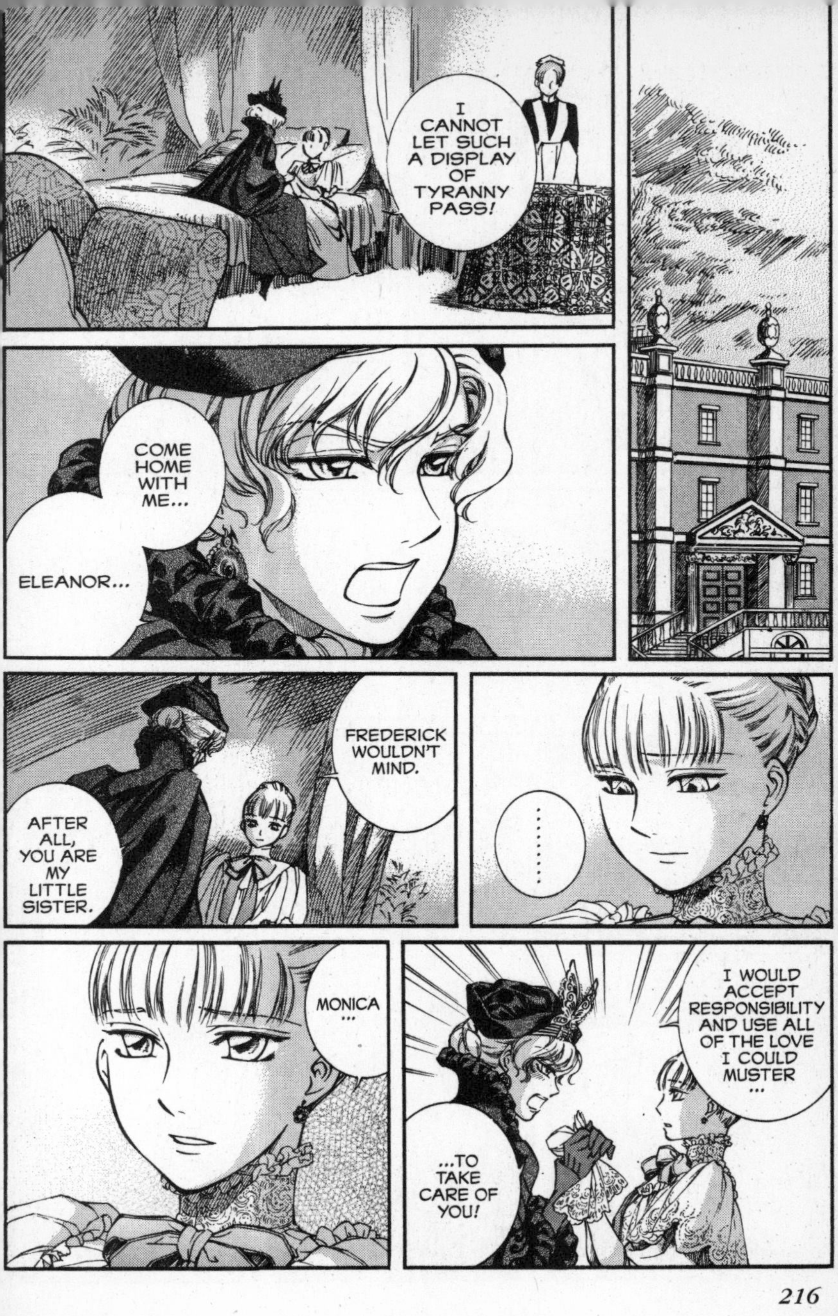
I CANNOT LET SUCH A DISPLAY OF TYRANNY PASS!
COME HOME WITH ME...
ELEANOR...
......
FREDERICK WOULDN'T MIND.
AFTER ALL, YOU ARE MY LITTLE SISTER.
I WOULD ACCEPT RESPONSIBILITY AND USE ALL OF THE LOVE I COULD MUSTER ...
...TO TAKE CARE OF YOU!
MONICA ...

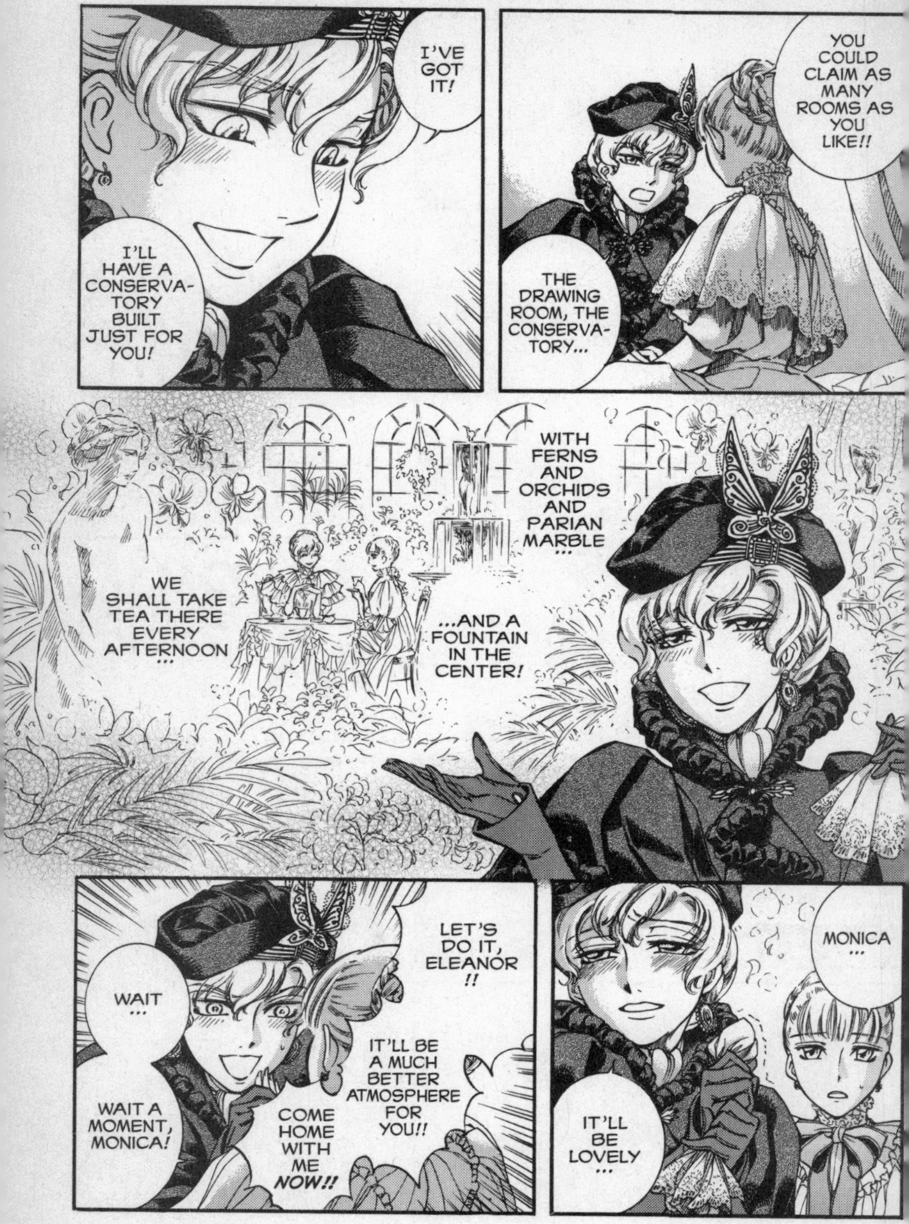
YOU COULD CLAIM AS MANY ROOMS AS YOU LIKE!!
THE DRAWING ROOM, THE CONSERVA-TORY...
I'VE GOT IT!
I'LL HAVE A CONSERVA-TORY BUILT JUST FOR YOU!
WITH FERNS AND ORCHIDS AND PARIAN MARBLE...
...AND A FOUNTAIN IN THE CENTER!
WE SHALL TAKE TEA THERE EVERY AFTERNOON...
MONICA...
IT'LL BE LOVELY...
LET'S DO IT, ELEANOR!!
IT'LL BE A MUCH BETTER ATMOSPHERE FOR YOU!!
COME HOME WITH ME NOW!!
WAIT...
WAIT A MOMENT, MONICA!

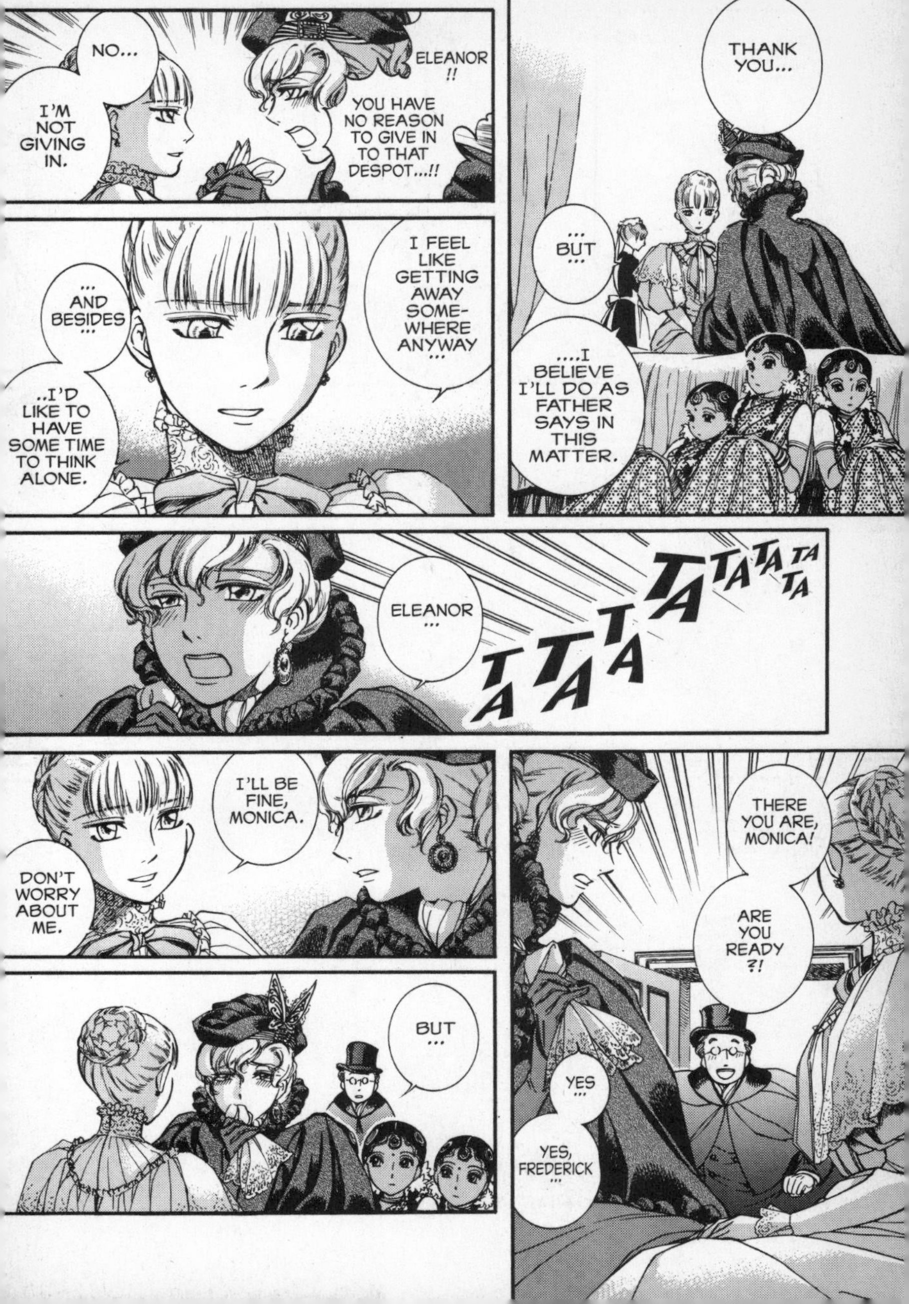
THANK YOU...
... BUT ...
....I BELIEVE I'LL DO AS FATHER SAYS IN THIS MATTER.
ELEANOR !!
YOU HAVE NO REASON TO GIVE IN TO THAT DESPOT...!!
NO...
I'M NOT GIVING IN.
I FEEL LIKE GETTING AWAY SOME-WHERE ANYWAY ...
... AND BESIDES ...
..I'D LIKE TO HAVE SOME TIME TO THINK ALONE.
TATATATATATATA
ELEANOR ...
THERE YOU ARE, MONICA!
ARE YOU READY ?!
YES ...
YES, FREDERICK ...
I'LL BE FINE, MONICA.
DON'T WORRY ABOUT ME.
BUT ...

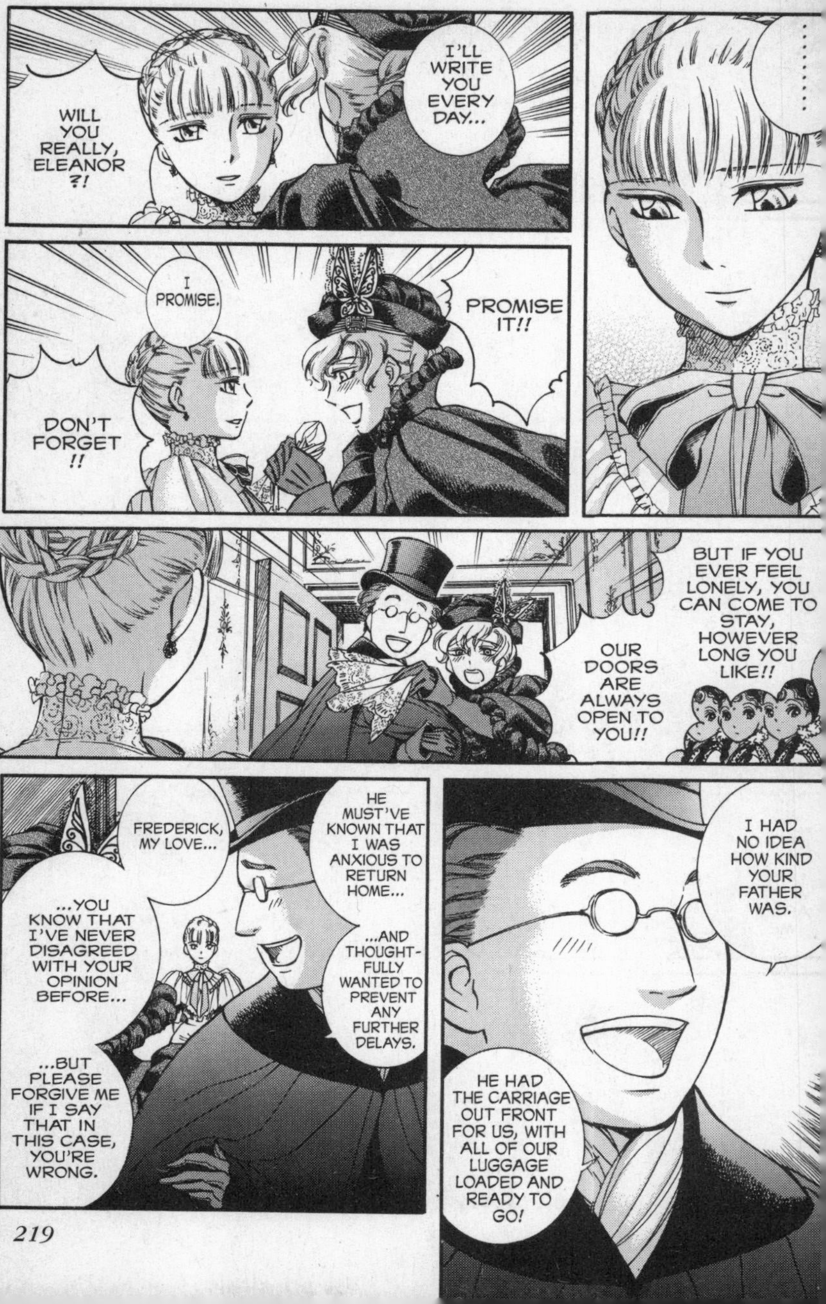
......
I'LL WRITE YOU EVERY DAY...
WILL YOU REALLY, ELEANOR ?!
PROMISE IT!!
I PROMISE.
DON'T FORGET !!
BUT IF YOU EVER FEEL LONELY, YOU CAN COME TO STAY, HOWEVER LONG YOU LIKE!!
OUR DOORS ARE ALWAYS OPEN TO YOU!!
I HAD NO IDEA HOW KIND YOUR FATHER WAS.
HE HAD THE CARRIAGE OUT FRONT FOR US, WITH ALL OF OUR LUGGAGE LOADED AND READY TO GO!
HE MUST'VE KNOWN THAT I WAS ANXIOUS TO RETURN HOME...
...AND THOUGHTFULLY WANTED TO PREVENT ANY FURTHER DELAYS.
FREDERICK, MY LOVE...
...YOU KNOW THAT I'VE NEVER DISAGREED WITH YOUR OPINION BEFORE...
...BUT PLEASE FORGIVE ME IF I SAY THAT IN THIS CASE, YOU'RE WRONG.

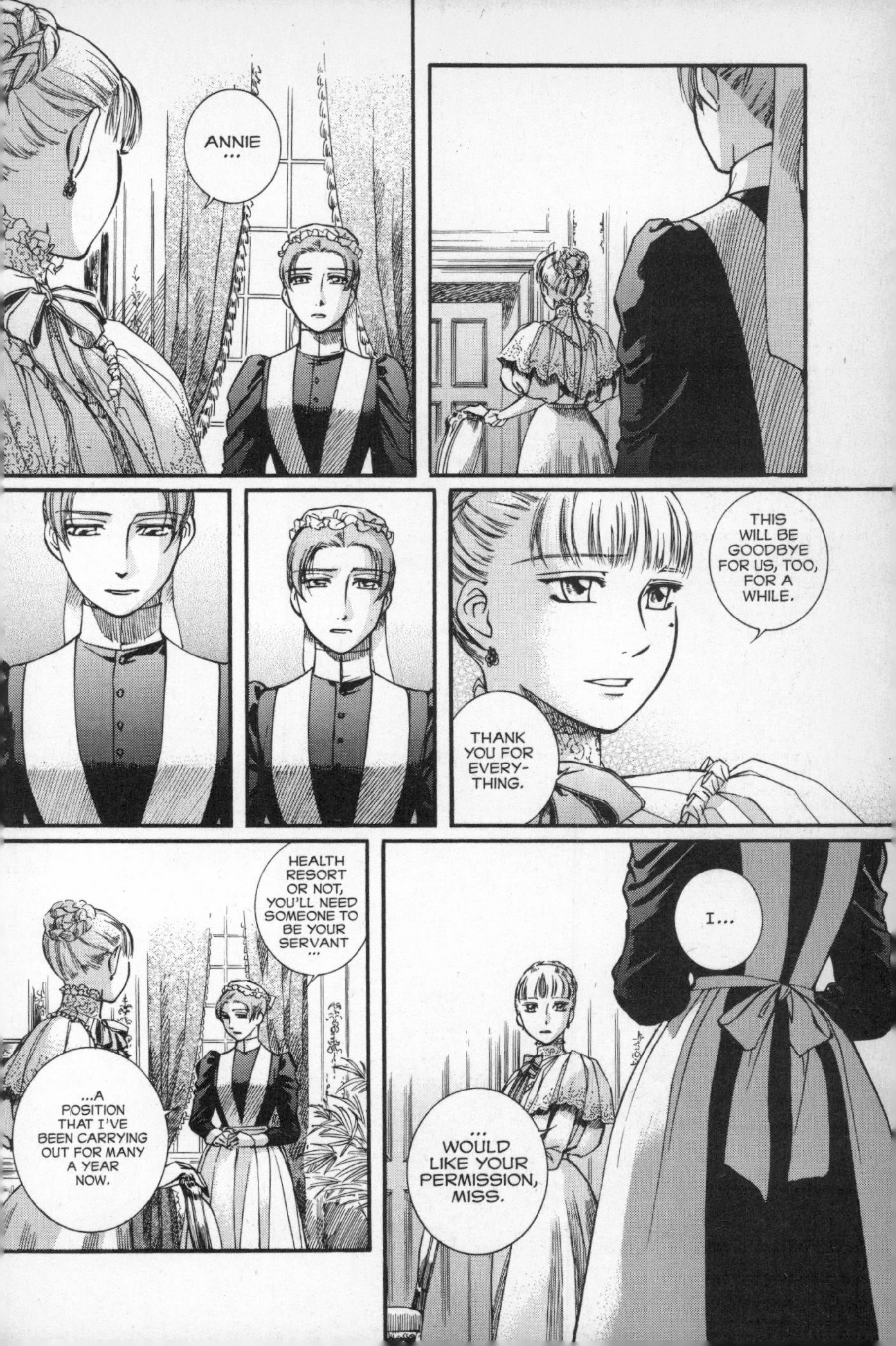
ANNIE ...
THIS WILL BE GOODBYE FOR US, TOO, FOR A WHILE.
THANK YOU FOR EVERY-THING.
I...
... WOULD LIKE YOUR PERMISSION, MISS.
HEALTH RESORT OR NOT, YOU'LL NEED SOMEONE TO BE YOUR SERVANT ...
...A POSITION THAT I'VE BEEN CARRYING OUT FOR MANY A YEAR NOW.

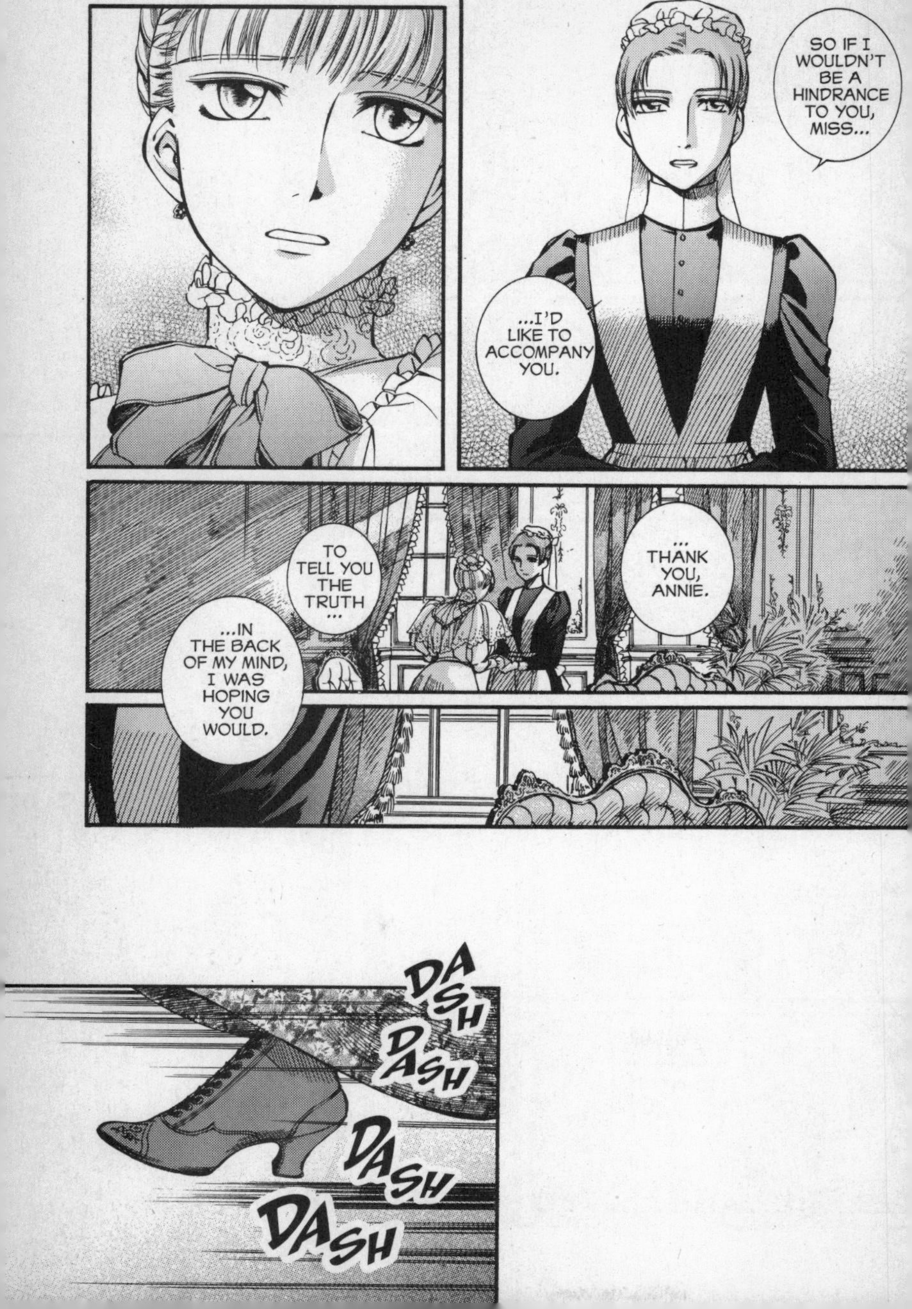
SO IF I WOULDN'T BE A HINDRANCE TO YOU, MISS...
...I'D LIKE TO ACCOMPANY YOU.
... THANK YOU, ANNIE.
TO TELL YOU THE TRUTH ...
...IN THE BACK OF MY MIND, I WAS HOPING YOU WOULD.
DASH DASH DASH DASH

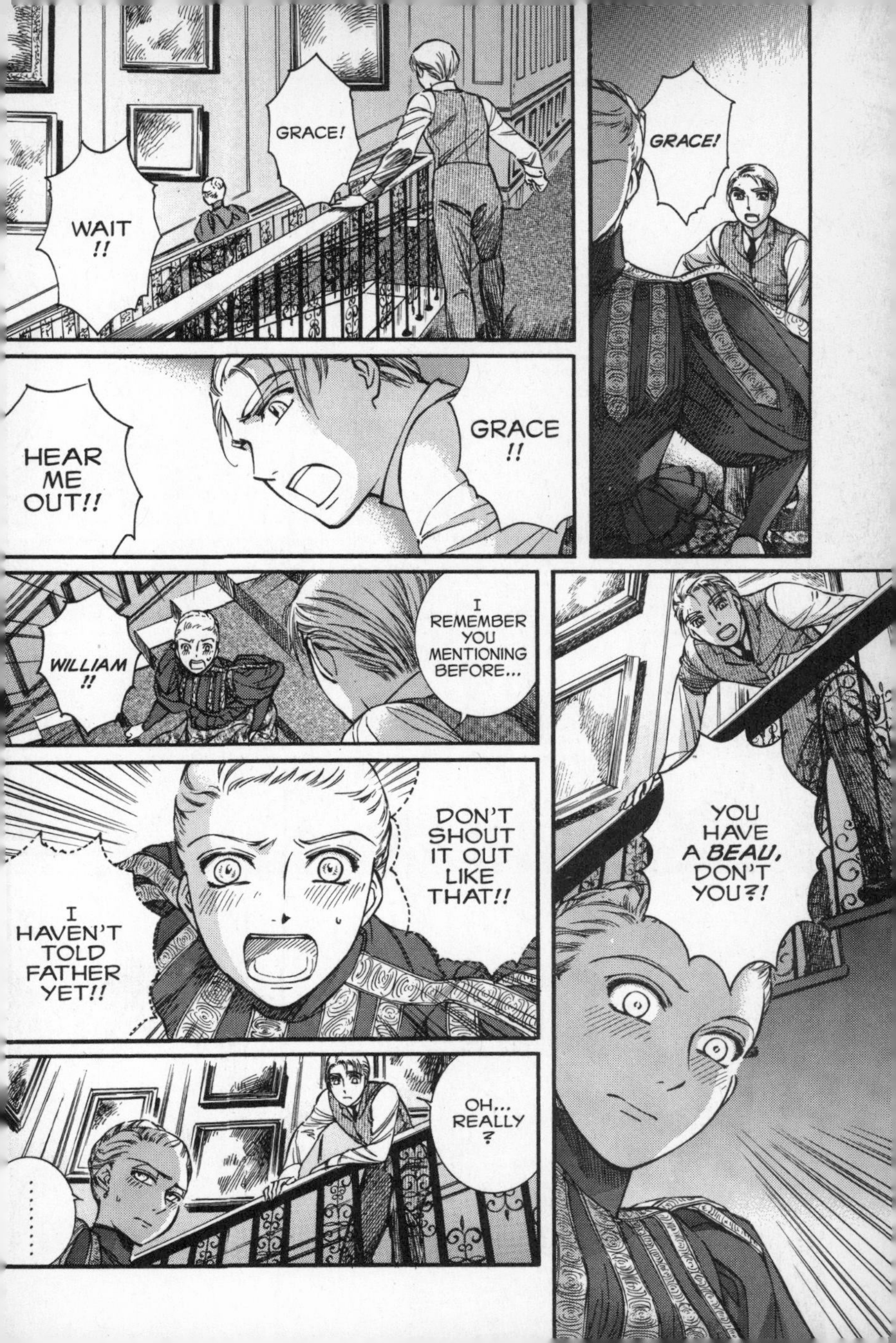
GRACE!
GRACE!
WAIT !!
GRACE !!
HEAR ME OUT!!
WILLIAM !!
I REMEMBER YOU MENTIONING BEFORE...
YOU HAVE A BEAU, DON'T YOU?!
DON'T SHOUT IT OUT LIKE THAT!!
I HAVEN'T TOLD FATHER YET!!
OH... REALLY ?
......

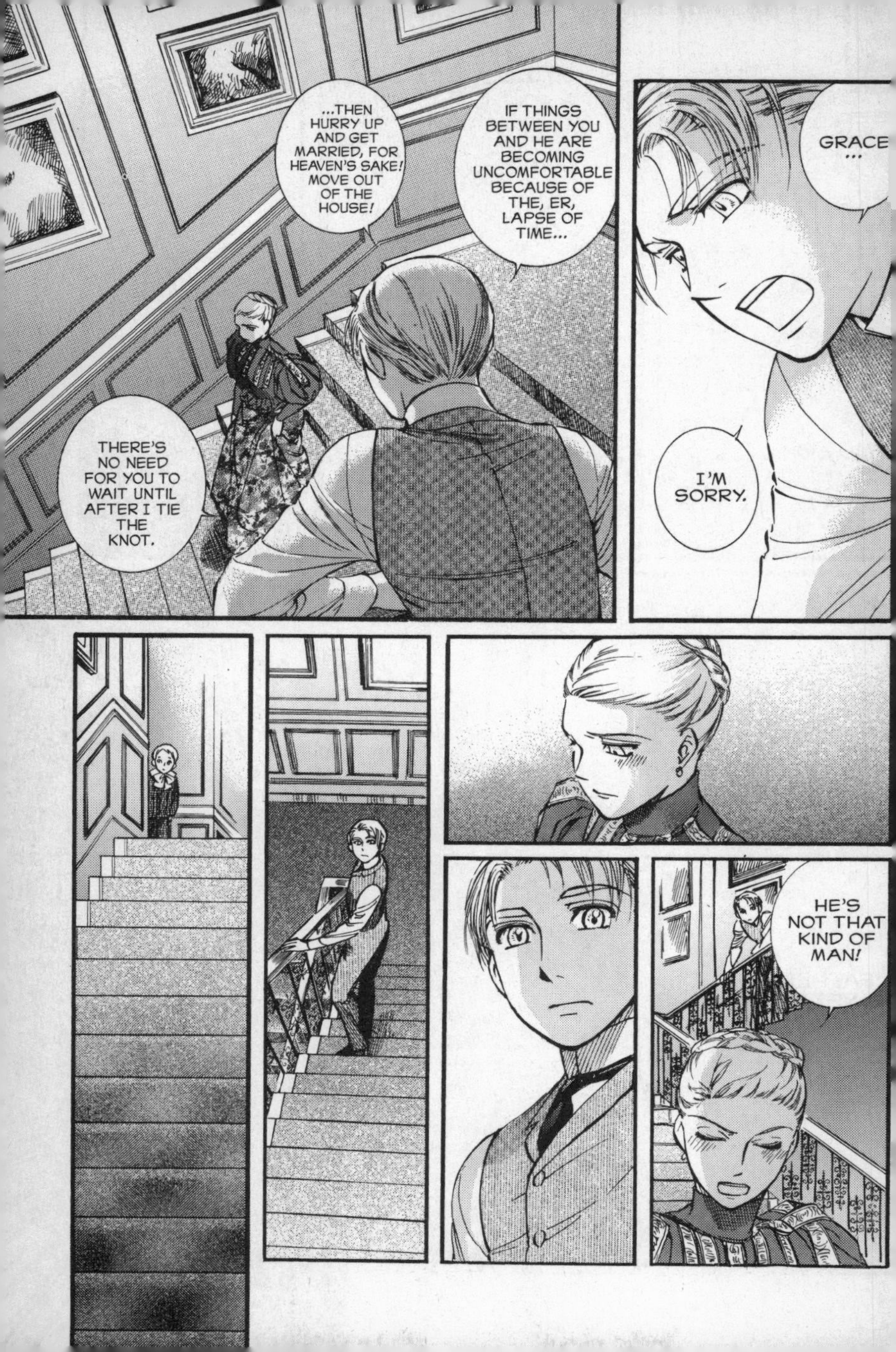
GRACE...
I'M SORRY.
IF THINGS BETWEEN YOU AND HE ARE BECOMING UNCOMFORTABLE BECAUSE OF THE, ER, LAPSE OF TIME...
...THEN HURRY UP AND GET MARRIED, FOR HEAVEN'S SAKE! MOVE OUT OF THE HOUSE!
THERE'S NO NEED FOR YOU TO WAIT UNTIL AFTER I TIE THE KNOT.
HE'S NOT THAT KIND OF MAN!

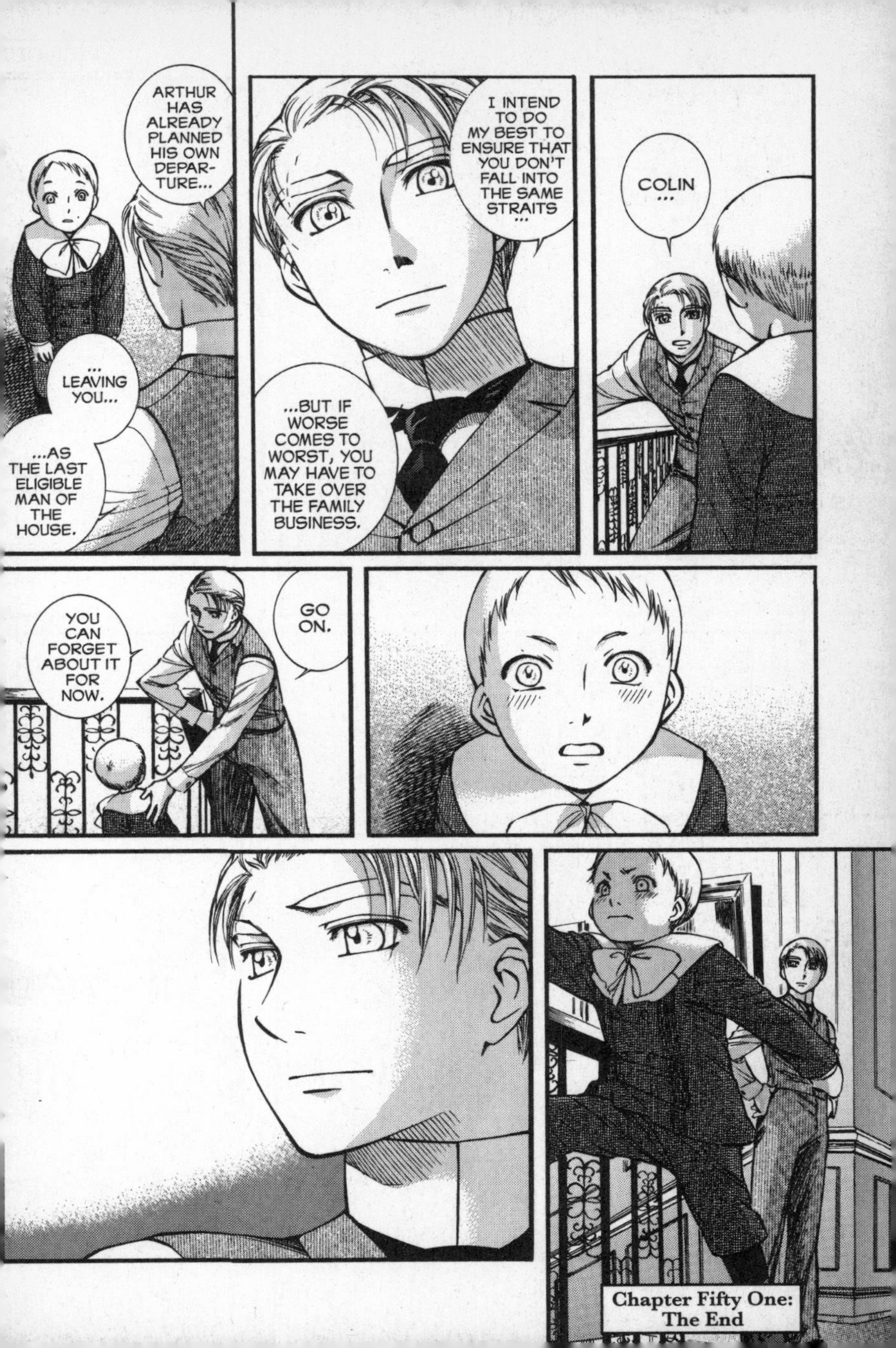
COLIN ...
I INTEND TO DO MY BEST TO ENSURE THAT YOU DON'T FALL INTO THE SAME STRAITS ...
...BUT IF WORSE COMES TO WORST, YOU MAY HAVE TO TAKE OVER THE FAMILY BUSINESS.
ARTHUR HAS ALREADY PLANNED HIS OWN DEPARTURE...
... LEAVING YOU...
...AS THE LAST ELIGIBLE MAN OF THE HOUSE.
GO ON.
YOU CAN FORGET ABOUT IT FOR NOW.
Chapter Fifty One: The End

EPILOGU

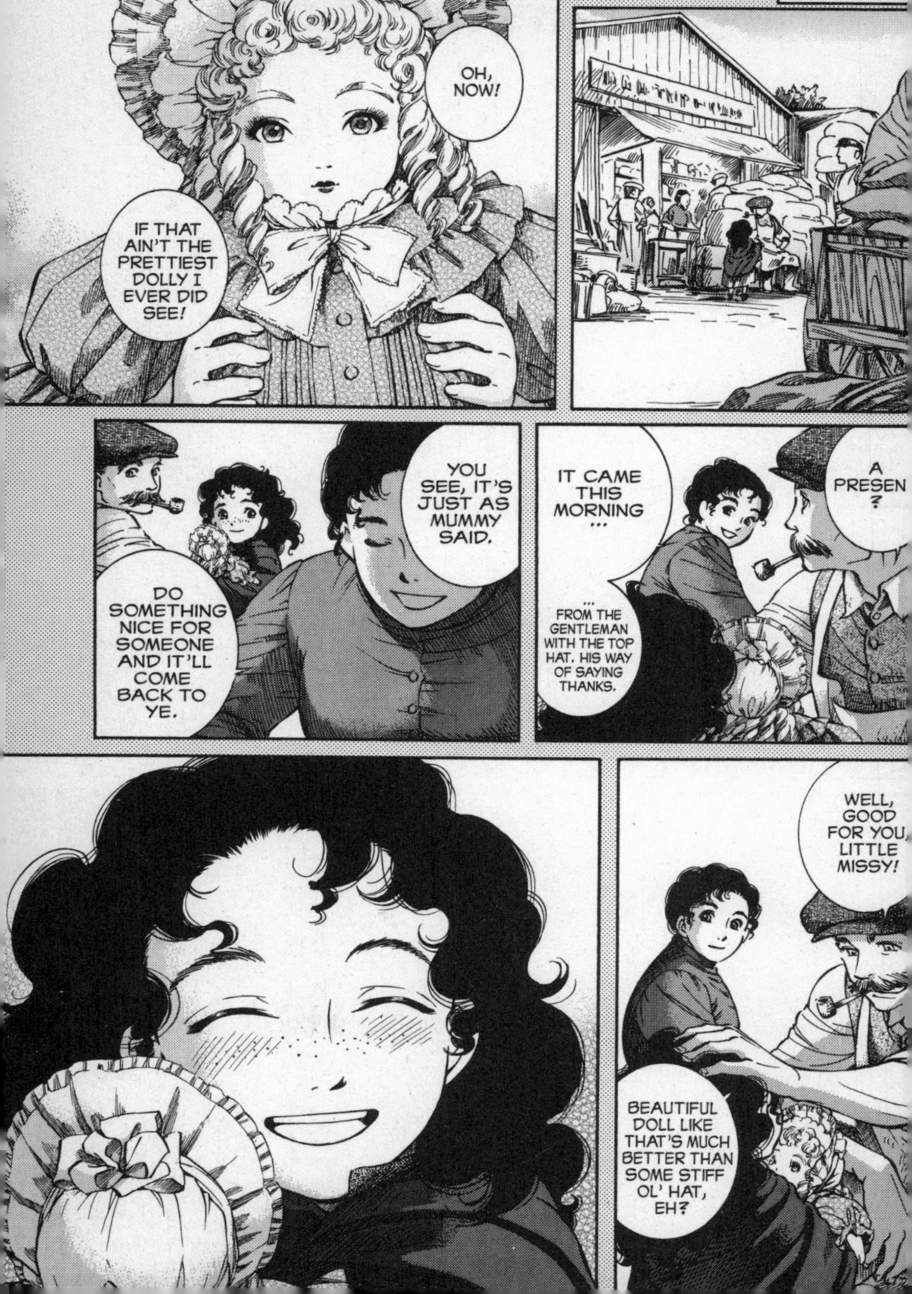

A PRESEN?
IT CAME THIS MORNING ...
... FROM THE GENTLEMAN WITH THE TOP HAT. HIS WAY OF SAYING THANKS.
OH, NOW!
IF THAT AIN'T THE PRETTIEST DOLLY I EVER DID SEE!
WELL, GOOD FOR YOU, LITTLE MISSY!
BEAUTIFUL DOLL LIKE THAT'S MUCH BETTER THAN SOME STIFF OL' HAT, EH?
YOU SEE, IT'S JUST AS MUMMY SAID.
DO SOMETHING NICE FOR SOMEONE AND IT'LL COME BACK TO YE.

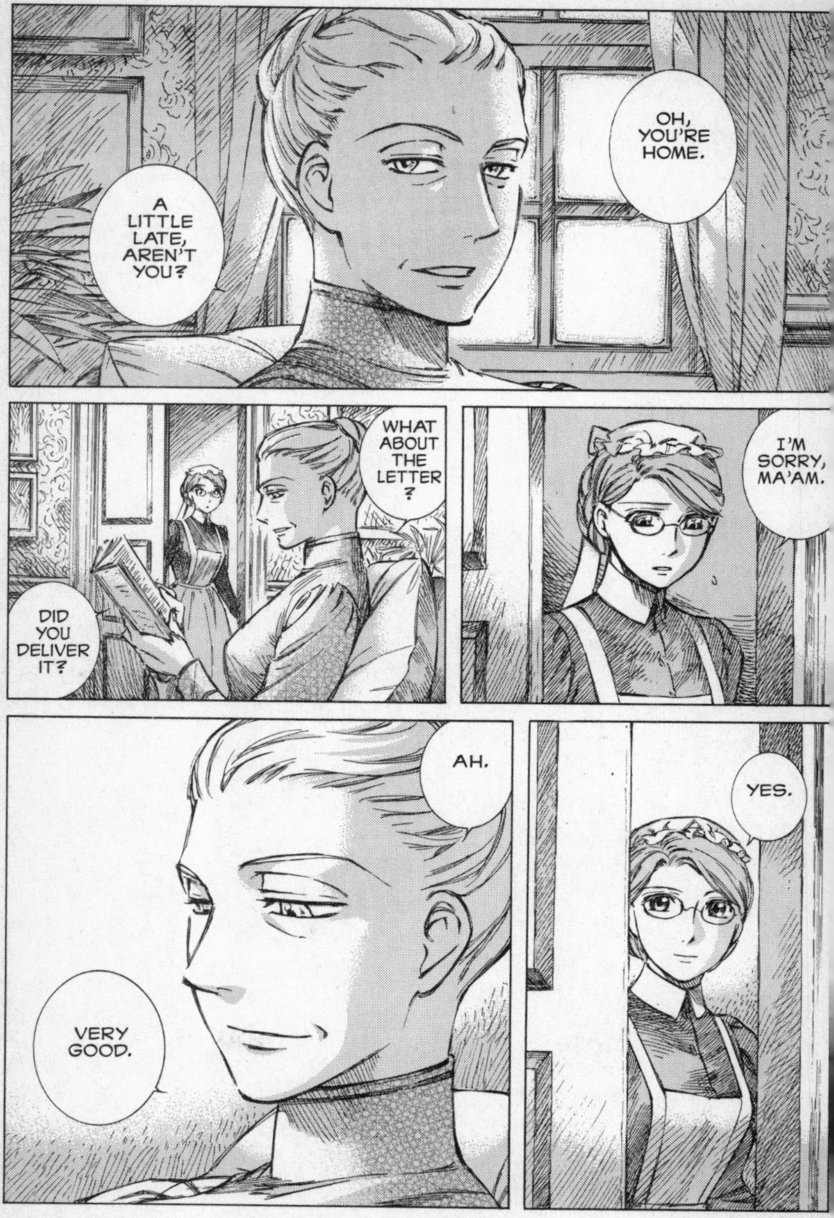
OH, YOU'RE HOME.
A LITTLE LATE, AREN'T YOU?
I'M SORRY, MA'AM.
WHAT ABOUT THE LETTER?
DID YOU DELIVER IT?
YES.
AH.
VERY GOOD.

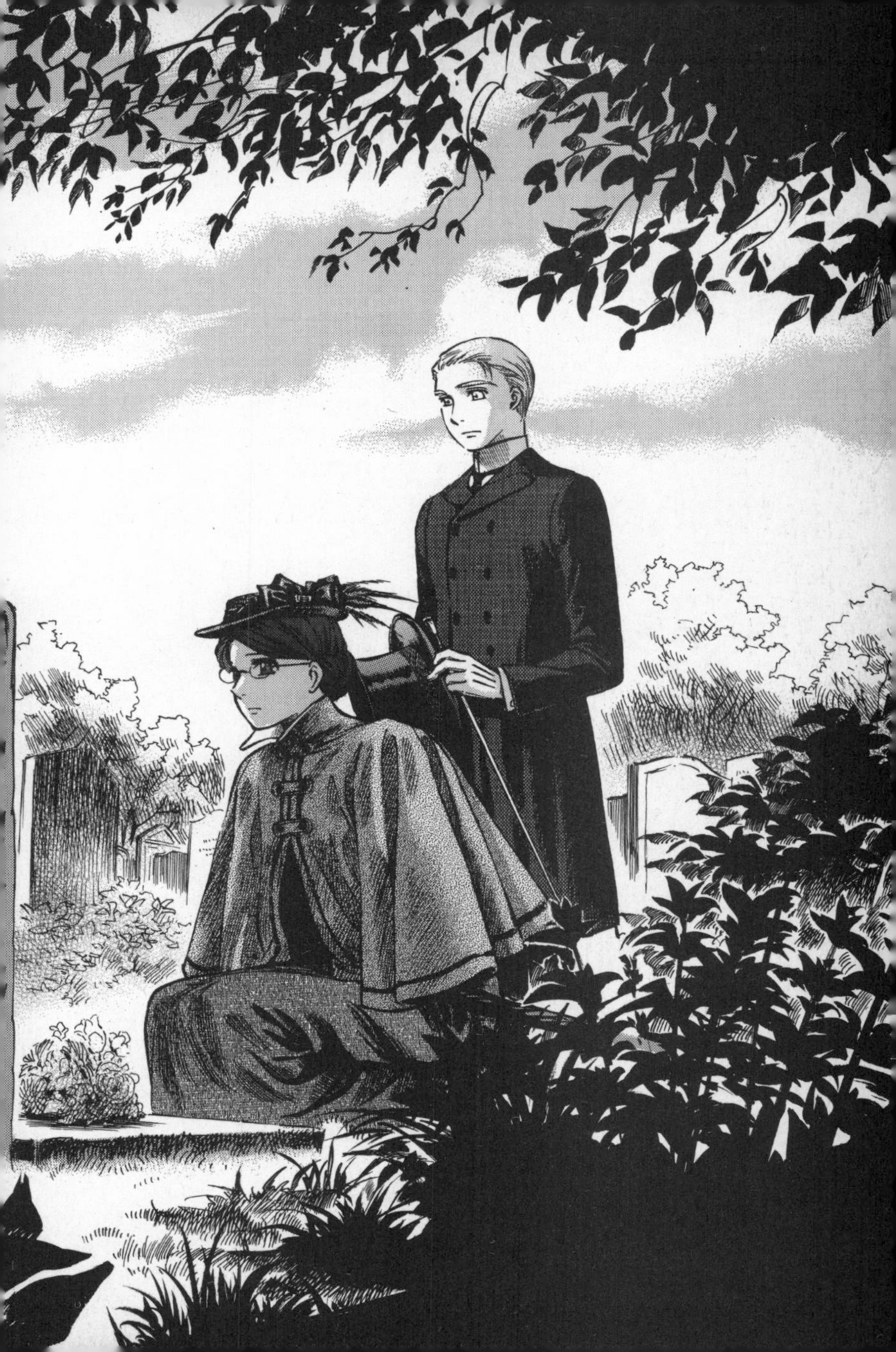

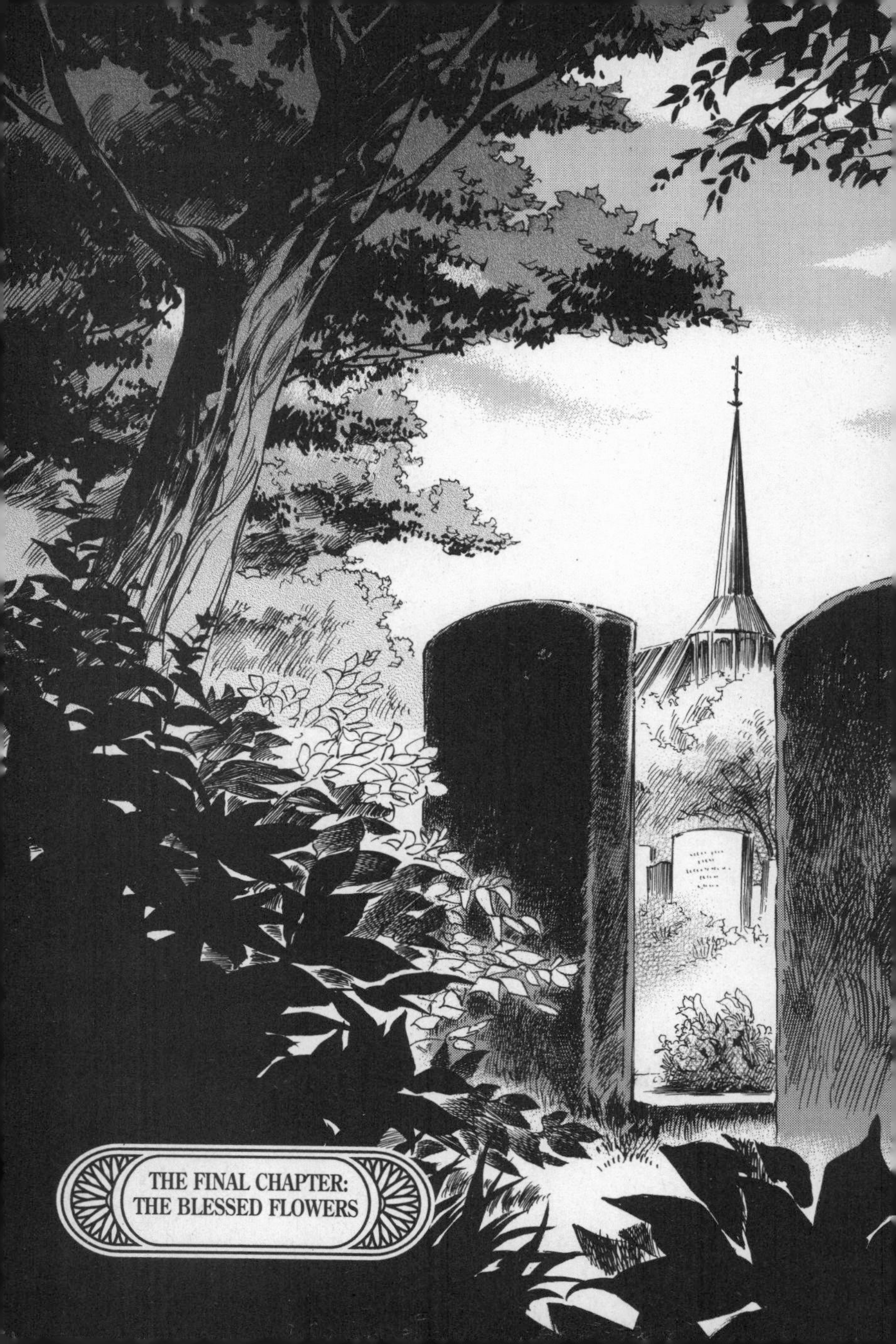
THE FINAL CHAPTER:
THE BLESSED FLOWERS

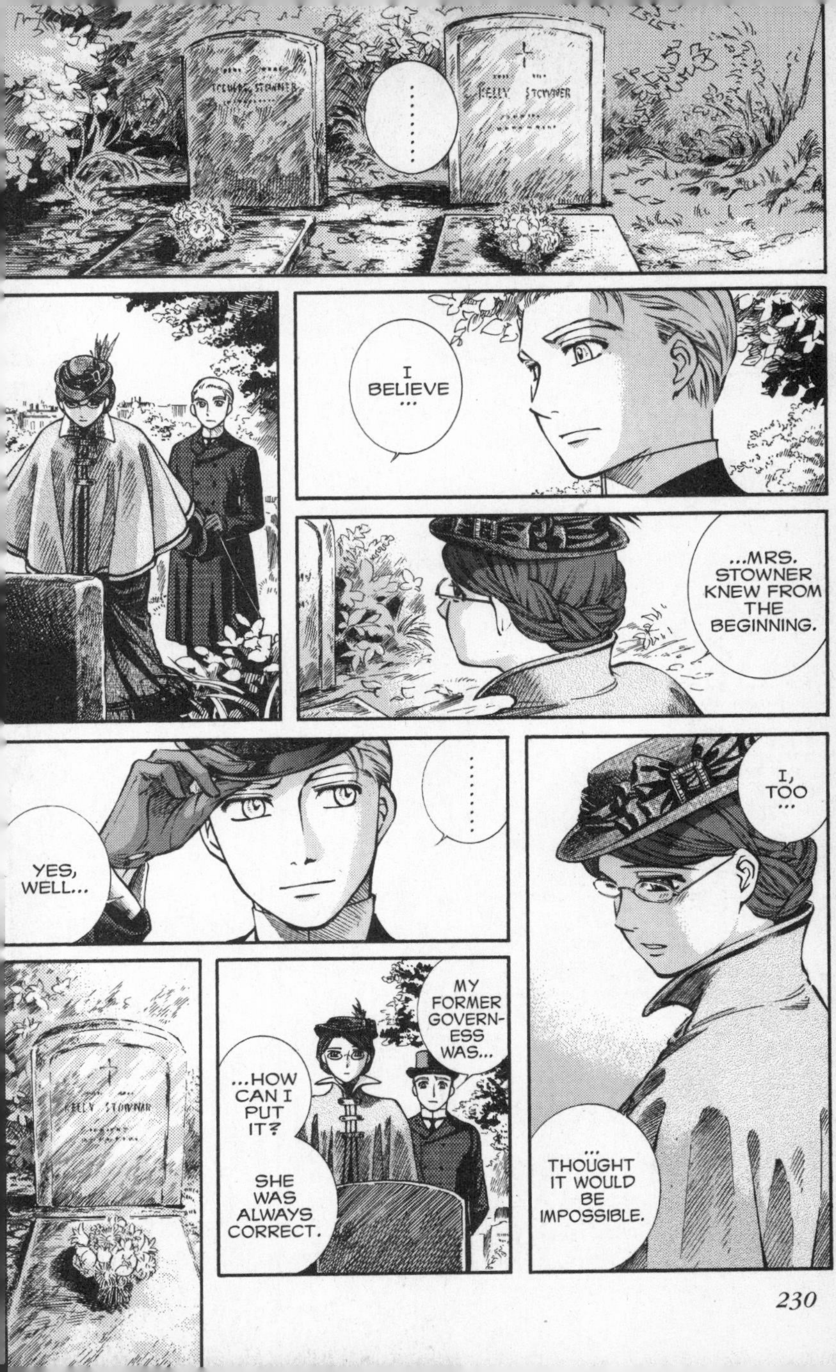
......
I BELIEVE ...
...MRS. STOWNER KNEW FROM THE BEGINNING.
I, TOO ...
... THOUGHT IT WOULD BE IMPOSSIBLE.
......
YES, WELL...
MY FORMER GOVERN-ESS WAS...
...HOW CAN I PUT IT?
SHE WAS ALWAYS CORRECT.

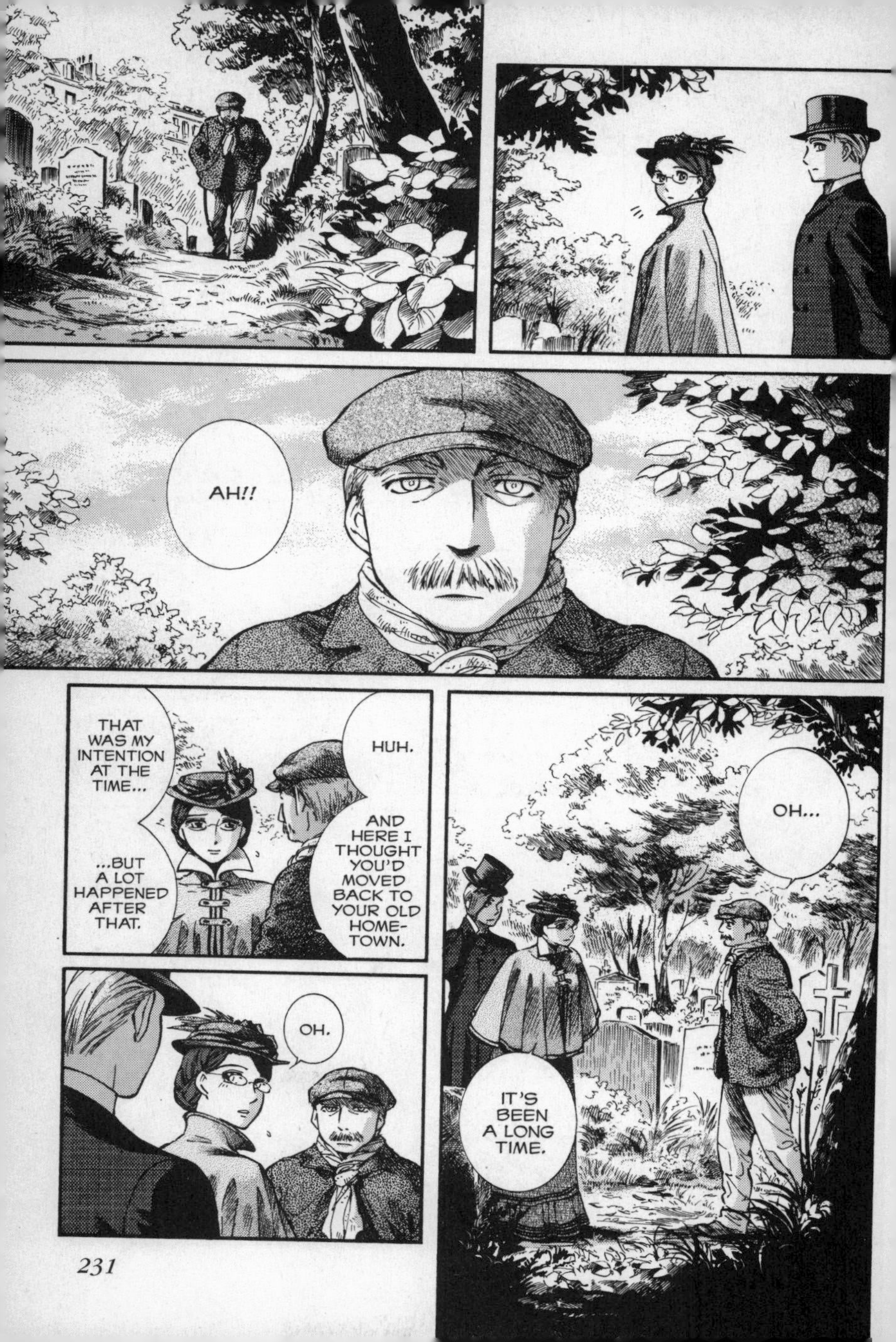
AH!!
OH...
IT'S BEEN A LONG TIME.
HUH.
AND HERE I THOUGHT YOU'D MOVED BACK TO YOUR OLD HOME-TOWN.
THAT WAS MY INTENTION AT THE TIME...
...BUT A LOT HAPPENED AFTER THAT.
OH.

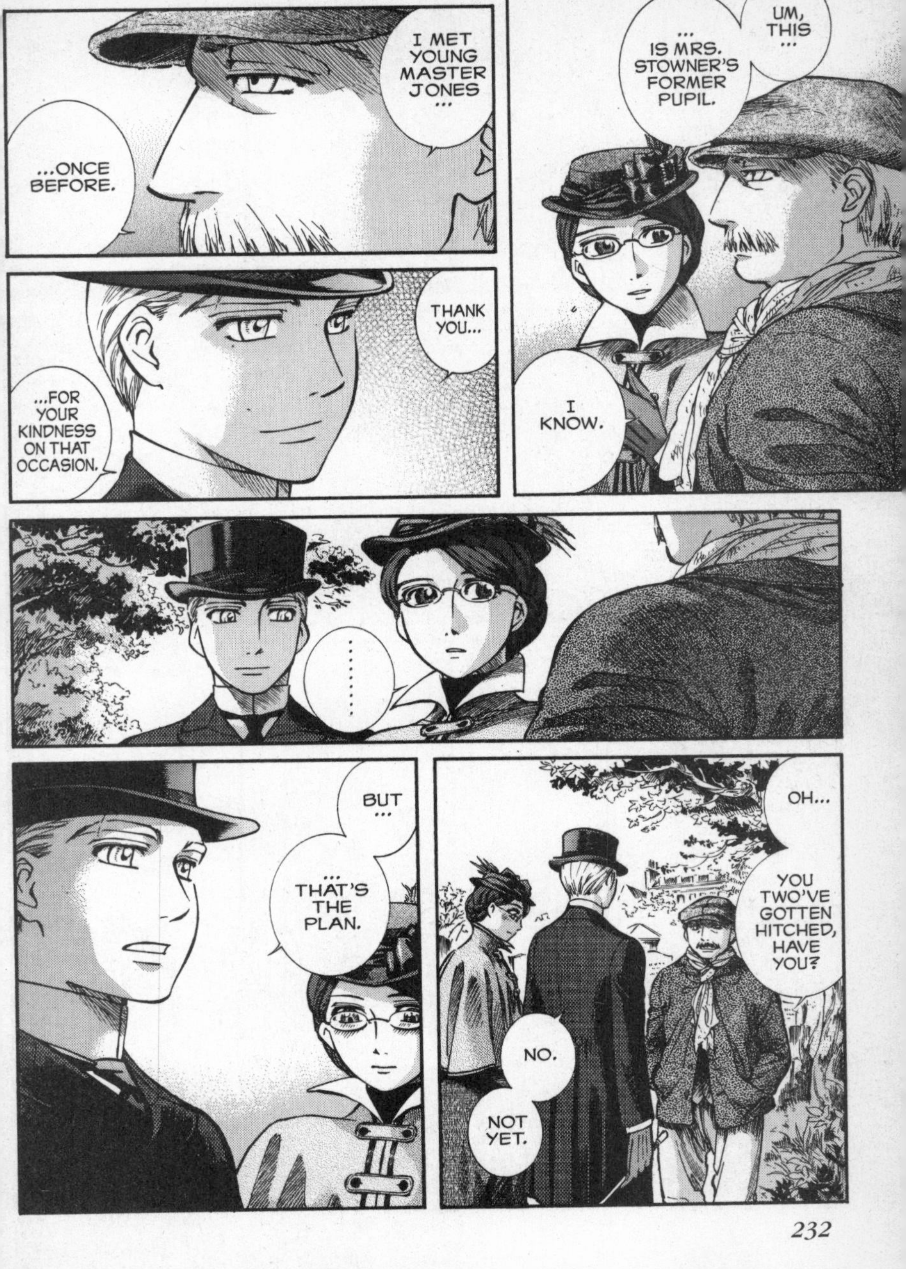
UM, THIS ...
... IS MRS. STOWNER'S FORMER PUPIL.
I KNOW.
I MET YOUNG MASTER JONES ...
...ONCE BEFORE.
THANK YOU...
...FOR YOUR KINDNESS ON THAT OCCASION.
......
OH...
YOU TWO'VE GOTTEN HITCHED, HAVE YOU?
NO.
NOT YET.
BUT ...
... THAT'S THE PLAN.

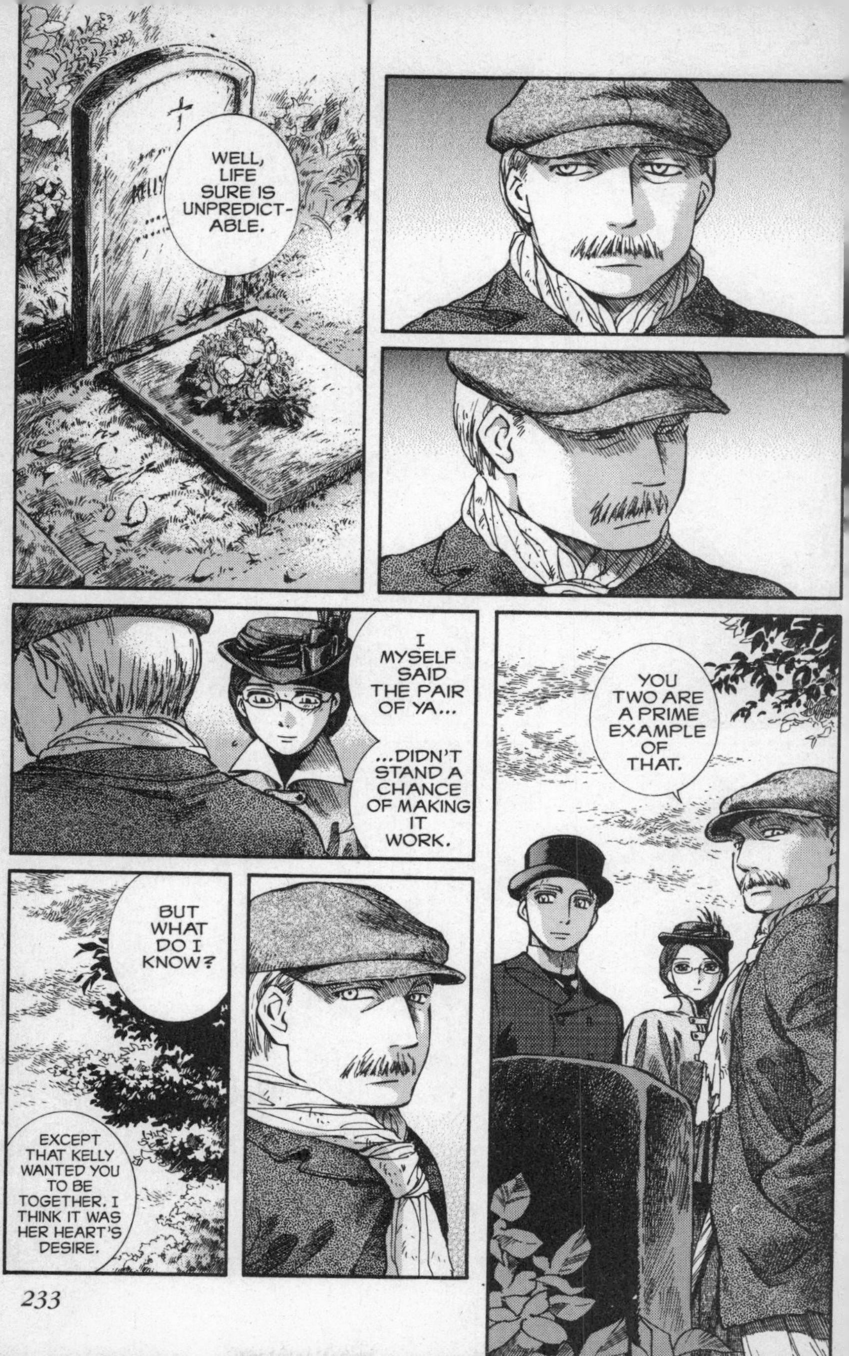
WELL, LIFE SURE IS UNPREDICT-ABLE.
YOU TWO ARE A PRIME EXAMPLE OF THAT.
I MYSELF SAID THE PAIR OF YA...
...DIDN'T STAND A CHANCE OF MAKING IT WORK.
BUT WHAT DO I KNOW?
EXCEPT THAT KELLY WANTED YOU TO BE TOGETHER. I THINK IT WAS HER HEART'S DESIRE.

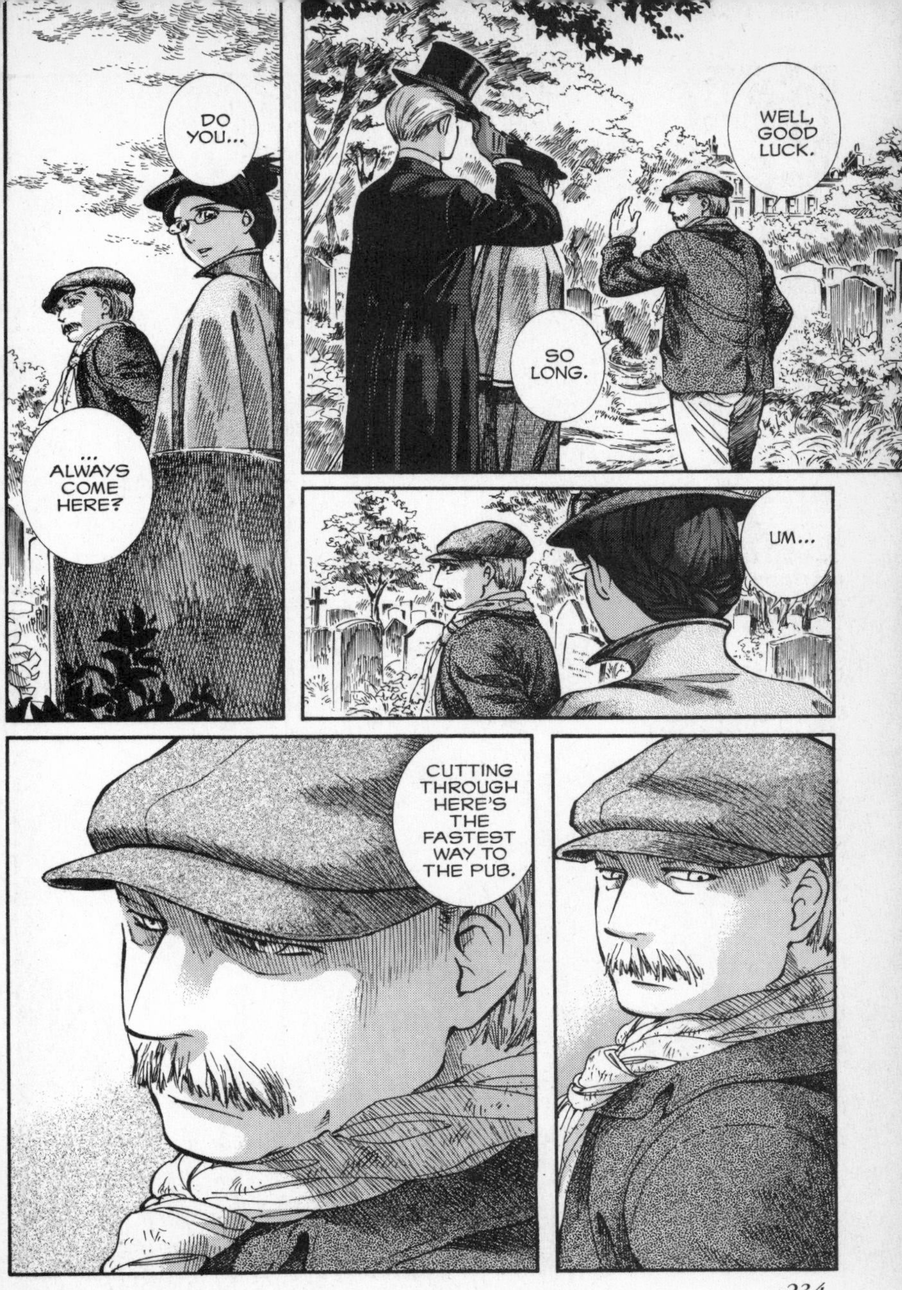
WELL, GOOD LUCK.
SO LONG.
DO YOU...
... ALWAYS COME HERE?
UM...
CUTTING THROUGH HERE'S THE FASTEST WAY TO THE PUB.

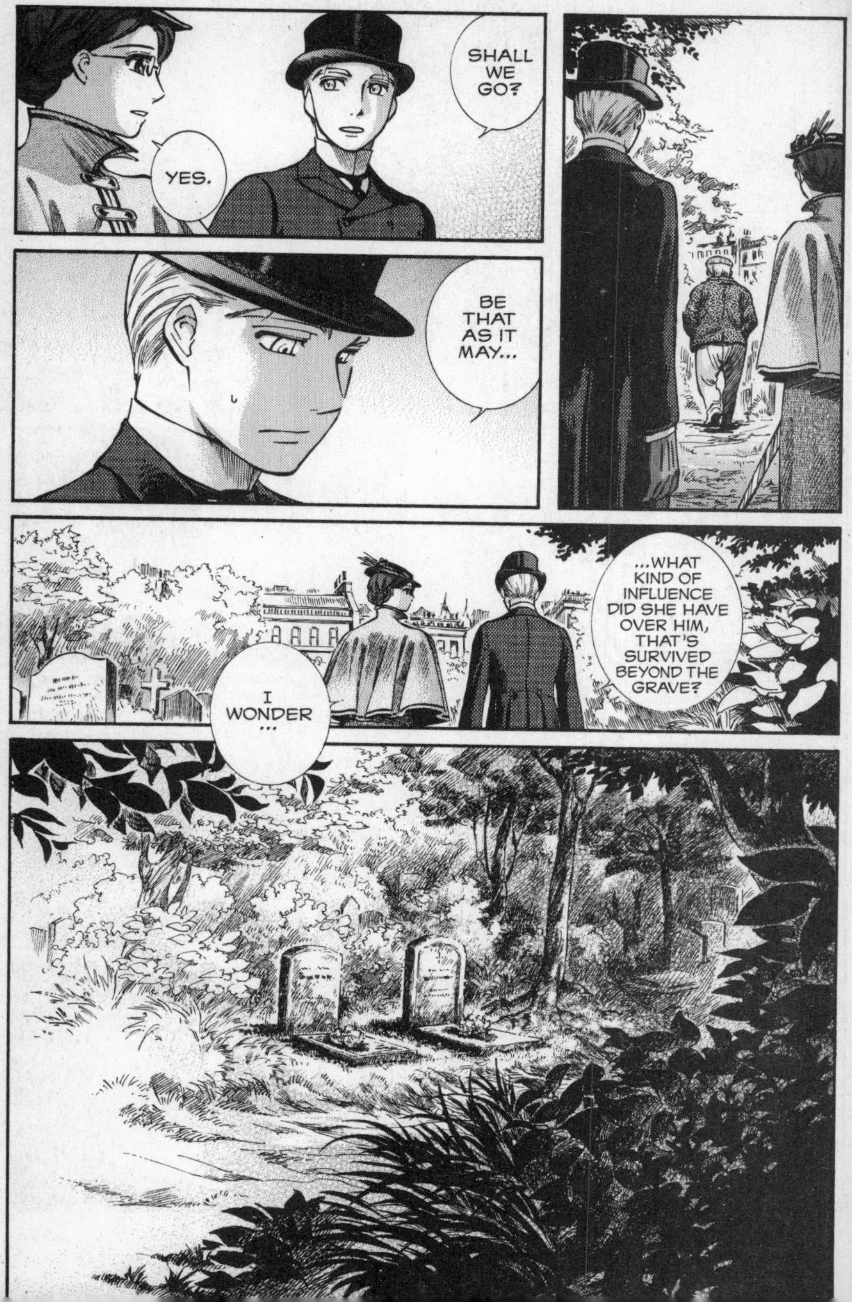
SHALL WE GO?
YES.
BE THAT AS IT MAY...
...WHAT KIND OF INFLUENCE DID SHE HAVE OVER HIM, THAT'S SURVIVED BEYOND THE GRAVE?
I WONDER ...

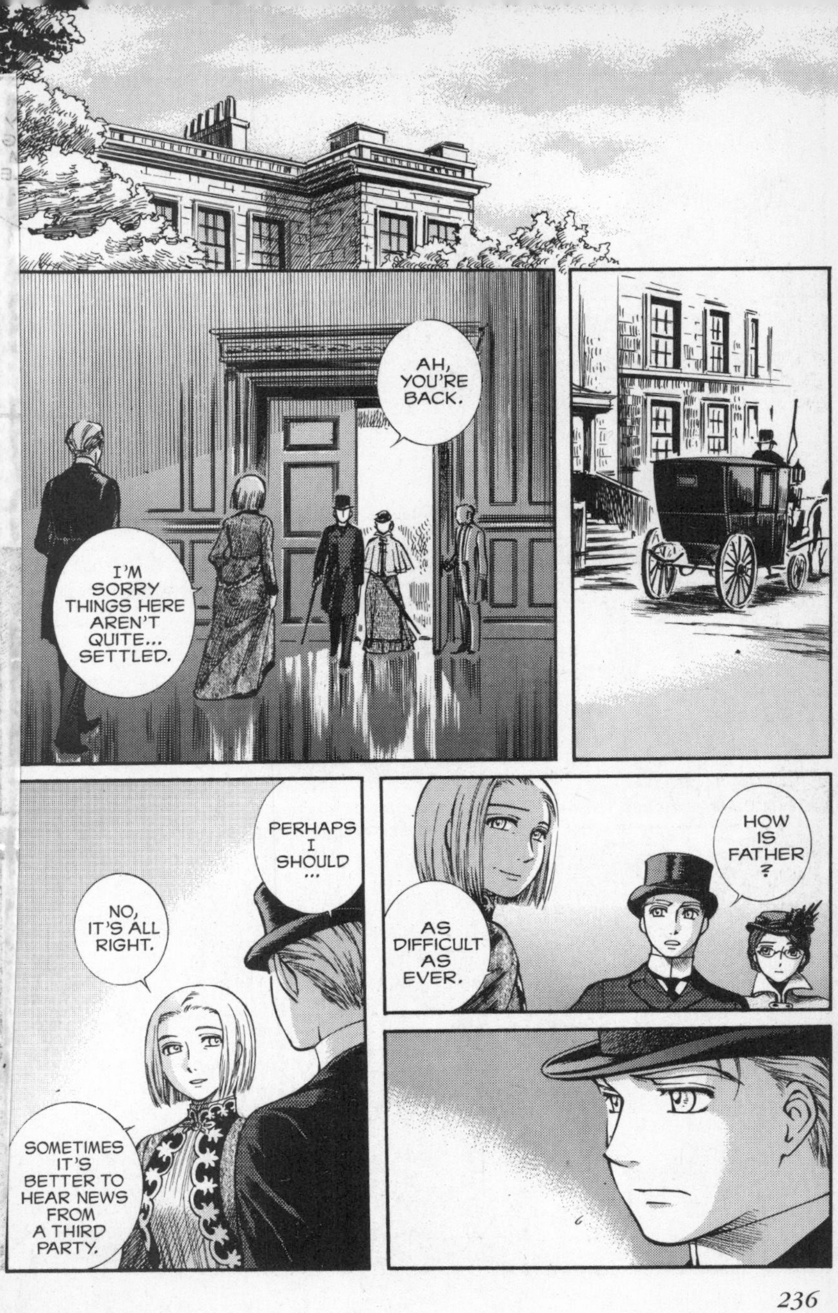
AH, YOU'RE BACK.
I'M SORRY THINGS HERE AREN'T QUITE... SETTLED.
HOW IS FATHER?
AS DIFFICULT AS EVER.
PERHAPS I SHOULD ...
NO, IT'S ALL RIGHT.
SOMETIMES IT'S BETTER TO HEAR NEWS FROM A THIRD PARTY.

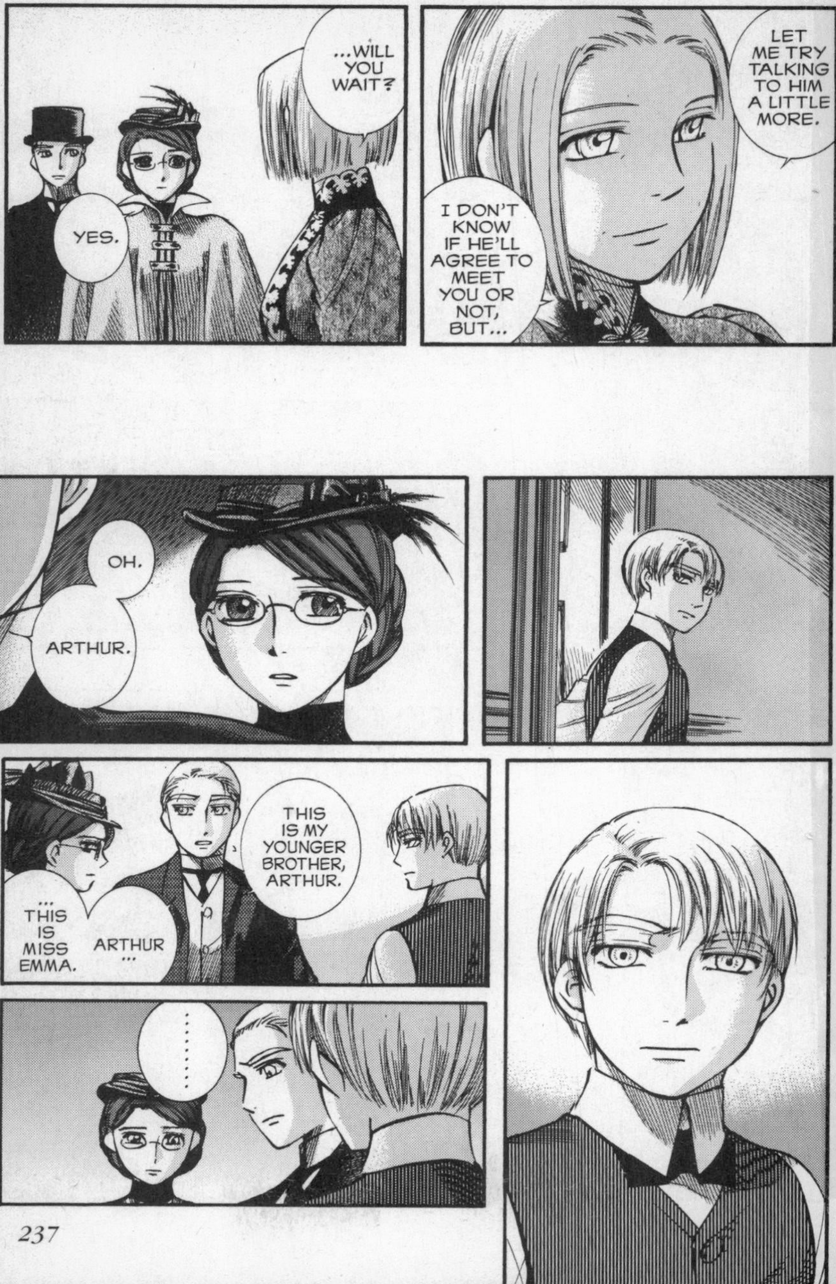
LET ME TRY TALKING TO HIM A LITTLE MORE.
I DON'T KNOW IF HE'LL AGREE TO MEET YOU OR NOT, BUT...
...WILL YOU WAIT?
YES.
OH.
ARTHUR.
THIS IS MY YOUNGER BROTHER, ARTHUR.
ARTHUR ...
... THIS IS MISS EMMA.
......

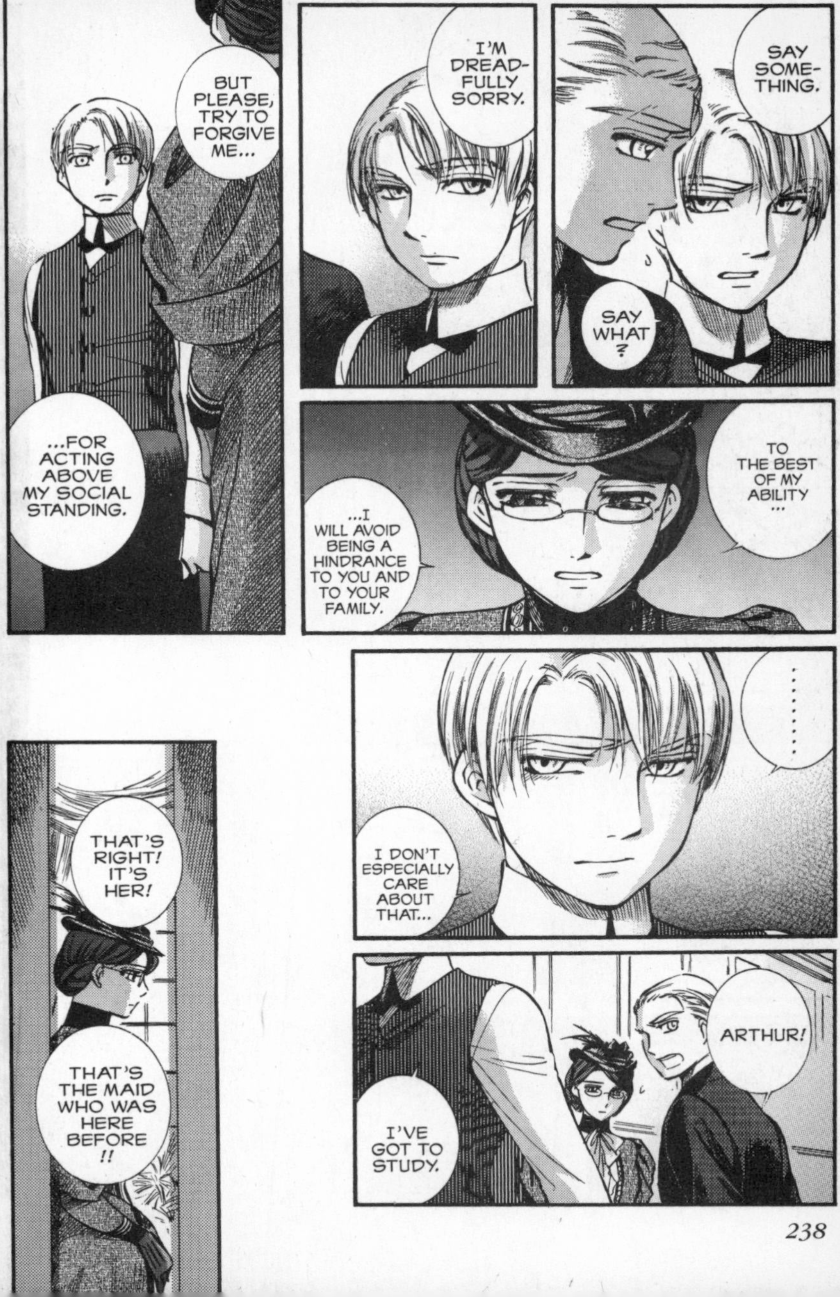
SAY SOME-THING.
SAY WHAT ?
I'M DREAD-FULLY SORRY.
TO THE BEST OF MY ABILITY ...
...I WILL AVOID BEING A HINDRANCE TO YOU AND TO YOUR FAMILY.
BUT PLEASE, TRY TO FORGIVE ME...
...FOR ACTING ABOVE MY SOCIAL STANDING.
....
I DON'T ESPECIALLY CARE ABOUT THAT...
ARTHUR!
I'VE GOT TO STUDY.
THAT'S RIGHT! IT'S HER!
THAT'S THE MAID WHO WAS HERE BEFORE !!

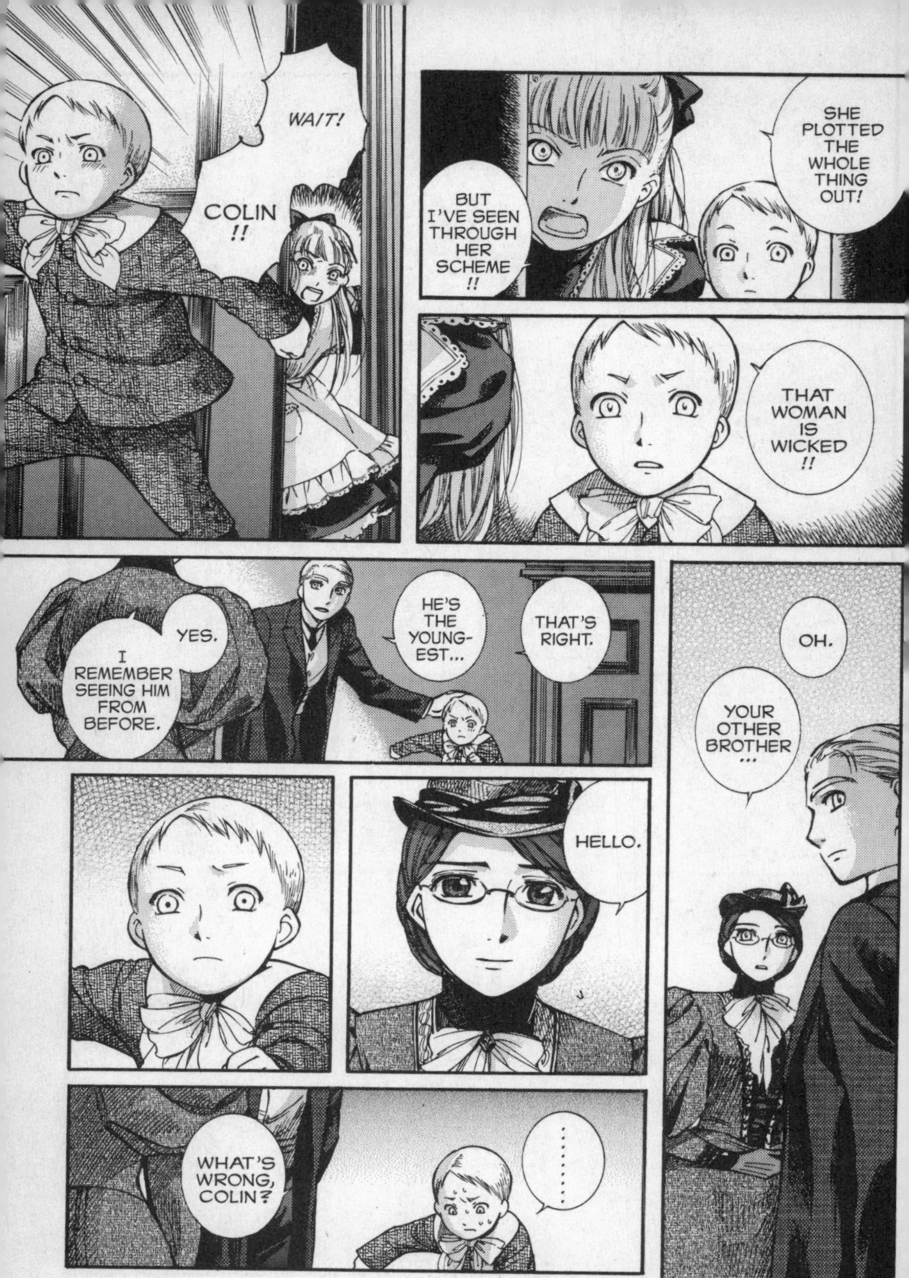
SHE PLOTTED THE WHOLE THING OUT!
BUT I'VE SEEN THROUGH HER SCHEME !!
THAT WOMAN IS WICKED !!
WAIT!
COLIN !!
OH.
YOUR OTHER BROTHER ...
THAT'S RIGHT.
HE'S THE YOUNG- EST...
YES.
I REMEMBER SEEING HIM FROM BEFORE.
HELLO.
....
WHAT'S WRONG, COLIN?

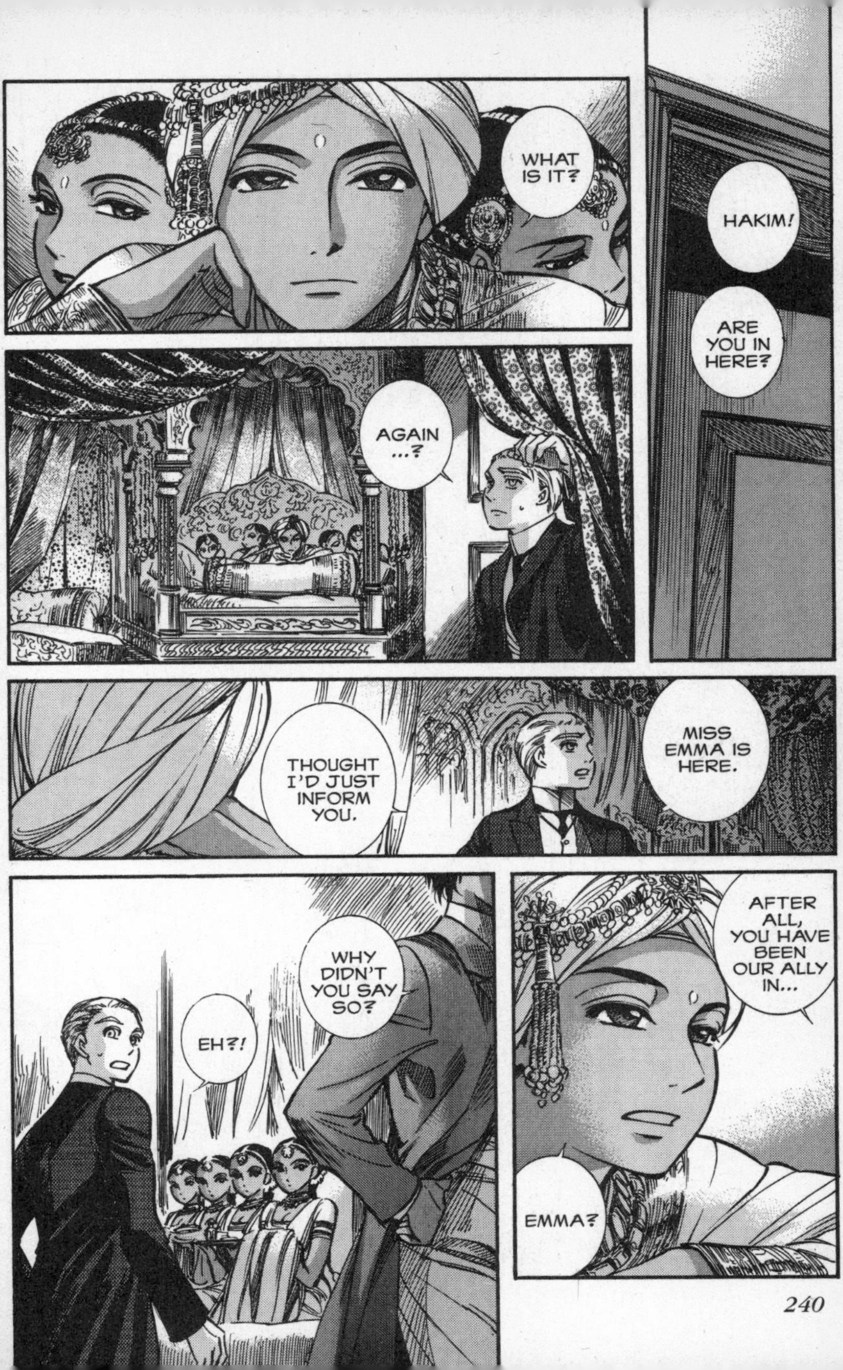
HAKIM!
ARE YOU IN HERE?
WHAT IS IT?
AGAIN ...?
MISS EMMA IS HERE.
THOUGHT I'D JUST INFORM YOU.
AFTER ALL, YOU HAVE BEEN OUR ALLY IN...
EMMA?
WHY DIDN'T YOU SAY SO?
EH?!

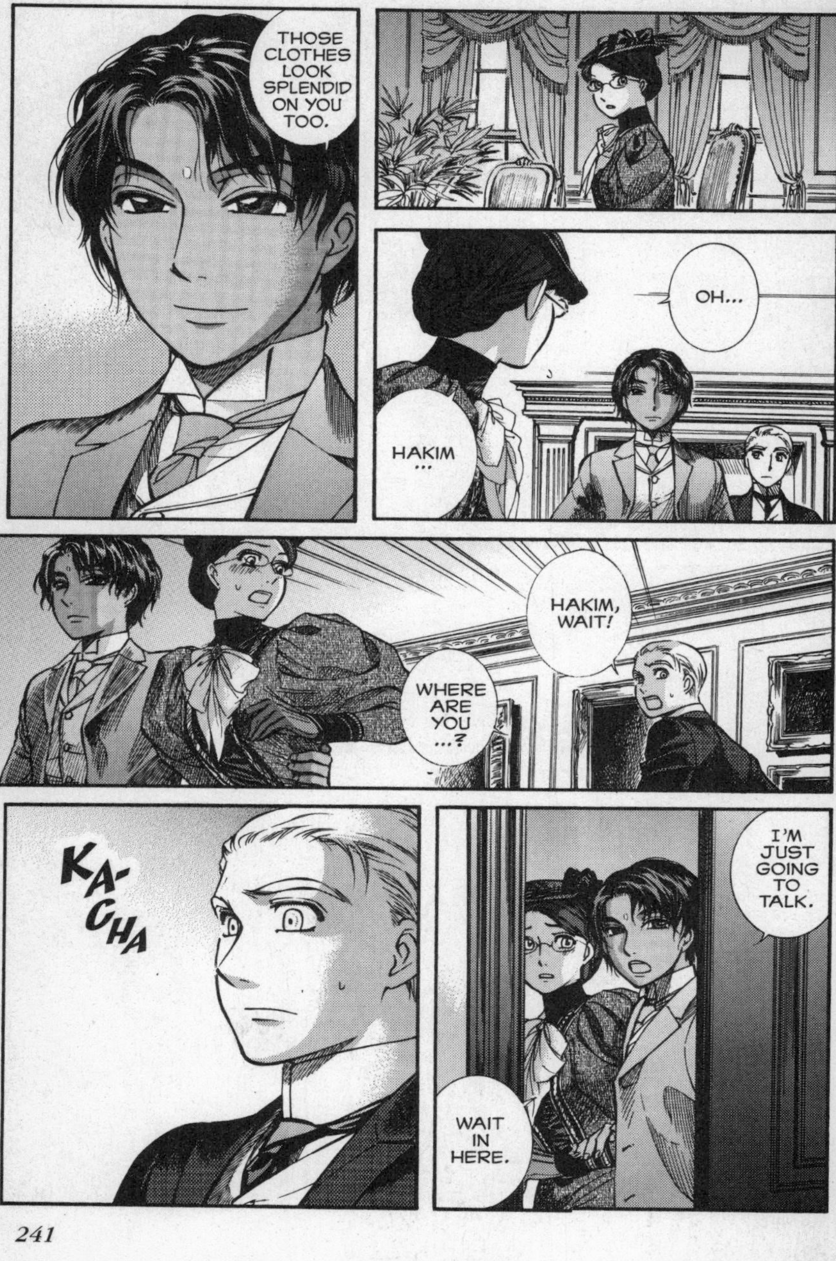
OH...
HAKIM ...
THOSE CLOTHES LOOK SPLENDID ON YOU TOO.
HAKIM, WAIT!
WHERE ARE YOU ...?
I'M JUST GOING TO TALK.
WAIT IN HERE.
KA-CHA

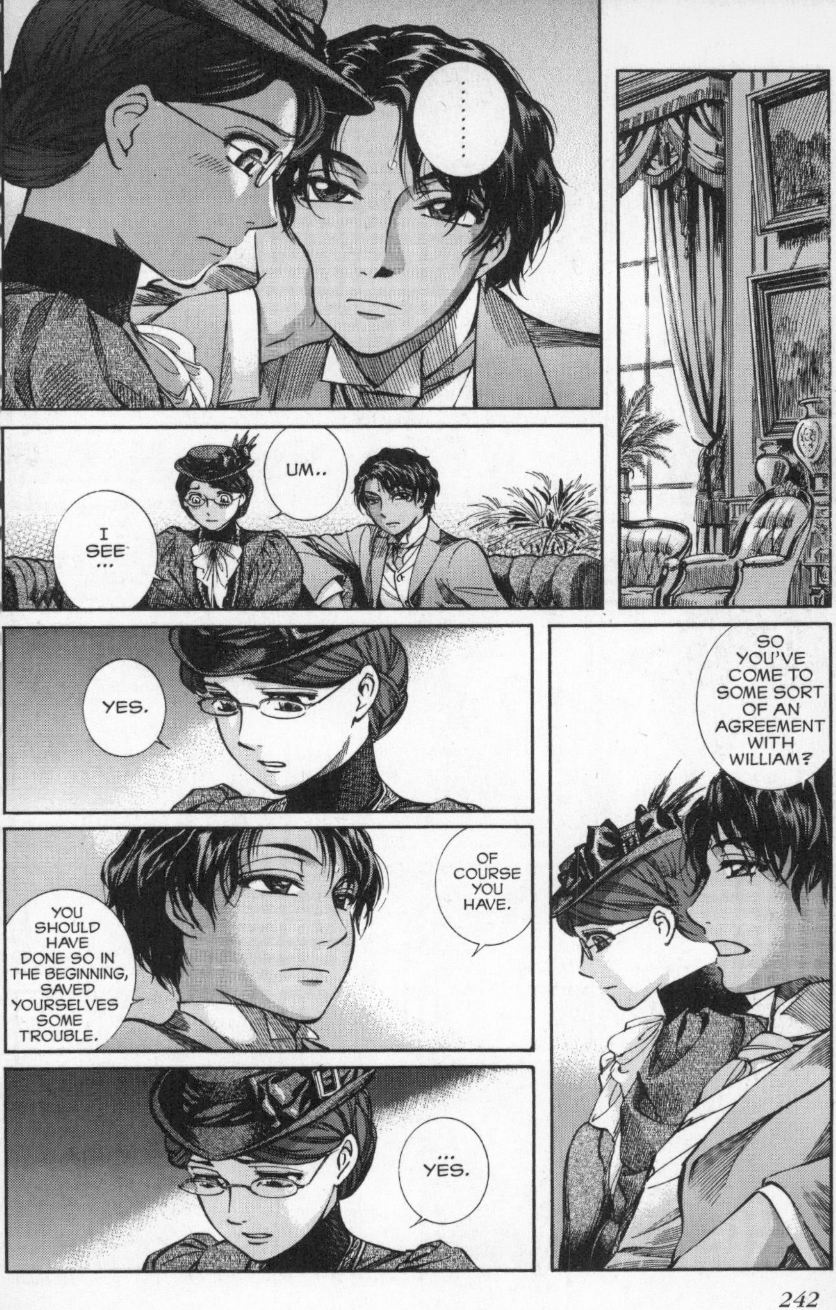
......
UM..
I SEE ...
SO YOU'VE COME TO SOME SORT OF AN AGREEMENT WITH WILLIAM?
YES.
OF COURSE YOU HAVE.
YOU SHOULD HAVE DONE SO IN THE BEGINNING, SAVED YOURSELVES SOME TROUBLE.
... YES.

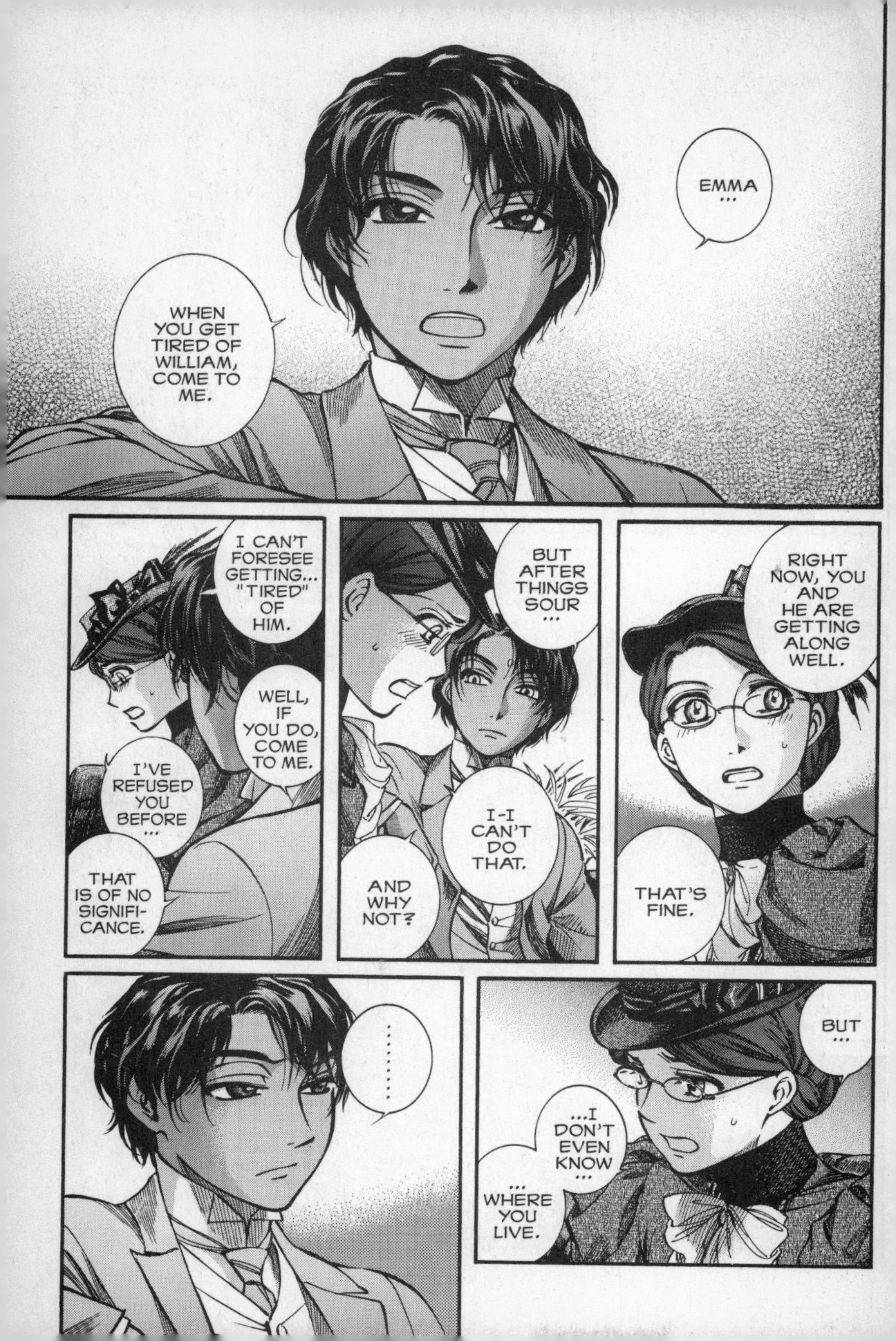
EMMA ...
WHEN YOU GET TIRED OF WILLIAM, COME TO ME.
RIGHT NOW, YOU AND HE ARE GETTING ALONG WELL.
THAT'S FINE.
BUT AFTER THINGS SOUR ...
I-I CAN'T DO THAT.
AND WHY NOT?
I CAN'T FORESEE GETTING... "TIRED" OF HIM.
WELL, IF YOU DO, COME TO ME.
I'VE REFUSED YOU BEFORE ...
THAT IS OF NO SIGNIFI-CANCE.
BUT ...
...I DON'T EVEN KNOW ...
... WHERE YOU LIVE.
......

·····

ASK WILLIAM.

···ALL RIGHT.

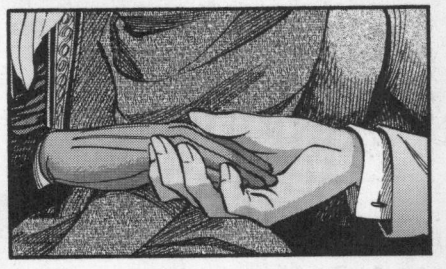

I GIVE YOU UP GRUDGINGLY.

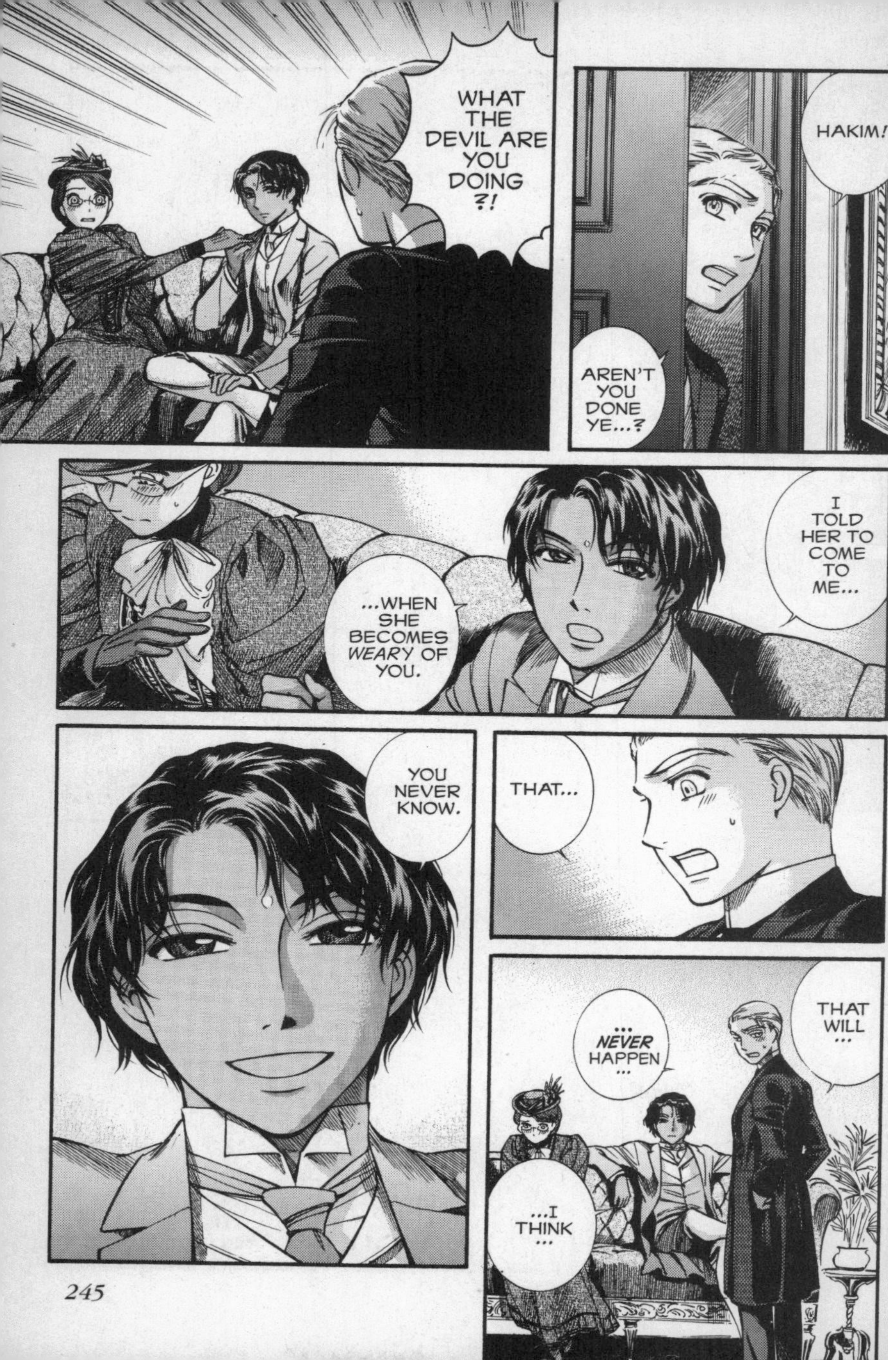
HAKIM!
AREN'T YOU DONE YE...?
WHAT THE DEVIL ARE YOU DOING ?!
I TOLD HER TO COME TO ME...
...WHEN SHE BECOMES *WEARY* OF YOU.
THAT...
YOU NEVER KNOW.
THAT WILL ...
... *NEVER* HAPPEN ...
...I THINK ...

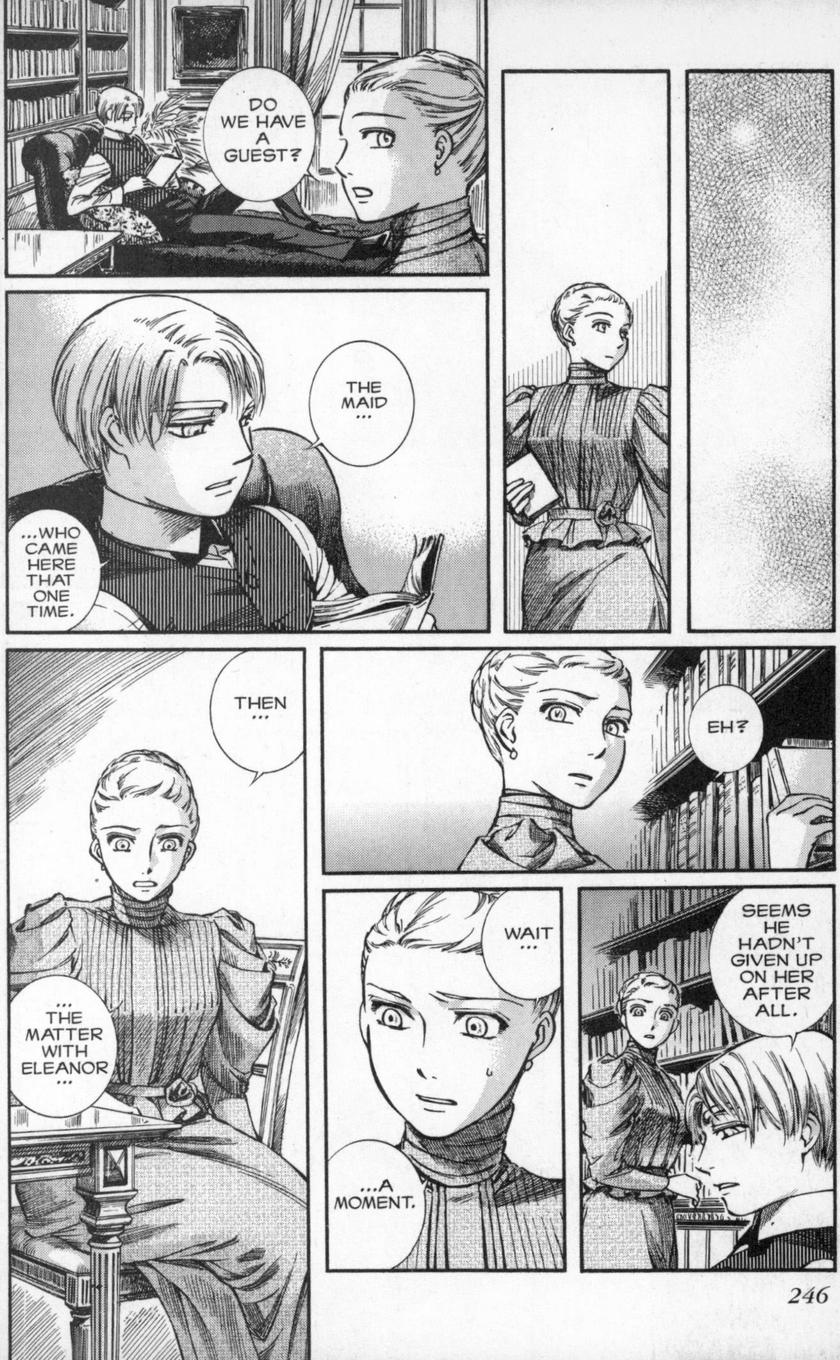
DO WE HAVE A GUEST?
THE MAID ...
...WHO CAME HERE THAT ONE TIME.
EH?
SEEMS HE HADN'T GIVEN UP ON HER AFTER ALL.
WAIT ...
...A MOMENT.
THEN ...
... THE MATTER WITH ELEANOR ...

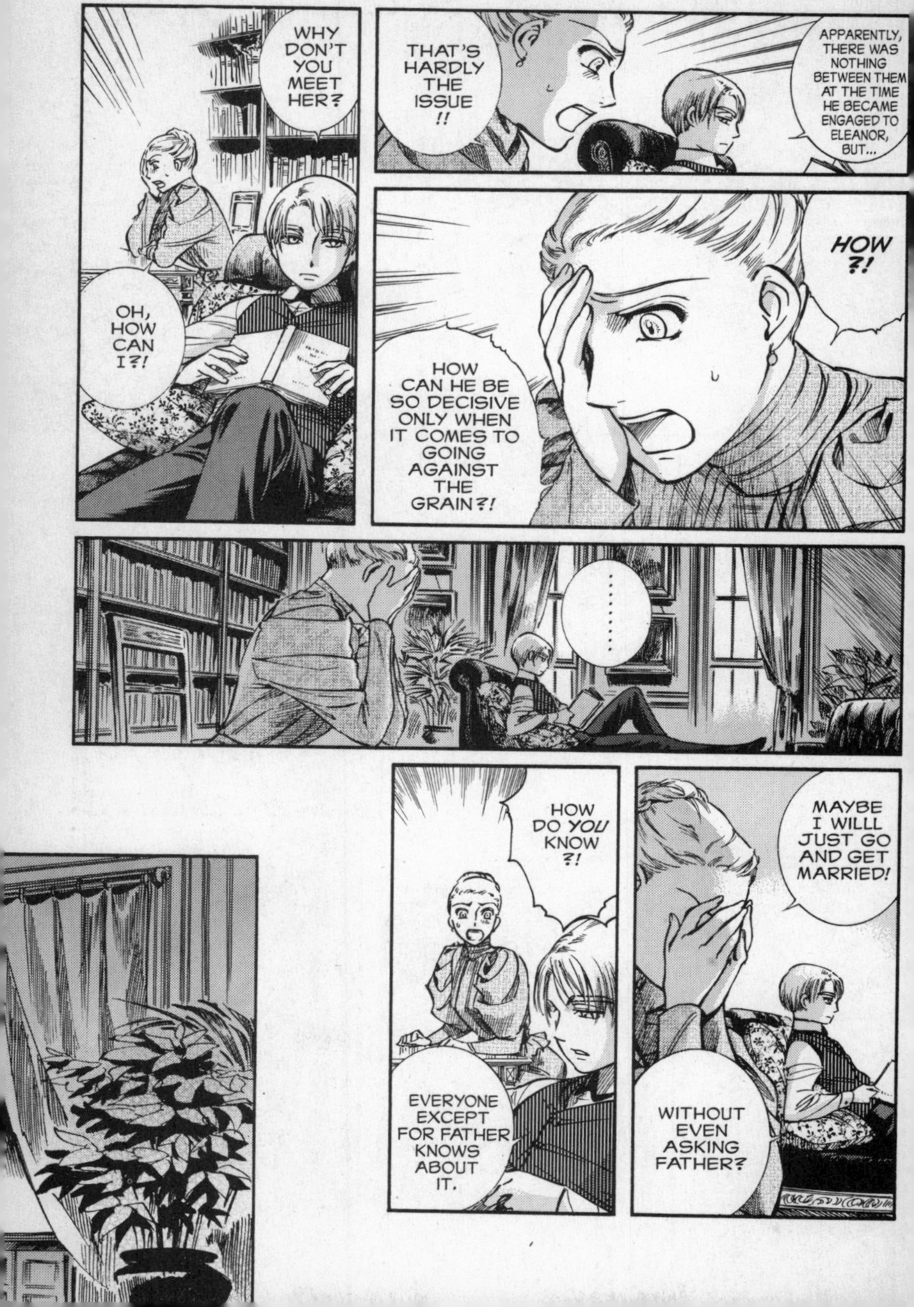
APPARENTLY, THERE WAS NOTHING BETWEEN THEM AT THE TIME HE BECAME ENGAGED TO ELEANOR, BUT...
THAT'S HARDLY THE ISSUE !!
HOW ?!
HOW CAN HE BE SO DECISIVE ONLY WHEN IT COMES TO GOING AGAINST THE GRAIN ?!
WHY DON'T YOU MEET HER?
OH, HOW CAN I ?!
......
MAYBE I WILL JUST GO AND GET MARRIED!
WITHOUT EVEN ASKING FATHER?
HOW DO YOU KNOW ?!
EVERYONE EXCEPT FOR FATHER KNOWS ABOUT IT.

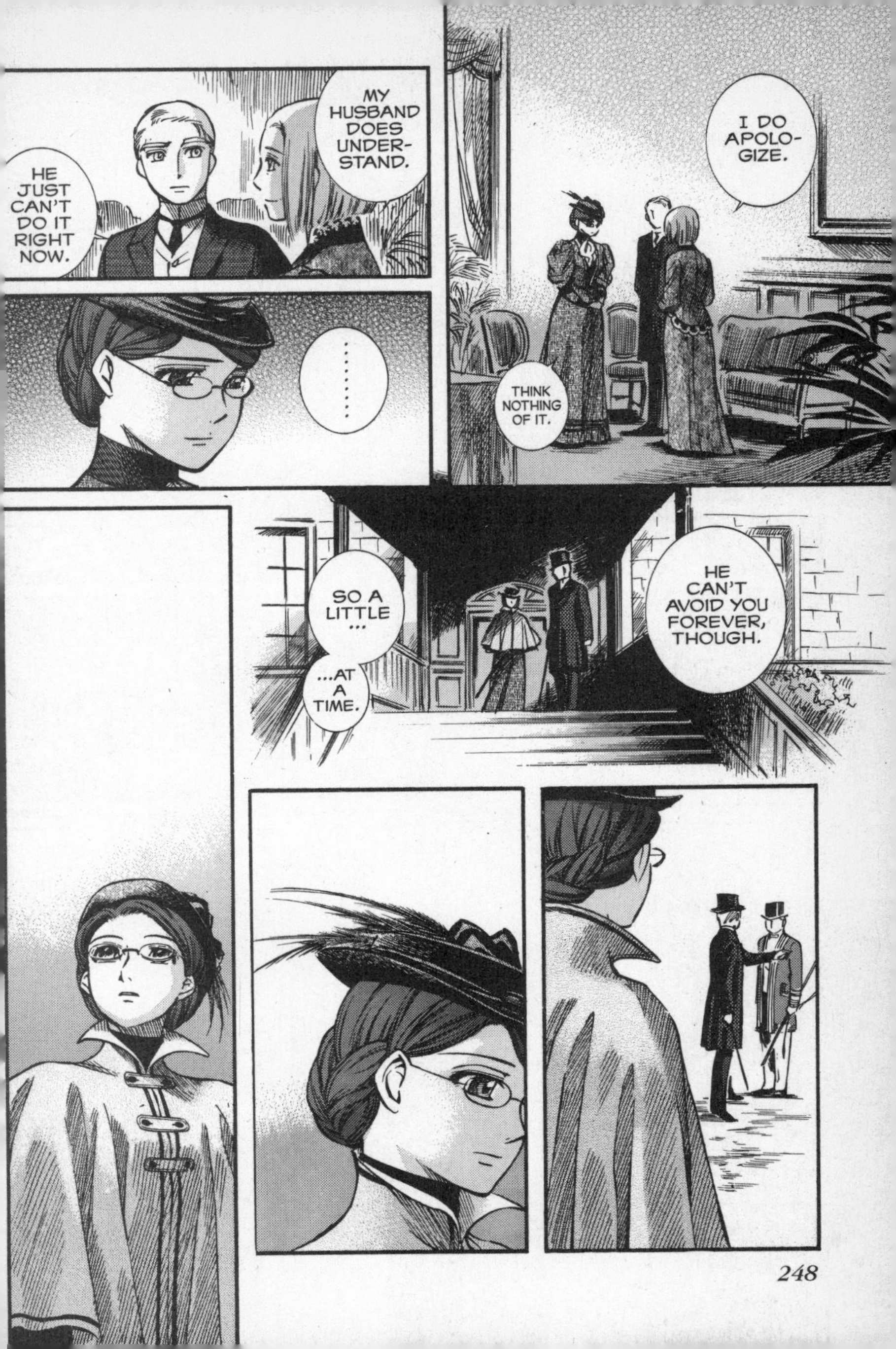
I DO APOLOGIZE.
THINK NOTHING OF IT.
MY HUSBAND DOES UNDERSTAND.
HE JUST CAN'T DO IT RIGHT NOW.
......
HE CAN'T AVOID YOU FOREVER, THOUGH.
SO A LITTLE ...
...AT A TIME.

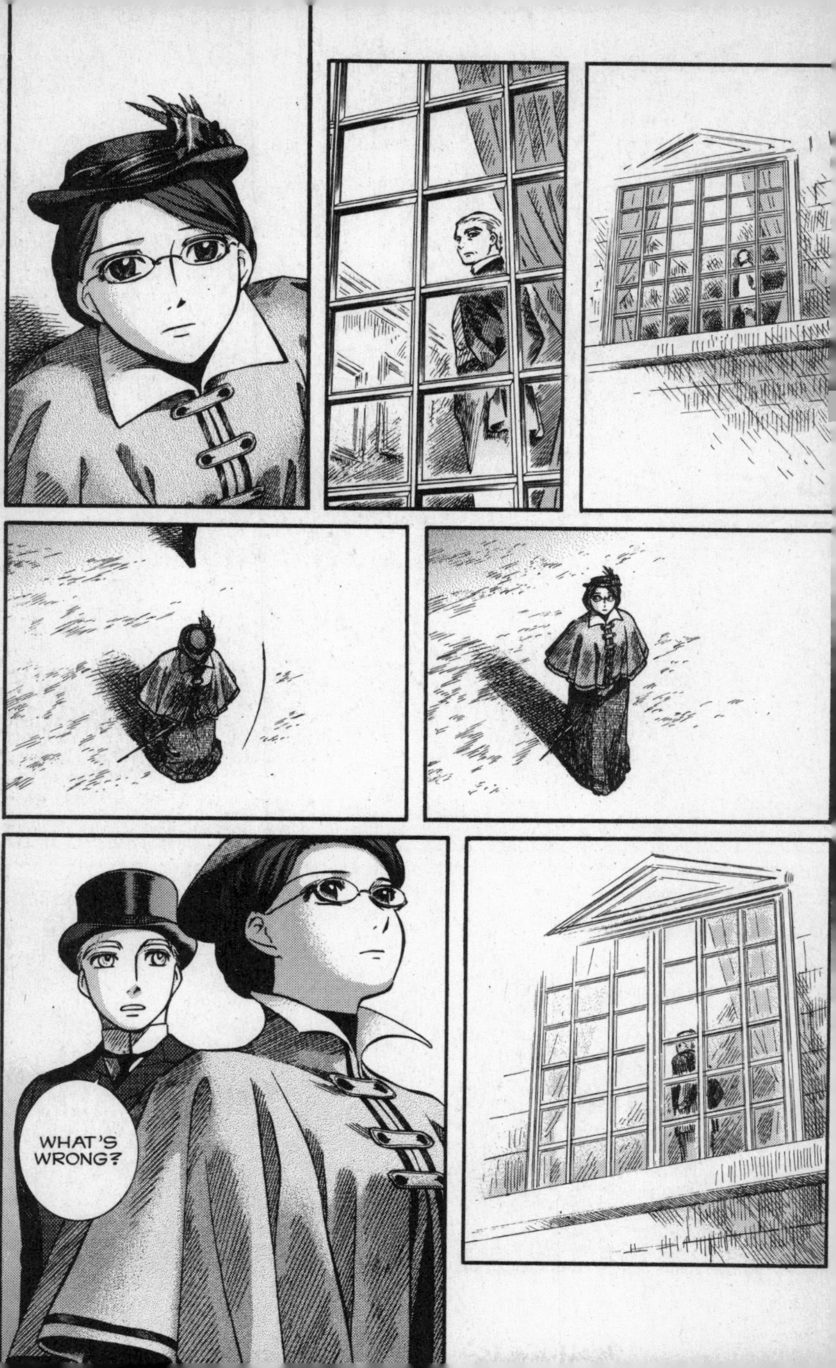
WHAT'S WRONG?

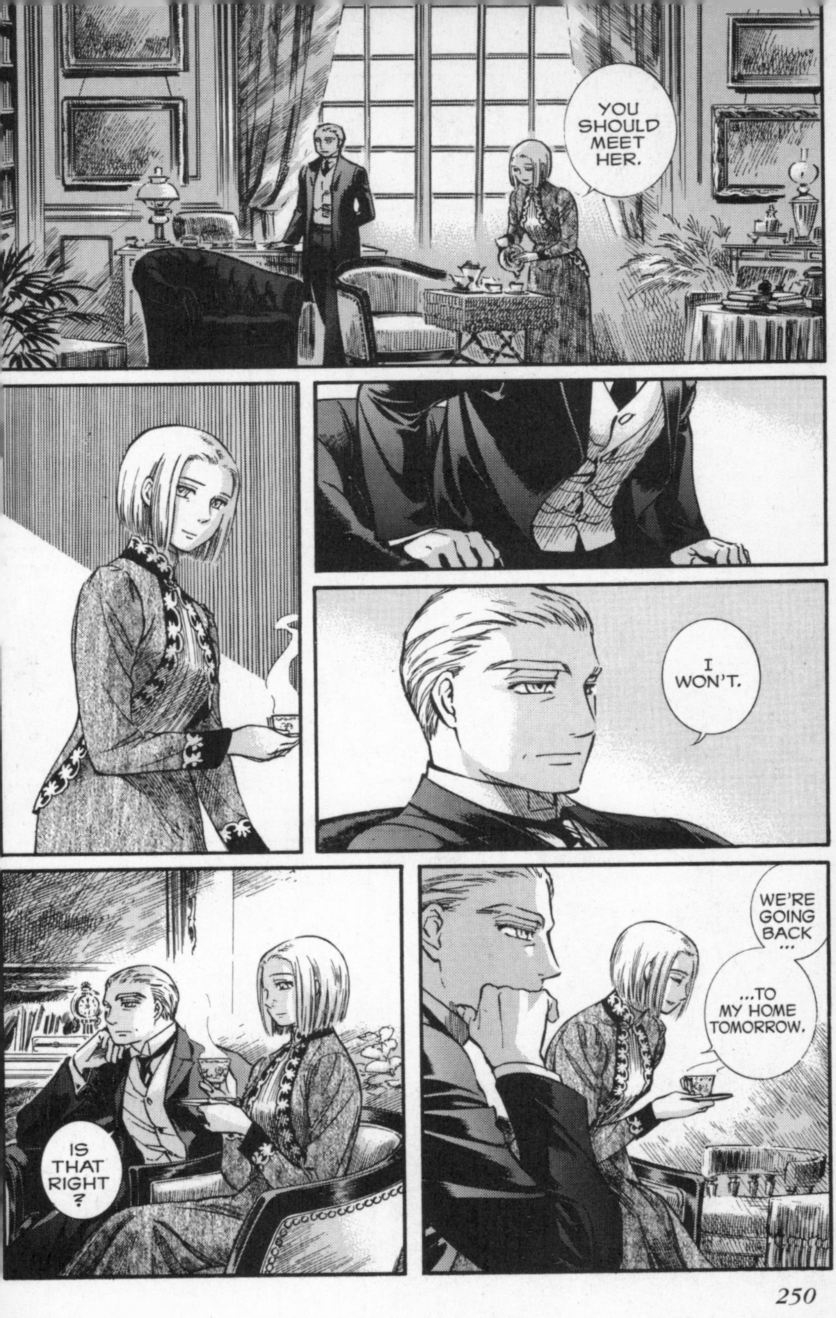
YOU SHOULD MEET HER.
I WON'T.
WE'RE GOING BACK ...
...TO MY HOME TOMORROW.
IS THAT RIGHT ?

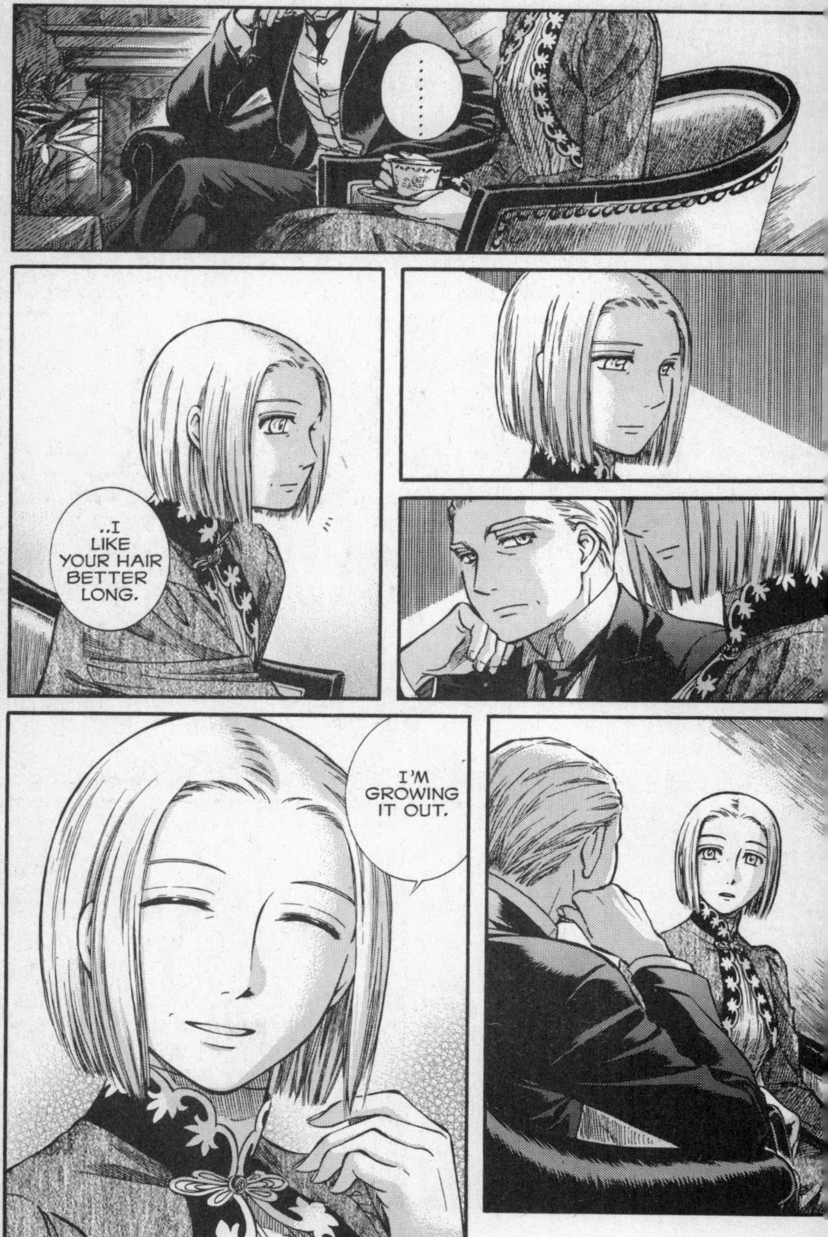
......
..I LIKE YOUR HAIR BETTER LONG.
I'M GROWING IT OUT.

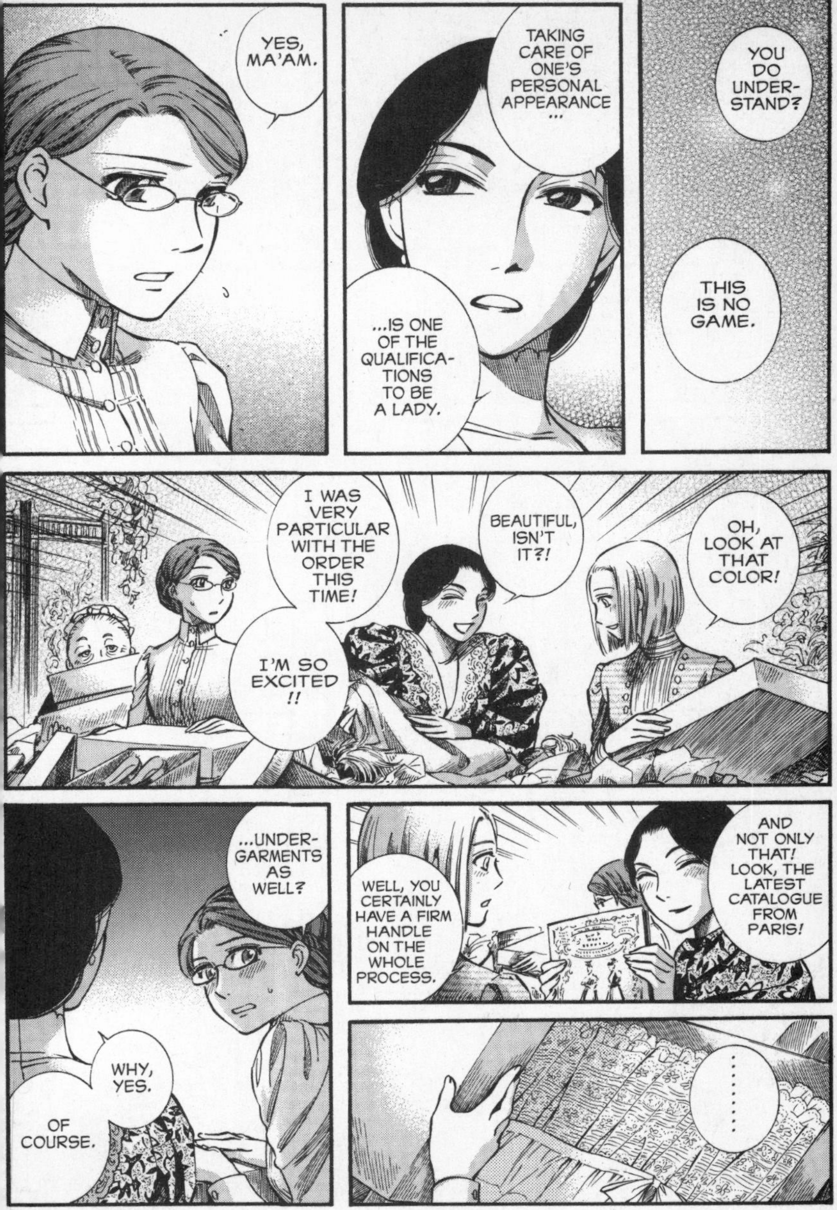
YOU DO UNDER-STAND?
THIS IS NO GAME.
TAKING CARE OF ONE'S PERSONAL APPEARANCE ...
...IS ONE OF THE QUALIFICA-TIONS TO BE A LADY.
YES, MA'AM.
OH, LOOK AT THAT COLOR!
BEAUTIFUL, ISN'T IT?!
I WAS VERY PARTICULAR WITH THE ORDER THIS TIME!
I'M SO EXCITED !!
AND NOT ONLY THAT! LOOK, THE LATEST CATALOGUE FROM PARIS!
WELL, YOU CERTAINLY HAVE A FIRM HANDLE ON THE WHOLE PROCESS.
......
...UNDER-GARMENTS AS WELL?
WHY, YES.
OF COURSE.

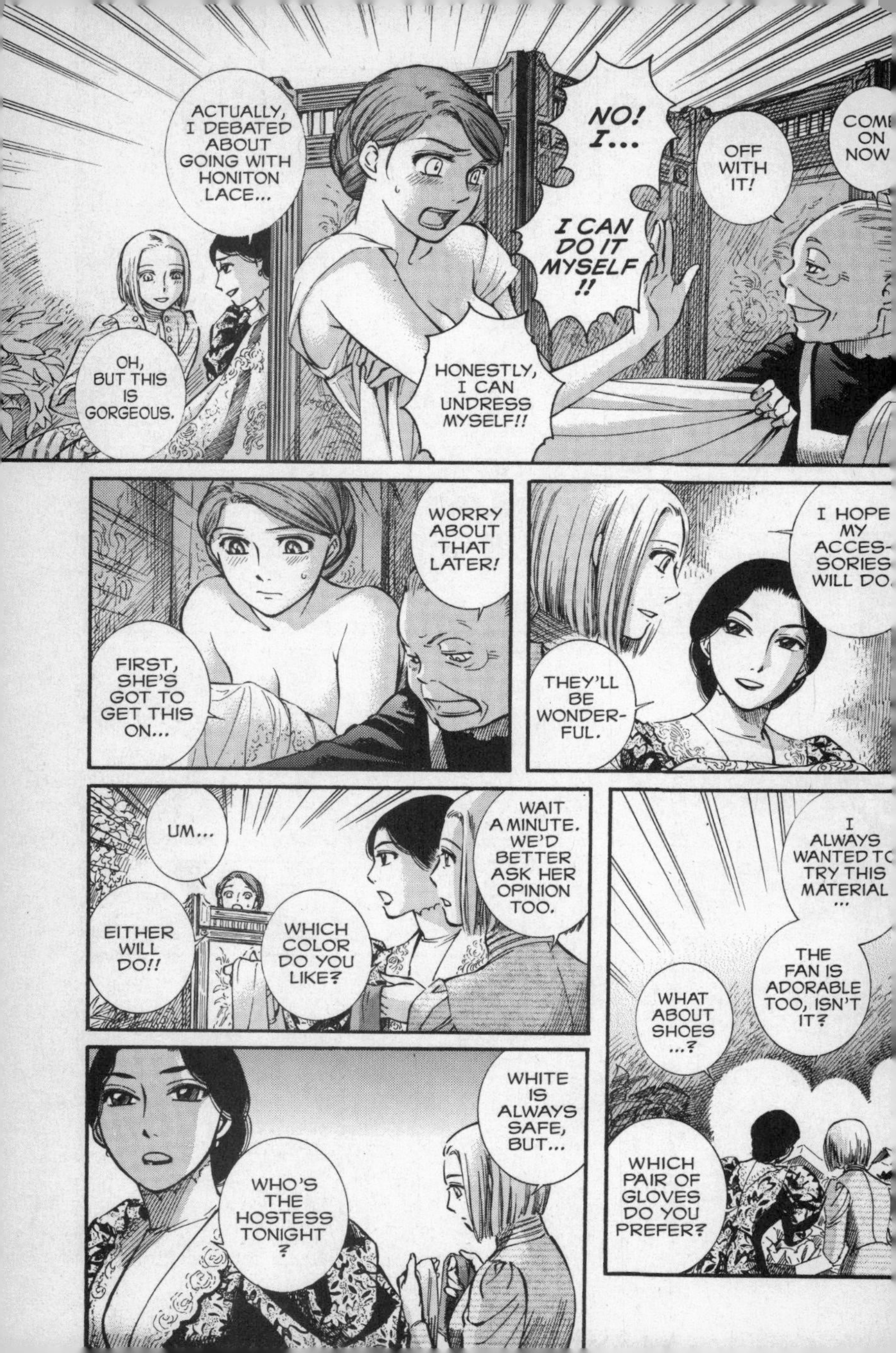
COME ON NOW
OFF WITH IT!
NO! I...
I CAN DO IT MYSELF!!
HONESTLY, I CAN UNDRESS MYSELF!!
ACTUALLY, I DEBATED ABOUT GOING WITH HONITON LACE...
OH, BUT THIS IS GORGEOUS.
I HOPE MY ACCES-SORIES WILL DO.
THEY'LL BE WONDER-FUL.
WORRY ABOUT THAT LATER!
FIRST, SHE'S GOT TO GET THIS ON...
I ALWAYS WANTED TO TRY THIS MATERIAL...
THE FAN IS ADORABLE TOO, ISN'T IT?
WHAT ABOUT SHOES...?
WHICH PAIR OF GLOVES DO YOU PREFER?
WAIT A MINUTE. WE'D BETTER ASK HER OPINION TOO.
WHICH COLOR DO YOU LIKE?
UM...
EITHER WILL DO!!
WHITE IS ALWAYS SAFE, BUT...
WHO'S THE HOSTESS TONIGHT?

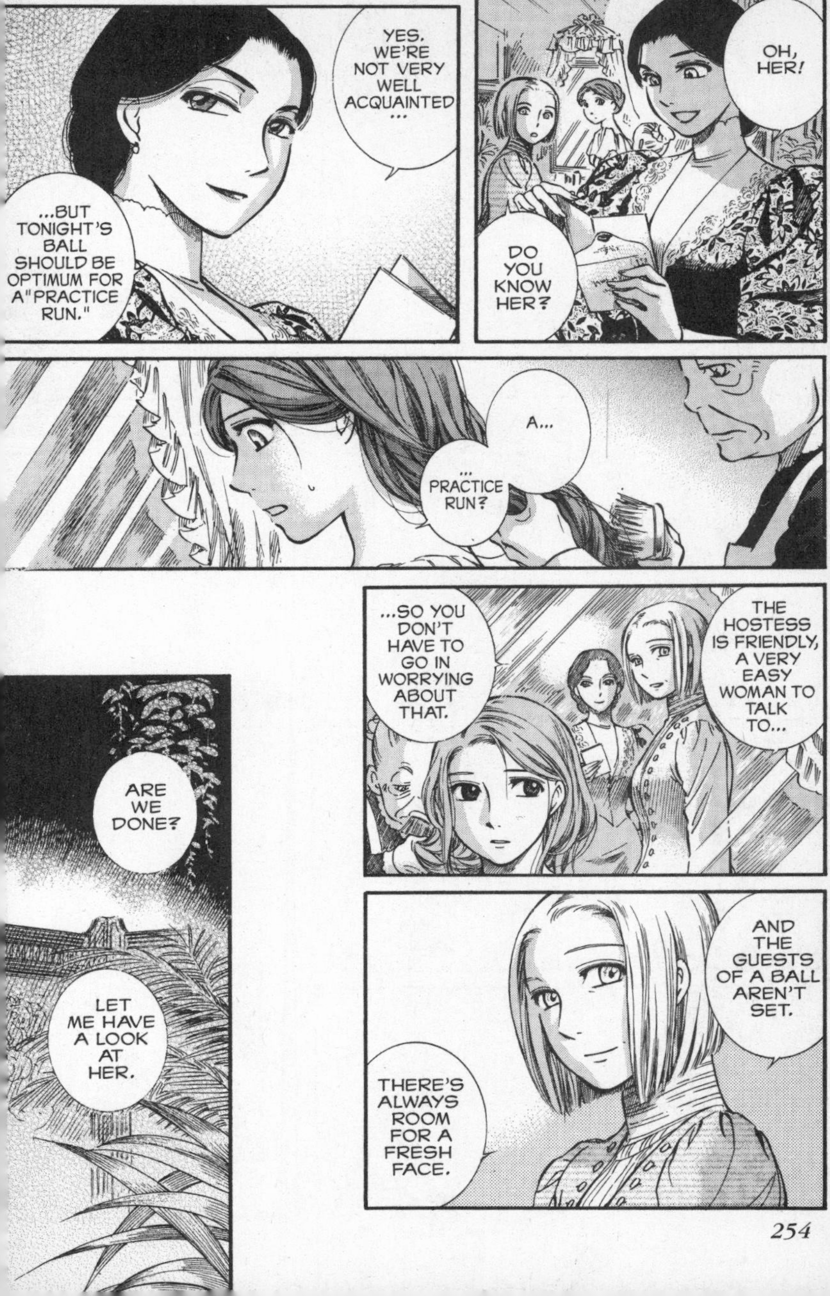
OH, HER!
DO YOU KNOW HER?
YES. WE'RE NOT VERY WELL ACQUAINTED ...
...BUT TONIGHT'S BALL SHOULD BE OPTIMUM FOR A "PRACTICE RUN."
A...
... PRACTICE RUN?
THE HOSTESS IS FRIENDLY, A VERY EASY WOMAN TO TALK TO...
...SO YOU DON'T HAVE TO GO IN WORRYING ABOUT THAT.
AND THE GUESTS OF A BALL AREN'T SET.
THERE'S ALWAYS ROOM FOR A FRESH FACE.
ARE WE DONE?
LET ME HAVE A LOOK AT HER.

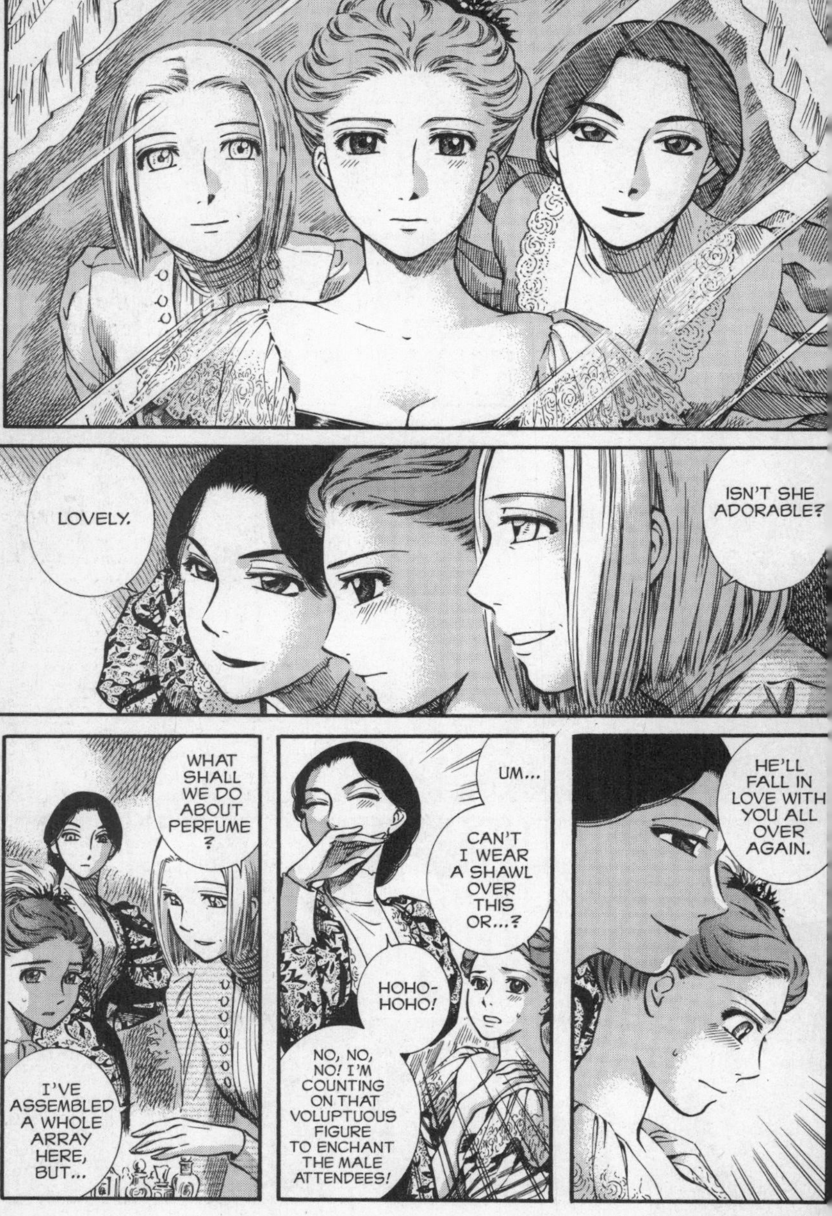
ISN'T SHE ADORABLE?
LOVELY.
HE'LL FALL IN LOVE WITH YOU ALL OVER AGAIN.
UM...
CAN'T I WEAR A SHAWL OVER THIS OR...?
HOHO-HOHO!
NO, NO, NO! I'M COUNTING ON THAT VOLUPTUOUS FIGURE TO ENCHANT THE MALE ATTENDEES!
WHAT SHALL WE DO ABOUT PERFUME?
I'VE ASSEMBLED A WHOLE ARRAY HERE, BUT...

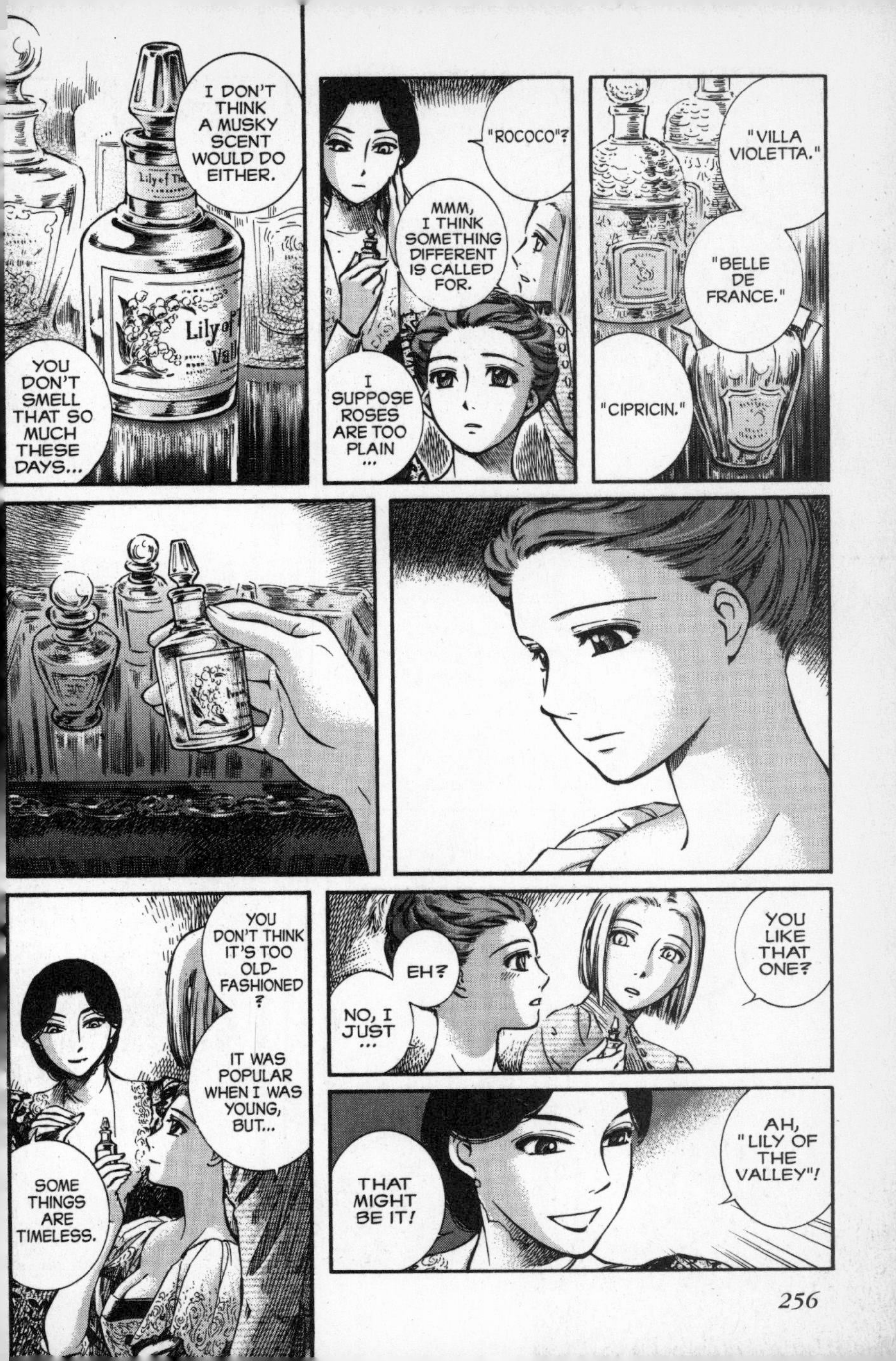
"VILLA VIOLETTA."
"BELLE DE FRANCE."
"CIPRICIN."
"ROCOCO"?
MMM, I THINK SOMETHING DIFFERENT IS CALLED FOR.
I SUPPOSE ROSES ARE TOO PLAIN ...
I DON'T THINK A MUSKY SCENT WOULD DO EITHER.
YOU DON'T SMELL THAT SO MUCH THESE DAYS...
YOU LIKE THAT ONE?
EH?
NO, I JUST ...
AH, "LILY OF THE VALLEY"!
THAT MIGHT BE IT!
YOU DON'T THINK IT'S TOO OLD-FASHIONED?
IT WAS POPULAR WHEN I WAS YOUNG, BUT...
SOME THINGS ARE TIMELESS.

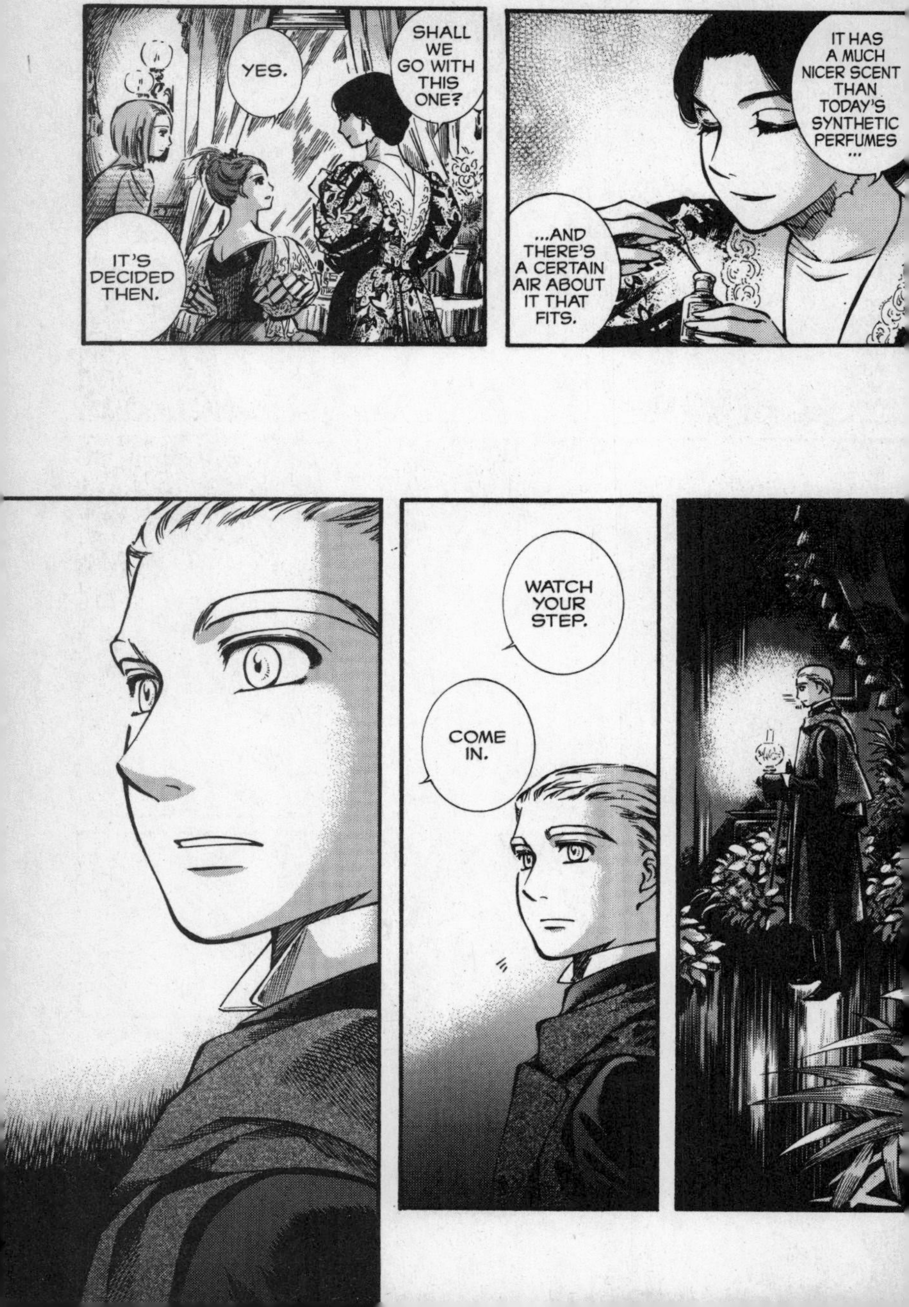
IT HAS A MUCH NICER SCENT THAN TODAY'S SYNTHETIC PERFUMES ...
...AND THERE'S A CERTAIN AIR ABOUT IT THAT FITS.
SHALL WE GO WITH THIS ONE?
YES.
IT'S DECIDED THEN.
WATCH YOUR STEP.
COME IN.

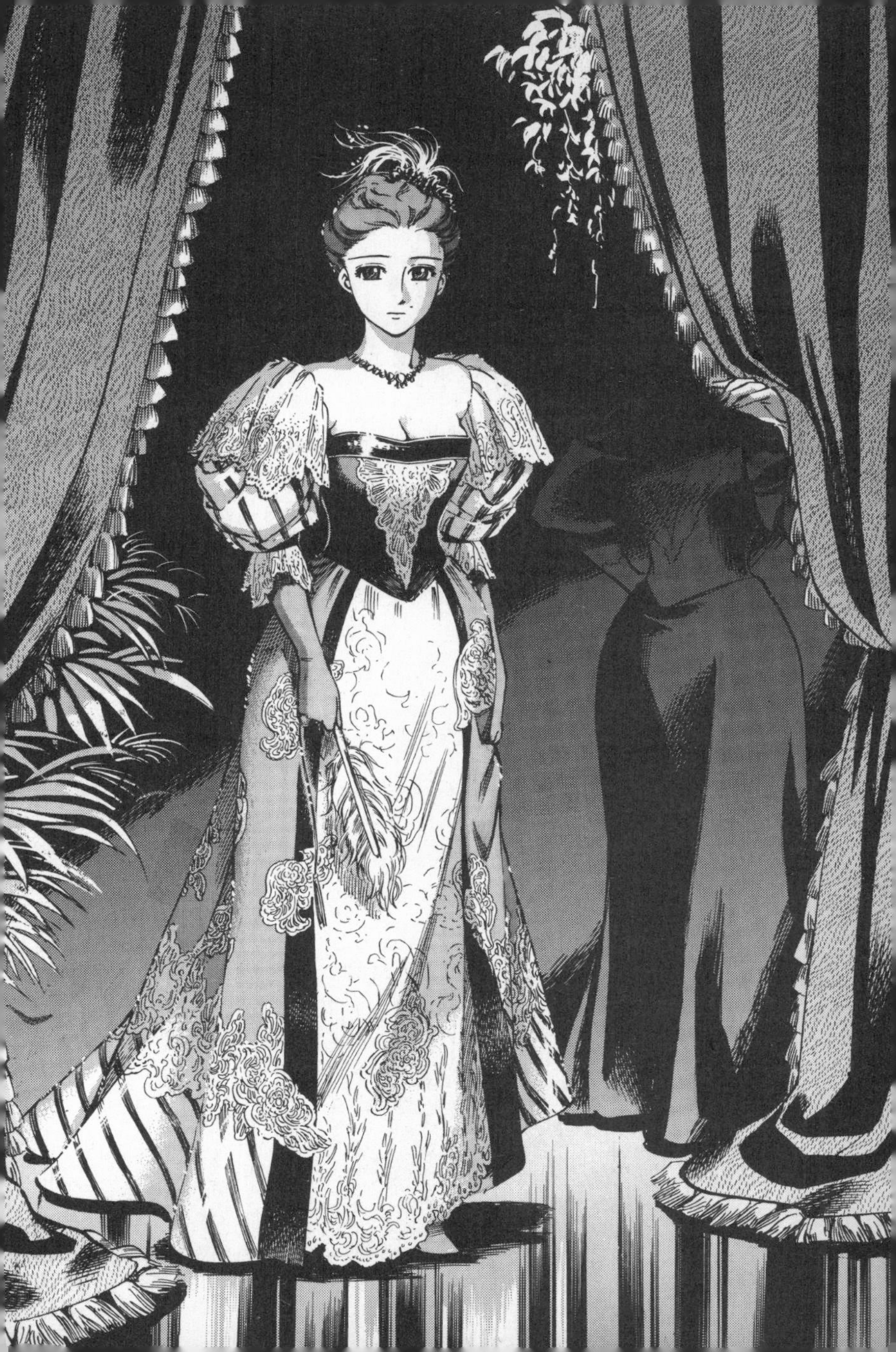

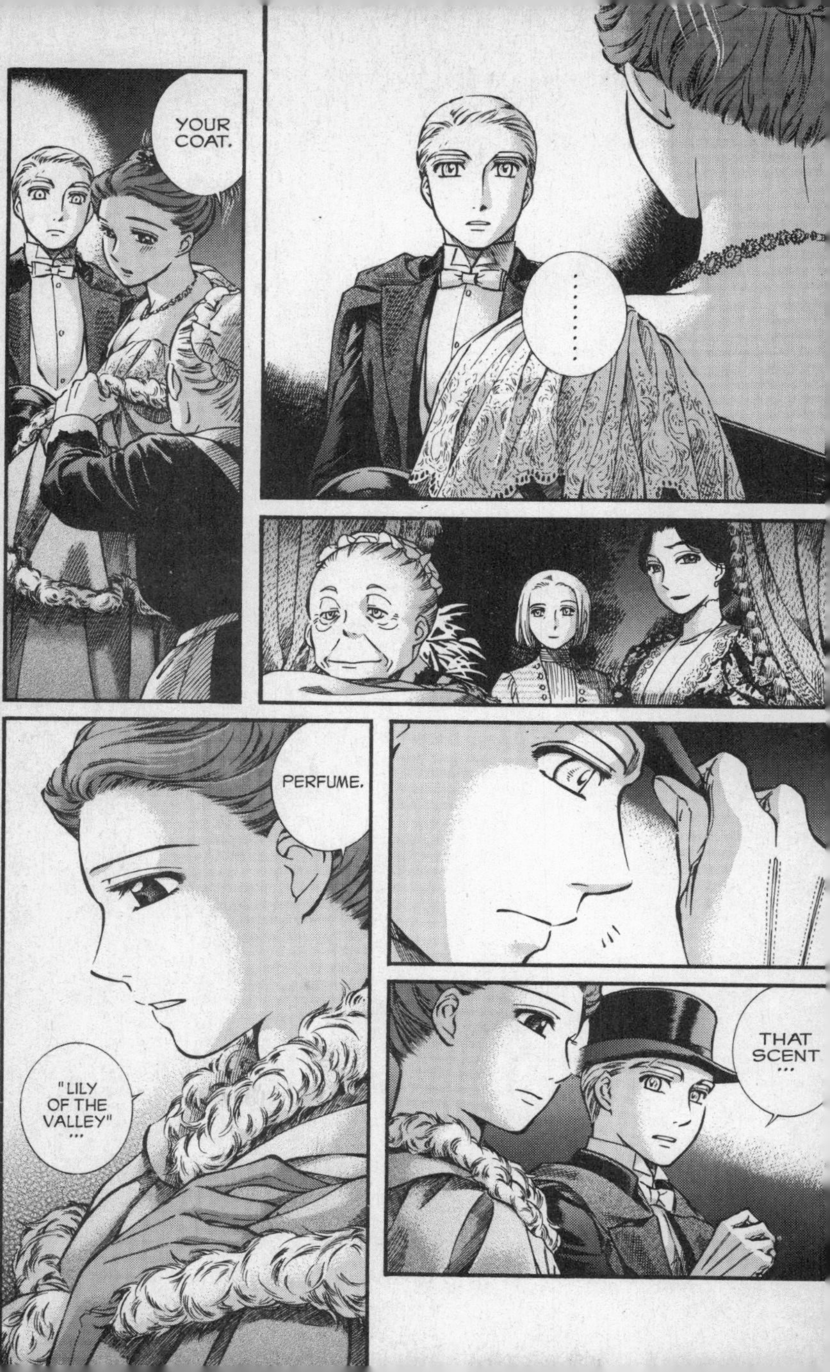
......
YOUR COAT.
THAT SCENT...
PERFUME.
"LILY OF THE VALLEY"...

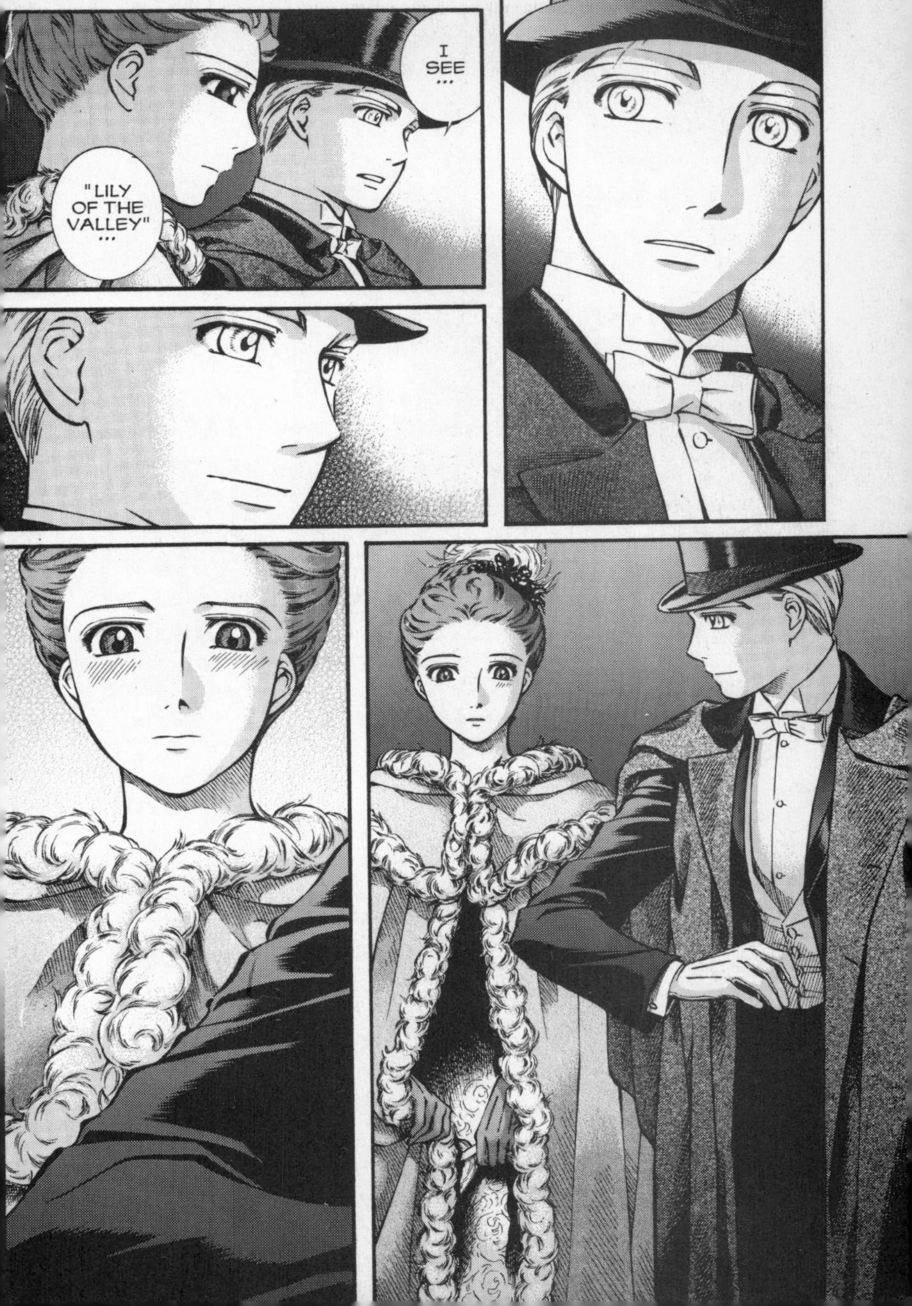
I SEE ...
"LILY OF THE VALLEY" ...

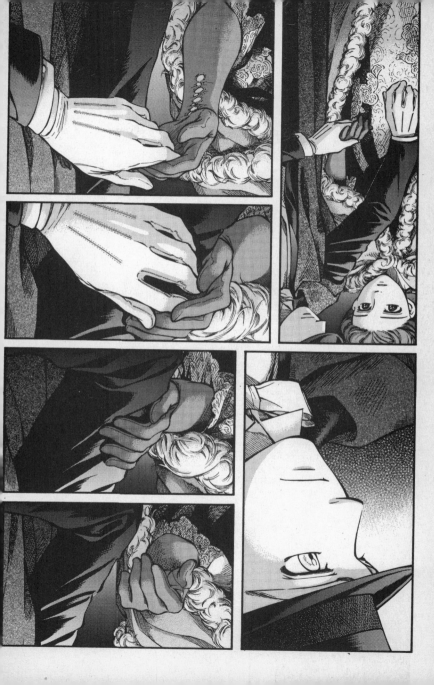

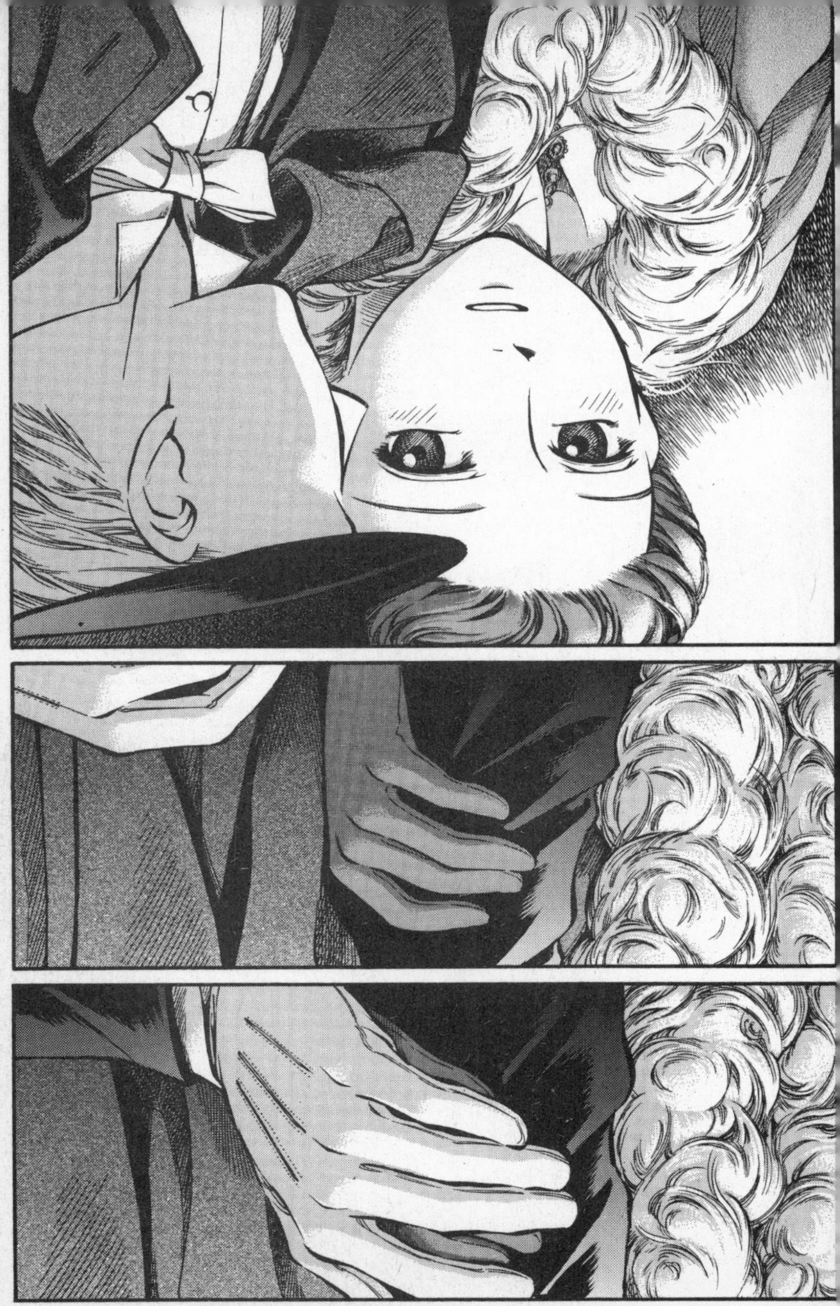

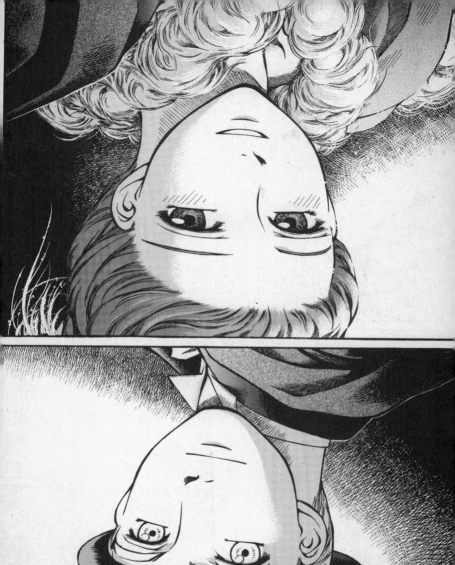

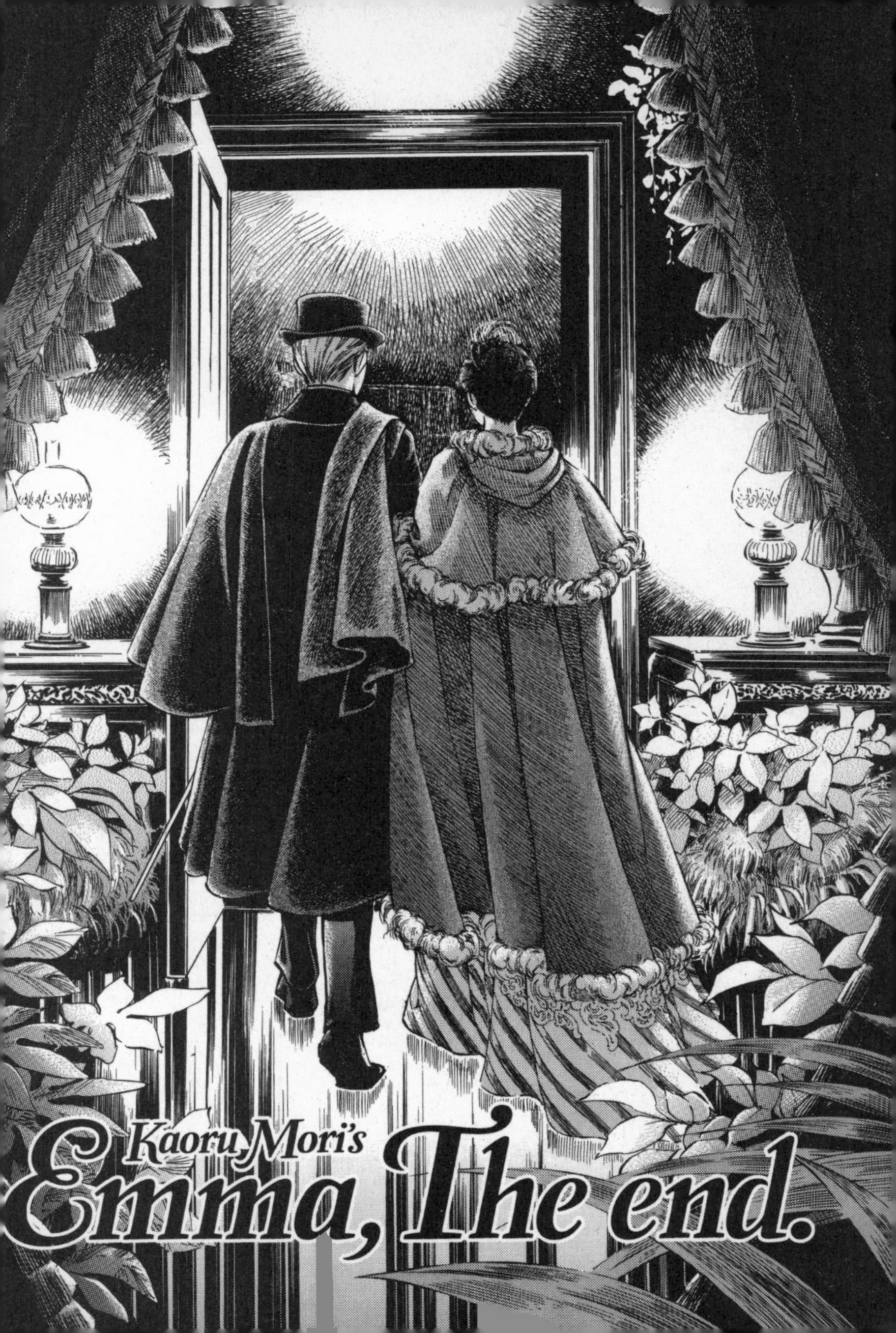
Kaoru Mori's
Emma, The end.

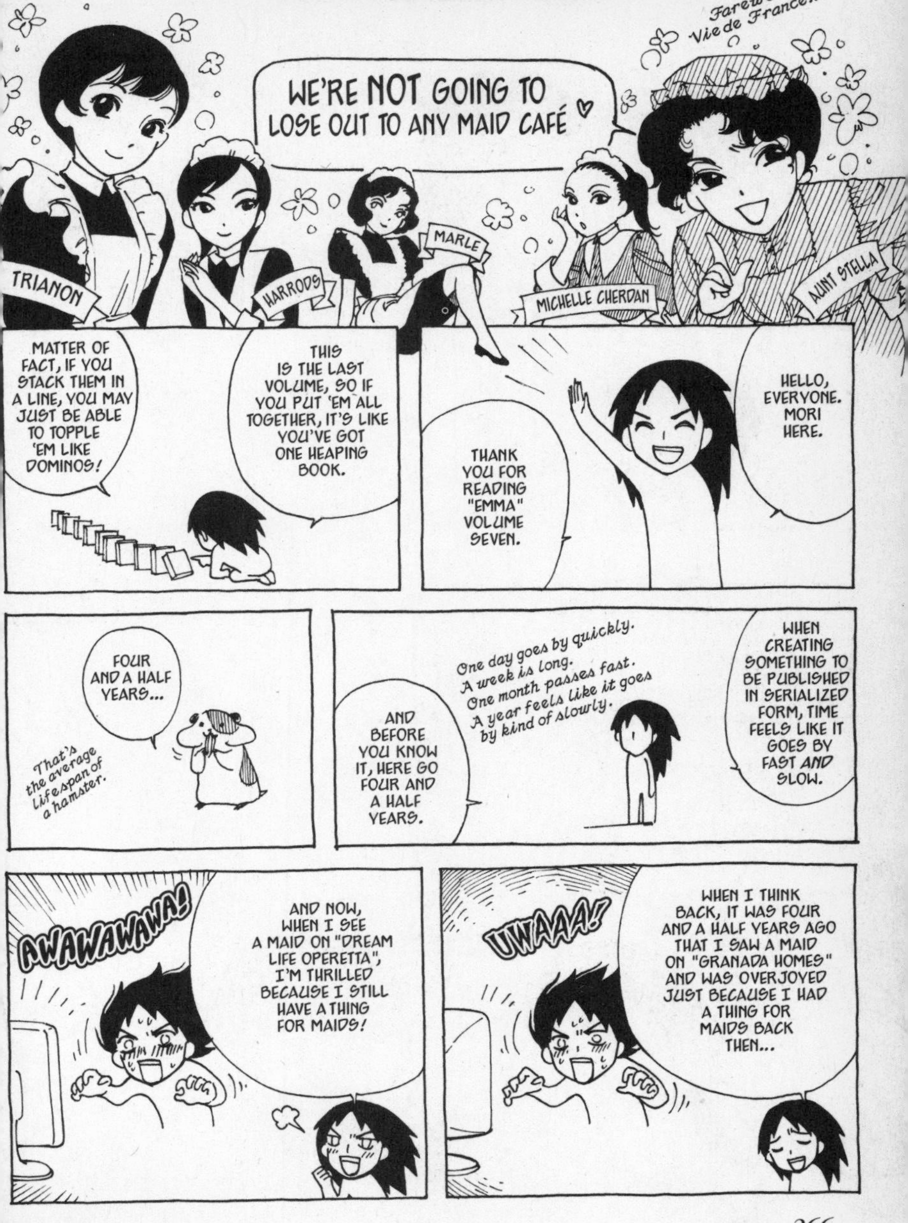
Farewell, Vie de France...
WE'RE NOT GOING TO LOSE OUT TO ANY MAID CAFÉ
TRIANON
HARRODS
MARLE
MICHELLE CHERDAN
AUNT STELLA
HELLO, EVERYONE. MORI HERE.
THANK YOU FOR READING "EMMA" VOLUME SEVEN.
THIS IS THE LAST VOLUME, SO IF YOU PUT 'EM ALL TOGETHER, IT'S LIKE YOU'VE GOT ONE HEAPING BOOK.
MATTER OF FACT, IF YOU STACK THEM IN A LINE, YOU MAY JUST BE ABLE TO TOPPLE 'EM LIKE DOMINOS!
WHEN CREATING SOMETHING TO BE PUBLISHED IN SERIALIZED FORM, TIME FEELS LIKE IT GOES BY FAST AND SLOW.
One day goes by quickly. A week is long. One month passes fast. A year feels like it goes by kind of slowly.
AND BEFORE YOU KNOW IT, HERE GO FOUR AND A HALF YEARS.
FOUR AND A HALF YEARS...
That's the average lifespan of a hamster.
WHEN I THINK BACK, IT WAS FOUR AND A HALF YEARS AGO THAT I SAW A MAID ON "GRANADA HOMES" AND WAS OVERJOYED JUST BECAUSE I HAD A THING FOR MAIDS BACK THEN...
UWAAA!
AND NOW, WHEN I SEE A MAID ON "DREAM LIFE OPERETTA", I'M THRILLED BECAUSE I STILL HAVE A THING FOR MAIDS!
AWAWAWAWA!

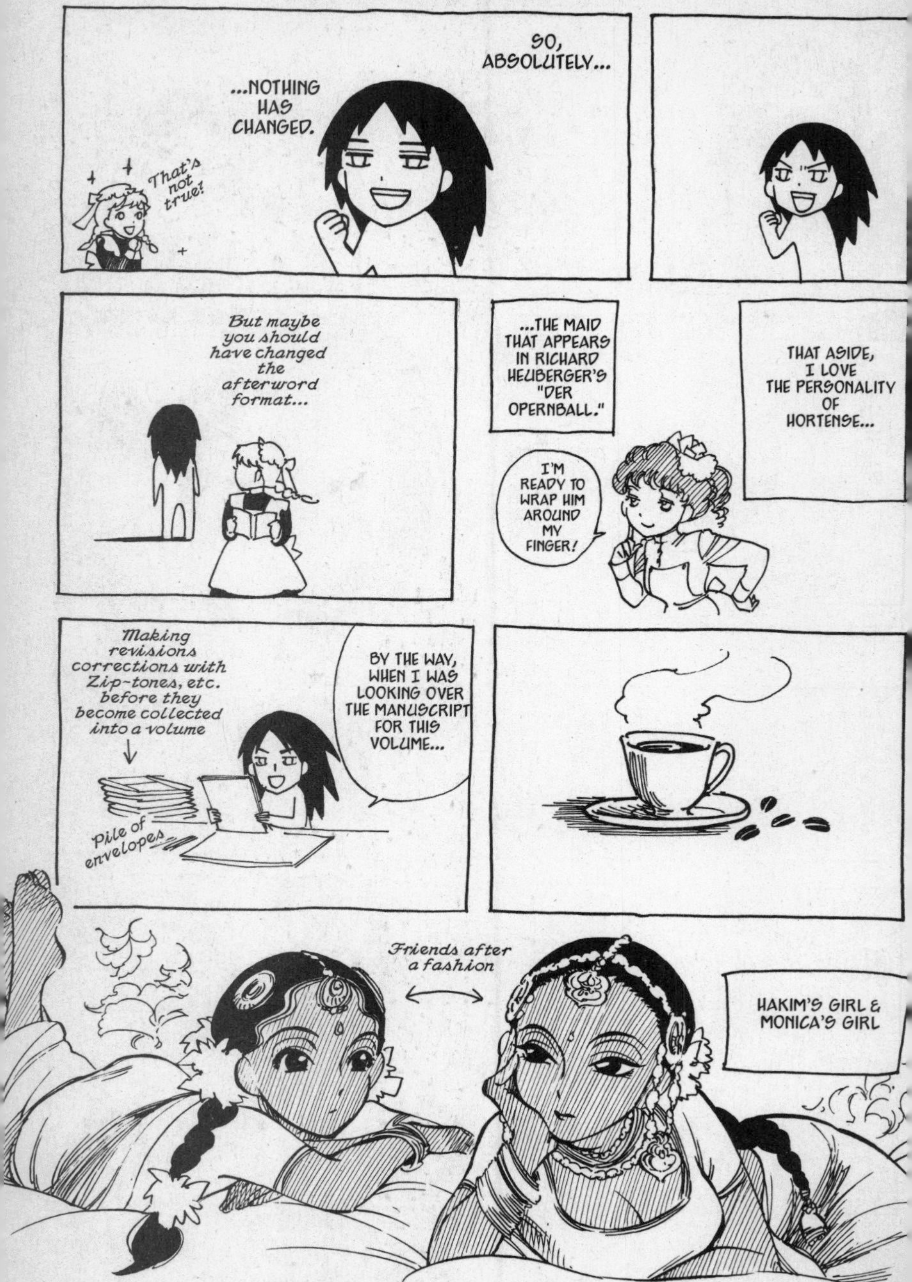
SO, ABSOLUTELY...
...NOTHING HAS CHANGED.
That's not true!
THAT ASIDE, I LOVE THE PERSONALITY OF HORTENSE...
...THE MAID THAT APPEARS IN RICHARD HEUBERGER'S "DER OPERNBALL."
I'M READY TO WRAP HIM AROUND MY FINGER!
But maybe you should have changed the afterword format...
BY THE WAY, WHEN I WAS LOOKING OVER THE MANUSCRIPT FOR THIS VOLUME...
Making revisions corrections with Zip-tones, etc. before they become collected into a volume
Pile of envelopes
HAKIM'S GIRL & MONICA'S GIRL
Friends after a fashion

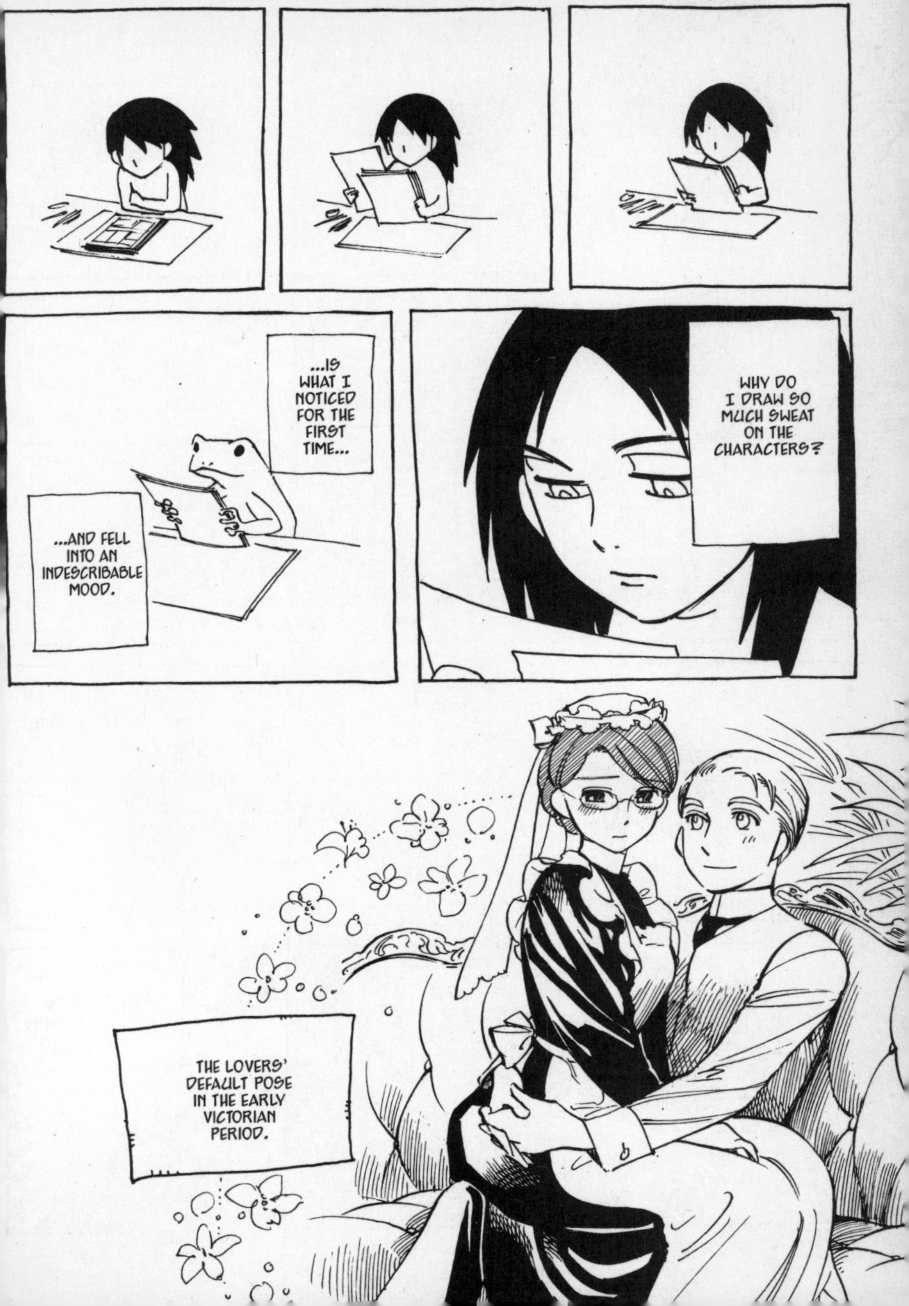
WHY DO I DRAW SO MUCH SWEAT ON THE CHARACTERS?
...IS WHAT I NOTICED FOR THE FIRST TIME...
...AND FELL INTO AN INDESCRIBABLE MOOD.
THE LOVERS' DEFAULT POSE IN THE EARLY VICTORIAN PERIOD.

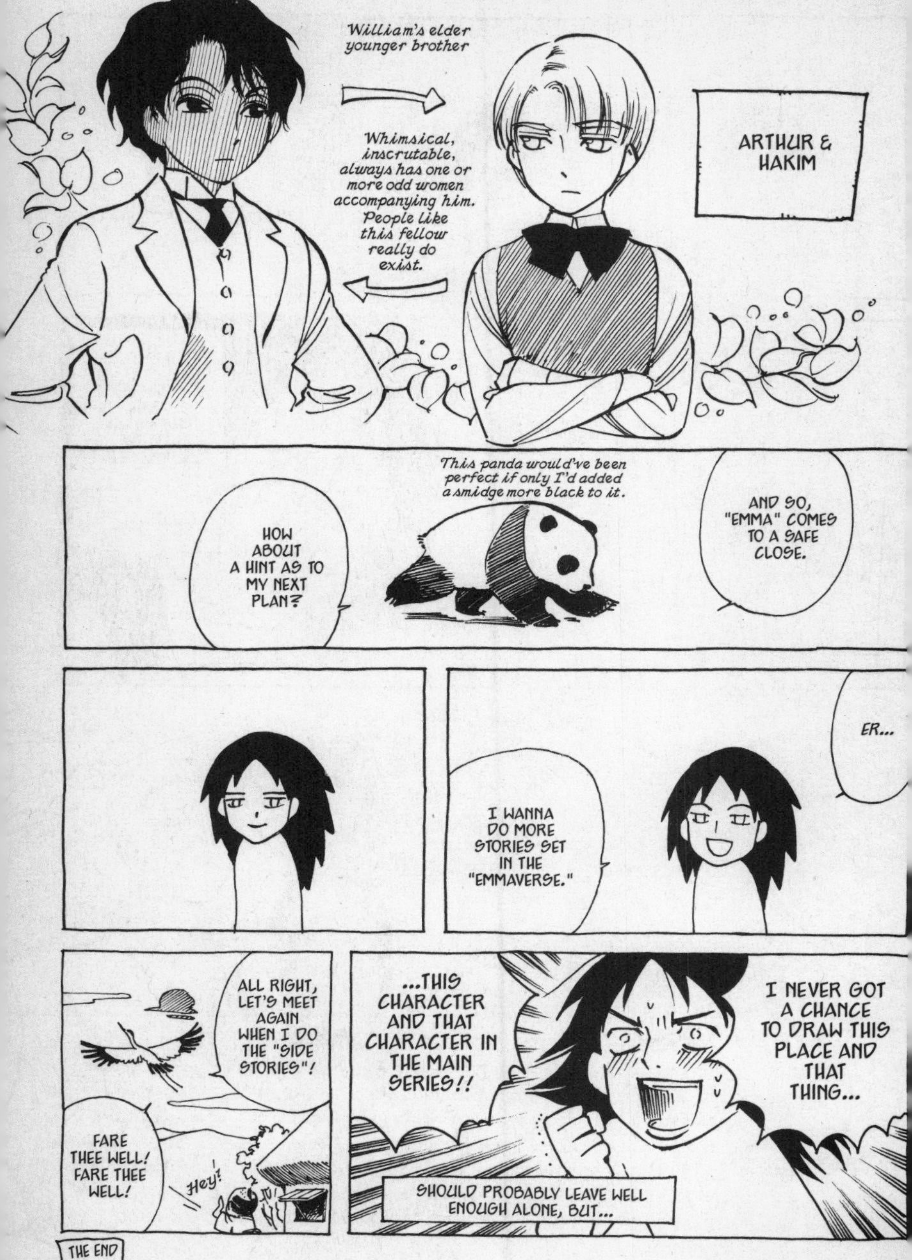
ARTHUR & HAKIM
William's elder younger brother
Whimsical, inscrutable, always has one or more odd women accompanying him. People like this fellow really do exist.
AND SO, "EMMA" COMES TO A SAFE CLOSE.
This panda would've been perfect if only I'd added a smidge more black to it.
HOW ABOUT A HINT AS TO MY NEXT PLAN?
ER...
I WANNA DO MORE STORIES SET IN THE "EMMAVERSE."
I NEVER GOT A CHANCE TO DRAW THIS PLACE AND THAT THING...
...THIS CHARACTER AND THAT CHARACTER IN THE MAIN SERIES!!
SHOULD PROBABLY LEAVE WELL ENOUGH ALONE, BUT...
ALL RIGHT, LET'S MEET AGAIN WHEN I DO THE "SIDE STORIES"!
FARE THEE WELL! FARE THEE WELL!
Hey!
THE END

EXPERIENCE THIS LOVE STORY FROM THE BEGINNING!

EMMA

By Kaoru Mori. If you've missed any of the six previous volumes in this series, now is the time to catch up! Start at the beginning to learn how a young girl named Emma is rescued from a life of destitution and raised to become a proper British maid. And when she meets William, the son of an upper class family, they develop a secret love their world will never allow them to express. Join us again next year for the return of EMMA with vol. 8—a collection of short stories focusing on some of the supporting characters introduced throughout the course of the series.

DON'T MISS THIS TITLE FROM THE CREATOR OF EMMA! COMING IN JULY!

![SHIRLEY]

By Kaoru Mori. This collection of short stories further explores the lives of English maids, portrayed through the experiences of several young women, including one named Shirley. Miss Bennett lives alone and keeps busy running the pub she inherited. Needing some help, she posts a notice for a maid. Along comes Shirley Madison, a girl who can clean and cook as well as any maid – even if she's only 13 years old!

THE LOVE FEST CONTINUES
AND IS AVAILABLE NOW!

VENUS in LOVE

Volume 2

By Yuki Nakaji. Fukami is convinced that there's chemistry between his friends Suzuna and Eichi, who just need a little push to become a couple. Little does he suspect that they both have a crush on him. But Fukami's got his own romantic distraction with a girl he keeps running into. When Suzuna realizes that she has a new rival for Fukami, she's going to have to act fast. Can she build up the nerve to tell him how she really feels?

IS A CO-WORKER OUT TO
GET KAZUHA? COMING IN APRIL!

I HATE YOU
more than anyone!
Volume 4

By Banri Hidaka. Now that she's finally decided to embark on a career as a hair stylist, Kazuha looks to Sugimoto for support. He warns her that it may not be as easy as she thinks, but still arranges for her to get a job at a salon. Kazuha quickly discovers that a fellow hairdresser she's just met already has it in for her. What's behind this woman's feelings...and what can Kazuha do to change her mind?

LOOKING FOR A HAPPY ENDING?
GET THESE COMPLETE SERIES NOW!

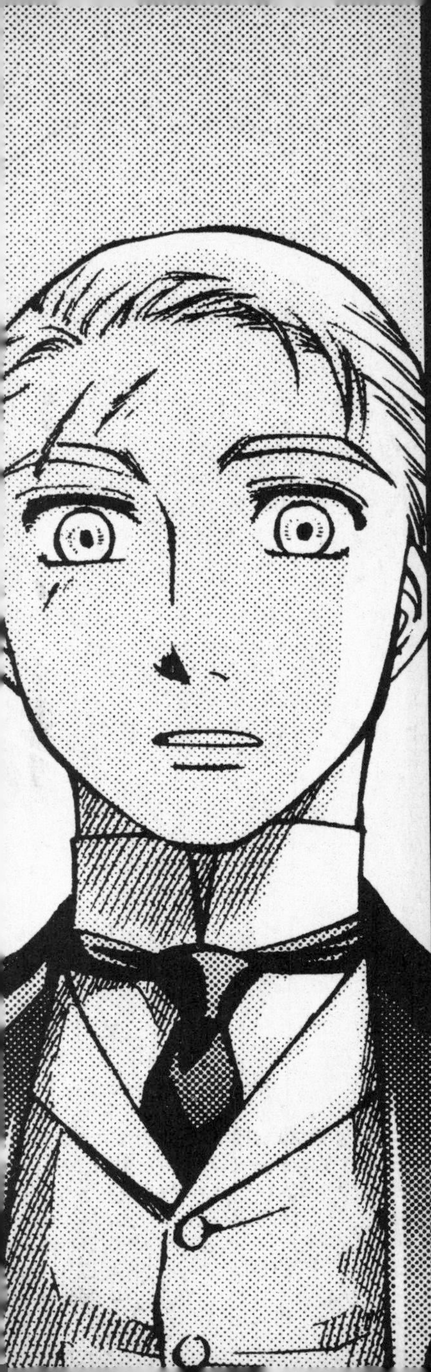

KNOW WHAT'S INSIDE

With the wide variety of manga available, CMX understands it can be confusing to determine age-appropriate material. We rate our books in four categories: EVERYONE, TEEN, TEEN + and MATURE. For the TEEN, TEEN + and MATURE categories, we include additional, specific descriptions to assist consumers in determining if the book is age appropriate. (Our MATURE books are shipped shrink-wrapped with a Parental Advisory sticker affixed to the wrapper.)

E

EVERYONE

Titles with this rating are appropriate for all age readers. They contain no offensive material. They may contain mild violence and/or some comic mischief.

T

TEEN

Titles with this rating are appropriate for a teen audience and older. They may contain some violent content, language, and/or suggestive themes.

T+

TEEN PLUS

Titles with this rating are appropriate for an audience of 16 and older. They may contain partial nudity, mild profanity and more intense violence.

M

MATURE

Titles with this rating are appropriate only for mature readers. They may contain graphic violence, nudity, sex and content suitable only for older readers.

CMX

EMMA Vol. 7 © 2006 Kaoru Mori. All Rights Reserved. First
published in Japan in 2006 by ENTERBRAIN, INC.

EMMA Volume 7, published by WildStorm Productions, an
imprint of DC Comics, 888 Prospect St. #240, La Jolla, CA
92037. English Translation © 2008. All Rights Reserved.
English Translation rights in U.S.A. and Canada arranged by
ENTERBRAIN, INC. through Tuttle-Mori Agency, Inc., Tokyo.
CMX is a trademark of DC Comics. The stories, characters,
and incidents mentioned in this magazine are entirely fic-
tional. Printed on recyclable paper. WildStorm does not
read or accept unsolicited submissions of ideas, stories or
artwork. Printed in Canada.

DC Comics, a Warner Bros. Entertainment Company.

Sheldon Drzka – Translation and Adaptation
Janice Chiang – Lettering
Larry Berry – Design
Jim Chadwick – Editor

ISBN: 978-1-4012-1737-2

All the pages in this book were created—and are printed here—in Japanese RIGHT-to-LEFT format. No artwork has been reversed or altered, so you can read the stories the way the creators meant for them to be read.

FLIP IT!

RIGHT TO LEFT?!

Traditional Japanese manga starts at the upper right-hand corner, and moves right-to-left as it goes down the page. Follow this guide for an easy understanding.

For more information and sneak previews, visit cmxmanga.com. Call 1-888-COMIC BOOK for the nearest comics shop or head to your local book store.

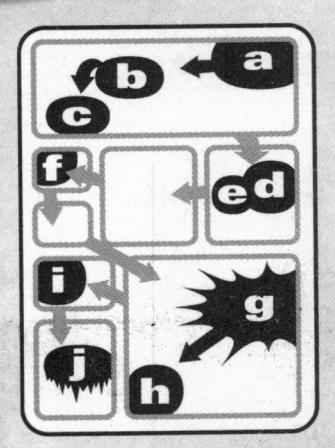